Digital Literacy at the Intersection of Equity, Inclusion, and Technology

Katelyn Burton Prager
Fashion Institute of Technology, USA

Nurhayat Bilge
Fashion Institute of Technology, USA

A volume in the Advances in Educational Technologies and Instructional Design (AETID) Book Series

IGI Global
PUBLISHER of TIMELY KNOWLEDGE

Published in the United States of America by
IGI Global
Information Science Reference (an imprint of IGI Global)
701 E. Chocolate Avenue
Hershey PA, USA 17033
Tel: 717-533-8845
Fax: 717-533-8661
E-mail: cust@igi-global.com
Web site: http://www.igi-global.com

Library of Congress Cataloging-in-Publication Data

CIP DATA PROCESSING

2024 Information Science Reference
hcISBN: 9798369325919
scISBN: 9798369345764
eISBN: 9798369325926

British Cataloguing in Publication Data
A Cataloguing in Publication record for this book is available from the British Library.

All work contributed to this book is new, previously-unpublished material.
The views expressed in this book are those of the authors, but not necessarily of the publisher.

For electronic access to this publication, please contact: eresources@igi-global.com.

Table of Contents

Detailed Table of Contents

This chapter embarks on a comprehensive exploration of the equity challenges entailed in learning management systems (LMS) within the domain of online education, under the critical gaze of social reproduction theory. The significance of this inquiry arises from the recognition that while LMS have emerged as potent instruments for course administration, they are not immune to perpetuating or ameliorating existing social inequalities. Within this chapter, the author undertakes an extensive analysis of these equity challenges, examining facets such as access, content accessibility, design, assessment, and various dimensions of online learning, all framed within the conceptual framework of social reproduction theory. This narrative endeavors to provide a holistic understanding of the intricate interplay between LMS, social reproduction dynamics, and equity within educational settings.

Article 24 of the Convention on the Rights of Persons with Disabilities outlines the responsibilities that individual governments have in ensuring equitable access to quality inclusive education for people with disabilities, including accessibility and reasonable accommodations. One example of reasonable accommodations is the use of assistive technology. This chapter provides a brief literature review of assistive technology in the field of English language education before providing a set of practical recommendations for using assistive technology in the English language classroom. These recommendations are divided into three categories: using assistive technology to increase accessibility, using assistive technology as an accommodation, and using assistive technology to promote digital literacy, which has been promoted by the OECD as an essential 21st century skill. The chapter concludes with some implications for stakeholders at various levels in using assistive technology to promote digital literacy in compliance with international policy guidance.

This chapter explores the integration of digital technology to enhance classroom equity. Examining the impact on diverse learning needs, it delves into how technology foster inclusivity supports personalized learning and addresses potential disparities. Concentrating on the possibility of overcoming educational gaps. It looks at how technology can improve accessibility to resources, emphasizing the possibility of closing educational gaps. It looks at how technology may enhance accessibility to resources. It emphasizes the role of digital tools in promoting equal access to educational recourses, ultimately contributing to a more equitable and inclusive classroom environment. It investigates the effective implementation of digital technology in classroom settings, considering teacher professional development and infrastructure requirements. The chapter also provides insight into the transformative potential of digital integration for achieving greater equity in education.

In this section, the needs of refugee children are discussed within the framework of Maslow's hierarchy and family systems theory, and explanations of children's participation in educational processes, the use of technology in educational processes, and teacher guidance are given. In addition, the study aims to determine the knowledge, awareness, and experiences of preschool teachers in Turkey about integrating technology into education in classrooms for refugee children. In this direction, the teacher interview form on technology integration into activities with refugee children in early childhood was developed by the researchers, and the current situation was revealed by interviewing preschool teachers working with refugee children. As a result of the research, it was seen that refugee children in Turkey have problems with language and communication, adaptation and behavior problems, self-care skills, and cultural differences. It was found that teachers used language translation programs and technology-assisted instruction to solve these problems and made arrangements such as making extra explanations for refugee children in the context of language and culture, using Arabic materials, and speaking English. It was stated that technology integration was beneficial for refugee children in terms of easier language acquisition. "easier instruction, more adaptability and motivation, and faster learning, and it was emphasized that it provided equal opportunities with Turkish children.

Nowadays, artificial intelligence (AI) has become a prevalent topic across the globe, particularly in academic institutions, as it has the potential to transform the teaching and learning process. Nonetheless, the emergence of AI also presents challenges that need to be addressed. This study delves into the role of AI in higher education, specifically in English as a foreign language (EFL) classrooms. The aim is to explore how AI tools affect learning experiences in this context. To that end, the research follows a qualitative approach, including semi-structured interviews and a questionnaire with students and teachers to gain insights into the influence of AI in EFL settings. Through a thematic analysis, the implications of AI in higher education were assessed. It is anticipated that the findings will provide new avenues for future research, shedding light on how the integration of AI could help level the language playing field.

Blending learning (BL) has emerged as one of the effective teaching and learning approaches in education, and research on the deployment of BL has been extensively conducted. This book chapter sets to present a mixed-methods study exploring Vietnamese L2 students' perceptions of the effects of BL on their English vocabulary enhancement. A cohort of 300 L2 students studying general English (GE) at a Ho Chi Minh City-based university in Vietnam took part in answering a questionnaire, and 15 of them participated in semi-structured interviews. Statistical analysis and content analysis were employed for quantitative and qualitative data analysis, respectively, and the sociolinguistic perspective was adopted for interpreting the results. The findings unraveled that Vietnamese L2 students perceived the effects of the deployment of BL in GE courses on their vocabulary enhancement as they could remember a wide range of vocabulary, recognize vocabulary meaning in context, and apply vocabulary in writing and speaking effectively.

This chapter explores the evolving role of pedagogical innovation in foreign language (FL) classes for media studies undergraduates at the School of Education (ESEV) of the Polytechnic Institute of Viseu (Portugal). It highlights the transformation of digital tools, initially seen as "icebreakers," into powerful aids for active methodologies, fostering both hard and soft skills essential for contemporary society and the job market. Teachers commonly integrate online applications, online platforms, and social networks to enhance FL learning. The narrative delves into challenges faced by teachers and students amid constant societal changes. The text emphasizes skills development, improvements over traditional methods, encountered difficulties, and the dynamics within the teaching-learning process. One relies upon gamification as a tool in FL classes, so as to look into its potential to contribute to the systematic exploration of successful educational innovations supported by digital tools in higher education, providing a foundation for future research.

Proficiency in writing is vital for EAP education. The COVID-19 pandemic prompted a shift from traditional classrooms to online platforms, leading higher education institutions to adapt their EAP courses accordingly. As students' perceptions and attitudes towards learning methods can significantly affect their effectiveness in acquiring knowledge, it is imperative to understand their perceptions of online EAP writing courses. This study, using surveys and interviews, revealed varied student reactions to online EAP courses. While online learning offers flexibility, it faces challenges including diminished motivation, lack of engagement, and limited interaction. Student satisfaction was linked to factors such as engagement, learning environment, instructor presence, and technology use. Moreover, structured online forums were found useful in enhancing critical thinking. Finally, the study offered three recommendations for the future development of online EAP instruction.

This chapter describes a teaching sequence in a course of English for English language learners. The participants developed a literacy project whose foundations integrated some of the principles of the educational model at Universidad Ean in Bogotá, Colombia. The guiding concepts that the instructor used to shape the instructional design were digital literacy, technology, and inclusion. These elements took precedence as students worked on each one of the phases of the class project. The chapter makes a claim for literacy instructors to work with a more comprehensive understanding of literacy instruction in classrooms.

Despite the widely recognized and acknowledged importance of communication, written, and presentation skills, students often struggle in this area, especially in connection with digital literacy. A noted disconnect between current skill sets, including digital literacy, and workplace needs supports an inquiry into how best to address this challenge in equitable and inclusive ways so as to strengthen both student awareness of the importance of transferable skills and the associated development of digital literacy and soft skills across disciplines. This chapter describes a course-long project that is grounded in principles of feminist digital pedagogy digital literacy, inclusive instruction, and equity and designed to support the development and transfer of written, presentation, and soft skills in a legal technology course developed at a two-year community college located in a large urban area and with a student population comprised primarily of minority and first-generation students. The project emphasizes equitable and inclusive reliance upon technology in all steps and components.

Preface

This collection aims to address a national and global need for furthering a deeper understanding of the complex relationships between equity, inclusion, and digital technologies in higher education. These issues impact students and faculty across disciplines and yet discussions and research in this area tends to be relatively siloed within individual fields. As educators negotiate this increasingly challenging relationship between educational technologies and equitable pedagogy, we believe there is value in crossing our disciplinary boundaries to foster a broader multidisciplinary conversation. This multidisciplinary book is intended as a reference guide and a practical resource for teacher-scholars in the fields of communication, rhetoric, composition, linguistics, TESOL, critical cultural studies, education, and beyond. While the chapters herein will focus primarily on these disciplines, the insights contained in this collection may also provide helpful lessons for educators beyond these fields and throughout academia. We hope that this collection will propel that larger pedagogical conversation, guiding teacher-scholars as they navigate the rapidly evolving digital landscape.

The chapters to follow will explore scholarship at the intersection of equity/inclusion and digital pedagogies. They will explore how educators can leverage technology to create more equitable learning environments (both on and offline), how they can combat inequities created and/or exacerbated by digital technologies, and how they can guide students to become more thoughtful digital citizens. This text merges theory and practice, including theoretical chapters on equitable digital pedagogies as well as a collection of practical materials including assignments, syllabi, and course designs for teachers who want to leverage technology to create equitable learning environments.

THE EVOLVING DIGITAL LANDSCAPE

This collection is propelled by our current moment of rapid technological innovation. The digital resources at our disposal in the classroom have never been greater. Generally speaking, today's technologies are more intuitive than ever, easier to learn and use. Moreover, many are open access or free and the capabilities of today's technologies would have been unimaginable just a few short years ago. This moment of innovation is heightened as we bare witness to the rapid evolution of generative artificial intelligence (AI) technologies, which have the power to upend education as we have traditionally known it. This rapid innovation has brought us to a point where technology can no longer be ignored, even by the most tech averse of educators.

Living (and teaching) in a world saturated with evolving technologies has created countless opportunities for pedagogical innovation. However, the pressures to use said resources have also never been greater. While technology can enhance classroom learning, to do so it must be integrated meaningfully. Is a given technology helping to achieve the student learning outcomes and enhance student learning? Or is it merely adding "flash" or excitement? Or, worse yet, is it working against the larger learning goals by confusing or frustrating students? Some of the chapters to follow will share examples of digital technologies that had unintended or even harmful consequences for students and educators alike. In this moment, we are surrounded by the tempting bells and whistles of new technology but, as we explore the potential of these programs and devices for our own teaching, we must also be mindful to use technology intentionally and with abundant caution.

EQUITABLE PEDAGOGY

Against this backdrop of technological innovation, we face many of the same equity challenges we've long encountered with our students. The students who enter our classrooms are often quite diverse, coming from varying cultures, embodying diverse races or ethnicities, speaking different languages with varying levels of proficiency, experiencing different socioeconomic norms, and more. Moreover, it is vital to remember that these individual identity traits do not exist in isolation. Rather, the complex intersections between these traits compound this diversity exponentially, creating further inequities. All of this difference merges into a single classroom working towards similar learning outcomes. However, these differences mean that each student enters our classroom with vastly different levels of preparedness, ability, and access to resources. And, therefore, with vastly different learning differences or needs.

Digital pedagogy has the capability to sway our classrooms in either direction: to create a more level playing field for all students or to exacerbate existing inequalities. Incorporating new digital technologies without careful thought and planning can create added burden–academically, emotionally, and financially–for students who are already struggling, serving to reify existing inequalities and often widening the gap between student groups.

This collection seeks to acknowledge and accommodate these differences by investigating digital pedagogical strategies and considering the ways they might serve to either exploit or rectify these differences. Ultimately, the chapters in this collection will offer insights into the disparities (often unintentionally) created in our teaching by emergent technologies and share innovative assignments, projects, and teaching strategies that work to dismantle these inequities.

CONTENTS AND ORGANIZATION

Our book offers insights into digital literacy and aspects of equity from an international and interdisciplinary standpoint. The contributing authors from diverse countries, including Portugal, Spain, Turkey, China, India, Vietnam, United States, Japan, and Colombia; represent different disciplines, such as education, linguistics, sociology, and psychology. Moreover, chapters vary in their demonstration of critical, theoretical, and practical perspectives. As such, we organized the book to begin with critical and theoretical works and build upon their examinations. We continue with chapters offering empirical studies and practical applications regarding digital literacy and equity. Thus, the book has three parts, each containing five contributing chapters: (1) Theorizing Digital Equity: Opportunities and Limitations of Digital Technologies in the Classroom, (2) Scholarly Examinations of Digital Equity, and (3) Practical Applications and Resources for Educators: Activities, Assignments, Syllabi, and Course Design.

The first part of our book, "Theorizing Digital Equity," starts with Laura E. Mendoza's chapter entitled "Equitable Digital Practices for Multilingual Learners," which provides a critical examination of equity in the classroom. The author argues that in the face of a growing need for technology in the classroom, the burden of ensuring equity for students falls on the educators in addition to the many challenges already present. The chapter's focus is multilingual classrooms, where "finding the balance between including differentiated instruction through technology and empowering students through various digital literacy practices might be even harder."

Steven D'Agustino's chapter, "Social Reproduction and Equity Challenges in Learning Management Systems (LMS) within Online Education," continues the critical examination of digital equity through Social Reproduction Theory. Thus, the author analyzes equity challenges through a sociological lens, while demonstrating "the importance of understanding digital platforms not just as technological advancements but as phenomena deeply intertwined with socio-educational issues that demand critical examination."

Next, in the chapter "Leveraging Assistive Technology to Promote Inclusive English Language Teaching and Digital Literacy," Davey Young provides a critical analysis of assistive technology and equity in the context of persons with disabilities. Additionally, the author offers recommendations that are "divided into three categories: using assistive technology to increase accessibility, using assistive technology as an accommodation, and using assistive technology to promote digital literacy."

Authors Amina Parveen, Aamir Naziir Ganie, Fazila Bashir, Phayaola N. Zimik and Shazia N. Jan contribute two chapters to this volume. Analyzing the concept of digital equity in-depth, the authors offer one theoretical and one practical work, each in corresponding sections. The research team's first chapter, "Enhancing Classroom Equity through the Integration of Digital Technology," examines the positive impact of digital technology while addressing current discrepancies and inequities in the classroom. The authors' argument exhibits ways digital technology can be utilized to address diverse learning needs, foster inclusivity, support personalized learning, and address potential disparities to possibly overcoming educational gaps.

The final theoretical chapter of the book, entitled "Machine Intelligence in Translation Studies: Transformative Digital Approaches for Culturally Inclusive Education," is authored by Berra Nur Acay, Tuğba Nur Küçük, Aylin Yardımcı, and Eda Başak Hancı-Azizoglu. The authors critically analyze digital equity from the applied linguistics disciplinary perspective, offering a thorough examination of the use of technology in translation studies, where a cultural understanding and linguistic connotation are key components of accuracy.

The second part of the book demonstrates a collection of "Scholarly Examinations of Digital Equity." The first chapter of this section, authored by Kübra Engin, Kadriye Selin Budak, Emine Bozkurt Polat, Feyza Aydin Bölükbaş, and İlkay Ulutaş, is entitled "Linking with Technology in the Education and Adaptation Processes of Refugee Children." Following the influx of refugees and consequently refugee children in Turkey, the researchers discuss their study "within the framework of Maslow's Hierarchy and Family Systems Theory, and explanations of children's participation in educational processes, the use of technology in educational processes, and teacher guidance."

Next, Silvia Maria Bravo Palomares discusses the ways artificial intelligence (AI) impacts higher education, specifically English as a Foreign Language (EFL) classrooms. The chapter, entitled "Leveling the Language Field: A Qualitative Study of the Impact of AI on Learning English as a Foreign Higher Education," is an in-depth qualitative study offering insights of both students and educators in higher education.

Thao Quoc Tran and Thao Phuong Nguyen's chapter, "The Deployment of Blended Learning for English Vocabulary Enhancement: Voice of Vietnamese L2 Students," is "a mixed-methods study exploring Vietnamese L2 students' perceptions of the effects of BL on their English vocabulary enhancement." The chapter demonstrates benefits of blended learning and technology use for students in language learning classrooms.

Similarly, authors Véronique Delplancq, Ana Maria Costa, José Pereira, Romain Gillain, and Susana Fidalgo examine advantages of technology use in foreign language classes in their chapter entitled "Using Digital Tools to Innovate in Higher Education: From Icebreakers to Various Skills Development." Additionally, the researchers analyze challenges regarding the use of technology in foreign language classes and provide a thorough discussion of "skills development, improvements over traditional methods, encountered difficulties, and the dynamics within the teaching-learning process."

In the last chapter of the section, "Exploring Students' Perceptions of Online EAP Writing Courses in the EMI Context in Mainland China," authors Luyue Wang, Chenghao Wang, and Bin Zou analyze technology use and its effectiveness in English for Academic Purpose (EAP) courses in English as the medium of instruction (EMI) programs. The study exhibits the impact of and challenges raised by the shift from traditional classrooms to online platforms in higher education, especially after the COVID-19 pandemic.

The final part of our book, "Practical Applications and Resources for Educators," starts off with the second piece by Amina Parveen, Aamir Naziir Ganie, Fazila Bashir, Phayaola N. Zimik and Shazia N. Jan. In this chapter, "Pedagogical Strategies for Developing Digital Literacy," the authors expand on their analysis through "a holistic approach for cultivating digital literacy skills in students by employing innovative pedagogical strategies." To this end, they offer two case studies resulting in applicable strategies to enhance digital equity and minimize the educational gap in the classroom.

José Manuel Correoso-Rodenas's chapter, "The Last Frontier(s): Teaching Archive-Based, Historical Texts in a Digital Context," offers "a case-study about the educational exploration of some pieces of archival material related to the Spanish exploration of Northwestern America." The chapter both offers practical strategies and critical analyses of access and equity in the context of technology and, in particular, digital archives.

Next, Héctor Manuel Serna Dimas discusses an instructional design example of digital literacy, technology, and inclusion in the chapter, "Scaffolded Literacy Instruction for English Language Learners: Using Technology to Transform the Playing Field." The author examines a literacy project, which calls for "a more comprehensive understanding of literacy instruction in classrooms."

Author Jennifer Schneider's contribution "Authentic Presentation Experiences as a Tool to Develop Transferable Skills" offers applicable insights into teaching digital literacy. The chapter "describes a course-long project that is grounded in principles of feminist digital pedagogy, digital literacy, inclusive instruction, and equity," which is designed to teach students written and oral communication competence as well as presentation skills.

The concluding chapter of the section and the book, "The Internet Problem: Pedagogical Solutions to the Information Problem," is a comprehensive examination of higher education challenges regarding digital literacy and generative artificial intelligence. Author Julie Christina Tatlock discusses "the role formative assessment can play in making digital skills integrated into curriculum" and offers "a series of sample assignments demonstrating formative assessment and specifically formative assessment vis a vis the digital world."

FINAL THOUGHTS: BALANCING CAUTION AND HOPE

Taken together, this collection of theoretical, empirical, and practical chapters communicates a message of caution about the technologies that are rapidly becoming so deeply embedded into our institutions, our classrooms, and our lives. These technologies have the potential to deepen inequalities within our classrooms if used without careful consideration. The chapters presented here will unpack the theory of this inequity and provide empirical evidence of this disparity in academia. We hope this scholarship will serve as a reminder of the great power of technology, and the care and consideration required of educators when they decide to integrate technology in the classroom.

However, this collection is not a neo-Luddite's rejection of educational technologies, and we hope you'll see the innovation, enthusiasm, and, ultimately, hopefulness woven throughout each of the subsequent chapters. While educational technologies may carry risks, they also open both us and our students to new worlds of opportunities. We hope the chapters to follow will inspire educators to reconsider their own pedagogy and how technology might be integrated with both caution and hope to lift up all of our students.

Katelyn Burton Prager
Fashion Institute of Technology, USA

Nurhayat Bilge
Fashion Institute of Technology, USA

Section 1
Theorizing Digital Equity: Opportunities and Limitations of Digital Technologies in the Classroom

Equitable Digital Practices for Multilingual Learners

Laura E. Mendoza
https://orcid.org/0000-0001-8649-8775
University of Texas at El Paso, USA

ABSTRACT

Leveraging today's use of technology is a responsibility that educators, administrators, and policymakers should be sharing. Unfortunately, this task has been confluently left to educators, who, in addition to having to face many other challenges in their classrooms, have to plan accordingly how technology can represent a benefit and not a struggle for their students. In the multilingual classroom, where educators and students concurrently are facing a variety of types of marginalization, finding the balance between including differentiated instruction through technology and empowering students through various digital literacy practices might be even harder. The present chapter aims to contribute to the growing knowledge of the intersectionality that equity and digital literacy practices represent in the multilingual classroom. This chapter also aims to continue the conversation of the cultural competence educators and multilingual learners must navigate to be successful at school and outside of it.

INTRODUCTION

Leveraging today's use of technology is a responsibility that educators, administrators, and policymakers should be sharing. Unfortunately, this task has been confluently left to educators, who, in addition to having to face many other challenges in their classrooms, have to plan accordingly how technology can represent a benefit and not a struggle for their students. In the multilingual classroom, where educators and students concurrently are facing a variety of types of marginalization, finding the balance between including differentiated instruction through technology

DOI: 10.4018/979-8-3693-2591-9.ch001

and empowering students through various digital literacy practices, might be even more challenging. The present chapter aims to contribute to the growing knowledge of the intersectionality that equity and digital literacy practices represent in the multilingual classroom. This chapter also aims to continue the conversation on the cultural competence educators and multilingual learners must navigate to succeed at and outside school.

Many multilingual learners are constantly exposed to various technologies while performing non-academic tasks; concurrently, the instances where pedagogical practices appropriately use technology vary from institution to institution and from educator to educator. The current chapter presents information about the relevancy that interlinks equity, technology, and education in today's multilingual classrooms; it provides a brief historical background about the ways in which the term equity has made it to the digital world and distinguishes between digital practices and digital literacy practices. The chapter presents information about how the digital divide continues to be problematic and underseen. Still, it conjointly aims to provide a variety of pedagogical practices that pretend, as much as possible, to close the existent gap. Recommendations to inform the literature and to provide spaces for administrators, curriculum creators, and educators to think critically about the ways in which technologies are integrated into today's multilingual classrooms are present throughout the chapter in an effort to contribute positively to the ongoing discourse on effective pedagogical practices and equitable learning environments in diverse educational settings.

BACKGROUND

Equity in Today's Digital World

Equity, in this chapter, relates directly to what Papendieck (2018) identifies as retooling the educational status quo. The author highlights that to entirely interconnect technology and equity, we must refrain from reproducing pedagogies that disrupt broad social changes. Consequently, understanding the interconnectedness of equity and technology, particularly in the multilingual classroom, represents the integration of practices that are far from oppressive. First of all, we must fully understand that spaces like the multilingual classroom continuously fight against a wide variety of social injustices. For this reason, to fully connect equity with technology, we must start by utilizing resources and pedagogies that empower our multilingual students instead of continuing to hinder them.

Equity, nevertheless, looks different for all students. In Gorski's (2005) words: "students experience technology in very different ways" (p. 12). For multilingual students, for example, equity may take re-learning task-specific vocabulary in order to be able to navigate the devices provided at school because defaults are in English (Gorski, 2005; Peña-López, 2010). In terms of access to devices, those who are more fortunate may, for instance, be provided with a variety of devices (e.g., tablets, laptops, computers, cameras, and printers) by their new institutions. However, in their institutions, students commonly deal with having limited resources; therefore, this accessibility to devices does not differ from the circumstances students may face at home.

Taking the example of transnational students who come legally to the United States to continue their academic paths, these transnational students may be perceived as privileged at first instance since, first of all, they are entering a powerful country legally, and second of all, they are able to enjoy the benefits (e.g., having access to a number of devices) that their receiving country (The United States) can share with them through their institutions. Nevertheless, their circumstances may not be as fortunate and simplistic as they seem since other tensions are present in transnational students' lives. Added to the known complexities of navigating cultural identity, facing language barriers, and grappling with the impact of the digital divide, students whose life happens while physically traversing two countries (e.g., US/Mexico) constantly mobilize their political, social, and cultural issues from one side to another in the same way they mobilize their knowledges (Guerra, 2004; Fránquiz and Ortiz, 2017; Mendoza-Fierro, 2020). To illustrate, transnational (US/Mexico), particularly transfronterizx students (border commuters), have diverse types of access to technology on every border. Thus, although their American institutions are able to provide them with newer technologies (e.g., devices and educational platforms), transnational students lose all or some access as they go back home. To illustrate, while one side of the border may enjoy high-speed broadband, the other side of the border may contend with limited access, emphasizing the pronounced digital divide between the two regions (US/Mexico).

For the same reason but from a more positive perspective, transnational and transfronterizx students find equitable virtual spaces where they can simultaneously connect their lives on both sides at the border thanks to technology. For instance, Mendoza-Fierro (2020) states that students enrolled in and attending school in an American institution in the US highlighted how they can connect their two communities (school and home) by making use of their digital literacy practices. In this case, students learned to connect their communities specifically by using their institution's preferred educational platform (Blackboard). The transfronterizx students in this study could continue mastering school materials taught in the US by accessing them in Mexico.

Digital Practices

Although the terms digital practices and digital literacy practices are interrelated, the present chapter slightly differentiates between them. Broadly speaking, digital literacy practices are conveniently positioned within the giant umbrella of digital practices. In this chapter, digital practices should be understood following Jones et al. (2015) perspectives:

Digital practices, then, are these 'assemblages' of actions involving tools associated with digital technologies, which have come to be recognized by specific groups of people as ways of attaining particular social goals, enacting particular social identities, and reproducing particular sets of social relationships. The assumption is that digital technologies, because of the different configurations of modes and materialities they make available, both make possible new kinds of social practices and alter the way people engage in old ones (p. 3).

These practices radically distinguish themselves from those that occur equivalently offline; digital practices occur online and are always connected to various digital tools and technologies. In this sense, digital practices occur online despite their users' intentions to utilize them and, more importantly, despite their users' proficiency with each of them. Digital practices are tightly intertwined with cultural practices, shaping and reflecting how various communities use, learn, and construct digital technologies within the broader context of their cultural norms, values, and linguistic repertoires.

Critically linked to the purpose of the present chapter is the understanding of the existent connection between language learning and the aforementioned digital practices. Chik (2015) explains that the impact of new digital practices (e.g., learning a language using a website or application) relies heavily on these websites' attempts to be omnipresent. The author underscores that, notwithstanding the potential lack of scholarly credibility in the materials featured on these websites and applications, their usability and heightened interactivity have prompted practitioners to incorporate them as supplementary tools for language learning. In today's multilingual classrooms, the stretched connection between language learning and digital practices resonates because it opens the room to let students develop knowledge and skills that otherwise might be hindered and, additionally, to let students embed other collaborative practices that might be pretty common for them outside of academic contexts.

Digital Literacy Practices

For the purpose of the present chapter, digital literacy practices must be understood, as proposed by Jones (2016), who follows Gee's previous perspectives on 'New Literacy Studies.' Jones states:

These literacy practices involve new forms of social interaction, new kinds of texts, and new understandings of authorship and agency. The study of 'digital literacies' is the study of the everyday, vernacular literacy practices people engage in using digital technology and how these practices affect language learning and language use (p. 3).

The present chapter addresses the idea that digital literacy practices will go beyond the preconceived literacy practices of reading and writing. This chapter, therefore, adheres to the constraints that 21st-century skills like problem-solving, teamwork, productivity, curiosity, analysis, and cultural competency will always go hand in hand with newer practices that interwind with the use of technology, such as familiarity with office productivity software (e.g., Microsoft or Google packages), understanding of the use of varied Internet browsers (e.g., Mozilla, Google Chrome), and having a general familiarity with a variety of electronic devices (e.g., smartphones, tablets, laptops). In this sense, the chapter suggests that digital literacy practices help students better understand, mediate, and re-thinking texts, but conjointly, they are also becoming more effective users of technology. It is crucial for the understanding of the present chapter that digital literacy practices here always thrive for the agents to interact with these new literacies in an active way by critically analyzing, synthesizing, or creating/re-creating content in complex ways. To further the conversation, the following section provides deeper information regarding our current digital divide as well as today's meaning of cultural competence, both in relation to our current multilingual classrooms.

THE MAIN FOCUS OF THE CHAPTER

The Current Digital Divide and Its Relevancy in the Multilingual Classroom

Unfortunately, the digital divide may be connected to several factors that impact students. On the one hand, for example, the digital divide may impact students generationally (Salajan et al., 2010; Soomro et al., 2020; Volkom et al., 2014). On the other hand, the digital divide may impact students based on their socioeconomic status (Ancheta-Arrabal, 2021; Cullen, 2001; Ma, 2021). As part of the first scenario, those students who were born in an age where technology was not a need but a luxury may face a difficult time trying to learn again how to do something (e.g., doing math or writing an essay) they had previously mastered without the use of technology. Another crucial digital divide factor is gender issues (Ancheta-Arrabal, 2021; Ching et al., 2005). Our educators are responsible for providing as many opportunities as possible for our multilingual students to develop their digital literacy skills to close the gap that distances them from mainstream society. It is primarily crucial to open opportunities for women, especially those who might not even know that they have been threatened politically, socially, and culturally just because of who they are. Ancheta-Arrabal (2021) emphasizes: "ICT (Information and Computer Technologies) use determines people's professional and vital development. This makes digital gender exclusion a fundamental problem, affecting half of humanity—women—without a clear awareness of it" (p. 13). Consequently, considering our political, cultural, and social gender disparities, we must reinforce our support to our minoritized students at all given moments; it must be evident that our efforts to provide them with more inclusive experiences are built far from the misogynous realities they may encounter in other areas of their lives.

To gain a deeper understanding of what the term digital divide entails, this chapter uses the term as suggested by Gorski (2005, p. 5):

The "divide" refers to the difference in access rates among one or more groups. For example, the racial digital divide is the difference in computer and Internet access and usage rates (at home, school, work, or other locations) between those groups with higher rates of access and usage (White people and Asian Pacific Islander people) and those with relatively lower rates of access and usage (Native American, African American, and Latina[o] people). However, this traditional understanding of the digital divide fails to capture the complete picture of inequity and alienation recycled by these gaps and the resulting educational, social, cultural, and economic ramifications, primarily for groups already educationally, socially, culturally, and economically oppressed. Meanwhile, such a limited view of the digital divide serves the interests of privileged groups and individuals, who can continue critiquing and working to dissolve gaps in physical access and use rates while failing to think critically and reflectively about their personal and collective roles in recycling old inequities in a new cyber-form.

Our current digital divide cannot be minimized by overseeing its origins' many political, cultural, and social aspects. Centralizing the conversation to school, the digital divide should not be simplified as having or not having access to devices and the Internet in and outside of the classroom (Clark & Gorski, 2002); the conversation must go beyond these simplistic views. Our current digital divide must be understood by globalizing various factors that are not only interdependent but also subject to ongoing evolution and adaptation. Let us, for instance, consider the example of the geographical, social, and economic digital divide; as all of these interject and interact with the others, they all also fluctuate to evolve concurrently. This said, the digital divide gaps that we deal with currently are different from the ones from twenty years ago, and equally important, will not be the same that our future generations will be facing. The challenges and practices that were problematic decades ago have, at least for a fair fraction, been dismantled, leading the way to new challenges and practices that create today's digital divide.

The current digital divide then goes further than the diffusion of electronic devices, its accessibility, and the rapid growth of the Internet. Politically and culturally speaking, the current digital divide includes an underestimated agenda that continues to reproduce disparities at various systemic levels. To illustrate, Gorski (2005) highlights:

In the end, White students are increasingly likely to build confidence and mastery over computer and Internet technologies, known as "net savvy." They are being prepared for the highly digitized global economy and pushed to understand technology in a complex way. Students of Color, less likely to be exposed to these technologies, remain largely unaware of the power and complexity of techno-society and, therefore, outside the digital loop (p. 11).

This is a relevant situation in any classroom, as we may all have students who have been marginalized or racialized. However, in the language classroom, this circumstance is alarming because we are now distancing ourselves from the possibility of having students who have faced barriers due to privileged views to immerse ourselves in a space where all students have been direct victims of systemic inequalities. Consequently, we must carefully consider how to start fostering empathy and understanding to collectively create a more equitable and inclusive learning environment. By consciously addressing the digital divide, not only through accessible physical technology, but we also aim to empower all students, ensuring they have equal opportunities to thrive in the digital age. Suppose we are not building walls against these misconducts, as mentioned above. In that case, the multilingual learners in our classrooms will remain faithful to the belief that their voices, perceptions, and cultures continue to be irrelevant to mainstream societies.

For instance, the digital divide may also entail further unfortunate variables in the multilingual classroom. For example, efficiently using leisure time to learn to maneuver the capabilities of various electronic devices, platforms, software, and apps may translate to gaining skills that otherwise will not be acquired (Clark & Gorski, 2002). However, as leisure time becomes increasingly a luxury, students whose economic dynamics depend on many working hours have fewer opportunities to become competent users of the increasingly incoming technologies and digital practices. For this reason, Gorski (2005) suggests re-thinking our conceptualizations of how closing the digital divide should signify only providing students with more devices or the Internet; the author states: " In addition to its offensively patriarchal nature, the suggestion that increasing or improving physical access to computers and the Internet will close the divide is simplistic and shallow—a band-aid approach to a remarkably ill social and educational system" (p. 7). In other words, Gorski (2005) invites us to revisit the instances where we have been only reproducing old views instead of closing the gap for our students.

Cultural Competence in Today's Multilingual Classroom

Unfortunately, the scenarios in multilingual classrooms are often not as privileged as others in many different senses. On the one hand, students enrolled in multilingual classrooms generally come from underprivileged backgrounds. Therefore, coming from precarious backgrounds, where not all families have access to diversified electronic devices, may prompt them to have limited or more limited digital literacy practices. Equally significant, home and language classroom differences may evoke stressful situations for emergent bilinguals since their parents may pressure them to learn English quickly to obtain respectable jobs (Kazim, 2017). This circumstance, added to the fact that students might not be as proficient in terms of technology in comparison to some of their White classmates, can position emergent bilinguals in highly uncomfortable situations.

Another problem to be considered when acknowledging the various backgrounds in a classroom involves the representation of transnational students. In a multilingual classroom, we will likely encounter transnational students whose previous educational experiences are highly likely to differ from what they are currently experiencing (Hamann et al., 2010; Trejo et al., 2023; Zúñiga & Hamann, 2009). Tyack and Cuban (1997), for instance, remind us:

Most Americans have been to school and know what a "real school" is like. Congruence with that cultural template has helped maintain the institution's legitimacy in the public's minds. Nevertheless, trouble often ensued when schooling departed too much from the consensual model of a "real school" and failed to match the grammar of schooling. If teachers did not maintain strict discipline and consistently supervise students in class, if traditional subjects were neglected, and if pupils did not bring report cards home, reforms might be suspected (p. 9).

However, the situation for transnational students tends to be even more impactful. If, for many Americans, *real school* has not mirrored their education expectations, imagine how chaotic it has been for transnational and all underprivileged students. Nevertheless, although their experiences might differ, many of these transnational students learn how to navigate their new experiences and technologies, constantly negotiating their physical and digital spaces (Mendoza-Fierro, 2020; Monty, 2015). As educators, we must constantly reflect upon our cultural competence in all our multilingual classrooms if we want to serve our students' needs.

To conclude, we must critically consider that multilingual students, underprivileged students, transnational students, emergent bilingual students, and all those students who may be considered underserved are continuously bringing with them a variety of knowledge that can help them and others become successful students. We need to also keep in mind that having access to technology in the United States is different than having access to technology in other countries; consequently, talking specifically about having access to technology at school, remains an important conversation even in the United States. However, there is an imminent need to understand inclusivity for newer pedagogical approaches to stop underestimating multilingual learners' capabilities. In this sense, we should avoid stratifying our classrooms by thinking that multilingual learners will not be able to follow all the recent technologies they will see in a classroom because, on the contrary, they have been resisting many complexities and inequalities by integrating their day-to-day digital literacy practices in their classrooms. For this reason, the present chapter aims to contribute to the ongoing conversation on the importance of having appropriate cultural competence regarding the current digital literacy practices for underprivileged students to better serve the needs of the students in today's multilingual classrooms.

SOLUTIONS AND RECOMMENDATIONS

Inclusive Pedagogical Approaches When Using Technology

To diminish the integration of pedagogies that are far from being inclusive and remain stereotypical, we, as educators, must prioritize adopting culturally responsive teaching practices that honor and validate all students' diverse identities and experiences. By writing this chapter, and this section primarily, the author aims to contribute to the ongoing conversation of promoting a variety of inclusive technologies to multilingual learners, particularly those pedagogies which include equitable digital practices and equitable access to technologies as a whole. Said this, the present chapter is a recollection of perspectives that are heavily inclined to support multilingual learners' advancements in mainstream societies, not only from an academic perspective but concurrently from a sociopolitical one.

To deepen the conversation, we need to understand and recognize the many instances in which our roles as educators are primarily to empower our multilingual learners by providing them with inclusive pedagogical approaches that may be underutilized in other classrooms. Likewise, it is our responsibility as educators to provide as many opportunities as possible for our multilingual students to develop their digital literacy skills in an effort to close the gap that distances them from mainstream society. It is primarily crucial to open opportunities for women, especially those who might not even know that they have been threatened politically, socially, and culturally just because of who they are. Ancheta-Arrabal et al. (2021) reflects on these issues and state: "ICT use determines people's professional and vital development. This makes digital gender exclusion a fundamental problem, affecting half of humanity—women—without a clear awareness of it" (p. 13). Therefore, we need to continue the conversation as to who is most likely to have limited access to technologies, who is most likely to have limited digital competencies, and who is most likely to have interrupted teaching instances of various digital literacy skills. If we, as educators, are not able to recognize that these issues are continuously emerging in our multilingual classrooms, we are lost; if we, as educators, are not able to recognize that by not acknowledging the issues mentioned above and gaps are re-reproducing the same systemic issues, we are lost. With every step that we take toward the dissemination of knowledge and its interconnectedness with education and equity, we are moving forward. Although changing one multilingual classroom at a time may not seem sufficient, it means embracing the change for future professionals.

During the last decades, authors (Ahmadi, 2018; Cruz-Jesus, 2016; Gee, 2010; Golonka et al., 2014; Jones et al., 2015; Lankshear et al., 2014; Mendoza-Fierro, 2020) have been providing a variety of suggestions to improve the experiences of multilingual learners. Some recurrent and overlapping pedagogical practices are mentioned repeatedly through the literature, fostering additional opportunities for educators and curriculum creators to find new ways to teach; it is by carefully rethinking the digital practices and experiences that we emphasize in our classroom that we depower or empower our multilingual learners, and simultaneously, create more inclusive physical and virtual spaces for them. For example, Gee (2010) reminds us: "Digital tools are changing the balance of participation and spectatorship. More and more today, people do not have to play just the role of the spectator. Since they can now produce their music, news, games, and films, for example, they can participate in what used to be practices reserved for professional or elite musicians, filmmakers, game designers, and news people" (p. 12).

For this reason, it is crucial for us, as educators, to think critically about the number of opportunities that we are providing our multilingual learners to become producers of these new types of knowledge and not only recipients. Suppose we continue emancipating the nature in which communities, to include minoritized communities such as multilingual learners, currently interact and learn. In that case, we can aspire to cultivate more inclusive, equitable, and empowering educational environments that honor all learners' diverse linguistic and cultural backgrounds. In a similar fashion, Cruz-Jesus et al. (2016) state: "ICT (Information and Computer Technologies) are becoming a critical tool not only for politics but also for individuals to engage in public and political activities, serving as a bridge between political entities and citizens" (p. 73). If this is, therefore, the case, we need to pay special attention to the opportunities that we ground in our multilingual classrooms to master the use of ICT; as it has been stated in this manuscript, our language classrooms are already full of students who have been minoritized for various institutions of power, and not supporting our students' skills development is reinforcing the fact, that in the near future, they will remain out of the political and social conversations held. The authors continue: "The use of ICT for civic participation (eCivic) allows individuals to get information on public issues in a faster and easier way than with traditional (offline) methods, which ultimately facilitates political and civic engagements and minimizes social constraints." This previous example then it is clearly a call for all of us to start breaking the barriers for our multilingual learners through the use of equitable technologies. Presupposing an imperative need for having inclusive pedagogies in today's multilingual classrooms requires letting students explore their digital worlds.

Another way to continue breaking the barriers for multilingual learners and to provide them with more inclusive educational spaces and pedagogies is to allow them to work collaboratively. From firsthand experiences, and working for several year at the college level, the chapter's author has noticed how some older students must re-learn their manners because it may take them twice the time to submit an assignment as they are conjointly learning the class content while learning to navigate technology. Similarly, she has noticed how some tasks (e.g., sending an email, opening a Word processor) that younger students may navigate in an innate way, presuppose moments of anxiety for them. On the other hand, younger students need help communicating and presenting their ideas. One possible way to alleviate this specific type of generational digital divide is to provide enough opportunities during class periods for students to work in pairs or small groups; in this case, younger and older students are to be purposefully grouped in order for them to learn to appreciate one another's strengths, and more importantly, build from them. The incorporation of this type of grouping is a smooth transition in many classrooms since today's education correspondingly looks for the constant integration of teamwork, which might openly mirror what the workforce of the 21st century requires. Taking the example of creating a presentation (e.g., PowerPoint, Canva, Google Slides, to name a few.) to be shared with the whole class may, therefore, look as follows: While some students will be able to gain experience advancing their digital literacy and multimodal skills, others simultaneously will advance their professional and communicative skills.

Additionally, administrators, policymakers, and educators must pay close attention to the gap in student accessibility. Golonka et al. (2014) share: "Well-established technologies, such as the personal computer and internet access, have become nearly ubiquitous for foreign language (FL) learning in many industrialized countries" (p. 70). However, the inquiry persists: What implications arise for nations that lack the industrial development of their counterparts? As it has been discussed here, the political, cultural, social, emotional, and financial barriers that multilingual learners face commonly, distant considerably from the circumstances that non-minoritized students may encounter inside and outside their classrooms. For this reason, promoting inclusive pedagogies in multilingual classrooms must be treated differently from the administrators' and educators' perspectives; in these classrooms, inclusivity not only should list having culturally appropriate modalities of instruction and content, but at the same time, it should include having a deeper understanding of aggregates of the inclusivity. In these classrooms, for instance, inclusivity should merge accessibility with digital practices' proficiencies among educators and students; we must understand that if educators are not ready to lead, and most importantly, are not well-trained to lead, our multilingual learners will continue to be unreasonably perceived as the problem.

Interestingly, Golonka et al. (2014) say: "The literature on electronic grammar checkers suggests that language learners need training in order to use this technology effectively" (p. 81). This view, however, contrasts with results from other (Mendoza-Fierro, 2020) studies, which have proven that students, in fact, use grammar checkers (e.g., Google Translate) to verify the specific spelling of a word or its pronunciation. This discrepancy underscores the importance of considering different methodologies and contextual factors when interpreting research findings that deal with the utilization of language tools, particularly if the findings contrast different educational settings. It must be then considered that what may look equitable in what scenario may not represent an impactful change if present in a different context; for multilingual learners, equitable practices, digital or not, represent a different scaffolding process than other students. Given their diversified backgrounds, values, and experiences, multilingual learners experience inclusivity differently; therefore, when adding the technology variable to the equation, multilingual learners require not only varied instances of exposure to digital practices but conjointly, pedagogical practices that are engaging, adaptive, and preferably personalized. As such, the subsequent subsection furnishes additional insights into digital pedagogies.

Digital Pedagogies

Not surprisingly, as technologies and their linked practices evolve, pedagogies also move forward. As a consequence, our motivations and responsibilities in our multilingual classrooms unfold to open the path to pedagogies that are not exclusively culturally relevant but equally important, pedagogically effective, and conducive to fostering equitable learning environments for all students. To further the conversation of what digital pedagogies are, the present chapter describes them based on Toktarova and Semenova (2020), who state that digital pedagogy refers to:

A branch of pedagogical science that reveals the essence and regularities of digital education, the role of 'digitalized' educational processes in personal growth, develops practical ways and means of improving their effectiveness; a pedagogical trend related to the task of building digital economy and digital society; science and practice describing the arrangement of an educational process in the new conditions of a bifurcated reality; embedding computer-based digital technologies in the art of learning, which allow enriching the processes of learning, teaching and assessing throughout the course; building knowledge by the professor through planning education based on problem solving and higher-order thinking skills; pedagogy that provides high-quality education using computers and programs, while the use of information and communication technologies is a tool for creating new learning opportunities; the science of specially organized purposeful and systematic activity on human formation, the content, forms and methods of upbringing, education and teaching using information technologies and the Internet (p. 2).

In other words, these aforementioned digital pedagogies look to consciously leverage and actively connect users, learners specifically, with the tools that help them mediate their learning processes. Through various innovative perspectives, the use of apps, platforms, and websites, and the dissemination of devices with the capabilities to perform the required tasks, digital pedagogies allow educators to constructively and equitably contribute to the learner's ownership of learning. When planned strategically, digital pedagogies can foster learning environments that build or strengthen digital skills while simultaneously providing more agency to the learner. For these and other relevant reasons, providing spaces for multilingual learners to have access to appropriately and equitably aligned digital practices is essential.

Nevertheless, these digital pedagogies remain incomplete and relatively isolated in classrooms where educators are not well prepared to work with them. Ahmadi (2018) states: "Teachers should model the use of technology to support the curriculum so that learners can increase the true use of technology in learning their language skills" (p. 117). For this reason, educators should be the first to explore these digital pedagogies on their own in an effort to implement them in plenty of different ways, taking into consideration that, first, not all students learn in the same way, and second, that not all institutions and therefore students will be engaging in the same types of technologies. The opportunities and the conditions in which students, particularly multilingual students, will learn will depend drastically on their educators. Moreover, as we move forward embracing the transformative power of technology in education, we, as educators, need to be as prepared as possible in order to (1) improve our students' opportunities to navigate various digital practices efficiently, (2) co-teach our colleagues how to adapt their classrooms effectively; (3) connect students' academic lives with their lives outside the classroom; and (4) reconstruct our active participation as primary sources of these digital pedagogies for all our students.

As more digital resources are becoming rapidly available, educators and learners themselves start becoming more acquainted with practices that link their lives inside and outside the classroom. Some of the ways in which these newer pedagogical approaches can be integrated into our classrooms can be, for instance, through the integration of MOOCs (Massive Online Open Courses) within our own or also by adding lessons where students can use other tools they are highly likely to be familiar with already. For example, the usability of social media sites can be more heavily considered by administrators, curriculum developers, and educators conjointly when creating curricula. Chik (2015) highlights that Language Learning Social Network Sites (LLSNSs), even though they are relatively new, have been able to captivate an increasing number of users because they have proven a degree of interactivity that mirrors what they look for while using other social media sites. In this sense, if we, as educators, endeavor to promote the appropriate utilization of these newer digital pedagogies, we will be mirroring scenarios that are already familiar to many of our students, increasing the possibilities of a higher engagement while mastering a new language or added content. Although it may represent several systemic and unforeseen barriers, enhancing learning for multilingual learners resonates with the needs of today's classrooms; consequently, we need to consider our practices carefully and thoughtfully in our classrooms to foster community, collaboration, and technologies clearly.

FUTURE RESEARCH DIRECTIONS

Given the many injustices that multilingual learners, unfortunately, experience, having access to technologies and using them appropriately and efficiently to become competent professionals does not always make it to the list. In this sense, although the integration of technology in the classroom has been primarily researched, the existent literature that interconnects multilingual learners with equitable technologies still needs to be explored. To begin with, a future path for this type of research could be to explore equity amongst distinct levels of education. Another potential possibility could be to continue exploring gender issues and the digital divide. In any of the cases, and because multilingual learners continue to be a minoritized community, all efforts to disseminate information that can foster better and more inclusive academic spaces for them should be thoughtfully taken into consideration.

CONCLUSION

As this chapter comes to an end, it is relevant to remind the reader that what has been explained through it affects particularly emergent bilinguals; in this sense, although most of the suggestions are beneficial for classrooms at all levels of education and from various subject matters, the classrooms which may encounter a higher number of recommendations would be those in which multilingual learners are enrolled in. Several examples in the chapter referred primarily to those emergent bilinguals whose primary language is one different from English since much of the existent literature is solely based on them. To illustrate, Gorski (2005) highlights: "Current or potential Internet users who do not speak English, or for whom English is not a native language, may find the Web to be a very lonely place" (p.30); consequently, without serving linguistically diverse populations like the ones we encounter in a daily basis in our language classrooms, we will not be able to close the gaps of the digital divide. By writing this chapter, the author reflected not only on the relevancy that the digital divide holds in contemporary educational landscapes but also on the imperative for proactive measures aimed at bridging this gap to ensure equitable access to educational opportunities for all students. The chapter provides various suggestions as to how to, on the one hand, contribute to closing the digital divide gap in our very own classrooms, but also how to support multilingual learners efficiently and effectively through the means of varied digital practices. Throughout the manuscript, the author highlights how re-shaping our pedagogical practices in the classroom can provide learners with opportunities to bridge their academic and non-academic knowledge, primarily in terms of technology.

Equally important, Golonka et al. (2014) state: "Using technology in delivering a lesson or instructional unit will not make bad pedagogy good. Nor does a lack of technological tools or applications prevent effective teaching" (p. 93). Having a positive impact on our students' academic and non-academic lives represents way more than just providing them with the necessary electronic devices that can come in handy when mastering content. To contribute to the lives of our multilingual learners further positively, we must take into consideration several factors including their background, previous knowledges, the various systemic inequalities they have been fighting with during their whole lives, and more importantly, the ways in which their digital practices tight closely to their experiences in our classrooms. As part of today's classroom, it takes crafting a good lesson and the appropriate integration of a variety of digital practices, which must be well-acquainted pedagogically; these digital practices must be carefully aligned with the course objectives in order for educators to be able to improve students' experiences while mastering new content (e.g., linguistic skills) while breaking down learning barriers through the use of equitable technologies.

REFERENCES

Ahmadi, D. M. R. (2018). The use of technology in English language learning: A literature review. *International journal of research in English education, 3*(2), 115-125.

Ancheta-Arrabal, A., Pulido-Montes, C., & Carvajal-Mardones, V. (2021). Gender digital divide and education in Latin America: A literature review. *Education Sciences*, 11(12), 804. 10.3390/educsci11120804

Chik, A. (2015). Recreational language learning and digital practices: Positioning and repositioning. In *Discourse and Digital Practices* (pp. 112–129). Routledge. 10.4324/9781315726465-8

Ching, C. C., Basham, J. D., & Jang, E. (2005). The legacy of the digital divide: Gender, Socioeconomic status and early exposure as predictors of full-spectrum technology use among young adults. *Urban Education*, 40(4), 394–411. 10.1177/0042085905276389

Clark, C., & Gorski, P. (2002). Multicultural education and the digital divide: Focus on Socioeconomic class background. *Multicultural Perspectives*, 4(3), 25–36. 10.1207/S15327892MCP0403_6

Cruz-Jesus, F., Vicente, M. R., Bacao, F., & Oliveira, T. (2016). The education-related digital Divide: An analysis for the EU-28. *Computers in Human Behavior*, 56, 72–82. 10.1016/j.chb.2015.11.027

Cullen, R. (2001). Addressing the digital divide. *Online Information Review*, 25(5), 311–320. 10.1108/14684520110410517

Fránquiz, M. E., & Ortiz, A. A. (2017). Co-editors introduction: Who are the transfronterizos and what can we learn from them? *Bilingual Research Journal*, 40(2), 111–115. 10.1080/15235882.2017.1329378

Gee, J. P. (2010). A situated-sociocultural approach to literacy and technology. *The new literacies: Multiple perspectives on research and practice, 165*, 193.

Gee, J. P. (2023). Discourse and 'the New Literacy Studies. In *The Routledge Handbook of Discourse analysis* (pp. 469–480). Routledge. 10.4324/9781003035244-39

Golonka, E. M., Bowles, A. R., Frank, V. M., Richardson, D. L., & Freynik, S. (2014). Technologies for foreign language learning: A review of technology types and their effectiveness. *Computer Assisted Language Learning*, 27(1), 70–105. 10.1080/09588221.2012.700315

Gorski, P. (2005). Education equity and the digital divide. *AACE Journal*, 13(1), 3–45.

Guerra, J. C. (2004). *Putting literacy in its place: Nomadic consciousness and the practice of transcultural repositioning*. University of Washington.

Jones, R. H. (2016). Digital literacies. In *Handbook of research in second language teaching and learning* (pp. 286–298). Routledge. 10.4324/9781315716893-21

Jones, R. H., Chik, A., & Hafner, C. A. (2015). *Discourse and digital practices: Doing discourse analysis in the digital age* (p. 262). Taylor & Francis.

Kazim, R. (2017). *The issue of multi-linguality and challenges faced by working class students studying in an English medium school in Hyderabad*. Research Gate.

Lankshear, C., & Knobel, M. (2014). Englishes and digital literacy practices. In *The Routledge Companion to English Studies* (pp. 451–463). Routledge.

Ma, J. K. H. (2021). The digital divide at school and at home: A comparison between schools by socioeconomic level across 47 countries. *International Journal of Comparative Sociology*, 62(2), 115–140. 10.1177/00207152211023540

Mendoza-Fierro, L. E. (2020). *The Digital Literacy Practices of Transfronterizx ESOL College Students: Los De ESOL* [Doctoral dissertation, The University of Texas at El Paso].

Monty, R. W. (2015). Everyday borders of transnational students: Composing place and space with mobile technology, social media, and multimodality. *Computers and Composition*, 38, 126–139. 10.1016/j.compcom.2015.09.013

Papendieck, A. (2018). Technology for equity and social justice in education: A critical issue overview. *Texas Education Review (Austin, Tex.)*.

Peña-López, I. (2010). From laptops to competences: Bridging the digital divide in education. *Rev. U. Soc. Conocimiento*, 7, 21.

Salajan, F. D., Schönwetter, D. J., & Cleghorn, B. M. (2010). Student and faculty inter-generational digital divide: Fact or fiction? *Computers & Education*, 55(3), 1393–1403. 10.1016/j.compedu.2010.06.017

Soomro, K. A., Kale, U., Curtis, R., Akcaoglu, M., & Bernstein, M. (2020). Digital divide among higher education faculty. *International Journal of Educational Technology in Higher Education*, 17(1), 1–16. 10.1186/s41239-020-00191-5

Toktarova, V. I., & Semenova, D. A. (2020, November). Digital pedagogy: Analysis, requirements and experience of implementation. *Journal of Physics: Conference Series*, 1691(1), 012112. 10.1088/1742-6596/1691/1/012112

Trejo Guzmán, N. P., Mora Vázquez, A., & Andrade Rubio, K. L. (2023). Navigating the transition from the American into the Mexican educational system: Transnational students' experiences. *Bilingual Research Journal*, 46(1-2), 142–157. 10.1080/15235882.2023.2225455

Tyack, D. B., & Cuban, L. (1997). *Tinkering toward utopia: A century of public school reform*. Harvard University Press. 10.4159/9780674044524

Volkom, M. V., Stapley, J. C., & Amaturo, V. (2014). Revisiting the digital divide: Generational differences in technology use in everyday life. *North American Journal of Psychology*, 16(3).

Zúñiga, V., & Hamann, E. T. (2009). Sojourners in Mexico with US school experience: A new taxonomy for transnational students. *Comparative Education Review*, 53(3), 329–353. 10.1086/599356

KEY TERMS AND DEFINITIONS

Digital Literacy Practices: These are literacy practices that directly deal with reading and writing using various newer modalities, such as texting, tweeting, etc. These literacy practices are embedded in the bigger umbrella of digital practices.

Digital Pedagogy: A type of pedagogy that centers its attention on working collaboratively through the means of various technologies. It resists traditional learning strategies and methodologies to embrace the co-creation of knowledge by constantly reflecting and critically thinking about various issues.

Digital Practices: Practices that refer directly to the instances in which individuals engage in activities that require the means of digital technologies.

Emergent Bilingual: The term *emergent bilingual* is favored over conventional designations like *Language Learner*, aiming to mitigate instances in which individuals are perceived and/or treated through the lens of their linguistic abilities.

Equity: Equity in this chapter refers to the instances in which purposefully users, primarily administrators, policy makers, and educators, leverage technology and its usage to help students develop specific skills.

Minoritized Students: Students whose experiences have been mandated by various systemic inequalities entirely based on their background, culture, and practices.

Multilingual Learner: Students whose first language is one different from English.

Chapter 2
Social Reproduction and Equity Challenges in Learning Management Systems (LMS) Within Online Education

Steven D'Agustino
https://orcid.org/0009-0008-4735-9922
Fordham University, USA

ABSTRACT

This chapter embarks on a comprehensive exploration of the equity challenges entailed in learning management systems (LMS) within the domain of online education, under the critical gaze of social reproduction theory. The significance of this inquiry arises from the recognition that while LMS have emerged as potent instruments for course administration, they are not immune to perpetuating or ameliorating existing social inequalities. Within this chapter, the author undertakes an extensive analysis of these equity challenges, examining facets such as access, content accessibility, design, assessment, and various dimensions of online learning, all framed within the conceptual framework of social reproduction theory. This narrative endeavors to provide a holistic understanding of the intricate interplay between LMS, social reproduction dynamics, and equity within educational settings.

DOI: 10.4018/979-8-3693-2591-9.ch002

INTRODUCTION

In the contemporary landscape of education, the emergence of online learning signifies a significant transformation characterized by the rapid proliferation of Learning Management Systems (LMS). These digital platforms have been lauded for their revolutionary impact on course administration and the delivery of education, fundamentally altering the pedagogical terrain. The integration of LMS into the fabric of educational delivery mirrors a broader digitization trend and highlights the intricate relationship between technology and educational equity. Within this context, a growing body of scholarly work critically examines the implications of LMS through the prism of Social Reproduction Theory, a theoretical approach that explores how educational systems can both mirror and perpetuate societal inequalities.

Originating from the critical sociology of education, Social Reproduction Theory provides a powerful lens for dissecting the ways in which LMS, as vehicles of online education, intersect with the dynamics of social reproduction, potentially deepening or bridging gaps in educational access, engagement, and outcomes. This exploration, drawing upon both seminal and recent studies, seeks to offer a thorough investigation into the complex interplay between technology, education, and social stratification.

The inquiry positions LMS at the intersection of technology and sociology, unraveling their role as both facilitators and products of social reproduction. It critically assesses how the design, accessibility, and pedagogical underpinnings of LMS may reinforce systemic biases or act as catalysts for educational equity. By examining aspects such as user access, content inclusivity, and assessment practices, the analysis reveals the nuanced ways in which LMS can influence educational outcomes across diverse learner demographics.

By weaving together insights from a wide spectrum of research, the investigation aims to shed light on the nuanced dynamics between LMS, social reproduction, and educational equity. It underscores the importance of understanding digital platforms not just as technological advancements but as phenomena deeply intertwined with socio-educational issues that demand critical examination. The discourse seeks not only to contribute to the evolving conversation on the role of technology in fostering equitable educational environments but also to guide the thoughtful design and application of LMS to actively address and mitigate equity challenges. Through this lens, the exploration underscores the potential of digital education tools to both challenge and reinforce existing educational paradigms and the societal disparities they reflect.

Social Reproduction Theory Background and Key Concepts

Social Reproduction Theory (SRT) offers a lens through which to examine how societies maintain and reproduce themselves over time, despite changes in their human and material components. Its roots are found in Karl Marx's critique of capitalist society characterized by an inherent drive towards accumulation. Initially, anthropologists drew from Marx to explore the reproduction of non-capitalist societies but gradually shifted their focus to capitalism, expanding the scope of SRT to include critical considerations of women's roles and domestic work in sustaining both current workers and future generations (Weiss, 2021).

Backer and Cairns (2021) revisited SRT within the context of education, integrating a feminist analysis of reproductive labor to address its complex relationship with capitalism. This expansion allows for a broader understanding of SRT, encompassing the reproduction of life under capitalist conditions. Key concepts in SRT include the processes through which societies ensure continuity, such as the biological reproduction of individuals, the reproduction of labor power, and the provisioning of care needs (Munro, 2019). Furthermore, Laslett and Brenner (1989) explored how macrohistorical processes shape and are shaped by gender relations and social reproduction, emphasizing the role of the family, market, community, and state in these dynamics.

SRT thus provides a comprehensive framework for understanding the reproduction of social hierarchies and inequalities, particularly through education and family structures. By examining the roles of various forms of capital, labor, and societal structures, SRT reveals the mechanisms through which social inequalities are perpetuated and offers insights into potential avenues for societal change. The theory has evolved to include a greater recognition of gender and domestic work, reflecting a shift towards a more inclusive understanding of social reproduction within capitalist societies (Weiss 2021; Backer & Cairns 2021; Collins 2009; Laslett & Brenner 1989; Munro, 2019).

In the exploration of Social Reproduction Theory (SRT), several key terms emerge as central to understanding its complexity and application across various fields. These terms, deeply rooted in the critical examination of societal structures, provide a framework for analyzing the perpetuation of inequalities and the mechanisms through which societies maintain continuity over time.

Social Reproduction: This core concept of SRT refers to the processes through which societies reproduce themselves, encompassing the biological reproduction of the population, the reproduction of labor power, and the provisioning of care needs necessary for the sustenance and maintenance of life. Originating from Karl Marx's critique of capitalist societies, social reproduction extends beyond economic reproduction to include the roles of gender, family structures, and educational systems in sustaining societal norms and hierarchies (Weiss, 2021).

If LMS are designed primarily to cater to the needs of privileged students—those with advanced technological skills, reliable internet access, and a conducive learning environment—they can inadvertently perpetuate social inequalities. This scenario aligns with Bourdieu's concept of social reproduction, where the educational system legitimizes and reinforces existing social hierarchies by privileging the cultural capital of dominant groups (Bourdieu, 1986). For instance, advanced LMS features that assume a high level of digital literacy or access to specific technologies may exclude or disadvantage students from less privileged backgrounds, thereby reinforcing educational and social stratification (Selwyn, 2010).

Habitus: As articulated by Pierre Bourdieu, habitus offers profound insights into the ways our life experiences shape our perceptions and actions. Reay (2004) describes habitus as the "deeply ingrained habits, skills, and dispositions that we possess due to our life experiences." This definition underscores the enduring influence of early socialization on our behaviors and outlooks. Maton (2008) elaborates on this by noting that "habitus provides a practical sense, a feel for the game, that is acquired through long-term immersion in a social field." This practical sense allows individuals to navigate their social environments intuitively. Nash (1999) highlights the significance of this concept in understanding social structures, stating that "Bourdieu's concept of habitus helps us to understand how social structures are internalized and how they shape individual actions." This internalization process explains how societal norms and values become second nature.

The implementation and use of LMS are significantly affected by the habitus of both students and educators. Students from technology-rich backgrounds, who have been exposed to digital tools and platforms from an early age, tend to find LMS more intuitive and accessible. Their familiarity with technology aligns with the design and functionality of most LMS, which often assume a certain level of digital literacy. This congruence between their habitus and the technological environment of LMS enables them to navigate these systems with ease, maximizing their learning potential and engagement.

Conversely, students from less privileged backgrounds, who may have had limited exposure to technology, often find themselves at a disadvantage. Their habitus, shaped by environments where digital tools are not prevalent, does not align with the demands of modern LMS. These students may struggle with basic navigation, become easily frustrated with technological glitches, and feel alienated by the implicit assumption of digital competence. This disparity in technological familiarity can exacerbate existing educational inequalities, as students with a less compatible habitus may experience reduced engagement and poorer academic outcomes.

Educators are similarly influenced by their habitus in their interactions with LMS. Teachers with a robust background in technology integration are more likely to effectively utilize the advanced features of LMS, such as interactive modules, multimedia resources, and data analytics tools. Their technological habits empower them to create dynamic and engaging online learning environments that enhance student learning experiences. In contrast, educators with limited digital proficiency may find LMS daunting, potentially leading to underutilization of the system's capabilities and less effective teaching practices.

Field: This concept offers a nuanced understanding of the social arenas where individuals and groups vie for various forms of capital. Hilgers and Mangez (2015) describe fields as "structured spaces of positions and the position-takings of actors who compete for the distribution of different kinds of capital," highlighting the competitive nature of these social spaces. This framework helps to elucidate how different actors maneuver and strategize to accumulate economic, cultural, social, and symbolic capital. Grenfell and James (1998) extend this idea to the realm of education, stating that "Bourdieu's concept of field provides a framework for understanding how educational institutions are sites of social struggle." Within educational fields, various stakeholders, including students, teachers, and policymakers, engage in struggles that reflect broader societal power dynamics. These perspectives underscore the critical role of fields in shaping social relations and maintaining hierarchical structures within society.

The educational field is a prominent example where such competition is evident, and within this field, LMS play a significant role in shaping educational experiences and outcomes. The implementation and utilization of LMS within the educational field can either serve to democratize education or reinforce existing social hierarchies. The design and governance of LMS are critical in determining their impact on educational equity. When LMS are implemented with a one-size-fits-all approach, without considering the diverse needs and resources of different educational institutions, they risk perpetuating inequalities. For instance, access to advanced LMS features—such as sophisticated data analytics, interactive simulations, and personalized learning paths—may be restricted to well-funded schools that can afford the associated costs. Conversely, under-resourced schools may only have access to basic LMS functionalities, thereby limiting the educational opportunities available to their students.

This disparity in access to LMS features exacerbates existing educational inequalities by providing students in wealthier schools with a competitive advantage. These students benefit from enriched learning environments that can enhance their academic performance and engagement, while their counterparts in less affluent schools may struggle with outdated or less effective tools. Such inequalities in the educational field reflect broader social hierarchies and contribute to the reproduction of social stratification.

Social capital: As defined by Portes (1998), social capital "stands for the ability of actors to secure benefits by virtue of membership in social networks or other social structures." This concept is crucial in understanding how individuals and groups navigate social hierarchies and access resources. The role of social capital in educational settings is particularly significant, as highlighted by Stanton-Salazar and Dornbusch (1995), who emphasize that "the critical role of significant others in status attainment continues to be interpreted mainly in functionalist terms." This perspective suggests that the social networks and relationships students form can heavily influence their educational and social outcomes. Woolcock (1998) further expands on this idea, stating that "social capital refers to the norms and networks that facilitate collective action," which underscores the importance of social cohesion and collective efficacy in achieving both individual and community goals. Together, these insights illustrate how social capital operates within educational contexts to perpetuate or challenge existing inequalities, shaping the trajectories of students based on their social connections and the support they receive from their networks.

LMS possess the potential to enhance social capital by fostering interactions among students, teachers, and peers. However, the efficacy of these systems in promoting equitable access to social capital is contingent upon their design and implementation. LMS can serve as powerful tools for building and enhancing social capital within educational communities. Features such as discussion forums, group projects, and collaborative tools enable students to engage in meaningful interactions that transcend the traditional classroom setting. Discussion forums allow students to share knowledge, ask questions, and receive feedback from both peers and instructors, thereby creating a rich tapestry of academic discourse. Group projects facilitated through LMS can foster a sense of community and collective responsibility, as students work together to achieve common goals. Collaborative tools, such as shared documents and virtual meeting spaces, further support these interactions by providing platforms for real-time communication and cooperation.

Despite the potential of LMS to enhance social capital, disparities in social capital can influence how effectively students are able to leverage these networks for academic support and opportunities. Students from privileged backgrounds often enter educational settings with a higher degree of social capital, having access to well-established networks that can provide academic guidance, mentorship, and resources. In contrast, students from marginalized or less affluent backgrounds may lack these connections, making it more challenging for them to navigate academic environments and access support.

Cultural and Economic Capital: These terms, integral to the analysis of social reproduction, describe the non-financial and financial resources individuals possess, which influence their social mobility and position within societal hierarchies. Cultural capital can include education, skills, and other non-material assets that contribute to social status, while economic capital refers to material wealth and financial assets. Bourdieu's theory of cultural capital highlights how these forms of capital contribute to the reproduction of social classes across generations.

Students possessing greater cultural and economic capital often have prior exposure to technology, access to high-quality educational resources, and a conducive learning environment, all of which facilitate their navigation and utilization of LMS platforms. This prior exposure results in enhanced digital literacy, a familiarity with online learning tools, and the ability to access supplementary educational materials that can bolster their academic performance. For instance, students from affluent backgrounds are more likely to have personal computers, reliable internet access, and a quiet space for study, which collectively contribute to their ease of engagement with LMS (Bourdieu, 1986; Lareau, 2003). Conversely, students with less cultural and economic capital may encounter significant barriers when engaging with LMS. These students often lack prior technological exposure, face challenges in accessing digital devices and reliable internet, and may not have a supportive learning environment. These disparities can hinder their ability to effectively participate in online learning, potentially exacerbating educational inequalities (Bourdieu, 1986; DiMaggio, 1982).

Gender and Social Reproduction: These terms explore how gender relations and the organization of social reproduction—encompassing biological reproduction, care work, and the socialization of children—are shaped by and shape macrohistorical processes. Feminist theories of social reproduction extend the analysis to consider how societal reproduction involves not only the perpetuation of economic and social structures but also the reinforcement of gender norms and inequalities (Laslett & Brenner, 1989).

Studies have shown that male students tend to dominate online discussions, while female students participate less frequently and receive less acknowledgment for their contributions, which can lead to perceived higher competence in males (Lim et al., 2020; Jungwirth, 1991). Additionally, female students are more likely to request information but offer fewer explanations and opinions, resulting in less impactful participation (Li, 2002). Furthermore, educational materials that predominantly feature male perspectives and authors marginalize female students and reinforce the notion that male contributions are more valuable (Wu et al, 2020). Although the design features of LMS and their assessment do not differ significantly between genders, usage patterns indicate higher engagement among male students, potentially leading to a lack of representation and engagement for females (Aditya & Permadi, 2020).

Institutional Mechanisms: Social reproduction theory provides a critical lens through which to view the role of educational institutions in society. According to Collins (2009), "social reproduction theory argues that schools are not institutions of equal opportunity but mechanisms for perpetuating social inequalities." This perspective challenges the idealistic view of schools as levelers of social disparity, suggesting instead that they function to maintain and reproduce existing social hierarchies. In alignment with this, Giddens (1979) posits that "institutions are the principal means by which social practices are routinized across time and space." Schools, as key institutions, therefore play a crucial role in embedding and normalizing these practices, ensuring that the social order is consistently reproduced. Together, these insights underscore the powerful role of educational systems in shaping and sustaining societal structures.

LMS platforms, as tools for administering and delivering education, are deeply influenced by the institutional mechanisms of the schools and universities that adopt them. When LMS policies are rigid and standardized, they may inadvertently exclude non-traditional learners, such as adult students, part-time students, or those from diverse socio-economic backgrounds. These learners often have unique needs and constraints that rigid policies fail to accommodate. For instance, strict deadlines, synchronous learning requirements, and limited access to support services can create significant barriers for non-traditional learners, exacerbating educational inequalities.

Educational stratification: This is the process by which education systems perpetuate social inequalities, is a deeply ingrained issue within many societies. Collins (2009) succinctly asserts that "schools are not institutions of equal opportunity but mechanisms for perpetuating social inequalities," highlighting the role of educational institutions in maintaining existing social hierarchies. This perspective is echoed by Bowles and Gintis (1976), who argue that "education reproduces the social relationships of economic life, functioning to integrate youth into the labor force." Their work underscores the idea that schools prepare students to fit predetermined economic roles, thereby reinforcing class structures. Bourdieu and Passeron (1990) further elaborate on this by stating, "every pedagogic action is, objectively, a symbolic violence insofar as it is the imposition of a cultural arbitrary by an arbitrary power." This concept of symbolic violence reveals how educational practices impose dominant cultural values on students, subtly perpetuating inequality.

LMS, as integral components of contemporary educational infrastructure, have the potential to either exacerbate or mitigate educational stratification. When LMS are designed and implemented without a critical awareness of existing social disparities, they can inadvertently favor students from privileged backgrounds—those with better access to technology, reliable internet, and supportive learning environments. Such students are more likely to navigate LMS platforms effectively, engage fully with digital learning resources, and benefit from the advanced features these systems offer. Conversely, students from underprivileged backgrounds often lack the necessary technological infrastructure and digital literacy skills to fully utilize LMS. This digital divide can lead to lower engagement, decreased academic performance, and a sense of alienation among these students. The unequal access to technology and the digital competencies required to thrive in an LMS-mediated educational environment thus contribute to the maintenance and deepening of educational stratification.

Symbolic capital: This form of capital is not tangible like economic capital, but it significantly influences social interactions and hierarchies. Symbolic capital can manifest in various forms, such as titles, awards, or reputations, and is often accrued through achievements that society values highly. It enables individuals and groups to assert influence and maintain their social positions, as their status is continually validated by societal recognition. The accumulation of symbolic capital thus reinforces existing social structures, as those with high levels of this capital are more likely to access opportunities and resources, further perpetuating their social dominance.

LMS, while designed to democratize access to education, can inadvertently reinforce existing structures of symbolic capital by privileging certain forms of knowledge and participation over others. LMS platforms typically reward digital literacy and online engagement, creating an environment where students proficient in navigating digital tools and resources are more likely to receive recognition and opportunities. These students often find it easier to engage in online discussions, submit assignments through digital platforms, and utilize advanced features of LMS, thereby accruing symbolic capital in the form of higher grades, positive feedback, and increased visibility among peers and instructors. This digital proficiency, however, is not uniformly distributed among all students. Those from underprivileged backgrounds or with limited access to technology may struggle to adapt to the digital demands of LMS, resulting in marginalization and a lack of recognition for their efforts and potential. The privileging of digital literacy in LMS can perpetuate educational inequalities by reinforcing the symbolic capital of students who are already advantaged. This dynamic underscores the importance of designing LMS that not only cater to diverse student abilities but also recognize and reward various forms of engagement and achievement.

Symbolic violence: This concept, developed by Pierre Bourdieu, refers to the subtle, often unnoticed forms of domination and oppression that are embedded within everyday social interactions and cultural norms. Bourdieu (2001) highlights this in the context of gender, noting that "masculine domination is so deeply embedded in our collective unconscious that we no longer even see it." This illustrates how societal norms can perpetuate gender inequalities without overt coercion. Bourdieu

(1991) further expands this concept to the realm of language, asserting that "language is not only an instrument of communication or even of knowledge, but also an instrument of power." This perspective underscores the power dynamics inherent in linguistic exchanges, where language can reinforce social hierarchies. Jenkins (1992) supports this by explaining that "Bourdieu's concept of habitus explains how social structures are internalized by individuals and shape their perceptions and actions," indicating how deeply ingrained these power structures can become within individuals' worldviews. Collectively, these insights reveal how symbolic violence functions to maintain and legitimize social inequalities through the internalization of dominant cultural norms and values.

In the context of LMS, symbolic violence can manifest through the standardization of content and assessment methods that fail to reflect the cultural diversity and varied experiences of the student body. LMS platforms, by design, often prioritize uniformity and standardization in their educational delivery. This standardization typically aligns with the dominant cultural norms and educational practices, which can marginalize students from diverse cultural backgrounds. For instance, standardized curricula and assessments may overlook the unique cultural knowledge, values, and learning styles of minority students, compelling them to conform to an educational paradigm that does not acknowledge or validate their identities. This imposition can result in students feeling alienated and devalued, undermining their academic engagement and self-esteem.

These key terms, derived from the interdisciplinary efforts of sociologists, anthropologists, and feminist scholars, enrich our understanding of Social Reproduction Theory. By integrating these concepts, SRT provides a comprehensive lens through which to examine the intricate ways in which societal inequalities are maintained and challenged, highlighting the roles of education, family, and labor in these processes. The contributions of Weiss (2021), Munro (2019), and Laslett & Brenner (1989) are instrumental in defining these terms and expanding the scope of SRT beyond its Marxist origins to include a broader analysis of societal dynamics.

The Social Development of Learning Management Systems (LMS)

The exploration of Social Reproduction Theory in the context of educational technology, specifically Learning Management Systems (LMS), requires an in-depth examination of its core concepts, historical underpinnings, and practical implications. At the heart of this inquiry is the idea that LMS, as technological embodiments of educational practices, are not merely tools for managing learning processes but are also implicated in the broader socio-economic and cultural dynamics of knowledge production and dissemination. This perspective invites a critical analysis of how

LMS can either reinforce traditional educational hierarchies and inequities or provide new opportunities for challenging and transforming them.

Relevant literature provides a rich tapestry of insights into the application of Social Reproduction Theory across various educational contexts. For instance, Rafalow & Puckett (2021) and Rafalow (2020) delve into the interplay between digital technologies and educational practices, shedding light on the ways in which technological innovations can both reflect and reshape social hierarchies within educational settings. Similarly, Collins (2009) and Croizet et al. (2017) offer valuable perspectives on the role of educational systems in perpetuating social inequalities, while Flecha (2011) and Wildhagen (2010) explore the potential for educational practices to contribute to social transformation. Further, Backer & Cairns (2021), van de Werfhorst & Hofstede (2007), Demaine (2003), and Emmerich & Hormel (2021) provide a broader historical and theoretical context for understanding the complex dynamics of education, technology, and social reproduction.

Learning Management Systems (LMS) play a crucial role in digital learning environments, acting as the backbone of online education. Their potential to either mitigate or exacerbate the digital divide is a critical area for examination. Studies by Rafalow & Puckett (2021) and Rafalow (2020) delve into how digital technologies, including LMS platforms, interact with educational practices and societal structures. They highlight the potential of these technologies to reflect and reshape social hierarchies within educational settings. Collins (2009) also explores the role of educational systems in perpetuating social inequalities, underscoring the significance of technological access in this dynamic.

Cultural Capital and the Digital Divide

The issues related to Learning Management Systems (LMS) and social reproduction fall under the broader rubric of the digital divide, which refers to the gap between individuals who have access to modern information and communication technology and those who do not. This divide manifests in disparities in access to hardware, internet connectivity, and digital literacy skills, which are crucial for effective participation in online learning environments (Warschauer et al, 2004; Selwyn, 2010). Students with greater cultural and economic capital are more likely to have the resources and prior exposure needed to navigate LMS successfully, thereby benefiting more from these educational technologies. Digital literacy is often assumed in LMS design, privileging students who have prior exposure to technology and are proficient in using digital tools. Their familiarity with digital environments aligns with the platform's expectations, thereby reinforcing their symbolic capital (Selwyn, 2010). Conversely, students from marginalized backgrounds often lack these resources, exacerbating existing educational inequalities and perpetuating the cycle of social reproduction (Bourdieu, 1986; DiMaggio, 1982). Addressing these disparities requires deliberate efforts to design LMS that are inclusive and accessible, providing necessary support and resources to all students to bridge the digital divide and promote equitable educational outcomes (Meyer, Rose, & Gordon, 2014; Selwyn, 2011).

The digital divide extends beyond mere access to devices, encompassing reliable internet connectivity, digital literacy, and the capacity to effectively utilize technology for learning. Economic disparities significantly impact students' ability to afford necessary computers and internet connectivity, with varied digital proficiency further disadvantaging students from lower socioeconomic backgrounds (Severiens & Ten Dam, 1998). The quality of educational content on LMS platforms can also vary, reflecting the resources available to different educational institutions, which affects engagement and learning outcomes (Gustavsson & Eriksson, 2010). Research by Croizet et al. (2017) and Flecha (2011) examines the cognitive and social dimensions of educational inequalities, emphasizing the need to address these broader aspects of the digital divide to ensure equitable access to online education. Additionally, Wildhagen (2010) and Backer & Cairns (2021) stress the necessity of a critical analysis of educational technologies, including LMS platforms, to understand their impact on reinforcing traditional educational hierarchies and inequities or creating new opportunities for transformation.

Considering the digital divide within the context of Social Reproduction Theory involves analyzing the policies and practices that govern the implementation and use of educational technologies. Van de Werfhorst & Hofstede (2007) and Demaine (2003) discuss the policy implications of educational inequalities, suggesting that a nuanced understanding of the digital divide can inform more equitable educational policies and practices. Furthermore, Emmerich & Hormel (2021) advocate for the integration of insights from social reproduction theory into the development and deployment of educational technologies to address the foundational causes of the digital divide.

Teacher training and support play critical roles in the effective use of LMS. Schools in more affluent areas are often better equipped to provide comprehensive training for teachers on LMS use, unlike their counterparts in under-resourced schools, highlighting a disparity that extends into the classroom (Ridgeway, 2001). Parental involvement and support further influence the effectiveness of online learning, with variability in parents' education levels, time availability, and comfort with technology impacting student success (Rogers, 2006). Assessment and evaluation biases within LMS platforms can also disadvantage students more accustomed to traditional learning settings, emphasizing the need for assessment methods that accurately reflect student understanding and learning processes (Boring, 2017).

Design practices and the user interface of LMS platforms are crucial in determining their accessibility and usability. Non-intuitive design conventions can hinder usability for students with limited digital experience, with culturally biased iconography potentially alienating students unfamiliar with certain symbols (Shekhar & Marsden, 2018). Assumptions about student learning styles that underpin LMS designs may not align with the diverse needs of the student population, disadvantaging those whose learning styles do not match the platform's delivery methods (Clegg, 2001).

Accessibility issues remain a significant concern, as a lack of features like screen reader compatibility and alternative text for images can exclude students with disabilities, underscoring the importance of designing LMS platforms that are accessible to all users (Messmer & Schmitz, 2004). The necessity for specific, often expensive, hardware or software to fully utilize LMS features can be a barrier for students from economically disadvantaged backgrounds, exacerbating the digital divide (Rogers, 2006).

Gender also plays a critical role in the design and perception of LMS. Studies have found no significant differences in how male and female students assess the design features of LMS, suggesting potential for gender-inclusive design strategies (Aditya & Permadi, 2020). However, structural gender differences in LMS use patterns reveal gender-based disparities, with male students using LMS more than females, indicating the need for gender-sensitive approaches in LMS design and implementation to ensure equitable access and engagement (Lim et al., 2020).

Through the lens of SRT, this analysis underscores the importance of addressing the digital divide in LMS from a comprehensive perspective that considers socioeconomic, cultural, and gender-specific factors. By adopting multifaceted and inclusive approaches in the design and implementation of LMS, educators and developers can work towards creating platforms that are accessible, engaging, and effective for all students.

Symbolic Violence and Accessibility in LMS

Symbolic violence refers to the subtle imposition of the dominant culture's values and norms onto marginalized groups, leading to internalized inferiority and perpetuating social inequalities (Bourdieu & Passeron, 1977). Within Learning Management Systems (LMS), symbolic violence manifests in ways that can significantly impact students with disabilities, reinforcing existing disparities and hindering their educational experiences. Students with disabilities often face substantial barriers in accessing and effectively using LMS platforms. These systems, typically designed with able-bodied users in mind, may lack essential features that make content accessible to all students. For instance, many LMS platforms do not fully support screen readers, which are crucial for students with visual impairments. This oversight can render digital content inaccessible, forcing these students to navigate an educational environment that does not accommodate their needs, thus perpetuating feelings of exclusion and inferiority (Burgstahler, 2015; Seale, 2014). The reliance on certain forms of knowledge and participation that align with dominant cultural norms within LMS further exacerbates these issues. Educational materials and assessments that are heavily text-based or require extensive use of visual aids can disadvantage students with disabilities. For example, students with dyslexia might struggle with large volumes of text, while those with hearing impairments may find it difficult to engage with audio-based content if captions or transcripts are not provided (Meyer, Rose, & Gordon, 2014).

Utilizing Social Reproduction Theory (SRT) as a framework offers a profound lens through which to understand the barriers to accessibility in Learning Management Systems (LMS) for learners with disabilities. SRT suggests that educational institutions play a pivotal role in perpetuating societal structures and inequalities. When examining the design and implementation of LMS through this lens, several key barriers emerge that not only hinder accessibility but also reflect broader societal attitudes toward disability.

Firstly, non-compliance with web accessibility standards in LMS design is not merely an oversight but a manifestation of societal disregard for the diverse needs of individuals. This reflects a broader pattern of marginalization and exclusion of individuals with disabilities, reinforcing existing social hierarchies (Collins, 2009). Similarly, the lack of screen reader compatibility and inadequate keyboard navigation support in LMS platforms mirrors the structural inequalities that individuals with disabilities face daily, echoing societal tendencies to overlook or underestimate their capabilities (Backer & Cairns, 2021).

Moreover, the absence of video and audio content transcriptions and captions, along with limited alternative text for visual content, exemplifies a form of symbolic violence. This exclusion devalues the learning experiences of students with auditory and visual impairments, perpetuating the social hierarchies that privilege able-bodied individuals (Croizet et al., 2017). Additionally, the design of complex and time-constrained assessments, along with inflexible content presentation, highlights the rigidity of educational systems that do not accommodate diverse learning needs, reinforcing the notion that traditional forms of learning and assessment are the most valued (Demaine, 2003). The lack of educator training on accessibility practices and insufficient policies on accessibility underscores a systemic failure to prioritize the needs of individuals with disabilities. This neglect reflects a broader societal issue, contributing to the ongoing marginalization of students with disabilities within educational systems and beyond (Taylor, 1982). Furthermore, the insufficient provision of support and accommodations within LMS platforms exemplifies the structural barriers to equality in education, indicative of the broader societal failure to provide equitable resources and opportunities for all individuals (Flecha, 2011).

By examining these barriers through the lens of SRT, it becomes evident that they are not isolated technical issues but are deeply intertwined with societal structures and attitudes that perpetuate inequalities. Addressing these challenges requires a systemic approach that not only seeks to remove technical barriers but also aims to transform the underlying societal attitudes and structures that contribute to the marginalization of learners with disabilities. This transformation is essential for leveraging educational technologies as tools for social change, promoting equity and inclusion within educational settings and the broader society.

The Field of Assessment

In the context of Social Reproduction Theory (SRT), the *field* of learner assessment within Learning Management Systems (LMS) is a complex social arena where various actors—students, educators, administrators, and policymakers—compete for resources, recognition, and academic success. This field is structured by specific rules and norms that determine what forms of knowledge and skills are valued and how they are measured. Within this field, LMS can both challenge and reinforce existing social hierarchies through their design and implementation of assessment mechanisms. The journey toward implementing inclusive and flexible assessment options in online learning environments, especially those mediated by LMS, is both a challenge and a necessity in modern education. This endeavor, viewed through the critical lens of SRT, underscores the persistent gap between the ideals of educational equity and the realities of practice. The narrative of this journey reveals the complexities and nuances of adapting educational practices to meet the needs of a diverse student body. At the core of this narrative is the struggle to move beyond traditional assessment formats, which remain deeply entrenched in educational systems. Despite the potential of online learning to offer a variety of assessment formats, the inertia of longstanding practices often prevails, limiting the ability of educators to fully embrace alternative methods that cater to different learning styles (Collins, 2009). This resistance to change reflects broader societal and institutional norms that prioritize efficiency and uniformity over diversity and individuality. Students from technologically advanced backgrounds, whose habitus includes familiarity with digital tools, are likely to find LMS more intuitive and accessible. Conversely, students with limited technological exposure may struggle, highlighting the need for LMS to include comprehensive support and training to bridge these gaps (Bourdieu, 1986).

Educators may face myriad pressures in the realm of assessment. SRT provides a critical lens through which to understand how educational practices, including assessment strategies, can either perpetuate societal inequalities or serve as a conduit for challenging and potentially transforming them. One of the primary challenges in implementing alternative and authentic assessments in online environments is the pervasive pressure to conform to standardized assessment formats. These formats, often easier to administer and grade at scale, are deeply entrenched in educational systems. However, they may not adequately capture the depth and breadth of students' understanding or skills. The reliance on standardized tests and quizzes can reflect broader societal and institutional valuations of efficiency over authentic learning, potentially marginalizing students whose strengths lie outside the narrow confines of traditional assessments (Rafalow, 2020; Collins, 2009).

Technical constraints within LMS platforms also pose significant challenges to implementing diverse assessment strategies. While LMS have evolved to offer a range of functionalities, the technical infrastructure may still limit the types of assessments that can be effectively designed and delivered. These constraints can hinder the adoption of innovative assessment methods, such as project-based learning, portfolios, or simulations, that require complex interactions or the submission of varied types of media (Croizet et al., 2017). Furthermore, the intricacies of grading alternative and authentic assessments in online courses can be a formidable challenge. These forms of assessment often require subjective judgment and a deep understanding of the criteria for success, demanding more time and expertise from educators. This complexity can be exacerbated in large-scale online courses, where the volume of assessments to be graded can be overwhelming, raising concerns about consistency and fairness in evaluation practices (Backer & Cairns, 2021).

Lastly, concerns related to academic integrity are amplified in the context of alternative and authentic assessments. The open nature of these assessments, while conducive to fostering critical thinking and application of knowledge, can also make it difficult to ensure that the work submitted is entirely the student's own. This challenge is compounded in online settings, where the distance and anonymity of the digital environment can make it easier for students to circumvent academic integrity policies (Emmerich & Hormel, 2021).

Habitus and Learner Engagement

Among the Social Reproduction Theory (SRT) concepts, habitus is particularly well-suited to examine learner engagement in Learning Management Systems (LMS). Habitus, as defined by Pierre Bourdieu, refers to the ingrained habits, skills, and dispositions that individuals acquire through their life experiences and socialization processes. This concept captures how deeply embedded personal and cultural backgrounds influence how students perceive, interact with, and engage in educational environments, including LMS (Bourdieu, 1986). It prompts a deeper examination of how the impersonal nature of LMS platforms can inadvertently reinforce existing social hierarchies and inequalities, especially when support services and meaningful interactions are lacking (Rafalow & Puckett, 2021; Collins, 2009). Research has shown that habitus significantly affects how students engage with digital learning environments. For example, a study by Margaryan, Littlejohn, and Vojt (2011) found that students' prior experiences with technology and their socio-cultural backgrounds influenced their patterns of engagement in online learning. These findings underscore the importance of considering habitus when designing and implementing LMS to foster inclusive and effective learning experiences.

LMS platforms often value assertive communication styles, encouraging students to actively participate in discussions, express opinions confidently, and engage in debates. These behaviors are typically rewarded with higher grades and recognition, aligning with the dominant cultural norms of assertiveness and individualism. However, students from cultures that value humility, collective participation, or reflective thinking may find it challenging to conform to these expectations. Their contributions might be overlooked or undervalued, leading to a sense of marginalization and internalized inferiority (Hofstede, 1986; Bourdieu & Passeron, 1977).

Support services in online education, such as tutoring, counseling, and technical assistance, are critical for student success. However, the digital divide—a term that encapsulates the disparities in access to technology and the internet—can hinder students' ability to benefit from these services. SRT compels us to recognize that the availability and quality of support services in online platforms are not just logistical concerns but are deeply tied to broader issues of social equity and access (Backer & Cairns, 2021). For students from marginalized backgrounds, the lack of personalized support can exacerbate existing educational disparities, perpetuating cycles of disadvantage.

Furthermore, the interactions between educators and students in online courses often lack the spontaneity and depth of face-to-face engagement, potentially impacting the learning experience and outcomes. SRT challenges us to consider how this reduction in direct interaction can affect students differently, depending on their socio-economic background, learning styles, and prior experiences with technology. For some, the transition to online learning is seamless, while for others, it represents a significant barrier to participation and engagement (van de Werfhorst & Hofstede, 2007).

The impersonal nature of LMS platforms often results in a reliance on written communication as the primary mode of interaction between educators and students. This privileging of writing can inadvertently exacerbate existing social hierarchies and educational disparities. Students who excel in verbal expression may find their strengths underutilized in an environment that predominantly values written communication. This scenario underscores a broader equity concern, as the ability to articulate ideas effectively in writing is often influenced by factors such as educational background, socio-economic status, and primary language, thereby impacting students differently based on their individual circumstances (Backer & Cairns, 2021).

The predominance of written communication in online settings, as discussed by Jaldemark (2008), highlights the constitutional patterns of exchange in higher education where the participation of students is heavily reliant on their ability to articulate thoughts in writing. This dynamic underscores the need for a conscious effort to broaden the scope of communication genres within online courses, moving beyond text-based interactions to include more varied and inclusive forms of communication.

Furthermore, the work of Lillis and Turner (2001) delves into the challenges faced by 'non-traditional' student writers, shedding light on the broader cultural and historical context of academic writing. Their findings underscore the importance of reconsidering traditional academic practices to accommodate the diversity of student backgrounds and writing abilities in online education.

Bello, Brandau, and Horne (2020) contribute to this discussion by identifying strategies that can create higher levels of immediacy and connection between online instructors and their students through written communication. Their research suggests that encouragement, personalized feedback, and assurances of instructor availability are highly valued by students, indicating that even within the constraints of written communication, there are opportunities to enhance the sense of closeness and support in online learning environments.

Lea and Street's (1998) academic literacies approach further challenges the implicit models used to understand student writing in higher education. By acknowledging the conflicting and contested nature of writing practices, this approach provides a valuable framework for developing more inclusive and equitable writing assessments and pedagogies in online courses.

The enhancement of verbal immediacy in online university classes, as explored by Sparks, Song, Brantley, and Liu (2014), emphasizes the need for next-generation assessments that recognize the multifaceted nature of writing proficiency. Their operational definition of writing proficiency includes social and rhetorical knowledge, domain knowledge, language use, and writing processes. This comprehensive view of writing underscores the importance of diversifying assessment methods to capture the broad spectrum of students' writing abilities and preferences.

Together, these insights underscore the urgency of addressing the privileging of written communication in online education. By integrating a variety of communication and assessment methods, online courses can become more inclusive, recognizing and valuing the diverse ways in which students learn and express their understanding. This approach not only aligns with the principles of equity and social justice but also enriches the educational experience for all students, ensuring that online learning environments are conducive to the full spectrum of learning styles and preferences.

As we navigate the intricacies of online education, it becomes evident that these challenges are deeply embedded in the fabric of societal structures and norms. SRT compels us to critically examine online learning environments through an equity-focused lens, highlighting the need for holistic approaches that prioritize inclusivity, equity, and the well-being of all students. By addressing the privilege accorded to written communication and ensuring equitable access to support services and protections for student data, online education providers can move toward a more inclusive and just educational paradigm.

LMS and the Culture of Surveillance

The integration of surveillance mechanisms within LMS is a phenomenon that not only reflects but potentially exacerbates broader societal trends toward increased monitoring and data collection. The concept of *institutional mechanisms* is particularly appropriate. This concept encompasses the policies, practices, and organizational structures within institutions that sustain social hierarchies and perpetuate inequalities. By focusing on institutional mechanisms, we can critically analyze how surveillance practices embedded within LMS contribute to the maintenance of existing power dynamics and social stratifications.

Similarly, the concept of "system avoidance," where individuals who have encountered the criminal justice system subsequently avoid institutions that keep formal records, suggests parallels in educational settings where LMS surveillance could lead to student disengagement (Brayne, 2014).

Moreover, the application of machine learning for surveillance in healthcare, based on social media data, echoes the potential for LMS platforms to employ student data in ways that raise ethical concerns about privacy and autonomy (Gupta & Katarya, 2020). The cultural critique of surveillance as a disciplinary apparatus (Pecora, 2002) further contextualizes the impact of LMS surveillance, suggesting it could contribute to a culture of observation where students learn to navigate an environment of constant monitoring. Research into "surveillance as cultural practice" highlights how surveillance is embedded within, and generative of, social practices in specific cultural contexts (Monahan, 2011), indicating that surveillance in LMS might not only mirror but actively shape educational cultures. Institutional mechanisms encompass the surveillance policies and practices embedded within LMS. These include monitoring student activity, tracking logins and participation, and using data analytics to assess performance and behavior. Such practices reflect broader institutional goals and power dynamics, often prioritizing efficiency, accountability, and control over educational equity and student autonomy (Foucault, 1977; Gilliom & Monahan, 2013).

The implementation of surveillance tools in LMS can reinforce existing power structures by maintaining strict oversight of student activities. This surveillance can create an environment where students feel constantly monitored, which can impact their behavior and engagement. The institutional drive for surveillance often stems from a desire to maintain order and discipline, reflecting broader societal trends towards increased monitoring and control (Lyon, 2022). Surveillance mechanisms can disproportionately affect marginalized students, exacerbating educational inequalities. For example, students from disadvantaged backgrounds may feel more acutely the pressures of being monitored, potentially leading to disengagement or resistance. Additionally, the data collected through LMS surveillance can be used to enforce punitive measures, further entrenching existing social hierarchies (Hope, 2018).

Institutional mechanisms within educational settings dictate the extent and nature of surveillance practices in LMS. These mechanisms often reflect institutional priorities such as maintaining academic integrity, ensuring student participation, and improving educational outcomes. However, the emphasis on surveillance can lead to a culture of mistrust and control, where student autonomy and privacy are compromised (Selwyn, 2011). The use of surveillance in LMS can be seen as a form of social control, where institutions exert power over students through continuous monitoring. This aligns with Foucault's concept of the panopticon, where visibility is a tool for enforcing discipline and compliance. Surveillance in LMS thus becomes a means of reinforcing institutional authority and maintaining hierarchical relationships within the educational field (Foucault, 1977). Surveillance practices can have significant implications for educational equity. Students who are already disadvantaged may be further marginalized by surveillance mechanisms that do not take into account their unique circumstances and challenges. For instance, students who lack reliable internet access or face other barriers may be unfairly penalized for their inability to meet the surveillance criteria set by the LMS (Hope, 2018).

The surveillance of teachers, with its implications for identity and pedagogy, serves as a cautionary parallel for student surveillance in LMS platforms, suggesting that such practices might not only detect but also simulate desired behaviors, thus influencing the very nature of teaching and learning. This raises critical questions about the balance between educational oversight and individual freedoms, highlighting the need for a nuanced approach to surveillance in online education that respects student privacy and dignity while acknowledging the diverse impacts of these practices across different student

CONCLUSION

Through the lens of Social Reproduction Theory (SRT), the examination of Learning Management Systems (LMS) in online education has revealed a complex interplay between technology, educational practices, and social equity. This synthesis of key findings and insights illuminates the multifaceted challenges and opportunities that LMS platforms present in the pursuit of equitable online education.

SRT, with its focus on how societal inequalities are perpetuated through educational systems, provides a critical framework for understanding the dynamics of online learning environments. It underscores the necessity of critically examining LMS not merely as technological tools but as significant factors in the broader socio-educational landscape that can either reinforce or challenge existing social hierarchies.

One of the primary insights from this exploration is the recognition of the digital divide as a significant barrier to equity in online education. This divide, reflecting broader societal inequalities, is exacerbated by disparities in access to technology, reliable internet connectivity, and digital literacy. The role of LMS platforms in either mitigating or exacerbating these disparities is crucial, highlighting the need for these systems to be designed and implemented with a keen awareness of their potential to influence educational equity (Rafalow & Puckett, 2021; Collins, 2009).

Furthermore, the analysis has shown that the impersonal nature of online learning, facilitated by LMS, poses challenges to fostering meaningful interactions between educators and students. The predominance of written communication within these platforms can inadvertently privilege certain forms of knowledge and expression over others, thereby marginalizing students whose strengths may not align with this mode of communication. This situation calls for a diversification of communication and assessment methods within LMS to ensure inclusivity and to accommodate diverse learning styles and preferences.

Additionally, the exploration has highlighted the impact of the emphasis on standardized assessment formats as barriers to equity. These aspects of LMS design and instructional practice can alienate students not well-versed in specific linguistic codes or those whose learning achievements may not be adequately captured by traditional assessments. Addressing these challenges requires a conscientious effort to design LMS platforms and online courses that are accessible, inclusive, and capable of supporting a wide range of assessment strategies that value diverse student capabilities.

The surveillance mechanisms embedded within LMS platforms also raise concerns about privacy and autonomy, underscoring the need for a balanced approach to educational oversight that respects student rights and dignity. These concerns, examined through the SRT framework, highlight the potential for surveillance practices to reinforce power structures and inequalities within educational settings.

In conclusion, the application of Social Reproduction Theory to the analysis of Learning Management Systems in online education has revealed the critical need for these platforms to be designed and utilized in ways that prioritize equity and inclusivity. By addressing the highlighted challenges, educators and technologists can leverage LMS platforms to not only facilitate effective online learning but also to challenge and transform the social inequalities that pervade educational systems. This endeavor aligns with the transformative potential of SRT, offering a pathway toward a more equitable and just educational landscape.

Recommendations and Future Directions

The essential quandary of constructing a standardized online learning environment, particularly within the confines of Learning Management Systems (LMS), lies in balancing the efficiency and scalability inherent in standardization with the imperative to respect and nurture the individual agency, complexity, and diversity of learners. This challenge is at the heart of modern educational discourse, as educators and technologists grapple with creating digital spaces that are both universally accessible and deeply personal.

Standardization in LMS typically involves creating uniform structures and processes for content delivery, assessment, and interaction to ensure consistency and manageability across diverse educational settings. However, this approach often overlooks the unique perspectives, learning styles, and needs of individual students. The agency of learners, or their capacity to act independently and make their own choices, can be stifled by a one-size-fits-all model that prioritizes efficiency over personalization. The quandary here is how to design LMS platforms that empower students as active participants in their learning journey rather than passive recipients of standardized content.

Learners come from a myriad of backgrounds, each bringing a unique set of experiences, knowledge, and cultural perspectives to the educational table. This diversity enriches the learning environment, offering opportunities for deeper understanding and engagement. However, it also introduces complexity into the design and implementation of LMS. The challenge lies in accommodating this diversity without resorting to overly simplistic or reductive models of instruction and assessment that fail to capture the richness of individual experiences. Striking a balance requires an approach that is both flexible enough to adapt to varied learning needs and robust enough to maintain a coherent educational experience.

One potential solution to this quandary is the integration of adaptive learning technologies and personalization features within LMS platforms. These technologies can analyze individual learning patterns and preferences to tailor content, suggest resources, and adjust assessment strategies accordingly. By embracing personalization, LMS can better support the individual agency of learners, allowing them to navigate content in ways that align with their personal learning goals and preferences.

Furthermore, providing a range of communication and collaboration tools can enhance the social dimension of learning, enabling students to engage with peers and instructors in diverse ways. This not only supports the complexity and diversity of learners but also fosters a sense of community and belonging within the online learning environment.

Moreover, the role of educators is pivotal in navigating the balance between standardization and individual agency. Educators must be adept at leveraging the capabilities of LMS while remaining attuned to the needs and voices of their students. This may involve adopting a more facilitative role, guiding learners through personalized learning pathways and fostering an environment where diverse perspectives are valued and explored.

The concept of extending deadlines and offering flexible scheduling represents a beacon of hope for accommodating the varied circumstances of online learners. Yet, this flexibility often encounters barriers in the form of rigid institutional policies and accreditation standards, highlighting a disconnect between the potential of online learning to provide equity and the structural constraints that limit its realization (Backer & Cairns, 2021).

The potential for alternative assessment methods to empower students by allowing them to leverage their strengths and interests remains largely untapped. This approach challenges the traditional educational paradigm by recognizing the diverse capabilities of the student population. However, realizing this potential requires a cultural shift within educational institutions, moving away from a monolithic approach to education towards a more personalized and inclusive model (Taylor, 1982).

Providing personalized feedback and support in online settings emerges as a critical yet challenging component of inclusive education. The scalability of personalized feedback is constrained by factors such as class size and faculty digital literacy, underscoring the need for targeted professional development and resources to support effective online teaching practices (Demaine, 2003).

The adoption of Universal Design for Learning (UDL) principles in LMS platforms is essential for creating accessible and inclusive online learning environments. However, the implementation of UDL often faces challenges related to limited resources, technical constraints, and a lack of awareness among educators and instructional designers (Flecha, 2011).

This narrative reveals that the path to inclusivity in online education is fraught with challenges that stem from deeply ingrained societal and institutional norms. Overcoming these challenges requires a systemic approach that not only addresses technical barriers but also fosters a cultural transformation within educational institutions. Such a transformation would prioritize diversity, inclusivity, and equity, aligning educational practices with the principles of social justice.

As this journey unfolds, it becomes clear that bridging the gap between the ideals of inclusive education and the realities of its implementation is a collective endeavor. It necessitates a commitment from all stakeholders—educators, administrators, policymakers, and students—to advocate for and enact change. Through this collective effort, the transformative potential of online education can be realized, offering a more equitable and inclusive learning experience for all students.

Addressing these challenges requires a multifaceted approach that not only involves rethinking assessment strategies but also entails a broader cultural shift within educational institutions. By embracing alternative and authentic assessments, educators can move towards a more inclusive and equitable assessment practice that recognizes and values the diverse capabilities and learning styles of students. This shift, while challenging, aligns with the transformative potential of SRT, offering a pathway to disrupt the social reproduction of inequalities and foster a more just educational landscape.

REFERENCES

Aditya, B., & Permadi, A. (2020). Gender factor in designing features of a learning management system in higher education. *Proceedings of the International Conference on Online and Blended Learning 2019* (ICOBL 2019) IEEE. 10.2991/assehr.k.200521.006

Backer, D. I., & Cairns, K. (2021). Social reproduction theory revisited. *British Journal of Sociology of Education*, 42(7), 1086–1104. 10.1080/01425692.2021.1953962

Bello, R., Brandau, F., & Horne, D. (2020). The enhancement of verbal immediacy in online university classes: A student-generated taxonomy. *International Journal of Communication*, 14, 17. 10.22237/ijoc.2020.14.17

Boring, A. (2017). Gender biases in student evaluations of teaching. *Journal of Public Economics*, 145(C), 27–41. 10.1016/j.jpubeco.2016.11.006

Bourdieu, P. (1986). The forms of capital. In Richardson, J. (Ed.), *Handbook of Theory and Research for the Sociology of Education* (pp. 241–258). Greenwood. https://www.marxists.org/reference/subject/philosophy/works/fr/bourdieu-forms capital.htm

Bourdieu, P., & Passeron, J.-C. (1977). *Reproduction in education, society, and culture*. Sage.

Bowles, S., & Gintis, H. (1976). *Schooling in capitalist America: Educational reform and the contradictions of economic life*. Basic Books.

Brayne, S. (2014). Surveillance and system avoidance: Criminal justice contact and institutional attachment. *American Sociological Review*, 79(3), 367–391. 10.1177/0003122414530398

Burgstahler, S. (2013). Preface. In Burgstahler, S. (Ed.), *Universal design in higher education: Promising practices*. DO-IT, University of Washington. www.washington.edu/doit/preface-0

Clegg, S. (2001). Theorising the Machine: Gender, education and computing. *Gender and Education*, 13(3), 307–324. 10.1080/09540250120063580

Collins, J. (2009). Social reproduction in classrooms and schools. *Annual Review of Anthropology*, 38(1), 33–48. 10.1146/annurev.anthro.37.081407.085242

Croizet, J. C., Goudeau, S., Marot, M., & Millet, M. (2017). How do educational contexts contribute to the social class achievement gap: Documenting symbolic violence from a social psychological point of view. *Current Opinion in Psychology*, 18, 105–110. 10.1016/j.copsyc.2017.08.02528865350

Demaine, J. (2003). Social reproduction and education policy. *International Studies in Sociology of Education*, 13(2), 125–140. 10.1080/09620210300200107

DiMaggio, P. (1982). Cultural capital and school success: The impact of status culture participation on the grades of U.S. high school students. *American Sociological Review*, 47(2), 189–201. 10.2307/2094962

Emmerich, M., & Hormel, U. (2021). Unequal inclusion: The production of social differences in education systems. *Social Inclusion (Lisboa)*, 9(3), 432–442. 10.17645/si.v9i3.4322

Flecha, R. (2011). The dialogic sociology of education. *International Studies in Sociology of Education*, 21(1), 7–20. 10.1080/09620214.2011.543849

Foucault, M. (1977). *Discipline and punish: The birth of the prison*. Pantheon Books.

Gilliom, J., & Monahan, T. (2013). *SuperVision: An introduction to the surveillance society*. University of Chicago Press.

Gupta, M., & Katarya, R. (2020). Social media based surveillance systems for healthcare using machine learning: A systematic review. *Journal of Ambient Intelligence and Humanized Computing*, 11(10), 4053–4069. 10.1007/s12652-020-01881-z32622833

Gustavsson, M., & Eriksson, A. F. (2010). Gendered learning environments in managerial work. *Studies in the Education of Adults*, 42(2), 141–158. http://urn.kb.se/resolve?urn=urn:nbn:se:liu:diva-64270. 10.1080/02660830.2010.11661594

Hilgers, M., & Mangez, E. (Eds.). (2015). *Bourdieu's theory of social fields: Concepts and applications*. Routledge.

Hofstede, G. (1986). Cultural differences in teaching and learning. *International Journal of Intercultural Relations*, 10(3), 301–320. 10.1016/0147-1767(86)90015-5

Hope, A. (2018). Creep: The growing surveillance of students' online activities. *Education and Society (Melbourne)*, 36(1), 55–72. 10.7459/es/36.1.05

Jaldemark, J. (2008). Participation and genres of communication in online settings of higher education. *Education and Information Technologies*, 13(2), 129–146. 10.1007/s10639-008-9057-9

Jenkins, R. (1992). *Pierre Bourdieu.* Routledge. 10.4324/9780203317471

Jungwirth, H. (1991). Interaction and gender — Findings of a microethnographical approach to classroom discourse. *Educational Studies in Mathematics*, 22(3), 263–284. 10.1007/BF00368341

Laslett, B., & Brenner, J. (1989). Gender and social reproduction: Historical perspectives. *Annual Review of Sociology*, 15(1), 381–404. https://www.jstor.org/stable/2083231. 10.1146/annurev.so.15.080189.00212112316382

Lea, M., & Street, B. (1998). Student writing in higher education: An academic literacies approach. *Studies in Higher Education*, 23(2), 157–172. 10.1080/03075079812331380364

Lillis, T., & Turner, J. (2001). Student writing in higher education: Contemporary confusion, traditional concerns. *Teaching in Higher Education*, 6(1), 57–68. 10.1080/13562510020029608

Lim, K., Nam, Y.-O., Eom, S., Jang, Y., Kim, D., & Kim, M. (2020). Structural gender differences in LMS use patterns among college students. *Sustainability (Basel)*, 12(11), 4465. 10.3390/su12114465

Lyon, D. (2022). Surveillance. *Internet Policy Review*, 11(4). Advance online publication. 10.14763/2022.4.1673

Margaryan, A., Littlejohn, A., & Vojt, G. (2011). Are digital natives a myth or reality? University students' use of digital technologies. *Computers & Education*, 56(2), 429–440. 10.1016/j.compedu.2010.09.004

Maton, K. I. (2008). Empowering community settings: Agents of individual development, community betterment, and positive social change. *American Journal of Community Psychology*, 41(1-2), 4–21. 10.1007/s10464-007-9148-618175215

Messmer, R., & Schmitz, S. (2004). Gender demands on e-learning. *WIT Transactions on Information and Communication Technologies*, 31. Advance online publication. 10.2495/CI040261

Meyer, A., Rose, D. H., & Gordon, D. (2014). *Universal design for learning: Theory and Practice.* CAST Professional Publishing.

Monahan, T. (2011). Surveillance as cultural practice. *The Sociological Quarterly*, 52(4), 495–508. 10.1111/j.1533-8525.2011.01216.x22175064

Munro, K. (2019). Social reproduction theory, social reproduction, and household production. *Science and Society*, 83(4), 451–468. 10.1521/siso.2019.83.4.451

Nash, R. (1999). Bourdieu, "Habitus", and educational research: Is it all worth the candle? *British Journal of Sociology of Education*, 20(2), 175–187. 10.1080/01425699995399

Pecora, V. P. (2002). The Culture of surveillance. *Qualitative Sociology*, 25(3), 345–358. 10.1023/A:1016081929646

Portes, A. (1998). Social capital: Its origins and applications in modern sociology. *Annual Review of Sociology*, 24(1), 1–24. 10.1146/annurev.soc.24.1.1

Rafalow, M. H. (2020). *Digital divisions: How schools create inequality in the tech era*. University of Chicago Press. 10.7208/chicago/9780226726724.001.0001

Rafalow, M. H., & Puckett, C. (2022). Sorting machines: Digital technology and categorical inequality in education. *Educational Researcher*, 51(4), 274–278. 10.3102/0013189X211070812

Reay, D. (2004). It's all becoming a habitus: Beyond the habitual use of habitus in educational research. *British Journal of Sociology of Education*, 25(4), 431–444. 10.1080/0142569042000236934

Ridgeway, C. L. (2001). Gender, status, and leadership. *Journal of Social issues, 57*(4), 637-655. https://psycnet.apa.org/doi/10.1111/0022-4537.00233

Rogers, A. (2006). Lifelong learning and the absence of gender. *International Journal of Educational Development*, 26(2), 189–208. 10.1016/j.ijedudev.2005.07.025

Selwyn, N. (2010). Looking beyond learning: Notes towards the critical study of educational technology. *Journal of Computer Assisted Learning*, 26(1), 65–73. 10.1111/j.1365-2729.2009.00338.x

Selwyn, N. (2011). *Education and technology: Key issues and debates*. Continuum International Publishing Group.

Severiens, S., & Ten Dam, G. (1998). Gender and learning: Comparing two theories. *Higher Education*, 35(3), 329–350. Advance online publication. 10.1023/A:1003033003124

Shekhar, A., & Marsden, N. (2018). Cognitive walkthrough of a learning management system with gendered personas. *Proceedings of the 4th Conference on Gender & IT.* ACM. 10.1145/3196839.3196869

Sparks, J. R., Song, Y., Brantley, W., & Liu, O. L. (2014). *Assessing written communication in higher education: Review and recommendations for next-generation assessment* (ETS Research Report No. RR-14-37). Princeton: Educational Testing Service. 10.1002/ets2.12035

Stanton-Salazar, R. D., & Dornbusch, S. M. (1995). Social capital and the reproduction of inequality: Information networks among Mexican-origin high school students. *Sociology of Education*, 68(2), 116–135. 10.2307/2112778

Taylor, S. (1982). Schooling and social reproduction. *Australian Journal of Education*, 26(2), 144–154. 10.1177/000494418202600204

van de Werfhorst, H. G., & Hofstede, S. (2007). Cultural capital or relative risk aversion? Two mechanisms for educational inequality compared. *The British Journal of Sociology*, 58(3), 391–415. 10.1111/j.1468-4446.2007.00157.x17727500

Warschauer, M., Knobel, M., & Stone, L. (2004). Technology and equity in schooling: Deconstructing the digital divide. *Educational Policy*, 18(4), 562–588. 10.1177/0895904804266469

Weiss, H. (2021) "Social reproduction". In Stein, F. (Ed) *The Open Encyclopedia of Anthropology* Facsimile of the first edition in *The Cambridge Encyclopedia of Anthropology*. Cambridge. 10.29164/21socialrepro

Wildhagen, T. (2010). Capitalizing on culture: How cultural capital shapes educational experiences and outcomes. *Sociology Compass*, 4(7), 519–531. 10.1111/j.1751-9020.2010.00296.x

Woolcock, M. (1998). Social capital and economic development: Toward a theoretical synthesis and policy framework. *Theory and Society*, 27(2), 151–208. 10.1023/A:1006884930135

Wu, T. J., Wang, L. Y., Gao, J. Y., & Wei, A. P. (2020). Social support and well-being of chinese special education teachers-An emotional labor perspective. *International Journal of Environmental Research and Public Health*, 17(18), 6884. 10.3390/ijerph17186884 32967136

Chapter 3
Leveraging Assistive Technology to Promote Inclusive English Language Teaching and Digital Literacy

Davey Young
https://orcid.org/0000-0002-8837-0924
Sophia University, Japan

ABSTRACT

Article 24 of the Convention on the Rights of Persons with Disabilities outlines the responsibilities that individual governments have in ensuring equitable access to quality inclusive education for people with disabilities, including accessibility and reasonable accommodations. One example of reasonable accommodations is the use of assistive technology. This chapter provides a brief literature review of assistive technology in the field of English language education before providing a set of practical recommendations for using assistive technology in the English language classroom. These recommendations are divided into three categories: using assistive technology to increase accessibility, using assistive technology as an accommodation, and using assistive technology to promote digital literacy, which has been promoted by the OECD as an essential 21st century skill. The chapter concludes with some implications for stakeholders at various levels in using assistive technology to promote digital literacy in compliance with international policy guidance.

DOI: 10.4018/979-8-3693-2591-9.ch003

INTRODUCTION

Article 24 of the Convention on the Rights of Persons with Disabilities (CRPD) outlines the responsibilities that individual governments have in ensuring equitable access to quality inclusive education for people with disabilities, most notably to provide reasonable accommodations to students with disabilities. In 2016, the UN's Committee on the Rights of Persons with Disabilities drafted an addendum to the CRPD titled General comment no. 4 (GC4), "the most comprehensive and authoritative instrument explaining the human right to inclusive education" (Graham, 2020, p. 11), to elaborate on the CRPD's Article 24 in the interest of attaining Sustainable Development Goal 4, which is to achieve quality inclusive education. GC4 improves upon previous policies' shortcomings by providing a clear definition of inclusive education and specific guidance on how inclusive education can be implemented.

A central concept in the CRPD that is elaborated in GC4 is reasonable accommodations. The term reasonable accommodation is defined by the CRPD as "necessary and appropriate modification and adjustments not imposing a disproportionate or undue burden, where needed in a particular case, to ensure to persons with disabilities the enjoyment or exercise on an equal basis with others of all human rights and fundamental freedoms" (United Nations, n.d., article 2). Additionally, Article 29 of GC4 recalls a distinction made in General Comment 2

between the general accessibility duty and the obligation to provide reasonable accommodation. Accessibility benefits groups of the population and is based on a set of standards that are implemented gradually. Disproportionality or undue burden cannot be claimed to defend the failure to provide accessibility. Reasonable accommodation relates to an individual and is complementary to the accessibility duty. An individual can legitimately request reasonable accommodation measures even if the State party has fulfilled its accessibility duty. (p. 8)

By way of example, Article 30 further states that

accommodations may include: changing the location of a class; providing different forms of in-class communication; enlarging print, materials and/or subjects in signs, or providing handouts in an alternative format; and providing students with a note taker or a language interpreter or allowing students to use assistive technology in learning and assessment situations. (Committee on the Rights of Persons with Disabilities, 2016, p. 9)

From this we can understand that accessibility and reasonable accommodations are separate concepts, but also that accommodations made in advance or in anticipation of specific learner needs as a new standard can constitute accessibility. Importantly, assistive technology is one such way to accommodate or increase accessibility for students with disabilities, and is also immensely effective in reducing barriers to learning for such students worldwide (UNESCO, 2023).

UNICEF (2022) notes that assistive technology is a multi-faceted and somewhat ambiguous concept, but one that is growing increasingly important in educational contexts around the globe. World Health Organization (2024)

> *defines assistive technology as the application of organized knowledge and skills related to assistive products, including systems and services. According to WHO's definition, an assistive product is any external product, especially produced or generally available, the primary purpose of which is to maintain or improve an individual's functioning and independence, and thereby promote their well-being.*
>
> *Assistive products include devices, equipment, instruments or software from 6 functional domains: mobility, vision, hearing, communication, cognition and self-care. Examples of assistive products are physical products such as wheelchairs, spectacles and hearing aids, and digital products such as software and apps. (paras. 1-2)*

The present chapter will use WHO's definition of assistive technology; in keeping with the scope of the current volume, there will also be a particular focus on digital products when referring to assistive technology. While there is a clear need for more comprehensive research into the applications of assistive technology for achieving inclusive education, recent reviews of existing research have found that assistive technology does indeed increase academic participation and performance of students with disabilities across various learning contexts, particularly for students with sensory impairments (Chambers, 2020; Fernández-Batanero et al., 2022).

Disability and Assistive Technology in English Language Learning and Teaching

Because making reasonable accommodations for students with disabilities, including the use of assistive technology, is context-dependent, specific consideration for how students with disabilities experience language learning must be made before an understanding of best practices for using assistive technology in English language teaching can be achieved. Various forms of disability can interact with language learning in unique ways. Compared to students without sensory impairments, for instance, students with sensory impairments experience language learning differently and have different learning preferences.

Blind or visually impaired students outperform their sighted peers in verbal recall tasks, and English language learners with visual impairments have a strong preference for gaining information through auditory input, which in turn supports reading and writing ability (Arslantas, 2017). A study by Wesołowska and Jedynak (2014) with three groups of English language learners—one without visual impairments, one with moderate visual impairments, and one of fully blind students—found that each group employed different strategies when learning vocabulary. There is even evidence to showing that blind English language learners have different motivation to learn English compared to peers without any form of visual impairment (Khodadady & Gholamian, 2014). Blind students also experience physical learning environments differently than their sighted peers, which can result in exclusion from shared learning spaces and group activities and difficulty accessing on-campus resources such as support centers for students with disabilities (Carpenter, 2024). Blind and visually impaired students have also reported more successful English language learning experiences when assistive technology was used effectively (Carpenter, 2020; Khan & Mahmood, 2022).

Compared to their peers without hearing impairments, English language learners with hearing impairments may have greater difficulty receiving instructional information (Iwai, 2024), learning vocabulary (Domagała-Zyśk, 2019; Mpofu & Chimhenga, 2013; Murphy & Dodd, 2010), using correct grammatical forms (Murphy & Dodd, 2010), and speaking (Iwai, 2024; Mpofu & Chimhenga, 2013). According to Swisher (1989),

> *hearing loss itself acts as a drastic filter on the linguistic data, and information obtained from aided residual hearing, as well as from visual sources such as lip-reading and signed representations of spoken language, is typically fragmentary. In addition to the limitations of input, the very difficulty of the task of learning an auditory language with severely restricted information is likely to lead to loss of motivation. (p. 239)*

Findings from Csizér and Kontra (2020) also suggest that deaf and severely hearing impaired English language learners rely more strongly on the teacher and friends and family when learning English compared to their peers, and that barriers they face in the English language classroom can have a negative impact on their language learning motivation; from these findings, the authors concluded that the affective domain may play a more significant role in determining engagement in the language learning experience for students with hearing impairments compared to their hearing peers. Some common barriers that deaf or hearing-impaired English language learners may experience are decreased social interaction with other students (Mpofu & Chimhenga, 2013; Murphy & Dodd, 2010), communicative breakdowns, and heightened anxiety (Iwai, 2024).

In addition to sensory impairments, consideration must be made for how specific learning difficulties (SLDs) such as ADHD and dyslexia interact with language learning. First of all, "language learners with SLDs show significant differences in their working memory and phonological short-term memory capacity," compared to their peers without SLDs (Kormos, 2017a, p. 47). Depending on the exact nature of the SLD and other factors in the learner profile, students with SLDs may have difficulty processing input, automatizing lexical chunks, creating long-term memory, and producing output (Borodkin & Faust, 2014; Kormos, 2017a). Students with dyslexia, for example, may experience greater difficulty understanding and internalizing syntactic and phonological rules when learning a foreign language (Sparks et al., 1991), while children with ADHD generally have lower working memory, difficulty self-regulating, and related difficulty with L1 acquisition (Barkley, 1997). SLDs are less visible than other forms of disability, and the overlap of characteristics of different SLDs indicates that they often co-occur, meaning a student with one SLD is very likely to have at least one other; additionally, among all students with disabilities, those with SLDs are the most likely to appear in regular classes in primary and secondary contexts, as well as to go unnoticed in postsecondary ones (Kormos, 2017a; Kormos 2017b; Smith, 2018).

Fortunately, there is evidence that assistive technology and other accommodations can help foster classroom participation and learning for English language learners with sensory impairments and SLDs. Tsukamoto (2024), for instance, was able to accommodate a blind EFL student at a Japanese university by keeping a learning journal to reflect on her practice, keeping in constant contact with the student about their needs, integrating assistive technology, and making accommodations to the classroom layout, routines, and learning materials. Similarly, Iwai (2024) reported on a battery of accommodations for an English language learner with a hearing impairment at a private university in Tokyo. These included differentiating materials and tasks, routinizing instructions and tasks, using assistive technology and multimodal materials and tasks, modifying directions, staying in contact with the student about her needs, arranging the classroom with the student's impairment in mind, allowing extra time to complete activities, making assessment accommodations, creating a supportive environment, and coordinating closely with the university's student support center. One form of assistive technology, a type of reusable writing tablet called a Boogie Board, was also supplied to the teacher by the university's support center and allowed the student to participate in discussion activities. Finally, in a classroom observation of 17 secondary Israeli EFL students, 16 of whom had SLDs,

Cohen (2011) attributed a high degree of participation to the teacher's ability to modify, scaffold, and present multisensory texts using assistive technology.

There are even cases of assistive technologies being designed specifically for English language learners. One example is English Eye, a mobile app with speech recognition and synthesis, translation, and Braille input capabilities that was developed specifically to promote English language learning among Sri Lankan students with vision impairments (Jayakody et al., 2016). In other instances, assistive products made for L1 English speakers have been used for L2 English learners. Lerga et al. (2021), for instance, inventoried a number of mobile applications for children with dyslexia that can also be used for English language learners, but noted that because they were created for children whose first language is English, there may be additional and unanticipated challenges in using these technologies with other populations. Such possibilities further underscore the notion that disability and relevant accommodations are context-dependent.

A common feature of assistive technologies in education, especially in language learning contexts, is their capacity for multimodality. Multimodality refers to the use of different channels of communication to convey meaning, and has received substantial attention in the field of English language teaching in recent decades (Kessler, 2022). Multimodality is also a common feature of various reified sets of inclusive practices such as Universal Design for Learning, Universal Design for Instruction, and Universal Instructional Design (Evans et al., 2017), and has been advocated as an inclusive practice in the field of English language teaching specifically (Kormos & Smith, 2024; Young & Burke, 2024). The need for multimodality to make learning experiences and environments more accessible for English language learners with sensory impairments is self-evident, though multimodal materials can also improve learning for students with SLDs (Kormos & Smith, 2024), as well as students without disabilities (Kessler, 2022).

Despite the benefits of assistive technology in language education, there is evidence to suggest that many English language teaching contexts are poorly prepared to use assistive technology to promote inclusivity. In a review of nearly 30 papers on teaching EFL to students with visual impairments, Boltenkova et al. (2020) found that individual and external factors such as country of origin and access to assistive technology played a significant role in these students' learning experience, further arguing that the lack of a specific pedagogy for blind learners within the TESOL field may be a hindrance to their inclusion in English language learning environments. In a survey of 186 English language teachers in Saudi Arabia, most respondents reported insufficient training to teach English as a foreign language to deaf students and felt that the educational environments in which they worked were not, in terms of assistive technology, properly equipped to accommodate such learners (Khasawneh, 2021).

The use of assistive technology in English language teaching can be further hindered by poor digital literacy among teachers and/or students.

Digital literacy involves the confident and critical use of a full range of digital technologies for information, communication and basic problem-solving in all aspects of life. It is underpinned by basic skills in ICT: the use of computers to retrieve, assess, store, produce, present and exchange information, and to communicate and participate in collaborative networks via the Internet. (UNESCO, 2024)

Digital literacy is an increasingly important 21st century skill (OECD, 2021), and one that necessitates greater and greater consideration for multimodality in the face of a rapidly evolving technological landscape (Sindoni et al., 2022). As such, language teachers should include the development of digital literacy in their goals for student learning. This is especially important as educators in many contexts face the possibility that their students enter their classrooms with insufficient digital literacy, a concern that is further exacerbated by the possibility that many teachers themselves lack sufficient digital literacy to impart relevant skills to their students. Increasing the awareness of assistive technologies and their applications for English language learning are therefore paramount for helping the field of English language education meet its obligation to provide quality inclusive education as necessitated by international policy guidance and ensure the right to education for all learners. Fortunately, assistive technologies themselves allow easy entry points to help students develop their digital literacy. Furthermore, "[t]his approach represents a shift from the technocratic model of technology integration in learning through a more human centered model" (UNICEF, 2022, p. 81).

Recommendations for Using Assistive Technology in the English Language Classroom

This section will provide a set of practical recommendations for using assistive technology in the English language classroom. These recommendations are further divided into three categories: guidelines for using assistive technology as general accessible practice, guidelines for using assistive technology as accommodations on an as-needed basic, and guidelines for using assistive technology to promote students' digital literacy. These guidelines are not mutually exclusive. There is also some overlap across these three lists, and many are mutually reinforcing. Readers should also keep in mind that applications of inclusive educational principles are context-dependent, meaning that not all of these guidelines will be appropriate or even possible for every teaching context, and so modifications may be necessary.

Prior to following these guidelines, teachers should first and foremost identify any and all available institutional resources. These resources should include "hard" resources like embossing printers to create Braille materials, as well as "soft" resources like support from ICT or disability support personnel. Secondly, teachers need to familiarize themselves with a variety of assistive technologies in order to use them effectively and to help students use them as well. Once all available resources have been catalogued and teachers have familiarized themselves with available assistive technologies, teachers will have an easier experience following the guidelines listed below.

Using Assistive Technology to Increase Accessibility

- Develop and communicate clear guidelines for the use of assistive technology to all students.
- Engage multiple modalities when creating and giving input to students. This includes but is not limited to:
    - Using visual content to represent new words and concepts.
    - Using closed captioning or subtitles for all video materials.
    - Making transcripts of audio, including in formats that can easily be converted into Braille using an embossing printer (this depends on the software being used, so ask students who use such accommodations which format is best for them).
    - Raising students' awareness of free and open access software to convert formats of input and output, e.g. text-to-speech, speech-to-text, and text/speech-to-Braille (e.g., https://www.brailletranslator.org), as well as generative AI such as ChatGPT, though this last form of software must be utilized with appropriate caution.
- Follow accessibility guidelines for inclusive formatting for materials. For example, a minimum of 1.15 line spacing, ragged-right indentations, and sans-serif fonts are more accessible to learners with dyslexia, while color coding should be avoided for materials to be more accessible for students with colorblindness. Because SLDs are not visible forms of disability and may go undiagnosed well into adulthood, it is crucial to follow such guidelines as a matter of standard practice.
- Use adjustable formatting in digital materials so that students can change things like font, spacing, and background color to make them more readable.

- Check that digital materials are readable on different devices, as many students are just as likely to access course content on a smartphone as they are on a computer.
- Allow for the use of multiple modalities in students' output. This includes, but is not limited to:
  - Recording video or audio of spoken output.
  - Using speech-to-text or dictation software to complete writing assignments.

Using Assistive Technology as an Accommodation

- Communicate with students about their needs and what assistive technologies can best help meet them. Give students' agency over what assistive technologies they can use, and be flexible with students if they are navigating a particular assistive product for the first time.
- Identify impairment-specific assistive products (e.g., LexiPal for students with dyslexia) that can be used as specific accommodations on an as-needed basis.
- Allow students to use low vision aids like hand-held telescopes and magnifiers.
- Allow students to use talking tactile tablets (T3s). (Designed for visually impaired learners, T3s are a type of graphic tablet that uses a touch-sensitive surface that can create raised icons to represent illustrations or serve as pressure-sensitive buttons to play audio when pressed.)
- Allow students to use writing tablets such as Boogie Boards.
- Follow up with students regularly to ensure that their assistive technologies continue to meet their needs, and keep a record of your own observations related to how students are using their assistive technologies.

Using Assistive Technology to Promote Digital Literacy

- Include clear and concrete learning objectives related to digital literacy in course outlines and syllabuses.
- Provide explicit instruction on how to use:
  - Text-to-speech and speech-to-text or screen reading features of commonly used software and applications like Word and Google Chrome.
  - Organizational features of commonly used software and applications. Some examples are automated tables of contents and bullets and numbering.

- Editing tools within commonly used software and applications, for example Tracked Changes in Word.
- Organizational principles such as file naming conventions and folder partitioning, as well as how to create and keep track of secure passwords for different digital products and services.
- Generative AI products in a way that supports rather than undermines learning objectives.

- Give assignments that require using the features listed above. Depending on the class profile and learning objectives, these assignments can be short and simple or longer and complex. In any case, these assignments should be assessed formatively so that students receive feedback on their ability to use the technologies themselves. One example is to give students a short passage of text that they must digitize into an accessible format, for example by representing the content multimodally. This could include adding images to the text, changing the font or file type, or converting the text into a video with closed captioning. Such assignments can also target specific language skills. For example, teachers aiming to develop speaking skills could require students to create accessible video content, while those focusing on reading or writing could ask students to track changes in a Word file or Google Doc or revise text created using generative AI. Such assignments have a secondary benefit of raising students' awareness of barriers to learning for students with different support needs or forms of disability, thereby fostering a greater inclusive ethos within the class and creating a more supportive learning environment for a variety of student profiles.
- Encourage students to collaborate in their use of assistive technologies so that they can troubleshoot and learn new ways to use these technologies from each other.
- Create space for collaboration, group work, and class discussion using technology itself, for example through the use of online discussion forums.

It is also important to note that most if not all of the assistive technologies and guidelines listed above can benefit students from other groups, which is to say, students from groups for which the assistive technology was not originally designed. Writing tablets, for instance, are helpful not only for deaf and hard of hearing students, but those with communicative anxieties that may or may not be related to an SLD. Using the same example, any student, including those without disabilities, may struggle with the pronunciation of a new word, either productively or receptively, and in such instances something like a Boogie Board or text-to-speech software can aid in the acquisition of that word, especially as pertains to mapping phonemes to graphemes.

There any many more such instances in which assistive technology can benefit all students, and so teachers should reflect critically on its uses and applications.

Also, it is important to remember that assistive technology should be used to assist and not replace basic communicative skills and modalities. Generative AI, for instance, can support learning or be used inappropriately by students eager to find a shortcut. A university student using text-to-speech software and an embossing printer may still need to know the conventions of a basic research essay. Assistive technology should, in other words, be another means by which teachers help learners achieve learning aims. In this way, a plurality of literacies can be simultaneously developed, and students will have a greater awareness of how these literacies are interrelated. Furthermore, assistive technology "should be introduced as an integral part of the learning environment and a tool for participation like any other learning tool" (UNICEF, 2022, p. 84). Inclusive approaches, including the use of assistive technology, benefit everyone!

CONCLUSION

The above recommendations are not necessarily possible in all educational contexts, as access to financial and technological resources are not the same around the world, or even between schools in the same location. Many countries in the Global South, for instance, have extremely limited access to both assistive technology and relevant training for teachers, and the COVID-19 pandemic further exacerbated the digital divide for students with disabilities between developed and developing countries (UNESCO, 2021). Students who require but are unable to receive assistive technology as an accommodation therefore encounter barriers related not only to their disability, but to their country of origin and/or socio-economic status. At present, the use of inclusive assistive technology is a privilege.

Shi et al. (2022), however, note that assistive technology can go a long way in closing the digital divide, increasing opportunities for social participation for children with disabilities, and advancing the United Nations' Sustainable Development Goals, particularly in developing regions such as South East Asia. Sustainable Development Goal 4 itself leaves room for assistive technology and digital literacy in achieving its aim of eliminating educational disparities between majority and minoritized groups worldwide. Target 4.B, for instance, explicitly calls for expanding training in ICT in developing countries (United Nations, 2024). While these formal declarations do not automatically ensure that such aims are met, they can help provide a roadmap for educators at the local level. GC4 and UNICEF (2022), for example, call for a whole school approach in utilizing assistive technology to include students with disabilities, including equitable allocation of resources, collaboration between stakeholders, and relevant teacher training. Awareness of inclusive education policy can help improve English language teachers' self-efficacy, but many of these teachers lack such awareness (Young, 2024).

Wider research reviews into the use of assistive technology in inclusive education have also emphasized the importance of the schooling environment and teacher training on how to use such technologies, though further research in this respect is still sorely needed (Chambers, 2020; Fernández-Batanero et al., 2022). Regardless, ensuring equitable and quality inclusive education in any context requires both willingness and capability of all stakeholders. If assistive technology and digital literacy are to be part of the educational paradigm as is called for at the international policy level, then teachers, teacher trainers, and school administrators must themselves have a sufficient degree of digital literacy and familiarity with relevant assistive technologies. Broader progress in educational and economic development must also be achieved to ensure sustainable educational development worldwide. In the meantime, and because the implementation of quality inclusive education is context-sensitive, English language teachers need to consider the unique features of their wider field, as well as their individual teaching contexts, before real progress can be made.

REFERENCES

Arslantas, T. K. (2017). Foreign language education of visually impaired individuals: A review of pervasive studies. *Ihlara Journal of Educational Research, 2*(2), 95-104. http://ihead.aksaray.edu.tr/tr/download/article-file/396670

Barkley, R. A. (1997). Behavioral inhibition, sustained attention, and executive functions: Constructing a unifying theory of ADHD. *Psychological Bulletin*, 121(1), 65–94. https://sciences.ucf.edu/psychology/childrenslearningclinic/wp-content/uploads/sites/24/2013/08/Barkley-1997-Psych-Bulletin.pdf. 10.1037/0033-2909.121.1.659000892

Boltenkova, J., Nevolina, A., Koksharov, V., Li, S., Rasskazova, T., Tkachuk, G., & Baliasov, A. (2020). Teaching EFL to blind and visually impaired students: An overview. *ICERI2020 Proceedings*, (pp. 5616-5623). IEEE. 10.21125/iceri.2020.1209

Borodkin, K., & Faust, M. (2014). Native language phonological skills in low proficiency second language learners. *Language Learning*, 64(1), 132–159. 10.1111/lang.12032

Carpenter, J. (2024). The social accomplishment of the right to an education: Interviews with people who are blind in Japan. In Burke, A., Young, D., & Cook, M. (Eds.), *Barrier-free Instruction in Japan: Recommendations for Teachers at All Levels of Schooling* (pp. 164–179). Candlin & Mynard. 10.47908/30/8

Chambers, D. (2020). Assistive technology supporting inclusive education: Existing and emerging trends. In Chambers, D. (Ed.), *Assistive Technology to Support Inclusive Education* (pp. 1–16). Emerald. 10.1108/S1479-363620200000014001

Cohen, I. (2011). Teacher-student interaction in classrooms of students with specific learning difficulties learning English as a foreign language. *Journal of Interactional Research in Communication Disorders*, 2(2), 271–292. 10.1558/jircd.v2i2.271

Committee on the Rights of Persons with Disabilities. (2016). *General comment no. 4*. OHCHR. https://www.ohchr.org/en/hrbodies/crpd/pages/gc.aspx

Csizér, K., & Kontra, E. H. (2020). Foreign language learning characteristics of deaf and severely hard-of-hearing students. *Modern Language Journal*, 104(1), 233–249. 10.1111/modl.12630

Domagała-Zyśk, E. (2019). Vocabulary teaching strategies in English as a foreign language classes for Deaf and Hard-of-Hearing students. In Domagała-Zyśk, E., & Kontra, E. H. (Eds.), *English as a foreign language for Deaf and Hard-of-Hearing persons: Challenges and strategies* (pp. 135–150). Cambridge Scholars Publishing.

Evans, N., Broido, E. M., Brown, K. R., & Wilke, A. K. (2017). *Disability in higher education: A social justice approach*. Jossey-Bass.

Fernández-Batanero, J. M., Montenegro-Rueda, M., Fernández-Cerero, J., & Garcia-Martinez, I. (2022). Assistive technology for the inclusion of students with disabilities: A systematic review. *Educational Technology Research and Development*, 70(5), 1911–1930. 10.1007/s11423-022-10127-7

Graham, L. J. (2020). Inclusive education in the 21st century. In Graham, L. J. (Ed.), *Inclusive education for the 21st century: Theory, policy and practice* (pp. 3–26). Routledge. 10.4324/9781003116073-2

Iwai, K. (2024). Time to care: Teaching discussion to a hearing-impaired student. In Burke, A., Young, D., & Cook, M. (Eds.), *Barrier-free Instruction in Japan: Recommendations for Teachers at All Levels of Schooling* (pp. 205–218). Candlin & Mynard. 10.47908/30/11

Jayakody, A., Lokuliyana, S., Sampath, A. A. T., Silva, G. T. S., Rajanthika, S. A. L., & Seneviratne, H. M. T. B. (2016). Mobile application for vision impaired people to facilitate to learn the English language. *International Journal of Computer Applications*, 138(12), 12–17. https://www.ijcaonline.org/research/volume138/number12/jayakody-2016-ijca-909025.pdf. 10.5120/ijca2016909025

Kessler, M. (2022). *Multimodality*. ELT Journal. 10.1093/elt/ccac028

Khan, G. Z., & Mahmood, A. (2022). The role of assistive technology in the English language learning experience of blind and visually impaired students in Pakistan: A qualitative study. *Journal of Social Sciences Review*, 2(4), 313–321. 10.54183/jssr.v2i4.106

Khasawneh, M. A. S. (2021). Problems teaching English to deaf students. *Indonesian Journal of Creative Counseling*, 1(1), 32–42. 10.47679/ijcc.v1i2.107

Khodadady, E., & Gholamian, M. (2014). Motivations underlying blind students' English language learning: A theoretical and factorial analysis. *International Journal of Applied Psychology*, 4(5), 169–180. 10.5923/j.ijap.20140405.01

Kormos, J. (2017a). *The second language learning processes of students with specific learning difficulties*. Routledge.

Kormos, J. (2017b). The effects of specific learning difficulties on processes of multilingual language development. *Annual Review of Applied Linguistics*, 37, 30–44. 10.1017/S026719051700006X

Kormos, J., & Smith, A. M. (2024). *Teaching languages to students with specific learning differences* (2nd ed.). Multilingual Matters. 10.21832/9781800418622

Lerga, R., Candrlic, S., & Jakupovic, A. (2021). A review of assistive technology for students with dyslexia. *Proceedings of the 13th Conference on Computer Supported Education,* (pp. 64-72). ACM. 10.5220/0010434500640072

Mpofu, J., & Chimhenga, S. (2013). Challenges faced by Hearing Impaired pupils in learning: A case study of King George VI Memorial School. *IOSR Journal of Research & Method in Education*, 2(1), 69–74. 10.9790/7388-0216974

Murphy, J., & Dodd, B. (2010). A diagnostic challenge: Language difficulties and hearing impairment in a secondary-school student from a non-English-speaking background. *Child Language Teaching and Therapy*, 26(3), 207–220. 10.1177/0265659009349977

OECD. (2021). *21st-century readers: Developing literacy skills in a digital world.* OECD. https://www.oecd.org/publications/21st-century-readers-a83d84cb-en.htm

Shi, G., Ke, S., & Banozic, A. (2022). The role of assistive technology in advancing sustainable development goals. *Frontiers in Political Science*, 4, 859272. 10.3389/fpos.2022.859272

Sindoni, M. G., Adami, E., Karatza, S., Moschini, I., & Petroni, S. (2022). Theory and practice of the common framework of reference for intercultural digital literacies. In Sindoni, M. G., & Moschini, I. (Eds.), *Multimodal literacies across digital learning contexts* (pp. 166–184). Routledge. 10.4324/9781003134244-13

Smith, A. M. (2018). *Inclusive practices.* Oxford University Press.

Sparks, R. L., Ganschow, L., Kenneweg, S., & Miller, K. (1991). Use of an orton-gillingham approach to teach a foreign language to dyslexic/learning-disabled students: Explicit teaching of phonology in a second language. *Annals of Dyslexia*, 41(1), 96–118. https://link.springer.com/article/10.1007/BF02648080. 10.1007/BF0264808024233759

Swisher, M. V. (1989). The language-learning situation of deaf students. *TESOL Quarterly*, 23(2), 239–257. 10.2307/3587335

Tsukamoto, M. (2024). A student with visual impairment in an EFL reading classroom: The teacher and the student's experience. In Burke, A., Young, D., & Cook, M. (Eds.), *Barrier-free Instruction in Japan: Recommendations for Teachers at All Levels of Schooling* (pp. 180–191). Candlin & Mynard. 10.47908/30/9

UNESCO. (2021). *Understanding the impact of COVID-19 on the education of persons with disabilities: Challenges and opportunities of distance education*. UNESCO. https://iite.unesco.org/publications/the-impact-of-covid-19-on-the-education-of-persons-with-disabilities/

UNESCO. (2023). *2023 global education monitoring report*. UNESCO. https://gem-report-2023.unesco.org/

UNESCO. (2024). *Digital literacy*. UNESCO. https://uis.unesco.org/en/glossary-term/digital-literacy

UNICEF. (2022). *The use of assistive technology in education: A guide for teachers and schools*. UNICEF. https://www.unicef.org/eca/media/30671/file/Teacher's%20guide%20for%20building%20capacity%20for%20assistive%20technology.pdf

United Nations. (2024). *Goal 4: Quality education*. UN. https://unric.org/en/sdg-4/

United Nations. (n.d.). *Convention on the rights of persons with disabilities and optional protocol*. https://www.un.org/disabilities/documents/convention/convoptprot-e.pdf

Wesołowska, A., & Jedynak, M. (2014). FL vocabulary learning strategies used by blind, partially blind and normally sighted learners of English. In Paradowski, M. (Ed.), *Teaching Languages off the Beaten Track* (pp. 306–328). Peter Lang.

World Health Organization. (2024). *Assistive technology*. WHO. https://www.who.int/europe/health-topics/assistive-technology#tab=tab_1

Young, D. (2024). Awareness of inclusive education policy among postsecondary English language teachers in Japan. In Peking University-Waseda University Joint Research Initiative (Eds.), *Renewing Governance Mechanism in Asia-Pacific* (pp. 338-355). Waseda University Press.

Young, D., & Burke, A. (2024). Conceptualizing inclusive practices for English language teachers. In Burke, A., Young, D., & Cook, M. L. (Eds.), *Barrier-free Instruction in Japan: Recommendations for Teachers at all Levels of Schooling* (pp. 86–104). Candlin & Mynard. 10.47908/30/3

Chapter 4
Enhancing Classroom Equity Through the Integration of Digital Technology

Amina Parveen
https://orcid.org/0000-0002-5092-0011
University of Kashmir, India

Aamir Naziir Ganie
University of Kashmir, India

Fazila Bashir
University of Kashmir, India

Phayaola N. Zimik
University of Kashmir, India

Shazia N. Jan
https://orcid.org/0000-0003-2849-4463
University of Kashmir, India

ABSTRACT

This chapter explores the integration of digital technology to enhance classroom equity. Examining the impact on diverse learning needs, it delves into how technology foster inclusivity supports personalized learning and addresses potential disparities. Concentrating on the possibility of overcoming educational gaps. It looks at how technology can improve accessibility to resources, emphasizing the possibility of closing educational gaps. It looks at how technology may enhance accessibility to

DOI: 10.4018/979-8-3693-2591-9.ch004

resources. It emphasizes the role of digital tools in promoting equal access to educational recourses, ultimately contributing to a more equitable and inclusive classroom environment. It investigates the effective implementation of digital technology in classroom settings, considering teacher professional development and infrastructure requirements. The chapter also provides insight into the transformative potential of digital integration for achieving greater equity in education.

DIGITAL TECHNOLOGY

Digital technology is the processing, storing, transmitting, and manipulating of data through the use of digital systems, such as computers and other electronic devices. It includes an extensive variety of applications and technologies, including networks, hardware, software, and the internet. The growth and spread of information and communication technologies (ICT) are widely acknowledged by economists, sociologists, educators, and communication scholars to be having a significant impact on contemporary living. Because of the affordances of new digital media, which combine the interactive qualities of speech and the archival qualities of writings, it is possible for large-scale collaborative editing of texts and many-to-many communication among people without regard to time or space. It also makes it easier to create a global hyper-indexed multimodal information structure and allows for the production and distribution of writing and multimedia content on a scale that was previously unthinkable. (2008; Warschauer, 1999). rm of learning that makes use of technology is called digital learning. In the modern era, people use digital technologies widely and in all kinds of contexts. Digital technologies have an impact on people's learning experiences in terms of what, why, where, and how they learn from others. Digital technologies, such as computers, laptops, tablets, smart phones, mobile phones, and so on, are widely used. Digital technologies are primarily used to quickly, easily, and affordably establish connections between people. People can connect with each other through an extensive array of digital services and resources. While there are many advantages to using digital technologies for learning, there are also risks and challenges for the students .The obstacles to obtaining knowledge and information are real and can be attributed to digital challenges (Digital Technology, 2015). It is necessary to take action in order to address the issues and difficulties related to digital technologies. Digital technology integration in the classroom can improve equity by offering a variety of learning opportunities and resources. This strategy encourages inclusivity and supports individualized learning preferences (Cavanaugh, 2016;Darling-Hammond 2017).However, its essential to consider potential disparities in technology access among students and implement strategies to address them (Mossberger,Tolbert,&Stansbury,2003).Overall, the thoughtful integration of digital technology can contribute to a more equitable learning environment. Research indicates that digital technology can empower students in underprivileged communities by offering exposure to diverse educational content and cultivating essential digital literacy skills (Bebell&O'Dwyer,2010;-Fairlie, et al., 2017).Furthermore incorporating collaborative online platforms can encourage peer to peer learning, breaking down barriers and promoting a sense of community in the classroom(Hew& Brush, 2007, Warschauer, 2003).To maximize equity, educators should adopt inclusive instructional design principles and ongoing professional development to ensure all students benefit from technology integration (Castek et al.2019; Ertmer, Ottenbreit-Leftwich, & Tondeur,2015).Moreover, digital technology allows for differentiated instruction, catering to individual student needs through adaptive learning platform and personalized feedback (Pane et al,2017, Hattie, 2012).This flexibility in teaching approaches helps address diverse learning abilities, ensuring that no student is left behind (Tomlinson, 2000).Additionally, the integration of technology can contribute to a more student-centric learning environment, promoting active engagement and self –directed learning (Mean et al, 2013,Jonassen, 1999). Teachers can make learning more inclusive and equitable for all students by adopting these practices. The integration of digital technology enables collaborative learning, breaking down geographical and social barriers. Virtual classroom and online platforms foster a sense of inclusivity, where students can participate actively, regardless of physical location or socio-economic factors. This promotes a more level playing field for all learners.

Significance

Enhancing classroom equity through the integration of digital technology is a pivotal in fostering an inclusive and fair educational landscape. By leveraging digital tools, educators can bridge the gap in access to information, ensuring that students, regardless of their geographical or socio-economic background, have equal opportunities to educational resources. Moreover, the personalized learning experiences facilitated by technology cater to diverse learning styles, allowing each student to thrive based on their individual needs. Ultimately, the integration of digital technology in education not only prepares students for a technology-driven future but also contributes significantly to closing achievement gaps, promoting engagement, and empowering educators to create a more equitable and enriching learning environment. The socioeconomic divide, which can differ significantly in terms of educational resources between high-income and low-income families, is a major effect of inequality. Compared to low-income families, high-income families frequently give their kids access to superior educational opportunities, such as private schools, advanced tutoring programs, and specialized educational services

.These variations can widen the disparity by giving students from various socioeconomic backgrounds unfair playing fields. Apart from the disparity in educational opportunities brought about by inequality, there is also an effect on the caliber of education obtained.

HOW CLASSROOM EQUITY IS ENCOURAGED BY DIGITAL TECHNOLOGY

Providing access to technology alone won't achieve classroom equity through the integration of digital literacy; rather, it calls for a multipronged strategy that recognizes students' varied needs and experiences and fosters equitable and inclusive learning opportunities, digital literacy should encompass not only technical skills but also critical thinking and ethical considerations in using digital resources. Digital literacy should encompass not only technical skills but also critical thinking and ethical considerations in using digital resources Martin (2018),. Digital divide" disproportionately affects marginalized students, thus access to digital devices and reliable internet is essential for equitable learning opportunities, Warschauer (2006),. In today's increasingly digital world, proficiency in digital literacy is essential for academic success and future career prospects. However, disparities in access to technology and digital skills can exacerbate existing inequities in education. Therefore, addressing these disparities requires a comprehensive strategy that combines access to technology, digital skills training, curriculum integration, differentiated instruction, equitable resource allocation, collaborative learning, digital citizenship education, feedback and assessment, as well as parent and community engagement, As emphasized by Cuban (2001), equitable resource distribution is essential for addressing disparities in access to digital tools and narrowing the achievement gap. . By adopting such an approach with special attention to references and citations from scholarly sources, educators can ensure that digital literacy initiatives are grounded in evidence-based practices and contribute to creating a more equitable learning environment for all students, Involve parents and the community in supporting digital literacy initiatives. Building partnerships with families, as recommended by Epstein (2018), strengthens home-school connections and promotes equitable access to digital resources and support.

Digital literacy encompasses the ability to find, evaluate, utilize, share, and create content using digital technologies. Here's how integrating digital literacy can contribute to classroom equity:

1. **Access to Information**: Digital literacy ensures that students have access to a vast array of information and resources online. This levels the playing field for students who may not have access to traditional educational materials, such as textbooks or libraries, due to financial constraints or geographic limitations.
2. **Personalized Learning**: Digital tools allow for personalized learning experiences tailored to individual student needs. By integrating digital literacy, educators can provide diverse learning opportunities that cater to different learning styles, abilities, and interests, thus addressing the unique needs of each student and promoting equity in education.
3. **Critical Thinking and Evaluation Skills**: Teaching digital literacy involves teaching students how to critically evaluate online information for accuracy, bias, and credibility. These critical thinking skills are essential for navigating the vast amount of information available on the internet and empower students to become discerning consumers and creators of digital content.
4. **Empowerment and Engagement**: Integrating digital literacy empowers students to actively engage with technology and become creators of digital content rather than just consumers. This empowerment fosters a sense of ownership over their learning and encourages participation, particularly among marginalized groups who may feel disengaged from traditional educational practices.
5. **Closing the Digital Divide**: By ensuring that all students have access to digital literacy skills and resources, educators can work towards closing the digital divide—the gap between those who have access to technology and the internet and those who do not. Bridging this gap is essential for promoting equity in education and ensuring that all students have the skills necessary to succeed in a digital world.
6. **Preparation for the Future**: In today's increasingly digital world, proficiency in digital literacy is essential for success in both academic and professional settings. By integrating digital literacy into the classroom, educators can better prepare students, regardless of their background or circumstances, for future academic and career opportunities, thus promoting equity in access to higher education and employment.

Overall, integrating digital literacy into the classroom is essential for promoting equity in education by providing all students with the skills, resources, and opportunities they need to succeed in the digital age

APPLICATION OF DIGITAL TECHNOLOGIES IN CLASSROOM AND HOW TECHNOLOGY INFLUENCES THE CLASSROOM EQUITY

The way we teach and learn in the classroom is being profoundly changed by the integration of technology. Fundamentally, it is acknowledged that technology plays a critical role in enabling students to take ownership of their education by converting instructors into guides or facilitators and learners into explorers of knowledge (Armstrong, 2014). In response to the desire for more technology-enhanced, student-centered learning, several universities have asked faculty members to reevaluate how they teach their subjects and to think about creating significant online components. In response to the growing interest in technology integration in the classroom, for instance, teachers at a rural university in Australia are encouraged to implement a "flipped classroom" and include a range of online resources into their lectures. Digital tools are only useful when used in conjunction with efficient teaching methods. (Morgan, 2014). Technology has had a tremendous impact on education over the past 20 years. Nowadays, most students use internet-enabled devices like laptops and smart phones to complete their academic work, which includes taking notes, attending lectures, and organizing their assignments.. According to data from 2022, with 900 million active internet users and a 47% internet penetration rate, India is among the world's second-largest online markets. Reports indicate that by 2025, the proportion of internet users is expected to rise above 55%. We already use a lot of technology in our daily lives outside of school. It makes sense to involve them in the educational process. However, using technology in the classroom shouldn't be limited to PowerPoint lectures or online learning environments. These are a few inventive ways that educational technology can be applied.

Classroom equity and digital technology are interconnected in several ways, influencing educational outcomes and opportunities for students.

Digital technology can either exacerbate or mitigate equity gaps depending on access to devices and the internet. Students from lower-income backgrounds or rural areas may have limited access to technology, leading to disparities in learning opportunities (Warschauer, 2004). Digital tools can cater to diverse learning needs, offering personalized instruction that supports equity by addressing individual student strengths and weaknesses (Darling-Hammond, 2015).Technology can enhance engagement by providing interactive and multimedia-rich learning experiences that appeal to diverse learning styles and interests, thus promoting equity in participation and motivation (OECD, 2015).Proficiency with digital tools is increasingly important for future success, making it crucial to ensure all students have opportunities to develop these skills to prevent further marginalization (DiMaggio et al., 2004).

Equitable access to training and support for teachers in integrating technology into their teaching practices is essential. It ensures that all students benefit from innovative instructional methods (Ertmer et al., 2012).Technology enables educators to collect and analyze data on student performance, helping identify and address achievement gaps based on factors like socioeconomic status or race (Wayman et al., 2007).Efforts to bridge the digital divide, including providing devices and internet access to underserved communities, are critical for promoting equity in educational outcomes (Warschauer, 2004).Digital technologies can offer culturally relevant content and resources that resonate with diverse student populations, thereby promoting inclusivity and equity in the curriculum (Gay, 2000).Online platforms and tools facilitate collaborative learning environments where students can work together regardless of physical proximity, fostering teamwork skills and promoting equity in participation (Dillenbourg, 1999).Technology plays a crucial role in providing personalized learning experiences for students with special needs, ensuring they receive tailored support and accommodations to achieve academic success (Rose & Meyer, 2002). Digital tools can support language acquisition for English language learners through interactive language programs and translation tools, reducing language barriers and promoting equity in language proficiency (Cummins, 2000).Digital technology enables students to connect with peers and experts globally, fostering a broader worldview and promoting equity in access to diverse perspectives and knowledge (Zhao & Frank, 2003).Integrating technology into classrooms can enhance critical thinking and problem-solving skills, which are essential for equitable access to higher education and future employment opportunities (Harris, Mishra, & Koehler, 2009).Technology can facilitate communication between teachers and parents, particularly in underserved communities where traditional means of communication may be limited, enhancing parental involvement and supporting equity in educational support (Davies & Aurini, 2010).Addressing ethical considerations such as data privacy and digital citizenship is essential to ensure equitable access to technology without compromising students' rights or exacerbating existing inequalities (Selwyn, 2016).

These additional references and insights further illustrate how digital technology can support equitable educational opportunities by addressing diverse learning needs, enhancing collaboration, and fostering inclusive learning environments.

HOW TO PROMOTE INCLUSIVE PRACTICES

Inclusive Practice

Since inclusive practices acknowledge the diversity of students, they enable all students to participate fully in learning activities, obtain course materials, and demonstrate their abilities. It recognizes the diversity of the student body as a resource that enhances the educational experience. (Equality Challenge Unit, 2013). It is an approach where all children, regardless of their backgrounds, abilities, or limitations, receive the appropriate support in a school setting—both socially and academically. This may suggest that children with disabilities are placed in less restrictive settings than their able-bodied peers. Regarding the curriculum, this suggests that, because of the techniques employed, all students can access learning in the classroom.

Strategies to Promote Inclusive Practice in the Classroom

Curriculum delivery methods cannot be considered inclusive unless they accommodate the needs of every student, regardless of their perceived ability or disability. As we have already seen, it is somewhat challenging to define inclusion because various people would use it slightly differently depending on the situation. However, if it had a fixed definition, it wouldn't be flexible enough to the ever-changing world, particularly in the field of education. (Trussler and Robinson, 2015). Because British and global society is becoming more diverse, educators and educational institutions need to be flexible in their methods and policies to accommodate all students. Additionally, the methods that are the needs of assisting specific learners with their issues will change every day, so practitioners need to be adaptable and flexible in order to participate in an active, reflective process. (Trussler and Robinson, 2015). However, a common beginning point is essential to understanding the broad tenets of inclusion. Regardless of a student's challenges, educationally inclusive schools offer them new opportunities. They do this by regularly tracking each student's progress, identifying any past problems (or potential future problems), and addressing any obstacles by taking concrete action to support the student's learning while fostering tolerance, acceptance, and understanding. The Office for Standards in Education is the source of this data. (Ofsted, 2000, p. 7 cited in Trussler and Robinson, 2015). Schools that uphold this philosophy essentially demonstrate that every child matters, which raises young people's self-esteem and sense of self as is essential to the process of education. It is critical to understand that inclusive practices and inclusion encompass more than just providing for the special education needs of students. The inclusive ethos allows every student in a given setting to reach their full potential through participation in extracurricular and academic activities. All students, without exception, should be a part of this. Embracing diversity, celebrating it, and using difference as a motivator for learning are crucial components of inclusive practice (Falvey and Givner, 2005). All children must have access to the curriculum in order to provide an environment that supports their full potential for development (Sage, 2007; DfES, 2004). Every child needs to feel safe in the classroom, thus educators and institutions must take action to eliminate any real or imagined obstacles to learning and equal opportunities, including evaluating how resources are used to give all kids more access to educational possibilities (Centre for Studies in Inclusive Education [CSIE], 2015). Teachers also need to make sure that appropriate learning challenges are created to fit the needs of the students, always trying to provide the students the chance to get better. Regardless of the children's age, educators are vital in helping them cultivate a lifelong love of learning in the classroomIt is apparent that this must be done in a safe, welcoming environment where everyone is valued and differences are accepted, celebrated, and respected. All children should be able to actively participate in the curriculum as equal members of the community and engage with it, as this is what defines an inclusive teaching and learning environment. Furthermore, there must to be proof of significant accommodations that enable students with disabilities to fully integrate into the curriculum and the school community as a whole, including extracurricular activities. Because of the basic structure of the educational system, implies that while developmental milestones must be demonstrated by an assessment of students' abilities at particular times, this does not absolve schools of their duty to give students under their care with a well-rounded, holistic educationWith an emphasis on children's active engagement with learning in both formal academic and social contexts, practitioners and educational institutions must provide a variety of programs and strategies that maximize student involvement and advancement in order to achieve this. (Dumaresq and Tommasini, 2014). According to Dumaresq and Tommasini 2014), there are several key elements that make inclusive practice possible. They claim that educators need to be aware of these fundamentals since they are essential to establishing a setting where people can feel secure and at ease and where each person is valued. These elements are said to include instructional strategies, student placement, cooperative practices, family and community involvement, leadership, the school's structure and ethos, and extra support services.

EXISTING INEQUALITIES IN THE CLASSROOM

Inequality refers to the unequal distribution of advantages, resources, and opportunities within a society. These differences can manifest in a variety of ways, such as social discrimination on the basis of race, gender, or ethnicity; political injustice, which involves unequal representation and power; and economic inequality, which involves unequal wealth or income. These differences have a profound effect on people and society as a whole. They can cause social class divisions and stir up protests against the structures that support these discrepancies. To further their potential, people who are disadvantaged by inequality frequently require greater opportunities or resources. We should all strive for a society that is more just in this way. Inequality still poses a serious barrier to accessing high-quality education in many areas. A cautionary indicator is the unequal distribution of resources among the schools. Rich neighborhoods tend to have higher budgets than low-income neighborhoods when it comes to hiring teachers, purchasing supplies, and providing learning environments. Because of this, white students from wealthier socioeconomic backgrounds typically have access to better facilities, a lower dropout rate, a greater variety of educational options, higher earnings, and more advanced instruction than do black students. Lack of access to high-quality education is also impacted by gender and ethnic inequality. This can involve things like receiving unfair treatment in the classroom or not having enough funding set aside for educational supplies or materials that are tailored to a particular community. Anything less is beneath the standards to which our society ought to aspire; everyone should have equal access to the education they require and merit. Clearly, the ability of a student to obtain a top-notch education can be adversely affected by social and economic differences in a disproportionately negative way. Poor people, for example, are disadvantaged because they frequently lack access to the resources needed for studying, including textbooks, laptop computers, reasonably priced transportation, etc. Furthermore, the continuous stress brought on by their challenging home environments exacerbates this issue and may impede their academic success. It is imperative for educational institutions to resist these significant variations and ensure that all students have equitable access to the best possible public education. They should first give poor Black schools the same financial aid as White schools in order for them to have the same infrastructure as their wealthier counterparts. In addition, there ought to be no discrimination in the classroom, and strategies for making underachievers feel heard and included need to be established. If schools can develop strategies that appropriately address poverty, then every student has an equal chance to thrive in the classroom.

The Ways That Inequality Affects the Quality of Education

The quality of education in the modern world is significantly impacted by inequality. Pupils with privilege and those without differ greatly in that regard because of unequal access to opportunities, funds, and resources. Schools in low-income areas usually need more funding to provide their students with a high-quality education.

This could lead to a number of issues, including outdated technology, crowded classrooms, unclean settings, and inadequate learning supplies.

As a result, students in affluent school districts could obtain an education at a different level than students in other forms of educational disparities. Racism, sexism, and classism are just a few of the educational disparities that continue to shape students' individual learning experiences. In the past, US institutions have not always provided historically marginalized groups with the same resources or support as they have for majority groups. This creates a vicious cycle that prevents disadvantaged children from pursuing better opportunities. employment that require a college degree or to pursue further education options.

Application of the Study

The application of the study "Enhancing classroom equity through digital technology" lies in leveraging digital tools and technologies to create a more equitable learning environment for all students, regardless of their backgrounds, abilities, or circumstances, Here's how this study could be applied ;

1. **Technology's Role in Classroom Equity:**
    - o Technology supports classroom equity through access to resources, personalized learning, and inclusive environments. It enables data collection for analyzing student performance, engagement, and resource access to identify disparities and take targeted actions.
2. **Key Aspects of Classroom Equity and Inclusive Education:**
    - o Classroom equity ensures fairness in resource distribution and opportunities for all students, acknowledging diverse needs. Inclusive education accommodates all learners within the regular environment, adapting teaching methods and fostering respect and collaboration.
3. **Benefits of Personalized Learning with Digital Technology:**
    - o Digital tools personalize learning experiences, adapting instruction to individual needs, abilities, and learning styles, addressing disparities among students.
4. **Equity Promotion Through Access to Resources and Collaborative Learning:**
    - o Digital tools provide equal access to educational resources and facilitate collaborative learning, allowing students to work together regardless of location, thus promoting equity.
5. **Digital Tools for Assessment and Feedback to Support Equity:**
    - o Digital tools streamline assessment and provide immediate feedback, supporting all students in tracking progress and improving regardless of their academic background.

6. **Frameworks Supporting Educational Equity:**
    - o Frameworks like Universal Design for Learning (UDL), Culturally Responsive Teaching, Digital Citizenship, and Differentiated Instruction utilize digital technology to cater to diverse learning needs, promote cultural understanding, foster responsible digital behavior, and offer personalized instruction.

Technology's Role in Promoting Classroom Equity

- Technology plays a vital role in promoting classroom equity by providing access to resources, supporting personalized learning, and fostering inclusive environments. It enables educators to collect and analyze data on student performance, engagement, and resource access to identify disparities and take targeted actions.

Key Aspects:

1. **Personalized Learning:** Digital tools personalize learning experiences based on individual student needs, preferences, and learning styles, ensuring all students receive tailored support.
2. **Accessibility Features:** Technology offers features like screen readers and text-to-speech tools, enhancing accessibility for students with disabilities and diverse learning needs.
3. **Online Learning Platforms:** These platforms provide access to diverse educational resources, leveling opportunities for students lacking local resources.
4. **Virtual Classrooms:** Virtual environments promote collaboration and inclusion among students from varied backgrounds and locations.
5. **Digital Literacy Instruction:** Technology teaches digital skills crucial for navigating online environments safely and effectively.

Classroom Equity and Inclusive Education

- Classroom equity ensures fairness in resource distribution and opportunities, recognizing diverse student needs. Inclusive education accommodates all learners by adapting teaching methods and fostering a culture of respect and collaboration.

Key Components

1. **Classroom Equity:** Ensures fairness in resource allocation and support to meet diverse student needs for academic and social success.
2. **Inclusive Education:** Promotes acceptance, belonging, and participation for all students through adapted teaching methods and inclusive practices.

Additional Benefits of Digital Technology

- Digital technology supports personalized learning, provides universal access to resources, facilitates collaborative learning, and enhances assessment and feedback processes.

Some supportive frame works of our results

1. **Universal Design for Learning (UDL)**: UDL is a framework that emphasizes designing curriculum and instruction to meet the needs of all learners by providing multiple means of representation, expression, and engagement. Digital technology can be used to implement UDL principles by offering diverse learning materials, tools for expression, and interactive activities that cater to individual learning preferences and abilities.
2. **Culturally Responsive Teaching**: This framework recognizes the importance of acknowledging and incorporating students' cultural backgrounds and experiences into the learning process. Digital technology can support culturally responsive teaching by providing access to culturally relevant resources, promoting cultural exchange and understanding through online collaboration, and facilitating communication between teachers, students, and families from diverse cultural backgrounds.
3. **Digital Citizenship**: Digital citizenship frameworks promote responsible and ethical use of technology among students, empowering them to navigate digital spaces safely and equitably. By teaching students how to critically evaluate online information, respect diverse perspectives, and participate constructively in digital communities, digital citizenship education fosters equity by ensuring that all students have the knowledge and skills they need to succeed in an increasingly digital world.
4. .**Differentiated Instruction**: Digital technology enables teachers to differentiate instruction based on students' individual needs, interests, and learning styles. Through adaptive learning platforms, interactive multimedia resources, and

customizable learning pathways, educators can provide tailored instruction that meets students where they are and helps them progress at their own pace.

5. **Language Support for English Language Learners (ELL)**: Digital tools can offer language support for ELL students by providing translation services, language learning apps, and multimedia resources in multiple languages. By making learning materials accessible in students' native languages and providing scaffolding support as they acquire English proficiency, digital technology helps to promote equity for ELL students in diverse classrooms.
6. **Data-Informed Decision Making**: Digital technology allows educators to collect and analyze data on students' learning progress, engagement levels, and academic performance. By using data analytics and learning management systems, teachers can identify trends, monitor student growth, and make informed decisions about instructional strategies and interventions to support equitable learning outcomes for all students.
7. **Social-Emotional Learning (SEL)**: Digital technology can support SEL initiatives by providing resources and tools for promoting students' social and emotional well-being. Through online mindfulness activities, virtual counseling services, and digital storytelling platforms, educators can foster students' self-awareness, social skills, and resilience, creating a more supportive and inclusive learning environment.
8. **Community Engagement and Partnerships**: Digital technology can facilitate communication and collaboration between schools, families, and community organizations to support students' academic success and holistic development. Through online parent portals, virtual family workshops, and community resource directories, educators can strengthen partnerships with families and community stakeholders, ensuring that all students have access to the support and resources they need to thrive.
9. **Global Competence**: Global competence frameworks emphasize developing students' knowledge, skills, and dispositions to engage effectively and ethically in a diverse and interconnected world. Digital technology can support global competence by providing opportunities for cross-cultural exchange, virtual collaboration with peers from around the world, and access to global perspectives through online resources and virtual field trips.
10. **Equity-Minded Teaching Practices**: Equity-minded teaching frameworks encourage educators to critically examine their practices and biases to ensure that they are inclusive and equitable for all students. Digital technology can support equity-minded teaching by providing resources for culturally responsive pedagogy, implicit bias training modules, and online communities of practice where educators can share strategies and insights for promoting equity in their classrooms.

By integrating these applications and supportive frameworks into their instructional practices, educators can harness the power of digital technology to create more equitable learning environments where all students have the opportunity to succeed

CONCLUSION

Equity through digital literacy is not just a modern educational trend; it's a necessity in our increasingly digital world. Through digital literacy, students gain access to a vast array of resources and tools that can empower them academically and personally. However, to ensure equity, educators must address disparities in access, training, and support. By providing equitable opportunities for all students to develop digital literacy skills, we can bridge the digital divide and create a more inclusive learning environment where every student has the chance to thrive. Certainly! In conclusion, embracing digital literacy in the classroom is crucial for promoting equity among students. By integrating digital tools and resources into teaching practices, educators can cater to diverse learning styles and needs, fostering a more inclusive educational environment. Moreover, digital literacy equips students with essential skills for the 21st century job market, empowering them to navigate an increasingly digital world with confidence and competence. However, achieving true equity requires addressing systemic barriers such as access to technology and digital skills training. By advocating for equitable distribution of resources and providing support to marginalized communities, we can ensure that all students have the opportunity to harness the full potential of digital literacy for their academic and personal growth.

REFERENCES

Bender, W. N. (2002). *Differentiating Instruction for Students with Learning Disabilities: best practices for general and special educators*. Corwin Press.

Booth, T., Ainscow, M., Black-Hawkins, K., Vaughan, M., & Shaw, L. (2000) *Index for Inclusion: Developing Learning and Participation in Schools*. Bristol: Centre for Studies on Inclusive Education Centre for Studies on Inclusive Education. https://www.csie.org.uk/inclusion/what.shtml

Cornell University Center for Teaching Excellence. (n.d.). *Inclusive Teaching Strategies*. Cornell University. https://www.cte.cornell.edu/teaching-ideas/building-inclusive-classrooms/inclusive-teaching-strategies.html

Cummins, J. (2000). *Language, power, and pedagogy: Bilingual children in the crossfire*. Multilingual Matters. 10.21832/9781853596773

Darling-Hammond, L. (2015). *Equity and Excellence in Education: The Role of High-Quality Instructional Materials*. Stanford Center for Opportunity Policy in Education.

Dash, N. (2006). *Inclusive Education for Children with Special Needs*. Atlantic Publishers and Distributors.

Davies, S., & Aurini, J. (2010). *The Professionalization of Teaching in the Post-Secondary Sector*. Springer Science & Business Media.

Department for Education and Skills. (2004) *Removing Barriers to Achievement: The Governments Strategy for SEN* London: Department for Education and Skills Publications Department for Education and Skills [DfES].

Desai, , S. (2013). Integrated systems oriented student-centric learning environment: A framework for curriculum development. *Campus-Wide Information Systems*, 31(1), 24–45. 10.1108/CWIS-01-2013-0002

Dillenbourg, P. (1999). What do you mean by "collaborative learning"? In Dillenbourg, P. (Ed.), *Collaborative Learning: Cognitive and Computational Approaches* (pp. 1–19). Elsevier.

DiMaggio, P., Hargittai, E., Celeste, C., & Shafer, S. (2004). Digital Inequality: From Unequal Access to Differentiated Use. In Neckerman, K. (Ed.), *Social Inequality* (pp. 355–400). Russell Sage Foundation.

Dumaresq, C. C., & Tommasini, J. J. (2014) 'Inclusive Practices.' Retrieved 8th December 2016 from http://www.charterarts.org/wp-content/uploads/2014/09/Inclusive-Practices.pdf

Ertmer, P. A., Ottenbreit-Leftwich, A. T., Sadik, O., Sendurur, E., & Sendurur, P. (2012). Teacher beliefs and technology integration practices: A critical relationship. *Computers & Education*, 59(2), 423–435. 10.1016/j.compedu.2012.02.001

European Agency for Development in Special Needs Education. (2010) *Teacher Education for Inclusion: International Literature Review*. Odense, Denmark: European Agency for Development in Special Needs Education.

Gay, G. (2000). *Culturally responsive teaching: Theory, research, and practice*. Teachers College Press.

Grace, S., & Gravestock, P. (2009). *Inclusion and Diversity: Meeting the Needs of All Students*. Routledge.

Hajhashemi, K., Caltabiano, N., & Anderson, N. (2016). Integrating digital technologies in the classroom: Lecturers' views on the flipped classroom approach. *Australian and International Journal of Rural Education*, 26(3), 18–29. 10.47381/aijre.v26i3.74

Harris, J., Mishra, P., & Koehler, M. (2009). Teachers' technological pedagogical content knowledge and learning activity types: Curriculum-based technology integration reframed. *Journal of Research on Technology in Education*, 41(4), 393–416. 10.1080/15391523.2009.10782536

Hernandez, J. (2021). Teachers' Perceptions of Integrating Digital Technology Tools [Doctoral dissertation, Concordia University Chicago].

Holmes, W., Anastopoulou, S., Schaumburg, H., & Mavrikis, M. (2018). *Technology-enhanced personalised learning: Untangling the evidence*.

Kamran, T. (2007). Islam, Urdu and Hindu as the Other: Instruments of Cultural Homogeneity in Pakistan. In Chandra, P., & Mahajan, S. (Eds.), *Composite Culture in a Multicultural Society* (pp. 93–122). Dorling Kindersley.

Kapur, R. (2018). *Significance of digital technology*. Research Gate.

Kids Together. (2010) *Benefits of Inclusive Education*. Kids Together. http://www.kidstogether.org/inclusion/benefitsofinclusion.htm

Land, S. (2004). *Effective Teaching Practices for Students in Inclusive Classrooms*. WM. https://education.wm.edu/centers/ttac/resources/articles/inclusion/effectiveteach/

Lentz, B. K., Dreshler, D. D., & Kissam, B. R. (2004) *Teaching Content to All: evidence-based inclusive practices in middle and secondary schools*. Boston, MA: Pearson Education Merriam-Webster Dictionary. https://www.merriam-webster.com/dictionary/disadvantaged

Mossberger, K., Tolbert, C. J., & Hamilton, A. (2012). Broadband adoption| measuring digital citizenship: Mobile access and broadband. *International Journal of Communication*, 6, 37.

National Health Service. (2012). *What is Equality and Diversity?* NHS. http://www.faculty.londondeanery.ac.uk/e-learning/diversity-equal-opportunities-and-human-rights/what-is-equality-and-diversity

Organisation for Economic Co-operation and Development (OECD). (2015). *Students, Computers and Learning: Making the Connection*. OECD Publishing.

Riordan, D. P. (2022). *Emergency Remote Instruction During the COVID-19 Pandemic: An Analysis of Access and Learning Outcomes* [Doctoral dissertation, University of Houston].

Rose, D. H., & Meyer, A. (2002). *Teaching Every Student in the Digital Age: Universal Design for Learning*. Association for Supervision and Curriculum Development.

Sage, R. (2007). *Inclusion in Schools: Making a Difference*. Network Continuum Education.

Selwyn, N. (2016). *Is technology good for education?* Wiley.

Tomlinson, C. (2009). Differentiating instruction as a response to academically diverse student populations. *On excellence in teaching,* 247-268.

Trussler, S., & Robinson, D. (2015) *Inclusive Practice in the Primary School: A Guide for Teachers*. London: Sage Publications Ltd.

Walther-Thomas, C., Korinek, L., McLoughlin, V. L., & Williams, B. (2000). *Collaboration for Inclusive Education: Developing Successful Programs*. Allyn & Bacon.

Warschauer, M. (2004). *Technology and Social Inclusion: Rethinking the Digital Divide*. MIT Press.

Warschauer, M., & Matuchniak, T. (2010). New technology and digital worlds: Analyzing evidence of equity in access, use, and outcomes. *Review of Research in Education*, 34(1), 179–225. 10.3102/0091732X09349791

Wayman, J. C., Midgley, S., & Stringfield, S. (2007). *Technology Applications in Education: A Learning View*. Lawrence Erlbaum Associates.

Zhao, Y., & Frank, K. A. (2003). Factors affecting technology uses in schools: An ecological perspective. *American Educational Research Journal*, 40(4), 807–840. 10.3102/00028312040004807

Chapter 5

Machine Intelligence in Translation Studies:

Transformative Digital Approaches for Culturally Inclusive Education

Berra Nur Acay
https://orcid.org/0009-0005-4513-3872
Cappadocia University, Turkey

Tuğba Nur Küçük
https://orcid.org/0009-0008-8694-9474
Mediterranean (Akdeniz) University, Turkey

Aylin Yardımcı
https://orcid.org/0000-0003-3238-4646
Kahramanmaras Sutcu Imam University, Turkey

Eda Başak Hancı-Azizoglu
https://orcid.org/0000-0001-6937-5925
Mediterranean (Akdeniz) University, Turkey

ABSTRACT

Translation has had the effect of introducing texts into new contexts, which is praised for opening up literature and other cultural artifacts to new audiences. Now that machine translation's capabilities have rapidly advanced to deliver and explain the context of the receiver part of the communication, it has become useful to humans in this modern era. Although there has been research on machine translation that has so far concentrated on the issues in machine learning, there is a lack of research

DOI: 10.4018/979-8-3693-2591-9.ch005

paying attention to cultural aspects of translation with MT tools. Yet, the changes in the perception of language and culture along with the recent developments in technology have led to the question of whether AI tools are able to grasp the significance of culture in communication to be able to deliver the real meaning behind the context. Thus, the purpose of this applied linguistics study is to explore how transformative digital approaches may contribute to artificially intelligent language teaching styles by overcoming the weakness of the 21st century educational systems.

INTRODUCTION

Machine translation (MT) gained significant popularity in language acquisition and learning practices in recent years. In this technology-dominated era, the integration of transformative digital educational practices has become a necessity for all. The fast-paced and dynamic evolution of technology requires new-age educators to offer profound practices for today's multicultural and multilingual learners.

Without doubt, integrating AI into numerous fields has become popular due to its immense potential to augment human perspective, yet AI tools still need to be developed and applied strategically with human guidance and oversight. Understanding how these technologies work, including their strengths and limitations is an ultimate solution for achieving culturally appropriate translational works along with the benefits of AI (Siu,2023). It is therefore vital to evaluate the changes that impacted the progressive developments in translation studies from a historical perspective.

MT has surpassed four stages in the historical development of machine translation until AI has reached its potential benefits. MT's initial development phase, which spanned 1949 to 1966, saw the formation of the field and the rise of foundational theories modeling the direct translation method. The second phase of MT's evolution took place between 1967 and 1989, and it was marked by the creation of linguistic rule-based systems and the growing use of MT for business. In the third stage, corpus-based techniques have become more popular since the 1990s (Hutchins, 2023). Since the mid-2010s, the fourth stage has seen a revolution with the broad implementation of neural machine translation by employing deep learning strategies (Koehn, 2020).

After these four significant milestones in its developmental history, AI has become quite popular among scholars who were curious to find out how to use the benefits of AI. This current popularity gained by MT tools enabled linguistic and cultural aspects of conveying the correct form of words and thoughts related to linguaculture. This new perspective also helped understanding the importance of the linguistic units of foreign languages selected for a better translation outcome. In order for translators to be able to grasp the perception of intercultural differences, they require understanding and studying the ability to apply lexical, grammatical, and stylistic techniques of both target and source languages in accordance with the norms of translation to improve the quality of translation (Siu,2023). Therefore, the developments in the field of AI has fostered connections between people across different languages and communication channels. Since human translators have progressed in the field, AI has served as a powerful tool for unlocking human potential and transforming translation by supplementing human intelligence (Siu,2023). Thus, the task of the translator has become related to their ability to fully convey the author's goal in the source language in the outcome that requires to grasp the audience of the target language which he translates (Tursunovich,2022).

On the other hand, a new generation of technologically equipped learners are now called digital natives since they were born in the cyber-age with an inherent ability of rapid access to limitless information (Wang et al., 2019). The existing body of research recognizes cognitive similarities and differences between machines and humans (Cataleta, 2021; Korteling et al.; 2021, Kühl et al.; 2022). artificial intelligence (AI) functions as the framework through which people grasp the processes machines practice to imitate human beings' creative cognitive abilities during the translation act. In this dynamic world of opportunities, MT creates and sends information across languages within seconds; however, the human impact is culturally missing from this easy and high-technology learning style.

From another perspective, the supreme need for creating educational programs that offer a harmonious balance between technology and human connection is quite significant. Educators are indeed tasked with more than just transmitting information swiftly, and they surely play a crucial role in infusing cultural sensitivity into the learning journeys of today's diverse learners. Simply mastering digital literacies without an awareness for equity and inclusivity, fails to equip students with one of the most critical learning skills for the 21st century: Empathy (Hancı-Azizoglu, 2021).

In addition to this lacking skill in education, fostering a culture of appreciation for diverse cultures offers what machines cannot offer, which is nurturing deep understanding and respect for differences. Therefore, the lack of culture in machine learning is evident. From a linguistic perspective, the existing body of research recognizes cognitive similarities and differences between machines and humans. For instance, AI functions as the framework through which people grasp the processes machines practice to imitate human beings' creative and cognitive abilities during the translation act. Despite the growing interest in AI, the context and the definition of the term "culture" is yet often misunderstood and used to refer to different aspects of language use. Culture often encompasses both ancient and contemporary norms that pass from one generation to the next without officially documented rules (Brinkmann et al.,2023). Therefore, any educational system is incomplete without understanding the essence of cultural respect and tolerance for inclusive teaching regardless of the learners' cultural origin.

Furthermore, culture is often perceived cumulatively within the same community, influenced by specific surroundings and circumstances, without time limitations. To illustrate, certain actions or discourses may be timeless and universally accepted within a culture, and even a minor cultural change may necessitate significant socio-political alterations. From another perspective, people are adapted to the information age that brings along technological advancements faster than the speed of light when compared to the change experienced in cultural change. Without further knowledge of linguistic and cultural transfer despite technological innovations, understanding machine intelligence and the lack of cultural components in educational programs is not possible (Lahcen, 2023). Beyond question, language learning then cannot be evaluated free from the interaction between cultural and technological change regarding the information age people are very fast at adapting nowadays. Thus, the conceptual aim of this linguistic study is to internalize the relationship between culture and MT considering recent developments by exploring the following critical aspects:

- The Lack of Culture in Machine Translation
- The Lack of Empathy in Translation through Machine Intelligence
- Inclusive Machine Teaching for Promoting Equality

THE LACK OF CULTURE IN MACHINE TRANSLATION

It is well known that language is the bridge between communication and culture. The inevitable and in-depth connection between language and culture has been an increasingly intriguing area of research for numerous research fields lately. The reason why the relationship between language and culture became an area of interest is that, in verbal communication, certain factors prevent the receiver part of the communication from grasping the real meaning behind the sender's message. The cultural difference between the sender and the receiver is the biggest obstacle in better grasping the meaning behind the sender's message. Translation is then seen as a mental activity in which the meaning of a given linguistic discourse is rendered from one language to another (Xiu & Xeauyin, 2018). This cultural issue has become a particularly significant research topic for the translation field since the traditional sense of understanding translation has shifted along with the recognition and abundant development of both AI and cultural studies in the past decades. It has shifted from being perceived as a cross-linguistic activity to being perceived as cross-cultural or intercultural communication/exchange. Furthermore, human translation (HT) has been considered as the oldest form of translation, relying on pure human intelligence to convey the real meaning behind a message. With the recent advancements, and the addition of machine translation (MT) tools into the translation studies field, a new perception is acquired.

This new perception of language has transformed into a system of representing a particular culture as well as being a part of it since the perception of translation shifted due to technological advancements. Therefore, it has become inevitable to object to the fact that a culture is being introduced while translating a source language text (Sun, 2011). From this perspective, it has become clear that proper understanding and rendering of the conveyed message of a text is more likely to be a problem of cultural diversity than that of linguistic differences. The difficulties arising out of differences between cultures also seem to constitute the most serious problems for translators, and these semantic challenges have produced the most far-reaching misunderstandings among readers (Nida, 1993; Yao et al., 2023). Nonetheless, the differences between the two cultures' semantic equivalence are limited to a certain degree. It is difficult to locate their referents in the target culture for the culture-specific terms and expressions. A word can have opposite meanings in two different cultures, such as the word "dragon" having a positive connotation in Asian cultures - good luck and fortune- while in the Western world, it is a threatening animal or a symbol of overwhelming evil. Therefore, non-equivalence in intralingual meaning - such as sound, rhythm, unique patterns of phrase order, and techniques for linking clauses into sentences- reveals the impact of cultural differences in the translation process (Sun, 2011). The dilemma of how to reflect culture through expressing language by translation of written content also lead to the conclusion that translation is inevitably both influenced by the source language culture and the target language culture. That's why how to comply with cultural norms became one of the major problems in the field of translation. It has become evident that effective and compassionate cross-cultural communication is dependent on the correctness of the translation of cultural entities. Thus, it is also necessary for social cohesion and peace (Xiu & Xeauyin, 2018).

Consequently, there is a clear tendency among translators to be less sensitive to cultural quirks and less critical of MT quality due to globalization, internationalization, and the leveling of cultural differences. It makes perfect sense to focus on how to translate texts related to the humanities because should machines prove to be able to translate texts in specialized fields—especially those that rely solely on general information—this will become the market for future translators. For instance, the output from neural machine translation (NMT) tools has just been found to be as good as that of human translators with experience regarding the latest news released (Łoboda & Mastela, 2023). Thus, it can be considered that non-machine tools (NMT) translate more effectively in some specialized contexts including general information and educational texts from European Union institutions. Regardless of these fast-paced developments due to the use of MT, the performance of MT tools concerning literary texts is still a contentious issue. So far, only a human translator seems to be able to correctly reflect literary works because machines only do direct word-for-word translations (Xiu & Xeauyin, 2018). The use of the new generation NMT engines is associated with a general reduction in the lexical richness of MT output compared to translation by a professional translator. NMT systems 'do not perform disastrously' and 'they offer a passable attempt at what the human translator is capable of' (Łoboda & Mastela, 2023, p. 504). Therefore, these observations might lead to the conclusion that producing comprehensible culture-bound text translations, which contain some archaized language, can still only be achieved with post-editing carried out by humans. Thus, it is equally important to highlight the intricate processes involved in evaluating the quality of translations through the evaluation of both human and MT workflows due to investigating the following factors between the two:

- the differences in methodologies and practices between human and MT
- the differences in linguistic and extra-linguistic factors between human and MT

In light of this, the the question of whether AI can adapt sufficiently to understand culturally defined contexts is worthwhile to address. In order for this goal to be achieved, it is important to take a look at how machines essentially learn. Even in the advanced state of artificial intelligence (AI), language processing issues still arise, not to mention the difficulties and complexities that come with translating regarding the social and syntactic features of the language (Massey, 2017). Although machine learning (ML) had begun to draw interest in the 1990s, it was not until the 21st century that it truly took off, largely due to the efforts of groups such as the Linguistic Data Consortium (LDC), which made a vast amount of written and spoken data available for study. Due to this, significant datasets with a large amount of text and various types of annotations were created, such as the Penn Treebank and Prague Dependency Treebank (Marcus et al.,1993).

What's more, these resources were utilized by researchers to create new methods of language comprehension, such as summarizing text and determining the meaning of words in various contexts. By utilizing statistical techniques of maximum entropy and support vector machines, they also enhanced machine translation. Researchers then were able to create methods for machines to learn from data without labeling it. This improved the performance of machine translation systems even in the absence of large amounts of pre-annotated data (Lecun et al.,2015). Neural Machine Translation (NMT), which leverages neural networks to translate languages more rapidly and accurately, is one remarkable advancements that humans lack. Since NMT functions by feeding vast volumes of language data into several layers of a neural network, which enables it to comprehend and translate languages with remarkable accuracy (Cho et al.,2014), multiple languages are adapted to diminish the most compared parties in translation (Das,2020): Human versus Machine Translation.

The Differences Between Human and Machine Translation

The developments in technology and MT tools along with its associated software led these advanced tools to become the largest, and increasingly growing, proportion of translated text producers today. It has transformed communication and understanding across languages and cultures worldwide significantly. From one perspective, the MT tools are known for their powerful abilities including the practicality of use, fast results, and the low cost required to produce translation results in multiple languages within seconds. Nonetheless, the results of MT still have plenty of shortcomings even though technology tends to develop faster, and these tools become better day by day. On the other hand, the boundaries between human and MT are becoming increasingly blurred, with the rise of post-editing, interactive MT, and related techniques. These advancements lead to a progressively indistinct separation between professional human translation and MT. The traditional demarcation between professional human translation and MT is undergoing a transformative shift. The emergence of post-editing, interactive MT and related tools is rendering this distinction increasingly indistinct (Castilho et al., 2018). These technologies, marked by growing efficiency, signal a departure from a rigid separation between human and MT, paving the way for collaborative and integrated approaches.

In order to further understand the capacity of MT tools, a thorough understanding of how the human factor works in the translation field is required. It is a common assumption that human moderators with an understanding of not just the language but also the sensitive cultural and social dynamics at play would be vital for the true meaning of a text by the receiver. Since MT is becoming more and more integrated into social media platforms, the broader context of the written materials becomes even more important, yet it is also changing very rapidly. Online texts are increasingly capable of translating between languages in ways that were not intended by the writers who produced them, by instances assuming entirely new and unexpected meanings for their intended audience (Wells, 2022). Therefore, one significant variable that creates difference between machines and humans is that machines overcome humans on timing while humans are far better in finding the meaning-making intended. This can be supported with the conclusion that while the fundamental principles of translation quality assessment persist, the approaches diverge significantly between human and MT workflows.

Considering these differences between MT and HT, language instructors utilized machine translation (MT) tools by discussing their advantages associated with ethical considerations and drawbacks into language teaching and learning. They then demonstrated how to use these tools effectively and guided students through hands-on applications. To ensure mastery, students were tasked with individual or collaborative assignment utilizing MT tools. These tools were also woven into dynamic classroom activities to encourage peer interaction for better learning practices (Deng, X., & Yu, Z., 2022)

The distinctive challenges and opportunities posed by each learning style necessitate tailored evaluation methods. As technological advancements continue to reshape the translation landscape, understanding and adapting to these differences become crucial for stakeholders in the language industry. Therefore, it can be concluded that MT tools have yet to catch up with traditional approaches to translation because of their inability to reflect cultural elements. As the borderline between machine-aided human translation and human-aided MT becomes increasingly blurred, translators must adapt to the new reality by acquiring the ability to recognize the context in which machines are likely to fail.

Therefore, AI language models cannot be compared to the special traits and talents that humans possess to explore the main differences between AI tools and human beings in terms of cultural nuances for a couple of reasons: The first one is Emotional Intelligence. People are very emotional beings. They are able to feel and communicate through a vast array of emotions by establishing strong bonds with people. The second one is Creative and Innovative Thinking. Humans are creative thinkers by nature; they may come up with original ideas and use their imaginations to think beyond the box. The third one is Physical Interaction and Sensory Perception. Because of their bodily existence, humans may physically engage with their environment. The other trait of human beings is Contextual Understanding. Humans have contextual awareness that is molded by their own experiences, cultural upbringings, and viewpoints. Another unique characteristics of human beings is Moral and Ethical Reasoning. Thanks to their sense of morality and ethics, humans are able to form opinions and decisions based on their ethical values. The last one is Physical and Biological Abilities. Due to their physical and biological characteristics, humans are able to perform a vast array of tasks. Thus, AI language models are capable of processing data, exchanging ideas, and providing information, but they fall short of the richness and nuance of human experiences, feelings, and physical presence. Humans are unique, and this contributes to their creativity, personality, and the diversity of human connection. While the AI model can offer guidance and assistance, it is ultimately the learner's obligation to engage in deeper learning. Seeking deeper learning necessitates critical thinking, active involvement, and knowledge application that are solely specific to humans (Analytic Alpha, n.d.).

Extra-Linguistic Factors Between Human and Machine Translation

In seminal translation-related works, the researchers already accepted that intelligent devices have many potential applications, but the discipline's primary theoretical objective is to comprehend intelligent processes apart from their specific physical implementation (Goldstein & Papert, 1977). Dresher & Hornstein (1976) argued that despite intense hope, the initial attempts to use computers to help with natural language comprehension were not very successful. Bar Hillel (1964, as cited in Dresher & Hornstein, 1976) documented the failure of several MT initiatives, which ultimately demonstrated that the programs' fundamental methodology was flawed. According to this method, translating between natural languages is a reasonably simple procedure. All the computer needs to make translations of a respectable quality is the dictionaries of the two languages and some basic grammatical knowledge and because of the nature of this failure, it was thought that if computers were to deal with natural language at all, a more complex understanding of language would be necessary. This involved having access to a dictionary with the knowledge of grammatical rules, but semantic perspectives and experience through world knowledge failed the attempts of effective MT attempts. It had previously looked quite tractable, if not easy, to apply computers to natural language, but it suddenly seemed nearly impossible. When it comes to comparing human and AI in the process of activating languages in making translations, culture is undoubtedly one of the most important achievements that people learn through experience and acquisition as a result of their contact with the outside world. Cultural knowledge is then one of the most critical facts that must be activated during translation in order for the texts to be understood and interpreted correctly by any individual coming from a different culture when translating between two languages.

In another seminal significant work, the concept of making a mistake is investigated to see how AI differs from human intelligence (Hertzberg, 1990). An individual's mistake can be understood if it is considered within the framework of life experience, culture, and way of seeing the world. A computer's mistake rather cannot be understood since it lacks a life of its own, within which its conclusions might either fit or fall out of. This idea is later supported by a current study which states that one of the main objectives of AI is the development of autonomous entities capable of expanding their lifelong repertoires of abilities. A potential developmental method suggests designing intrinsically driven agents that generate and pursue their own objectives in order to learn new abilities, but the diversity of goals, exploration, generalization, and skill mix of current algorithms remain severely constrained in computers despite recent improvements (Colas et al., 2022).

With the recent developments in technology, time efficiency has become an essential aspect. Nowadays the use of automatic "assistant" machines is now widely relied on to make human work easier, even in the translation field. Humans created tools that will help them to translate faster and better because people now demand everything to be faster and easier. These tools - which are referred to as MT tools- have started as the product of a subfield of computational linguistics that studies the use of software to translate text or voice from one natural language to another at a higher speed. MT can then be described as the use of translating applications or software that are powered by AI to translate text from one language to another (Fitria, 2021). It is therefore important to be clear regarding the fact that one extra-linguistic factor that impact the act of translation is the ultimate speed machines offer versus the limited speed humans offer.

The pace distinctions between these two types of translations have prompted researchers to compare their efficiency in reflecting cultural elements in translated materials by igniting their interest in which type of translation is preferable. The lack of standardized quality assessment is also a significant obstacle that has yet to be addressed. Although MT evaluation has become an important aspect of research, no formula or user-friendly model for MT or HT quality assessment has been developed. While these evaluations are critical, they should be supplemented with detailed error analyses and component evaluations in order to generate causal analyses that pinpoint errors and thus lead to system improvements (Xiu & Xeauyin, 2018). Expanding on the aforementioned insights, one of the processes involved in evaluating the quality of translations is error-based evaluation models. It is perceived as a prominent approach employed within the landscape of human translation workflows in the industry. This method represents a meticulous and systematic process wherein errors within the translated text are not only identified but also subjected to a rigorous evaluation involving counting, classification, and weighting. The responsibility for this evaluative process typically rests with a seasoned senior translator or a qualified reviewer, who undertakes the critical task of gauging the severity of each identified error. By employing this approach, the industry aims to establish a comprehensive understanding of the quality of human-generated translations, acknowledging that the nature and impact of errors can vary widely (Castilho et al., 2018).

Another noteworthy perspective to be explained is the Functional Equivalence Assessment approach. This approach signifies a departure from traditional, often subjective, measures of translation quality, opting instead for a more functional standpoint. By emphasizing the assessment of functional equivalence, the system encourages a shift toward evaluating how well a translated text fulfills its communicative purpose and intent. This approach acknowledges that translation quality goes beyond mere linguistic accuracy, recognizing the importance of ensuring that the translated content serves its intended function effectively. Thus, the Functional

Equivalence Assessment enriches the discourse on translation quality by offering a lens that aligns with the functional aspects of communication, providing a nuanced understanding that extends beyond linguistic precision alone. (House, 2001). The trajectory of this evolution suggests that the boundary-blurring trend is set to expand across various domains. As parallel corpora and natural language processing tools become more accessible, the development of customized and domain-adapted statistical and neural MT systems gain momentum. This expansion extends to new language pairs, diverse text types, and an array of subject matters, showcasing the adaptability of MT technologies.

In short, MT is regarded as the paradigm task of Natural Language Processing (NLP) because MT approaches rely on discrete representations of words and sentences. Thus, in recent years, the natural language processing community has paid close attention to continuous representations of words and sentences since MT tools combine almost all NLP research areas: syntactic parsing, semantic disambiguation, knowledge representation, language generation, lexical acquisition, and morphological analysis and synthesis. Consequently, machines are not advanced enough to accurately render these nuances; instead, they can only do word-for-word translations, and the quality of fully automated systems falls short in other areas. As a result, their outcomes must be monitored and corrected by a human agent during the post-editing (PE) stage. Since the translator begins with an initial hypothesis that needs to be corrected, this working method is more productive than translating everything by hand. If people and the system work together to develop a common plan, efficiency rates can be raised (Xiu & Xeauyin, 2018).

THE LACK OF EMPATHY IN TRANSLATION THROUGH MACHINE INTELLIGENCE

Today's digital native learners are born into an advanced virtual world through engaging easily with the online world by using digital tools. Regardless of the fact that they are naturally adept at using digital tools, they may not always be good at grasping certain human traits that are not readily available to acquire as a set of behaviors in the school environment. Empathy is one of the most critical human traits that is not possible to self-learn through digital devices (Hancı-Azizoglu, 2021). Linguistically speaking, understanding the real meaning behind a sentence requires substantial knowledge and experience to develop a feeling of empathy in desired learning environments for a better and more peaceful world. In contrast, MT tools currently don't have the ability to respond to circumstances like the way human beings do. For instance, a skillful human teacher with goodwill could easily create new ideas and solutions for unexpected and non-standard challenges occurring due to different learning styles and social environments. Culturally sensitive educational policies that model unity rather than disputes is possible only if the concept of empathy for all is valued in educational institutions. Yet, current machine-created solutions for educational challenges would neither be a preferred expert nor an ideal match for humanly problems in the long run without empathy.

Without empathy embedded into digital literacy, developing awareness and tolerance for the "other" and understanding cultural nuances of different perceptions cannot be promoted. Similarly, fostering an environment of respect and inclusion cannot be achieved in the classroom environment without understanding the unwritten cultural rules across world's varying cultures. Understanding another culture without judgments and tolerance means being able to imagine the experience without needing to live the experience itself. Thus, merely acquiring proficiency in digital literacies, without considering equity and inclusivity, overlooks the essential aspect of preparing students with one of the key learning skills crucial for the 21st century: Empathy (Hancı-Azizoglu, 2021). First of all, automated direct translations through a machine are not humanized for the fact that written texts translated through AI lack the ability to contain and reflect the human traits. Additionally, there can be semantic shifts between languages when the written text is translated directly by a machine without any emotions.

Consequently, instilling the concept of empathy into educational programs involves considering the diverse human traits that people share. In this way, students may consider the challenges of individuals with different needs by respecting their uniqueness. But, integrating one culture into another is not a simple educational target to be achieved in today's technologically global but rather politically reserved world when comparing humans to machines in the process of meaning-making. Thus, MT tools can't be equipped with cultural equivalents in the target language. Humans can indeed acquire this sort of diversifying awareness for translation by acquiring culturally-determined experience and knowledge in the target language. Hence, machines teach students to mostly write with robotic expressions, which lacks the emotional traits that a human has when the students use MT to translate their mother tongue into the target language (Niño, 2009).

Therefore, MT tools seem to decrease the learners' creativity and turn them into less social human beings who are devoid of empathy by disabling them from producing their own and new ideas. Students yet claim only a few significant reasons for using machine tools to improve their language proficiency considering the negative sides of MT. First of all, students can easily check their grammatical accuracy while translating texts from their native language into the target language. According to students, another advantage of the MT tools is the accessibility feature that makes the tools ready wherever and whenever they are available. From the teachers' perspectives, the MT tool use in the translation field has brought up challenges and concerns for teachers about plagiarism and honesty in academic and language skills use (Ducar & Schocket, 2018). The most challenging issue is that the students often use machine tools without knowing the limitations of MT, so they don't receive and understand the utilities of the tool. Therefore, it is necessary for the teacher to explain the limitations to lead the students to acquire an awareness in the fact that the tool is just a helper that is needed for scrutiny of a produced written text.

To clarify this scholarly discussion further, the likelihood that readers will interpret translations as accurate representations of the original author's opinions and goals grows as machine technologies advance and become less obvious. The entire viewpoint of the translated material is that it is altered by the loss of human agency in the decision to translate an idea formed in words into the best matching idea through the concept of empathy. So, the ultimate goal is to catch the closest meaning of the original text regardless of the variety of translation whether it is human oriented, machine-oriented or hybrid of the both. From another diverse perspective, a human translating a text that is politically or culturally sensitive would probably exercise some caution, or it might be decided that not translating at all would be better given the potential for harm (Wells, 2022). Therefore, the possibility of an increase in the datasets of multiple languages by involving the concepts of culture and empathy in machine training for translation purposes would reduce the risk of misunderstandings, disputes, and the quick dissemination of false information.

In addition, the challenge of integrating culture into the texts to be translated even led to the separation of the culture of the target and main language parts in an anticipated translation as weak and strong cultures. It is originated through the comparison of languages and cultures. The separation of cultures mainly had a hidden political, economic, or ideological agenda governing the acceptance of the foreign language culture by eventually affecting translators' decisions. Some countries have known political or economic superiority (strong cultures) over some other disadvantaged language cultures (weak cultures). While translating, the translators of the strong culture often aim to dominate the weaker culture language by aiming to force other cultures' literary work to adapt to their style. To illustrate, English has become a hegemonic language - being the strongest and therefore able to control other languages – over time due to its market share and the gravitational force it exerts on other languages (Lane-Mercier, 2014).

Thus, the translators, whose source language is English, have become the translators of the strong culture, proving that culture is effective in the field of translation as well since the translation products reflect power relations among the source and target languages. From another perspective to the dominancy of English language, there is little to no language technology support exists for more than 90% of the world's languages, which are spoken by over a billion people collectively. The term "low-resource languages" in computer science refers to the fact that the models used to build MT and related technologies require large amounts of pre-existing "training text," or corpora, which are less easily accessible for many languages around the world (Wells, 2022). The inability of the MT tools to function effectively with the majority of languages reflects the need for "training" and "programming" of the tools to achieve global efficiency in the translation act whether it is conducted by a machine or a human. Thus, it would indeed a smarter solution to include the missing remaining 90% of the data into the current machine leading datasets to scientifically understand the dynamics of all logic-based relations in the world with more empathy.

INCLUSIVE MACHINE-TEACHING FOR PROMOTING EQUALITY

A common perception of AI is that it is a specialized discipline with the aim of programming machines to appear intelligent. While the aim of utilizing computers is to comprehend human intellect, AI is not limited to a series of technologically-savy techniques that may be seen in humans through biological means. It is also proposed that computer programs are very fast along with an extensive set of memory, yet their capabilities are limited by the intellectual mechanisms that programmers are sufficiently knowledgeable about to incorporate into their designs in mind. The fact that the cognitive sciences are yet unable to pinpoint the precise nature of human talents only serves to recognize the fact that AI's intellectual processes are organized differently from human intellectual mechanisms (McCarthy, 2007). While the main concern about AI seem to be on computer programs, language learning and cognitive processes about language activation in brain should be investigated under the umbrella of AI studies to be able to offer inclusive machine-teaching for promoting equality in innovative learning environments. One of the most common field that AI is actively used for languages is the translation programs that are actively used by people instead of translators all around the world. Yet, a detailed proofreading becomes necessary for all those translated texts as it includes mistakes and mostly lacks interpretation.

The main cause of this conflict is human translators can code-switch between source and target languages while machines are using the language of technology, English, as the only dominant source. This type of dominancy is highly likely to block the sense of equality when the current datasets and how they are used by the machines favor one culture over the others. The extensive research on teachers' perceptions of the MT tools emphasize that teachers also switch their native language to English when they explain technical, terminology related terms with MT tools and technology. In contrast, they feel much more comfortable by using their native language while they reflect on social human traits that are necessary to convey the real meaning of a text to the receiver in a more successful way. Therefore, it is clear that there is a conflict between MT tools' techniques and results when compared to the instructors' techniques and results in the outcome of a translation process (Clifford et al., 2013). Moreover, teachers explain the reasons why they use different approaches for translation and the process of their decision-making while giving feedback; however, MT tools surely cannot comment on the process stages of translated sentences.

To reflect the accurate meaning behind a translated work, it is necessary for MT tools to have the capability to understand the culture and context of the language. If the students can't use machine intelligence with an awareness of empathy, then they cannot reflect the correct meaning of the sentence. Otherwise, the words that are produced by MT tools can be recondite and ambiguous. Therefore, mastering the target language is also critical while mastering digital literacy skills to lead the students to determine the correct sentence translation (Lee, 2019). Yet, one language has always been dominant over other languages throughout the history of the translation studies when target versus source languages are compared within the act of translation. Until now, English has gained reputation about literacy, and almost all books can be translated into English easier than other languages due to the easy accessibility of translation materials and the widespread use of the English language on a global scale. In translated works, considering the differences between source and target language is yet another vital point in order to receive accurate outcomes. Translating English to French is not the same as translating French to English. English written texts are more common than other language products. UNESCO has listed one million translated books since its establishment, and only one-tenth have been translated into English while an astonishing two-thirds have been translated from English. Thus, the translated text is often in the English language (Bellos, 2012), and this brings along cultural gaps across cultures within the act of meaning-making during translation.

As the volume of text generated by AI increases, it contributes to the data required to train AI engines by increasing the likelihood of mistakes and decreasing the quality of the output. Cultural insensitivity is further exacerbated by particular cultural groups as being either underrepresented or absent from training datasets. The linguistic and cultural variances among disadvantaged populations or particular cultures may be missed by AI models if those groups are not well represented. Furthermore, additional risks associated with AI translations' cultural insensitivity is present. One problem with translating idiomatic phrases or metaphors that are culturally specific is that AI models may find it difficult to accurately capture the intended meaning of these idioms because they lack the cultural context. This could result in translations that are inaccurate or they can even entirely send the wrong message. In particular, insensitive translations can also arise when translating names that incorporate honorifics and cultural customs.

To illustrate, translation algorithms could translate names incorrectly or rudely if they don't take cultural connotations of those names into account. Misunderstandings, inadvertent insult, or even the erasing of cultural differences may arise from this overgeneralization process due to the nature of MT datasets. Moreover, the process of MT may encounter difficulties when it comes to cultural quirks of formality and politeness. Different cultures have different standards and expectations due to acceptable degrees of formality and civility in communication, and machines that lack training on a variety of datasets may not comprehend cultural etiquette. They may produce translations that are too formal, which may come off as cold or aloof, or excessively casual, which may then be interpreted as improper or insulting. Finally, misinterpretations of cultural quirks and emotional signals might lead to misunderstandings in AI translations. Some languages have unique ways of addressing delicate subjects or expressing emotions that are difficult to translate exactly. The translated information may not accurately express the intended attitude if AI modeled machines just use literal translations and neglect emotional or cultural context, which might cause to misunderstandings or even offensive language. Machine intelligence indeed fail on word sense disambiguation, which is the inability to separate the words that have multiple or irrelevant meanings because it attempts to deduce the meaning of the word from its context.

Furthermore, the level of vocabulary used by the students is indeed more basic while the texts written by the MT tools seem to contain a high-level proficiency vocabulary (Tsai, 2019). This can lead students to deceive themselves into thinking that they are at a higher level than their actual proficiency while submitting assignments. This poses a conflict for teachers since the students with even high-level proficiency might not be aware of the mistakes that were produced by MT tools. MT tools then possess insufficient vocabulary when machines face with synonyms and antonyms, which are the main representatives of human intellect in standard tests (Widhiarso, 2016). It is teachers who can highlight mistranslations to overcome the ambiguity created by machines to raise students' awareness of the limitations of MT (Steding, 2009). In order to justify the opinion that is concluded, it can be stated that there are plenty of previous research about the significant role of the teachers, one of which investigated the CALF measures (syntactic complexity, accuracy, lexical complexity, and fluency) in MT in foreign language classes. Mostly the researchers aimed to calculate whether the accuracy of the text is improved through MT. The researchers concluded that the outcomes that the students received by using the MT tool were accurate although there weren't lexical and syntactic advancements.

In other words, students were able to produce longer sentences thanks to MT tools; however, there has been a diminution in the way they express their ideas and emotions. While beginner-level students are able to receive the facilitated basic grammatical structures, advanced-level students couldn't get enough help with syntactic and lexical complexity. Thus, the findings showed that the perception of the students who have different levels of fluency in English varies in terms of the outcomes of MT tools when their performances are evaluated. The students with higher proficiency levels didn't like the outcomes that were produced by MT tools because they lacked the human traits which help to further reflect the complex structures the students aimed to use (Chung & Ahn, 2021). That's why, using MT tools still cannot contribute to the full needs of the students without the presence of actual language teachers.

All in all, the utilization of AI shows promising results in the realm of linguistics. Research suggests that AI positively impacts writing, grammar, and vocabulary acquisition, which is deeply rooted with translational fields. AI users appreciate its ability to provide contextualized learning while making the retention of new words easier. Yet, its effectiveness in improving speaking and listening skills seems limited. Nevertheless, learners find AI beneficial due to its instant feedback, which enhances motivation and engagement. Moreover, its versatility in various learning experiences, such as interactive learning and creative writing, adds to its appeal. Despite encountering technical issues and some limitations in aiding language learning, AI holds potential for enhancing language competency and learner engagement. Continued refinement of the system is crucial to address existing constraints and optimize the language acquisition process (Karataş et al., 2024)

In the light of the arguments presented above, it is crystal clear that there are several challenges of MT as it lacks enough cultural knowledge that help human beings to make meaning intuitively. What's more, the translation made through machines involve cultural insensitivity (Akorbi, n.d.). Biases in the training datasets used to create AI models are one of the key reasons why AI translations are culturally insensitive. Since the first major language models were all trained on preexisting written content that was fully authored by humans, AI algorithms may be based on a biased or unrepresentative corpus. Prejudices in society, historical inequalities, and the scarcity of inclusive and varied datasets are a few of the causes of bias in training data. Thus, the accuracy with which the AI is able to comprehend and interpret cultural quirks may be significantly impacted if the data utilized to train these algorithms is biased or unrepresentative. Therefore, teachers' knowledge of their own students' levels is currently the best smart solution to help students to realize this misunderstanding. That's why, MT tools can be as harmful as it can be helpful for students' language learning. This is where the importance of the teacher's role come on stage in the learning process. A teacher explaining to students how machine tools will facilitate their writing level can help them see the real benefits of an effective and technology-integrated classroom.

CONCLUSION

In the light of these information, it is safe to say that MT tools seem to have caught up with human translators in speed and accuracy with the recent advancements in technology. Human translator services are also not necessarily available all the time, and it takes time to produce the translations in addition to its added high costs. Considering these obstacles, it is not surprising that currently MT is used by many people and has become a necessity. It looks like MT is slowly shifting the human translator profession. This comprehensive resource serves as a valuable guide for understanding the multifaceted nature of translation quality assessment and its significance in both academic and industrial contexts. The entire viewpoint of the translated material is altered by the loss of human agency in the decision to translate a meaningful unit of expression into the best possible alternative without losing the essence of the message during the translation act. As a matter of fact, MT tools might be perceived as more useful and practical, yet these tools still don't have enough capacity to reflect the complex and culture-related context to the reader as well as a traditional human translator.

Since the first invention of AI tools, a few remarkable MT tools have also been produced into the market under the name of Google Translate, DeepL, Bab.la. With the continuous production of new MT tools and the development of both the quantity and quality of the works produced by these tools, there is a valid concern that technology may lead to a limited understanding of language among students, teachers, and the community. The understanding of language has indeed been reduced to a straightforward message that complicated the exchange between sender and receiver further. Furthermore, it is important to highlight the diversity of methodologies and approaches in both human and MT quality assessment (TQA). In essence, the collective insights from these various approaches contribute to the multifaceted nature of translation quality assessment. They underscore the importance of considering both linguistic and extra-linguistic factors, highlighting the necessity for a diverse array of methodologies to effectively address the intricate complexities inherent in the measurement of translation quality in both human and MT workflows (Castilho et al., 2018). Therefore, translation quality assessment plays a pivotal role in ensuring effective communication across languages; however, the methodologies employed differ significantly between human and MT workflows.

This fact disregarded the sociocultural embeddedness of both the speaker and the message when competence is seen as nothing more than a tool. Amplifying the use of these tools instead of relying on the tutors, who are specialized in the fields of applied linguistics and interpretation, means refusing the richness of the culture, human background, and interaction in addition to society (Urlaub & Dessein, 2022). Yet, this doesn't simply mean denying the developing means of technology or never taking advantage of it, it just means the role of professionals in the translation field still cannot be replaced by advanced machines. The ultimate reason why MT is preferred over human translation is the ease and accessibility; however, all students might not have the accessibility. Equality cannot exist if it is not attainable for every student. Its help doesn't include all students as well. Furthermore, all students may not be mastering digital literacy and need to get help for learning how to use MT. If they cannot be taught, they can just use it ineffectively. MT may make also errors in syntactic structures and lexical items. MT can expand learners' vocabulary but may lead to decreased utilization of complex and refined words (Chung & Ahn, 2021). Therefore, the technology carries opportunities for the learning process at a glance even though it brings invisible disadvantages after a while. According to students' proficiency level, it can be beneficial to suggest a new vocabulary or rewrite the sentence with the correct grammar. Nevertheless, the invisible disadvantages deprive the students of their human being skills. They might become unaware of the human traits that enable them to reflect what they aim to in their translation works. That's why, language teachers seem to be the only source who can guide them to incorporate digital literacy into their class, and they can guide students on how to utilize MT in their written work without plagiarism and without losing their ideas.

In light of these ideas, educators can instruct the students to internalize that today's nuanced, impressible, culture-embedded language can be specific for humans. The problem is not about using the MT tool while translating, it is more about assisting the students using MT and language skills regarding ethical reasons and connecting the 21st-century facilities (Ducar & Schocket, 2018). Integrating the technology into the class and showing the limitations and capabilities help students understand the reasons why and how they can use the MT tools. This can bring a sense of equality and inclusiveness along with the sense of empathy because students will realize that they receive equal opportunities with the ability to use MT tools anytime, anywhere. Teaching them how to check the MT tools' outcomes gives learners the control of benefitting from it, but not completely trusting it to do their assignments for them. One of MT tools' strong abilities is that it is good at lexical translation and technical informative sentences. Yet, its weakness in being good at only lexical translation and technical informative sentences enables it to only translate word-to-word, making the structure of the sentence its priority, and losing the essence of the meaning by using unusual or wrong vocabulary that cannot reflect the whole meaning of a sentence. Thus, the findings of this study can be summarized as follows:

- Low-level students can use the MT tools for improving their vocabulary skills or controlling their grammar while high-level students benefit from MT tools for more academic projects.

- MT favors word-to-word translation by focusing on the syntax of the target language while meaning-making is still a creative trait that is specific to real life teachers, not AI directed the virtual ones.
- Effective teachers need to understand how students may facilitate MT according to different levels and purposes for self-learning strategies.

REFERENCES

Akorbi. (2024, July 11). *The Risk of Cultural Insensitivity in AI Translations*. Akorbi. https://akorbi.com/blog/the-risk-of-cultural-insensitivity-in-ai-translations/

Analytic Alpha. (n.d.). *Artificial Intelligence in Language, Culture & Literature Teaching*. Analytic Alpha. https://www.analyticalpha.nl/artificial-intelligence-in-language-culture-literature-teaching/

Bellos, D. (2012). Is that a fish in your ear?: Translation and the meaning of everything. *Choice (Chicago, Ill.)*, 49(11), 49-6101. Advance online publication. 10.5860/CHOICE.49-6101

Brinkmann, L., Baumann, F., Bonnefon, J. F., Derex, M., Müller, T. F., Nussberger, A. M., Czaplicka, A., Acerbi, A., Griffiths, T. L., Henrich, J., Leibo, J. Z., McElreath, R., Oudeyer, P.-Y., Stray, J., & Rahwan, I. (2023). Machine culture. *Nature Human Behaviour*, 7(11), 1855–1868. 10.1038/s41562-023-01742-237985914

Castilho, S., Doherty, S., Gaspari, F., & Moorkens, J. (2018). Approaches to human and machine translation quality assessment. *Translation quality assessment: From principles to practice*, 9-38.

Cataleta, M. S. (2021). Artificial intelligence vs human intelligence. *Artificial intelligence vs human intelligence*, 107-116. NIH.

Cho, K., Van Merriënboer, B., Gulcehre, C., Bahdanau, D., Bougares, F., Schwenk, H., & Bengio, Y. (2014). *Learning phrase representations using RNN encoder-decoder for statistical machine translation.* arXiv preprint arXiv:1406.1078. 10.3115/v1/D14-1179

Chung, E. S., & Ahn, S. (2021). The effect of using machine translation on linguistic features in L2 writing across proficiency levels and text genres. *Computer Assisted Language Learning*, 35(9), 2239–2264. 10.1080/09588221.2020.1871029

Clifford, J., Merschel, L., & Munné, J. (2013). Surveying the Landscape: What is the Role of Machine Translation in Language Learning? *@tic. revista d'innovació educativa*, (10), 108-121.

Colas, C., Karch, T., Moulin-Frier, C., & Oudeyer, P. Y. (2022). Language and culture internalization for human-like autotelic AI. *Nature Machine Intelligence*, 4(12), 1068–1076. 10.1038/s42256-022-00591-4

Das, A. (2020). Neural Machine Translation (NMT): Inherent Inadequacy, Misrepresentation, and Cultural Bias. *International Journal of Translation*, 32(1-2).

Deng, X., & Yu, Z. (2022). A systematic review of machine-translation-assisted language learning for sustainable education. *Sustainability (Basel)*, 14(13), 7598. 10.3390/su14137598

Dresher, B. E., & Hornstein, N. (1976). On some supposed contributions of artificial intelligence to the scientific study of language. *Cognition*, 4(4), 321–398. 10.1016/0010-0277(76)90015-9

Ducar, C., & Schocket, D. H. (2018). Machine translation and the L2 classroom: PedagogicalSolutions for making peace with Google Translate. *Foreign Language Annals*, 51(4), 779–795. 10.1111/flan.12366

Fitria, T. N. (2021). A review of machine translation tools: The translation's ability. *Language Circle: Journal of Language and Literature*, 16(1), 162–176. 10.15294/lc.v16i1.30961

Goldstein, I., & Papert, S. (1977). Artificial intelligence, language, and the study of knowledge. *Cognitive Science*, 1(1), 84–123.

Hancı-Azizoglu, E. B. (2021). Emotional Intelligence and Empathic Linguistic Power in Times of Crisis. In *Rhetoric and Sociolinguistics in Times of Global Crisis* (pp. 100–115). IGI Global. 10.4018/978-1-7998-6732-6.ch006

Hertzberg, L. (1990). Artificial intelligence and the empiricist picture of thought. *Artifical Intelligence, Culture and Language: On Education and Work*, 9-12.

House, J. (2001). Translation quality assessment: Linguistic description versus social evaluation. *Meta*, 46(2), 243–257. 10.7202/003141ar

Hutchins, W. J. (2023). Machine translation: History of research and applications. In *Routledge encyclopedia of translation technology* (pp. 128–144). Routledge. 10.4324/9781003168348-7

Karataş, F., Abedi, F. Y., Ozek Gunyel, F., Karadeniz, D., & Kuzgun, Y. (2024). Incorporating AI in foreign language education: An investigation into ChatGPT's effect on foreign language learners. *Education and Information Technologies*, 1–24. 10.1007/s10639-024-12574-6

Koehn, P. (2020). *Neural machine translation*. Cambridge University Press. 10.1017/9781108608480

Korteling, J. H., van de Boer-Visschedijk, G. C., Blankendaal, R. A., Boonekamp, R. C., & Eikelboom, A. R. (2021). Human-versus artificial intelligence. *Frontiers in Artificial Intelligence*, 4, 622364. 10.3389/frai.2021.62236433981990

Kühl, N., Goutier, M., Baier, L., Wolff, C., & Martin, D. (2022). Human vs. supervised machine learning: Who learns patterns faster? *Cognitive Systems Research*, 76, 78–92. 10.1016/j.cogsys.2022.09.002

Lahcen, A. A. (2023). *The Impact of Machine Translation on Cultural Transfer in Literary Texts*. ResearchGate. https://www.researchgate.net/publication/374910874_The_Impact_of_Machine_Translation_on_Cultural_Transfer_in_Literary_Texts/citation/download

Lane-Mercier, G. (2014). Global and Local Languages. *A Companion to Translation Studies*, 217-229. Wiley.

LeCun, Y., Bengio, Y., & Hinton, G. (2015). *Deep learning. nature, 521*(7553), 436-444.

Lee, S. M. (2020). The impact of using machine translation on EFL students' writing. *Computer Assisted Language Learning*, 33(3), 157–175. 10.1080/09588221.2018.1553186

Łoboda, K., & Mastela, O. (2023). Machine translation and culture-bound texts in translator education: A pilot study. *The Interpreter and Translator Trainer*, 17(3), 503–525. 10.1080/1750399X.2023.2238328

Marcus, M., Santorini, B., & Marcinkiewicz, M. A. (1993). Building a large annotated corpus of English: The Penn Treebank. *Computational Linguistics*, 19(2), 313–330.

Massey, G. & Ehrensberger-Dow, M. (2017). Learning machines and teaching humans. International Conference: Points of View in Translation and Interpreting, Kraków, Poland. https://digitalcollection.zhaw.ch/handle/11475/3278

McCarthy, J. (2007). From here to human-level AI. *Artificial Intelligence*, 171(18), 1174–1182. 10.1016/j.artint.2007.10.009

Nida, E. A. (1993). *Language, Culture and Translating*. Shanghai Foreign Language Education Press.

Niño, A. (2009). Machine translation in Foreign Language Learning: Language Learners' and tutors' perceptions of its advantages and disadvantages. *ReCALL*, 21(2), 241–258. 10.1017/S0958344009000172

Siu, S. C. (2023). Revolutionizing translation with AI: Unravelling neural machine translation and generative pre-trained large language models. *SSRN* 4499768. 10.2139/ssrn.4499768

Steding, S. (2009). Machine translation in the German classroom: Detection, reaction, prevention. *Die Unterrichtspraxis/Teaching German, 42*(2), 178–189. 10.1111/j.1756-1221.2009.00052.x

Sun, H. (2011). On Cultural Differences and Translation Methods. *Journal of Language Teaching & Research*, 2(1), 160–163. 10.4304/jltr.2.1.160-163

Tsai, S. C. (2019). Using google translate in EFL drafts: A preliminary investigation. *Computer Assisted Language Learning*, 32(5–6), 510–526. 10.1080/09588221.2018.1527361

Tursunovich, R. I. (2022). Linguistic and cultural aspects of literary translation and translation skills. *British Journal of Global Ecology and Sustainable Development*, 10, 168–173.

Urlaub, P., & Dessein, E. (2022). Machine Translation and foreign language education. *Frontiers in Artificial Intelligence*, 5, 936111. 10.3389/frai.2022.93611135937139

Wang, H. Y., Sigerson, L., & Cheng, C. (2019). Digital nativity and information technology addiction: Age cohort versus individual difference approaches. *Computers in Human Behavior*, 90, 1–9. 10.1016/j.chb.2018.08.031

Wells, N. (2022). Translation as Culture in the Age of the Machine. *Wasafiri*, 37(3), 77–80. 10.1080/02690055.2022.2067244

Widhiarso, W. (2016). Comparing the performance of synonym and antonym tests in measuring verbal abilities. *TPM. Testing, Psychometrics, Methodology in Applied Psychology*, 23(3).

Xiu, P., & Xeauyin, L. (2018). Human translation vs machine translation: The practitioner phenomenology. *Linguistics and Culture Review*, 2(1), 13–23.

Yao, B., Jiang, M., Yang, D., & Hu, J. (2023). *Empowering LLM-based machine translation with cultural awareness.* arXiv preprint arXiv:2305.14328.

Section 2
Scholarly Examinations of Digital Equity

Chapter 6

Linking With Technology in the Education and Adaptation Processes of Refugee Children

Kübra Engin
https://orcid.org/0000-0003-2590-1115
Gazi University, Turkey

Kadriye Selin Budak
https://orcid.org/0000-0002-8161-7074
Bilecik Seyh Edebali University, Turkey

Emine Bozkurt Polat
https://orcid.org/0000-0002-1821-028X
Kahramanmaraş Sütçü İmam University, Turkey

Feyza Aydin Bölükbaş
https://orcid.org/0000-0002-4380-0134
Aksaray University, Turkey

İlkay Ulutaş
https://orcid.org/0000-0002-2234-0773
Gazi University, Turkey

ABSTRACT

In this section, the needs of refugee children are discussed within the framework of Maslow's hierarchy and family systems theory, and explanations of children's participation in educational processes, the use of technology in educational pro-

DOI: 10.4018/979-8-3693-2591-9.ch006

cesses, and teacher guidance are given. In addition, the study aims to determine the knowledge, awareness, and experiences of preschool teachers in Turkey about integrating technology into education in classrooms for refugee children. In this direction, the teacher interview form on technology integration into activities with refugee children in early childhood was developed by the researchers, and the current situation was revealed by interviewing preschool teachers working with refugee children. As a result of the research, it was seen that refugee children in Turkey have problems with language and communication, adaptation and behavior problems, self-care skills, and cultural differences. It was found that teachers used language translation programs and technology-assisted instruction to solve these problems and made arrangements such as making extra explanations for refugee children in the context of language and culture, using Arabic materials, and speaking English. It was stated that technology integration was beneficial for refugee children in terms of easier language acquisition. "easier instruction, more adaptability and motivation, and faster learning, and it was emphasized that it provided equal opportunities with Turkish children.

INTRODUCTION

The number of people forced to migrate and leave their country has increased considerably over the years. According to UN data, while there were 70 million refugees in the world in 2018, 108.4 million people were forcibly displaced by the end of 2022. The refugee population in Turkey, which started with 252 people in 2011 (Güçer et al., 2013), reached 3.7 million in 2018 (UHNRC, 2018). Data for 2023 show that the Islamic Republic of Iran and Turkey are the countries with the largest refugee populations in the world, hosting 3.4 million refugees. Germany ranks third with 2.5 million refugees. The number of refugee children aged 0-11 is close to 7.5 million (UNHCR, 2023). As a result of this significant increase, researching the quality of life of children is especially important for society, determining the educational needs of refugee and immigrant children, increasing the educational standards of the population flow, and determining the needs and difficulties of teachers in this process are important for both country researchers and the world public (Busch et al., 2023). It is important to ensure social integration in the context of universal human rights and equal opportunities, to support children in terms of developmental aspects, and to ensure sustainable social development (Baysar et al., 2023).

Although the terms migrant and refugee are often used in similar contexts, they have certain differences. While migrants usually change their country of origin voluntarily, refugees are forced to leave their country and seek a place under international protection. While migration is often motivated by economic or social reasons, refugee status is often associated with emergencies such as persecution, war, or human rights violations. When considered in this context, the needs of the two groups and the perspective of the society may differ. Increasing globalization trends may cause people to experience situations they do not want to experience, and diplomatic relations may expose families, the weakest link of society, to deep and traumatic experiences. Wars, armed conflicts, power conflicts, civil wars, political instability, economic inequalities, and raw material inadequacies, such as the forced departure of individuals who have difficulty in sustaining their lives in their own countries in line with material interests such as raw material inadequacies drag these individuals to the position of refugees (Amoako, 2023; Şeker & Aslan, 2015; Tunç, 2015; Lonn & Dantzler, 2017; Usta & Ergün, 2022).

Figure 1. Population pyramid for the selected population types

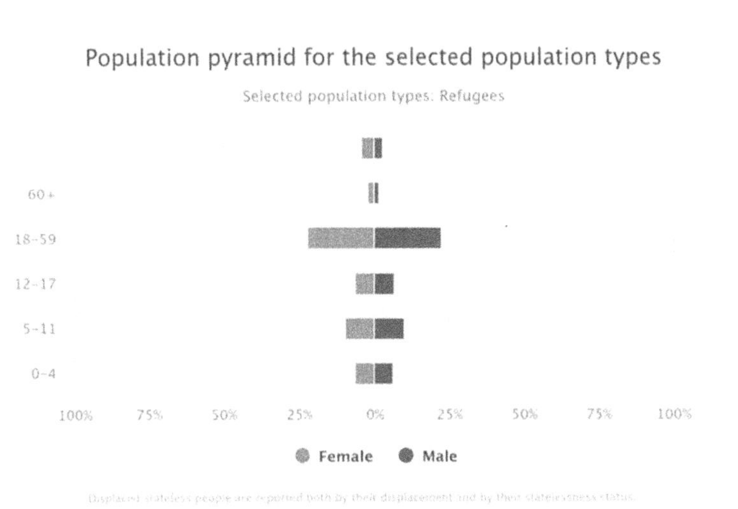

Note: This figure is taken from the https://www.unhcr.org/refugee-statistics/download/?url=K4StQ8

The internal crises and uncertainties emerging in the Middle East have triggered refugee mobility at a level that can affect the whole world and created one of the refugee crises for Turkey, especially due to being a neighboring country and its geopolitical position (Tunç, 2015). Refugee crises, which are seen as one of the biggest problems today, have put different systems in countries under pressure. One of these systems is the education system. The inclusion of refugees in the education process of the country they migrated to, their acceptance, and their adaptation to the existing order have seriously challenged the education systems. Serious difficulties have been faced in integrating all migrants into all systems of society (Montgomery et al., 2014). Refugee children, who have been left in a vulnerable situation due to the deprivation of their right to choice in their lives, have difficulties adapting to the education systems in the countries they migrate to. While developing countries and their existing education systems have difficulty in meeting all the needs of their own citizens, a serious population influx causes the existing systems to fail to function properly. This situation negatively affects not only the academic achievements of all individuals but also the psychological well-being of society (Cerna, 2019). Turkey, the country hosting the highest number of refugees in the world, is a country that is highly affected by these effects and needs work in this field (UNICEF, 2018). 2022-2023 MoNE data show that there are 730,806 Syrian children attending schools at the primary education level. Turkey, in terms of its geopolitical position, is faced with an increasingly intense mobility of people displaced for various reasons, such as war and security, and migrants who come to Turkey or move through Turkey in search of better opportunities. This situation necessitates the need for information sharing between national and international stakeholder institutions and the development of policies in cooperation for foreign children affected by the phenomenon of migration. If appropriate migration policies and social protection systems are structured, inequality created by internal migration and international migration within countries can be reduced (World Social Report, 2020).

Fundamental Needs of Refugee Children

Refugee children, like all children, have basic needs that need to be met to ensure their well-being and development, particularly in the context of displacement and resettlement (Sirin &

Figure 2. Maslow's hierarchy of needs

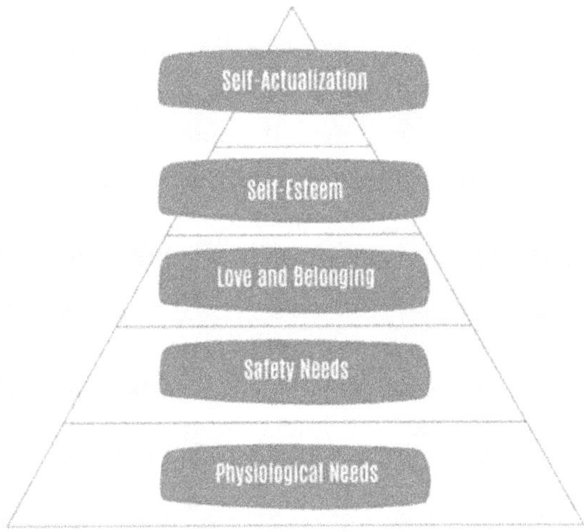

Rogers-Sirin, 2015). Meeting children's basic needs provides a basic structure for them to achieve a healthy, happy, and successful future. These needs should be an important priority of society and governments, and meeting them requires co-operation between policymakers, educators, health professionals, and social service providers (Busch et al., 2023). Research and policy development efforts are also important to fully understand children's needs and provide appropriate support and resources. This is because refugee children are seen as one of the most vulnerable populations in the world (Stevens et al., 2023).

According to Maslow's hierarchy, people's physiological needs should be met first. Maslow's hierarchy of needs provides a practical and humanistic framework for professionals working with this population (Lonn & Dantzler, 2017) and is also suggested as a potential framework to support wellness initiatives. Among the most basic needs of refugee children are physiological needs such as food, water, shelter, and medical care (Sirin & Rogers-Sirin, 2015; Morland et al., 2016). These children are deprived of their basic life needs due to war, natural disasters, or other challenging situations. They go through traumatic experiences such as war, violence, or forced migration. These children need a safe and secure environment away from violence, exploitation, and abuse. Providing shelter, family unity, and social security are important to meeting these needs. Provision of health services, vaccination, nutrition and food safety, medical care, psychosocial support, counseling processes, protection from exploitation and abuse, prevention of child labor, protection from negative experiences such as human trafficking and sexual abuse, play and recreation opportunities, and education opportunities should be provided.

Education is particularly important for refugee children as it helps them develop skills, knowledge, and resilience for the future. Access to quality education helps them to integrate into new communities, overcome trauma, and build resilience for their future.

Providing strong social support networks is critical for refugee children to feel a sense of belonging and safety. Reuniting with family members, maintaining cultural ties, and promoting social integration help mitigate the challenges of displacement and increase resilience. Parental separation, recognized as a risk factor for child health, cognitive development, and psychological well-being (Fellmeth et al., 2018), particularly affects refugee children. Family Systems Theory significantly emphasizes the role of the family in assessing the needs of these children and states that family support is a critical factor in the adaptation process of children (Samania, 2011). Family support is the most important foundation for children and plays an important role in meeting their psychological, emotional, and practical needs. Family communication and relationships, psychosocial cohesion, access to social support, and cultural and identity adaptation all play an important role in supporting children's adaptation process. Considering all these basic needs of children requires the collaborative efforts of governments, humanitarian organizations, communities, and individuals to ensure the promotion and protection of the rights and dignity of refugee children. It is among the humanitarian duties that individuals have to fulfill. Appropriately promoting early childhood experiences enables parents to increase their knowledge of early childhood education and learning and facilitates social contexts (Busch et al., 2023).

Participation of Refugee Children in School Processes

Considering the information on the consequences of the negativities experienced by refugee children in the early period due to the forced removal of their living conditions, it is necessary to take action to support the developmental characteristics of refugee children after their arrival at the migration points (Busch et al., 2023; Busch et al., 2022). In particular, it is stated that school environments are the ideal environment to meet the psychosocial needs of child refugees and to provide interventions and social support to help them adapt to society (Block et al., 2014; Murray, 2019; Sirin & Rogers-Sirin, 2015; Stevens et al., 2023; Votruba-Drzal et al., 2015). In early childhood, precarious environments potentially jeopardize children's successful transition from early childhood programs (Busch et al., 2022; Sirin & Rogers-Sirin, 2015). Although school environments for migrant children are generally stable and safe, they have difficulties in adapting to the new environment (Derince, 2019; Şeker & Aslan, 2015), although refugee children and youth are often referred to as 'stress-resistant' or 'resilient' (Maegusuku-Hewett et al., 2007) due to sudden migration processes, different cultural backgrounds and different language experiences (Derince, 2019; Şeker & Aslan 2015). It is seen that learning the majority language is the first among the many difficulties faced by refugee children (Stolk et al., 2023). In this context, educators need information on how to provide meaningful educational experiences for refugee children (Moinolnolki & Han, 2017). Failure of school environments to provide refugee children with the appropriate support and sensitivity they need may have deeper effects on the education and training processes of these children. Children who experience negative interaction processes may experience inadequate participation in the learning process, absenteeism, a sense of failure in establishing and maintaining negative social relationships, and low academic achievement and, consequently, poor long-term prospects in terms of employment and general socio-economic status (Block et al., 2014).

Refugee children need to benefit from the education of host countries in order to be able to adapt to the existing order, and in this direction, they need to acquire the relevant competencies in order to benefit from these education systems (Busch & Leyendecker, 2019). Refugee children's academic performance can be negatively affected by the traumatic effects of war, forced displacement, separation from family members, time spent in refugee camps, lack of education, little or interrupted education, and resettlement stress (Kaplan et al., 2016). As stated in many studies, these children have to cope with problems such as difficulty in focusing attention, anxiety, conflicts with peers, lower cognition-based performances and pre-academic skills, developmental disabilities, and language and speech disorders (Busch et al., 2021; Busch et al., 2022; Buchmüller et al., 2020). In a study in which teachers' opinions were taken, it was observed that they expressed the problems they perceived with refugee students, especially in the context of language problems, cultural differences, and emotional problems (Yurdakul & Tok, 2018).

It is known that supportive services provided in early childhood have the quality of improving children's development and well-being. These services should be both holistic and support children's learning. Parents, teachers, school administrators, and policymakers involved in the whole of these services should be in consensus in this context; educators who take an active role in the education process should provide positive and warm relationships and facilitate language and cognitive learning through rich, mutual, responsive interactions and content-based teaching. In order to ensure that educators can interact appropriately with children in this context, the right conditions must also be provided. These conditions include the ratio of refugee students to the number present in the classroom, staff training and support, and safe and stimulating facilities (Melhuish et al., 2014). It is important that these issues are adopted as common principles in all countries.

The Islamic Republic of Iran and Turkey have the largest refugee populations worldwide, hosting 3.4 million refugees each. Germany ranks third with 2.5 million (UNHCR, 2023). Findings from Germany reveal a higher rate of developmental disabilities in young children of refugee families (Buchmüller et al., 2018; Busch et al., 2021). Therefore, developmental needs should be met first. In many countries around the world, studies are carried out to meet the needs of these children. For example, in Germany, in response to this situation, state authorities have provided financial support for early childhood education programs for refugee children (Busch, 2023).

They have established "Bridging Projects" for refugee children. The project is designed to compensate for the lack of regular childcare places and to facilitate their transition to regular early childhood education programs. In Turkey, Syrian refugee children were receiving education in Temporary Education Centres in accordance with the curriculum of their home countries when they first arrived. However, when it became clear that the war and migration would be protracted, these centres were gradually closed and refugee children were supported to integrate into the Turkish education system. One of the biggest steps in this direction is the Supporting the Integration of Syrian Children into the Turkish Education System (PICTES) project, which is carried out in cooperation with the Ministry of National Education and the EU Delegation to Turkey. This project aims to facilitate Syrian refugees' access to education in Turkey and to help them integrate into the Turkish education system. Within the scope of PICTES, various activities such as Turkish and Arabic language training, provision of educational materials, administrative staff, and teacher training have been carried out (PICTES, 2021). In addition, according to the 2023-2028 Turkey Child Rights Strategy Document and Action Plan, the physiological needs of refugee children are trying to be met. It is seen as an important criterion that children whose physiological needs are met can adapt to social life and feel safe. Erdemir (2023) evaluated the effects of the Summer Preschools Programme on Syrian refugees aged 5-6 years and local children from vulnerable communities in Turkey. The program aimed to support the developmental well-being and school readiness of children with a history of forced displacement and poverty by supporting children's cognitive, language, and socio-emotional development. The study proved that the program is effective as a compensatory intervention strategy that can improve the developmental well-being, school readiness, and resilience of children exposed to adversity early in life. The "School Support Programme" operates in schools in Australia, facilitates partnerships between schools and institutions, and provides a holistic model for a whole-school approach that focuses on the learning, social, and emotional needs of students from refugee backgrounds. The interviews conducted as part of the project made it clear that raising educators' awareness of the special educational and developmental needs of refugee students is a crucial factor in motivating and facilitating changes in school practice. It was also found that the participation of parents as well as teachers in the education process is the key to effective education (Block et al., 2014).

When the intervention programs in different countries are examined, it can be said that the first objectives of the programs, in general, are to support language acquisition, increase social cohesion, provide psychosocial support, increase academic success, improve school-family cooperation, and apply sanctions to support social stability. In summary, it is possible to say that intervention programs have functions such as ensuring the successful integration of children and supporting their long-term success.

Technology in the Education and Adaptation Processes of Refugee Children

When the recommendations on supporting the participation of refugee children in early childhood are examined, it is emphasized that the educational environments offered to children should be reliable and stable, have clear routines and rules, and be predictable (Bouchane et al., 2018). Innovative solutions for providing this reliable environment for children in education and ensuring equal opportunities and access to quality education are critical, especially in early childhood. Technology is seen as an important bridge potential in meeting the educational needs of refugee children and ensuring equal opportunities. Today, with the increasing integration of technology in classrooms, it has become more important to address the language and cultural differences of refugee children in the context of technology and to use technology as a tool to ensure equal opportunities. The integration of refugee children into technology is seen as an important tool to help them overcome cultural, language, and adaptation difficulties. The opportunities offered by technology for children cover a wide range, from education to health services. Refugees are in constant interaction with technology (especially smartphones) to communicate with family and friends they left behind, access geolocation services, and learn the language, norms, and culture of the host country (AbuJarour et al., 2017).

United Nations Children's Fund (UNICEF) reports show that technology plays a critical role in migrant children's access to education. Mobile applications, online education platforms, and digital libraries allow these children to learn in the local language while preserving their own language and culture. This not only improves their academic achievement but also helps them to adapt more quickly to the integration process. In general, it has been suggested that technological devices be utilized to support the educational processes of refugee children.

Refugee children need to be able to adapt to social change as well as to the schools in the living spaces where they have to settle and to the education systems of society. In this process, it is thought that technology integration can provide support from different angles. Technology can increase refugee children's access to education, and providing appropriate integration opportunities can provide equal opportunities. It is known that these children especially need individualized teaching. In this context, technology integration can customize educational materials to better suit the individual learning needs of children. It can provide learning content according to student's abilities, interests, and speeds. The language learning of refugee children is seen among the most challenging factors in this process (Stolk et al., 2023; Ulukuş & Tümtaş, 2023).

For children who have to learn a new language, applications of technology that support language acquisition and translation can support this process positively. In this direction, a channel will be created for children's social interaction. The establishment of social interaction will support the increase of cultural understanding and adaptation in children. In this process, it would be a limited perspective to assume that technology provides support only in the context of children. Teachers with students with different language skills also need support in this process, and technology can support teachers in creating educational materials, monitoring student progress, and developing teaching strategies. For example, "Storybooks Canada," an open-access multilingual digital platform in Canada, is structured to improve students' reading skills. Having alternative language options, this program has proven to be a valuable tool in terms of sustaining both the country of immigration and the mother tongue (Gilman & Norton, 2020). However, migrant children's access to technology also faces some challenges. Financial constraints can limit access to technology, while the digital divide can deepen inequalities between refugee and settled children. Moreover, the lack of adequate education and guidance on the use of technology can pose safety risks, increasing children's exposure to harmful content. Wu (2022) emphasizes the importance of understanding the specific challenges and needs of refugee children in the educational context by examining the educational experiences of refugee children in European countries. In recent years, it has been seen that studies on refugee children and technology are related to virtual and augmented reality (Aman & Shiratuddin, 2020), digital gaming (Iakimova et al., 2022), child-computer interactive research methods for refugee children (Tahir & Wang, 2019), online learning experiences (Rice, 2023). Iakimova et al. (2022) developed the digital game "Antura and Letters" to develop literacy skills and psychosocial support for Syrian refugee children in order to examine the potential of digital games to support the educational and psychosocial needs of refugees. As a result of the study, it was concluded that the game improved early literacy (alphabetic knowledge, phonological awareness, reading fluency) and emotional well-being (decreased emotional and behavioral disturbances and increased positive peer relations, better social interactions, and a better sense of well-being).

Innovative technologies such as virtual reality and augmented reality can help these children adapt to a new environment and support them to cope with traumatic experiences. For example, virtual reality therapy can offer children affected by war or natural disasters the opportunity for emotional healing in a safe environment.

Teacher Guidance in Technology Integration of Refugee Children in Education and Adaptation Processes

It is thought that technology can provide a significant increase in refugee children's access to and quality of education and that teachers play a major role in ensuring quality technology integration. In order to ensure a sense of belonging to the community and to build trust between teachers and refugee populations, it is important to create inclusive and respectful learning environments where everyone is included (Nazzal et al., 2014). The role of teachers in the integration of technology in the education process of refugee children is vital. Teachers should first provide the necessary technological infrastructure, provide appropriate devices, provide internet access, and offer technical support. In addition, teachers should select or develop technology-based learning materials appropriate to the needs of refugee children. These materials can utilize a variety of media formats to improve children's language skills and strengthen their essential academic and social skills. Teachers should also teach students the skills to use technology effectively, provide individual support, monitor learning processes, and create creative learning environments incorporating technology (UNESCO, 2022).

Technology can also support educators' continuous professional development to effectively teach refugees or migrants and develop their subject matter expertise (UNESCO, 2022). As the most critical stakeholder in the teaching process, teachers should organize opportunities for technology integration at school, actively engage in technology integration in the family interaction process, and contribute to school-family cooperation. Collaborations with the community should enable educators to understand the specific experiences and needs of families and use community resources to develop culturally responsive environments and practices (Krakouer et al., 2017; Kardeş & Akman, 2018).

It is necessary to conduct studies to raise parents' awareness about preschools and to collaborate with experts working in different disciplines. It is suggested to employ bilingual staff from refugee communities and invite parents unfamiliar with play-based learning to participate in training and volunteer (Busch et al., 2018; Morland et al., 2016; Stolk et al., 2023). In this context, the research aims to reveal the difficulties experienced by preschool teachers working with refugee children in their classrooms in Turkey in the education and adaptation processes of these children and their experiences related to technology integration into the education process.

In the research, answers to the following questions were sought:

- What are the problems that refugee children face in their education and adaptation processes?
- How do teachers use technology to solve these problems?
- How do teachers make arrangements for refugee children in the context of language and culture during technology integration processes?
- What are the effects of technology integration on the education and adaptation processes of refugee children?
- How do teachers use technology to engage parents of refugee children in education?
- How do teachers share with their colleagues about the integration of technology in the education and adaptation processes of refugee children?
- What are teachers' opinions about teacher training regarding the integration of technology into the education and adaptation processes of refugee children?

METHOD

Research Model

The research was designed using a basic qualitative research design. Basic qualitative research is a type of research in which participants' daily experiences and how they make sense of them are described (Meriam, 2013). Within the scope of this research, since it is aimed to reveal the experiences and opinions of teachers about the use of technology in the education and adaptation processes of Syrian refugee children, the research was conducted as basic qualitative research.

Working Group

The study group of the research consists of 18 preschool teachers working with refugee children in their classrooms. Criterion sampling, one of the purposeful sampling methods, was used in the study (Gall et al., 2007; Patton, 2018). Critical situations can be the source of criterion sampling (Patton, 2018). For the first criterion of the participant selection criteria of the study, the data of the Republic of Turkey Ministry of Interior Directorate of Migration Management (2024) were used, and the participants were determined as working in one of the first ten provinces (Istanbul, Gaziantep, Şanlıurfa, Hatay, Adana, Mersin, Bursa, Konya, İzmir, and Ankara) where Syrian refugees under temporary protection are densely populated and having at least one refugee child in the classroom. In addition, the teachers' declaration that their technological competencies were at least at an intermediate level was also considered as a criterion. In addition, the researchers working in institutions affiliated with the Ministry of National Education and volunteering for the interview were also determined as criteria. A total of 18 preschool teachers, three from each province, working with refugee children in Istanbul, Gaziantep, Şanlıurfa, Bursa, Konya, and Ankara provinces were interviewed. Demographic data of the participant teachers are given in Table 1.

Figure 3. Demographic characteristics of the participants

	Participants	f
Gender		
Male	T15 T18	2
Woman	T1 T2 T3 T4 T5 T6 T7 T8 T9 T10 T11 T12 T13 T14 T16 T17	16
Age		
25-30	T2 T5 T6 T8 T9 T11 T13 T15 T16 T18	10
31-35	T1 T3 T10	3
36-40	T12 T14 T17	3
45-50	T7	1
Profession Year		
1-5 years	T2 T6 T9 T11 T13 T15 T16	7
6-10 years	T1 T3 T5 T7 T10 T14 T17 T18	8
11-15 years	T12	1
Technology Competence		
Medium level	T1 T2 T4 T7 T10 T12 T14 T17	8
High level	T3 T5 T6 T8 T9 T11 T13 T15 T16 T18	10
Participation of Refugee Children in Education Status of Participation in Education		
Yes	T11(MEB Inclusive Education) T14(MEB Inclusive Education)) T18 (PICTES)	3
No	T1 T2 T3 T5 T6 T7 T8 T9 T10 T16 T17 T15 T13 T12	15
Follow-up Status of Resources Related to Technology Integration in Refugee Children's Education Processes		
Yes	T13 (Youtube) T15 (Youtube, EBA, PICTES)	2
No	T1 T2 T3 T5 T6 T7 T8 T9 T10 T11 T16 T18 T17 T14 T12	16
Provinces of Duty		
İstanbul	T5 T6 T8	3
Gaziantep	T11 T13 T18	3
Şanlıurfa	T2 T4 T9	3
Bursa	T1 T3 T7	3
Konya	T14 T15 T17	3
Ankara	T10 T12 T16	3

Among the participants, two were male and 16 were female. Ten of the participants are between the ages of 25-30, 3 between 31-35, 3 between 36-40 and 1 between 45-50. While seven teachers have 1-5 years of experience, eight have 6-10, and 1 has 11-15 years of professional experience. Eight of the teachers stated that they have medium, and 10 of them have a high level of technological competence. Within the scope of the training organized by the Ministry of National Education on the participation of refugee children in education, two teachers stated that they received inclusive training, and 1 teacher stated that they received PICTES Adaptation Training. One teacher stated that he/she used YouTube for technology integration in the education processes of refugee children, and one teacher stated that he/she used EBA and PICTES resources in addition to YouTube.

Data Collection Tools

"Teacher Interview Form on Technology Integration in Activities with Refugee Children in Early Childhood" was used as a data collection tool in the study. The form was developed by the researchers and consists of two parts: demographic data and questions about technology integration. In the demographic data section, there are questions related to age, gender, years of service, graduated program, participation in education related to refugee children's education, resources related to the use of technological tools in the education of refugee children, and technological competence of the participant. In the second part, there are questions about the problems encountered in the education and adaptation processes of refugee children, the use of technology in solving problems, experiences about the use of technology with refugee children and its results, sharing with colleagues, and opinions about the content of training on the use of technology with refugee children. The prepared questions were sent to 5 preschool field experts, and the form was restructured to match the feedback received. With the finalized form, a pilot interview was conducted with one preschool teacher working with refugee children, and the comprehensibility of the questions was tested. According to Merriam (2013), the main purpose of qualitative research is to deepen understanding. Therefore, it emphasizes that validity and reliability criteria should be different from quantitative research. Among the validity and reliability standards that frequently stand out in qualitative research literature, there are elements such as providing diversity, participant verification, consulting expert opinions, long-term presence in the field, and detailed descriptions (Glesne, 2015; Patton, 2014). In the study, in order to ensure the reliability and validity of the form, care was taken to ensure the criteria of providing diversity, expert opinion, and detailed description.

Data Collection

In order to collect the data, teachers were informed about the purpose of the study, individual study calendars were created for the pre-service teachers who wanted to participate in the study voluntarily, and an appointment time was determined. The teachers were interviewed individually via telephone interviews in a quiet environment at the determined appointment time. During the data collection process, care was taken not to be directive while asking questions. The interviews with the participants were recorded using a voice recorder with the consent of the participants, and then the recorded data were transcribed.

Analysing the Data

The transcribed interviews were analyzed by the researchers using the content analysis method; firstly, the codes were determined by meticulously reading the answers given by the teachers, and then categories and themes were determined in accordance with the content of the codes. Content analysis refers to a process involving coding and categorization of data. This process aims to understand events and information in depth and present them in an organized way (Merriam, 2013; Patton, 2014). In this study, five randomly selected interviews were analyzed by two researchers, and the inter-rater coding reliability was calculated as .90. In addition, teacher opinions were presented with direct quotations without intervention and coded in accordance with ethical rules (Teacher 1: T1, Teacher 2: T2).

FINDINGS

In this section, the findings related to the problems experienced in the education and adaptation processes of refugee children and the technologies used in solving the problems, the arrangements made in the context of language and culture in the process of using technology with refugee children, the effects of the use of technology on the education and adaptation process of refugee children, the practices related to technology integration in the participation of refugee children's parents in education, the studies carried out at school on the use of technology in the education and adaptation processes of refugee children and the sharing with colleagues, opinions on teacher training for technology integration with refugee children and expectations from teacher training are included.

Problems Experienced in the Education and Adaptation Processes of Refugee Children and Technologies Used in Solving Problems

Figure 4. Problems experienced in the education and adaptation processes of refugee children and technologies used to solve problems

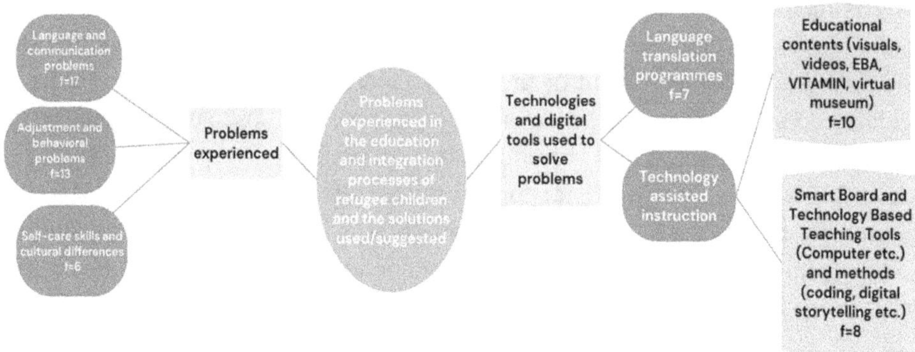

When the problems experienced by teachers in the education of refugee children are analyzed, it is seen that almost all of them (f=17) have language and communication problems with refugee children. Regarding this, T2 expressed his opinion: *"This is our biggest problem in this geography because they do not know the language, and we have difficulty communicating with them... They have adaptation problems with their friends because they do not understand the lessons."* At the same time, T11 stated, *"Children come to school without knowing Turkish. Therefore, they have difficulty understanding me and their friends. Because they do not understand me, they have crying crises, especially when they start school. They get bored and talk among themselves while reading books, especially in Turkish-language activities. I usually have difficulty giving instructions."* In addition, teachers mostly (f=13) stated that children had adaptation and behavioral problems. T5 expressed his opinion about this as follows: *"Since they usually cannot express themselves much, they can engage in more negative behaviors with other children. They push or pull the toy out of their hands, or they never listen to me, for example. Because they do not understand me, they can show such stubborn behaviors to me too much."*

However, it is seen that the number of refugee children in the class is also important in the adaptation problems experienced. In classes where there are more Syrian refugees than Turkish children, the teacher has difficulty giving instructions because the children speak their own language among themselves. Regarding this, T7 said, *"There are usually 11 Syrian children in my class; they speak their mother tongue all the time. I constantly give instructions, but no matter what I do, they still continue to speak their own language."* It was observed that in classes where Syrian children and Turkish children were equal, in-class segregation was high, while in classes with more Turkish children, children could adapt to the class more easily. T14 expressed his opinion on this as follows:

"For example, since I have 10 Syrian and 10 Turkish children, Turkish children set up games among themselves, and Syrian children set up games among themselves. Even if there is no speech, the child can set up a game on their own, continue the game together, sustain it."

When the opinions of the teachers were analyzed, it was determined that refugee children lacked self-care skills and had cultural differences. Regarding this, T15 said, *"They lack self-care skills. They don't pay much attention; the culture is very different; I mean, they have different roles at many points, from eating and drinking to playing games."* T14 expressed his opinion on this issue with the words, *"Children don't know the toilet bowl; they were very scared when they saw it and didn't want to go; they used to eat with their hands, now they have learned to use forks and spoons."*

Almost all of the teachers (f=17) stated that technology would be a useful tool in solving problems. T8 *"There, you know, children see through visual reading; they can do what they see better. There is also constant repetition there. For example, when teaching the color red, red balloons and red cars are constantly repeated, so children learn red in this way. I can say that my refugee student learned a few words through the smart board"*. T1 compared his two experiences in which he used and did not use technology as follows: *"Now I don't have a smart board in my classroom, but I had one in the first semester. I think it was better because it was a smart board. It was easier. For example, even if I explained something verbally, my refugee student understood at least what I meant by showing it on the smart board and supporting it by saying this is this.''* T7 also made a similar comparison: *"I worked in Urfa for four years before coming to Bursa, and the smart board was very useful for me there. I mean, I could open everything on it. The TV in my current classroom is small, so I can't present everything I want. Since I could access everything on the smart board, it was more functional."* On the other hand, S6 stated that technology could not be used effectively due to the language barrier: *I mean, I don't think it can be a very, very good tool. Because I open educational videos and stuff, I play games, but I didn't see much contribution. I try to play games physically. For example, we make refugee children sit side by side with their Turkish-speaking friends. They never let each other into the same space; we make them sit at the same table with the same chair, for example. You know, we can improve this by organizing more spaces and environments rather than technology. Numbers, geometric shapes, beautiful words, courtesy words that we need to use in the classroom, etc. I opened up a lot, but I didn't see much benefit because they didn't understand and didn't speak Turkish.*

When the opinions are examined, it is seen that language translation programs and technology-assisted instruction are used to overcome the problems experienced in the education and adaptation processes of refugee children. For technology-assisted teaching, it was determined that they included educational content (visuals, videos, EBA, VITAMIN, virtual museum, etc.) using smart boards and technology-based teaching tools and methods. T4 stated that he benefited from translation applications as follows: *For example, I used translation. How can I write in Turkish and say it in Arabic? Then, listening to it out loud. I think it facilitates children's language learning, especially in terms of language. When we open a cartoon, maybe we read a little bit of a story about exposure to language. It is undeniable that these also contribute to language development.*

Regarding technology-assisted instruction, T3 said, *"I mean, it is easier to get feedback from these educational videos or if you know the seasons one by one or if you know the animals, it is easier to show the visuals one by one and get feedback from the children in that way, and it actually attracts their attention more. Otherwise, it is boring for them too. They start talking among themselves. If the activities we do are less participatory, but when they are visually supported, I see that children are more interested and happier. And these technological tools provide visualization. Thus, it ensures their participation. Even when we are working, I may have to make an example of the book or activity myself and show it to them beforehand because they cannot understand what we are going to do. When I'm studying a book, I have to take care of them one-on-one, or I have to show them directly and make them do it. So frankly, we benefit a lot from these educational videos on Youtube."* and explained the educational content.

T8 exemplified the ways of utilizing educational content as follows: *In the art activity we are going to do, I first upload the board. So the children look at it, they do it there first. Or if I am going to introduce a new topic, they will watch a video or a presentation about it. Apart from that, if we are going to do an experiment, for example, I open the visuals of the materials of the experiment from there; they look from there to make it realistic. In storytelling, sometimes I read the story; sometimes we open interactive books, and we listen from the board in this way.* T13 explained his use of educational content with the following words and exemplified the various technology-based teaching tools he used: *I have a smart board in the game room. I set up a projection device in the classroom. I try to do it from there with a big screen or through the computer. Apart from that, I am also an EBA teacher. I gave all the students their passwords, and I logged in to the system with EBA and made sure that they followed the videos from there at regular intervals. I make daily assignments;*

I make them follow them from there. I mean, the subject we cover through games and stuff like that. There are things there; VITAMIN applications are already there, and I make sure they follow them. I use them, for example, in music class. For any subject, for example, I explained Mevlana. Let's say I show what kind of person he is related to that subject; I explain it there. Let's say I explained Konya.

Arrangements Made in the Context of Language and Culture in the Process of Technology Use With Refugee Children

Figure 5. Arrangements made in the context of language and culture in the process of technology use with refugee children

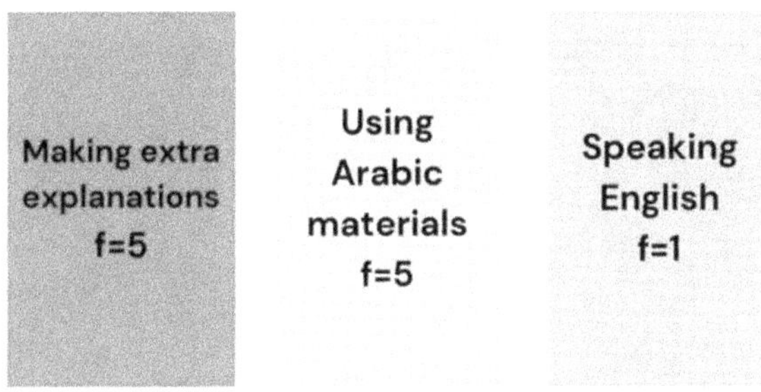

Half of the teachers (f=9) reported that they did not make any extra arrangements for refugee children during the technology integration process. The arrangements made were categorized as making extra explanations, using Arabic materials, and speaking in English. T1 stated that he stopped the process and made extra explanations: *I stopped at that moment. As a result, since they do not understand how to speak fluently, I stop and explain to them one by one, this is what he said; this is what he meant. Did you understand? I asked them if they understood more about this.*

T3 stated that he was able to communicate through English as another language: *We usually do not do anything different except show the visuals of all the activities. Because they adapt to what we do, or they can do it by looking at the person next to them. If they don't understand, sometimes I try to speak English, and they can talk to them. Yes, most of them speak English. Sometimes, we try to understand English words.*

T4: *"Sometimes I also play Arabic songs to make them feel very foreign, and they are very surprised. They are very happy. So, in this context, we can do such things so that children do not feel alone. We can turn it on in different languages. Apart from that, I cannot open anything informative for the lesson; unfortunately, they are in Turkish. I try to simplify it. I try to explain it by simplifying it in case they don't know this word."* She gave an example of using Arabic materials and giving extra explanations.

T5 stated that he had not been aware of such an arrangement before and, therefore, did not make an arrangement: *No. Unfortunately, unfortunately, I don't. I don't really sit down and do anything for it. When you asked me this question, I realized how lacking I was.* T6 emphasized that the class size did not allow for extra arrangements: *I cannot do extra. I cannot deal with them individually because it is too crowded. Whatever I did all at the same time, I can do, more precisely.*

The Effects of the Use of Technology on the Education and Adaptation Process of Refugee Children

Figure 6. The effects of the use of technology on the education and adaptation process of refugee children

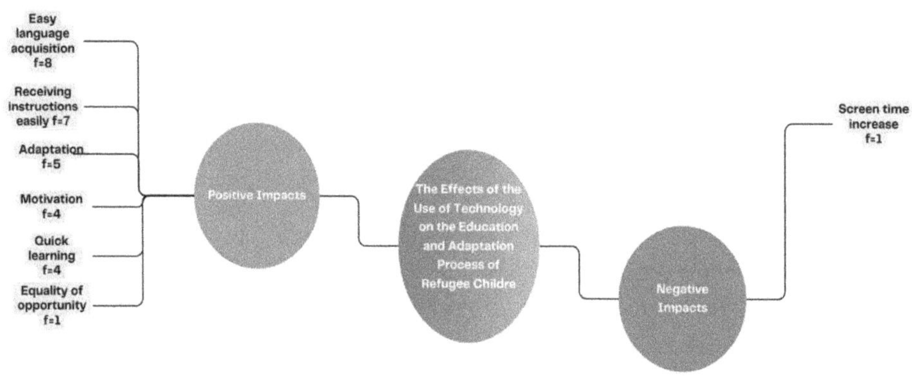

Participants stated that refugee children acquire language and receive instructions more easily, are more adaptable and motivated, learn faster, and have equal opportunities thanks to technology integration. However, they also evaluated the increase in screen time as a negative feature. T4 explained the contribution of technology to language acquisition with the following words: *"I think it facilitates children's language learning, especially in terms of language. When we open a cartoon, it is about exposure to language, and reading a story is the same way. It is undeniable that these contribute to language development. However, there may also be something that we can call negative. For example, when we tell children and their families to speak Turkish at home or produce something in Turkish when you think that this is done excessively when screen time increases, this can, of course, be negative."* T1 commented on receiving instructions more easily and motivation: *For example, when I show the worksheet in front of them from there, it is easier because it is a*

much bigger screen, the whole class sees it, and they see it more clearly. When I hold the worksheet in my hand and show it to the children, they can understand it, but Syrians sometimes find it difficult to do so on such a small piece of paper. Also, they have already been born into today's age of technology. I think phones are more attractive for children. Something like this seems to attract them more. It's a sports movement, something else, actually. For example, I make them do it, I turn it on and say let's do it or something like that, or with rhythm sticks, they become more like that. It's like they feel embarrassed when I'm in front of them, or for example, they look at me sometimes. They don't want to do it, but when I turn on the screen, and the person in front of me supports them with other birds, insects, covers, etc., and does something more like that, I think they do it better there. T18, on the other hand, provided examples of easy language acquisition, easy instruction taking, and equal opportunities with his explanation: *When we use technology, we overcome the language problem to a great extent because children see it visually. Apart from that, when we use technology in play activities, visuality is again at the forefront in games with technology. Children perceive things much more easily and play in-game activities much more easily. For example, when I want to give instructions for a game, the child can understand those instructions, but if they see how the game is played, I watch the video of the game being played. It enables that child to play that game immediately. So, these children are also disadvantaged. We want to take care of them as much as other children. But I can't pay enough attention to them, especially because we have language problems, and they are not at the same level. I think the quality of education that a Turkish student and a foreign student receive from a teacher is not the same. So, this technology can help reduce this difference.*

T9 stated that technology has enabled a decrease in adaptation problems: *As much as possible, I found short videos on YouTube for the mother, for example, about what she should do in school. The parent, for example, did not speak any Turkish. We interacted with the support staff at the school. I suggested that they watch short videos and Turkish channels as much as possible at home. In this way, he adapted to the class more easily, he started to participate in activities, and he did not have problems with his friends at first.* She also emphasized that it accelerated the learning process *because the child will most likely learn this situation faster when he/she encounters something visual. Because we cannot explain it in a moving way with cards. I mean, in the end, we are just trying to explain to the child that they should do this, that this is not right as much as they can understand. But with technological tools or cartoons and slides, we can probably reduce this in a shorter time.*

T15 emphasized the contribution of technology to the effective learning of refugee children: *"It is useful. I mean, it enables children to learn better and more actively. The child uses the technology there. Because many of them may not have seen or used this technology in their family life or in their previous life. So when the teacher does the activity with this child, it helps that child to learn faster, to be active, to learn; in other words, it helps the child to change that technology."*

T3 emphasized its effect on the acquisition of classroom rules, *Especially in the first months; for example, the visuals we show there about classroom rules or introductions are useful for children. We usually use them for these kinds of things.*

T6 stated that he could not see any benefit of using technology and attributed this situation to the children's lack of language skills: *I cannot say that it is very useful. I mean, they should know a little bit of language, but if they know a little bit of language, it works well. Mine didn't know any language at all, so it didn't have much effect. I mean, if they know a little bit of language, it can be useful, but I think it won't work because they don't know any language.*

Practices on Technology Integration in the Participation of Parents of Refugee Children in Education

Figure 7. Practices on technology ıntegration in the participation of parents of refugee children in education

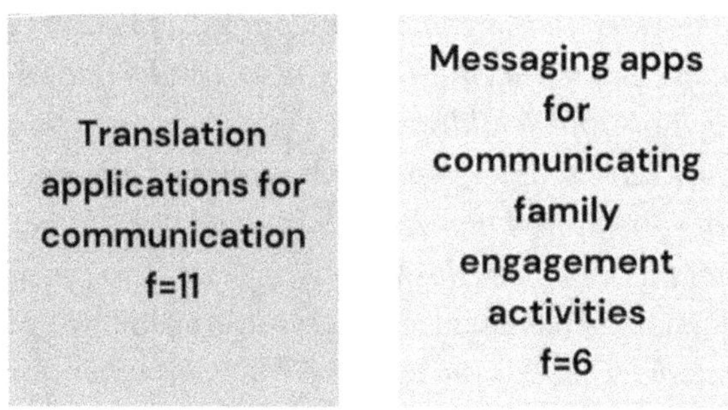

Teachers stated that they used translation applications for communication and messaging applications for communicating family involvement activities. Five teachers stated that they did not use technology for parent involvement. T3 stated that they could only communicate with the parents in written form as follows: *the rate of mothers who speak Turkish is very low. Unfortunately, in order to communicate with them, I usually send written messages from the WhatsApp group so that they can translate them into Arabic. With fathers, fathers can talk more. But with mothers, as I said, we only talk by writing. Because when I try to explain something at the door, they cannot understand.* T15 stated that he shared materials and content for family involvement activities through technology: *For example, we use it to introduce applications, to show applications, to send links, or when we hold parent-teacher*

conferences, we use it at parent-teacher conferences. I mean applications, sites. For example, there was a code site. It is a school about learning coding. At the very beginning, children at different levels up to high school could do activities for coding at this simple level through games, on the computer, or on the phone. There are digital stories, and we throw them away, saying they can use them. Regarding the subject, S8 said, *"Now we have a WhatsApp group. Through that group, I send videos to all the parents, but mostly, they pay more attention. Let's say we switched to the number 9. How to write the number 9? Here is the number 9. What is 9, how many are there? And they teach children how to represent it with objects. Or not colors or shapes but concepts. When I want to talk to the parents in Turkish, I write in Turkish, and they answer me in Turkish. But what I write probably goes to them in Arabic because they are Syrian. They reply to me with run-on sentences. I understand that, too; I think they have these translations on their phones."* T12 stated that she did not need to use technology because the family of the refugee child in her class could speak Turkish: *Nothing happened. I mean, I already have one student this year. His mother also speaks Turkish. She can answer our messages in Turkish.*

School Activities and Sharing With Colleagues on the Use of Technology in the Education and Adaptation Processes of Refugee Children

All of the teachers stated that there is no study on the use of technology in the education and adaptation process of refugee children in their schools. T5 summarized the issue as follows: *There are many refugee children in our school. Especially in our primary school, but I don't even hear them speaking Turkish properly like their siblings. I don't think anything is being done. I've never seen it.* T9 commented that *"there is no regulation, there is no practice."*

It was observed that teachers shared information about the education of refugee children with their colleagues, but the content related to technology integration was limited. T9 stated that the conversations focused on problems with the words, *"In general, I always talked about behavioral problems or learning difficulties, difficulties, language problems or the difficulties we had with parents, so we didn't really get to that dimension."*. T17 stated that the sharing developed within the framework of communication and harmony: *"I mean, how can we explain better? How can we communicate better? How can we minimize the issue of adaptation so that they can spend their education and training life successfully? I mean, we talk about these kinds of things in meetings when we come together with them.* T8 explained that they shared about the use of interactive whiteboards in the education of refugee children: *So yes, we are constantly having problems about how we can produce. Because we are teaching in a place with a very dense refugee population.*

We all try to communicate with them through the interactive board. I mean, we all have the interactive board in our classrooms, and we think that we can use it more easily. So, we had a conversation about how this would work better if we shared this with our colleagues.

T15 emphasized that the use of technology with refugee children depends on the technological possibilities of the school and stated that he shared with his colleagues about productive activities: *We have our own possibilities. When the school has facilities, we can use technology, but when the school does not have facilities when they are limited, we can use it in a limited way. We sometimes exchanged ideas with fellow teachers on this subject. We tried to do the activities they did, or we tried to implement a good activity we found, and they tried to do it too.*

Opinions on Teacher Training for Technology Integration With Refugee Children and Expectations from Teacher Training

All of the teachers stated that teacher training on technology integration in the education of refugee children was insufficient. T9 stated that he had not come across such a training before. He said, *"I actually follow these local trainings a lot; the trainings are open to teachers. But for example, I have not seen any training on this subject there yet.* T8 emphasized that children were distributed to classes without any training *(I mean, they never gave us such training before. They directly gave refugee children as students. This was confusing for us, but I wish it could be).* T15 stated that there is such training at different levels but not for the preschool period. *I thought it was insufficient because I had not heard about any training for foreign children, especially in terms of technology and education. To be honest, they were giving some training, but I heard that they were not for us, but rather for children to learn Turkish in the early stages and that Turkish teachers, especially teachers, were given training. But we were not given any training, whether in early childhood or in kindergartens, about what we should do for those children.*

Figure 8. Opinions on teacher training for technology integration with refugee children

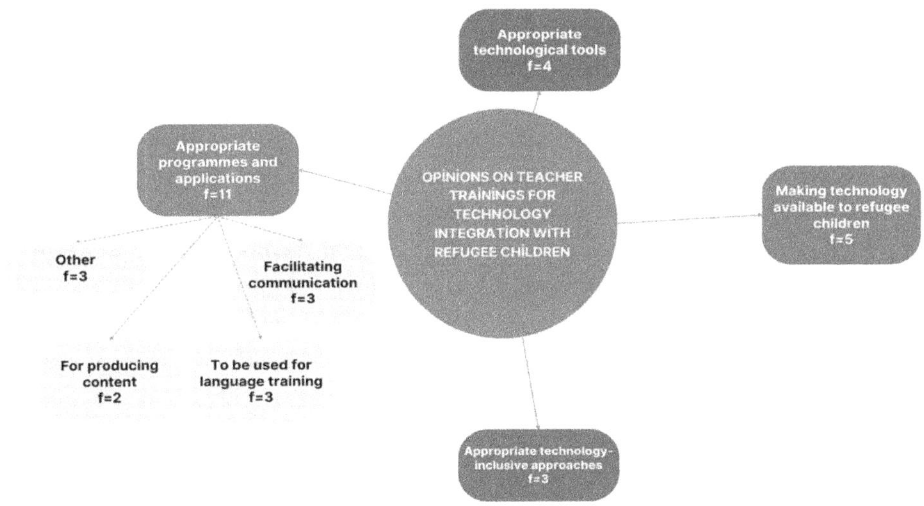

Teachers stated that they needed to be informed about programs and applications suitable for use with refugee children. Regarding the subject, T4 said, *"I mean, what I want is a solution, and I want a realistic solution. What can I do? What I can really do is to make sure that when I do this, it is useful in life. You know, sometimes it happens that we receive training on something, but you cannot apply it. But it is important that it is applicable."* and stated that useful information is needed. In this context, there is a demand for tools that will facilitate communication, be used for language education, and enable content production. T2 expressed the need for content related to communication and language education as follows: *"There will be materials, games, or interactive materials that will facilitate my adaptation to this region or that I can communicate better with those children. An application that can make my job easier. At least for preschool, I want to teach Turkish. You know, to teach our mother tongue."*

T13 described the content he expected from this kind of education, emphasized that he needed applications to be used for content creation, and stated that this would facilitate the language education process *(It is related to technology, but I think it should be briefly summarised from the beginning. We may have teachers who do not know about technology. For example, there were many of them in our school, and very few of their friends were interested. Whether it is a computer, smart board, programs, projects, etc., at least a short technology can be discussed. Afterward, with such summarised explanations, such as this is done with technology. It can also be used afterward. I think this could even be a video merging program. Because they are also doing animation, we can prepare something. There can be animation programs. I did a lot of them when I was at university; for example, they can be those. Animations can be prepared for children in Turkish and for foreign children in Turkish. At least we can make them more involved in the environment, and we can attract attention and make them learn Turkish better).*

T5 stated that he needed content about technological tools that can be used with refugee children and their presentation to children. *For example, even when you asked me which tools you wanted to use, I couldn't think of anything. I mean, what kind of tools can there be? How can we present them to refugee children at school or at work? What can we benefit from while presenting them? Or you said resources; in order to reach those resources, I think seminars would be very useful, and I think it would be beneficial to have such topics in seminars.* T18 emphasized that the training should be applied and stated that innovative technologies should be included in the training content: *The content of the training should be more practical. In other words, the theoretical part should be very little. It should be more about what can be done practically, and this should be followed up. What would I like to learn? Robotics, coding, artificial intelligence. For example, we are very weak in artificial intelligence. There may be something about augmented reality. There may be augmented reality applications that we can use with children.*

DISCUSSION AND RESULTS

The aim of the study is to determine the knowledge, awareness, and experiences of preschool teachers in Turkey about integrating technology into education in classrooms for refugee children. It is stated that access to quality education and innovative solutions are critical in the adaptation processes of refugee children (Iakimova et al., 2022; Tahir & Wang, 2019; Rice, 2023). In addition to these, in the adaptation processes of children, meeting the needs of teachers and identifying their difficulties and experiences is important in terms of better quality integration (Baysar et al., 2023). At this point, the opinions of teachers working in the classrooms where refugee children are present were taken in the study.

As a result of the research, it was determined that refugee children have problems with language and communication, adaptation and behavior, self-care skills, and cultural differences in education and adaptation processes. In their study, Kardeş and Akman (2018) drew attention to the problems related to learning Turkish and school adaptation in their interviews with teachers about Syrian children. Yurdakul and Tok (2018) similarly stated that teachers have language, cultural differences, and emotional problems with refugee children. Cultural differences pose some difficulties in classroom management and the inclusion of refugee children in educational environments. Teachers need to plan culturally sensitive educational processes related to these challenges (Roxas & Fruja, 2019). Since refugee children often come from trauma backgrounds, they need psychological support and trauma-based educational practices (Barrett & Berger, 2021). Although the results of the studies conducted are parallel to those of the current study, the complexity of this process also reveals that the problems experienced by teachers should be evaluated in a multidimensional and comprehensive manner.

In line with the themes, it was determined that technology was used in the teaching process and language and communication process to solve the problems experienced in the education and adaptation processes of refugee children. In addition, when the benefits of technology integration were examined, it was concluded that refugee children acquire language and receive instructions more easily, are more adaptable and motivated, learn faster, and have equal opportunities. When the studies on the integration of refugee children into education are examined, it is seen that studies have been conducted on mobile applications to teach the language of the countries where refugees are settled, especially related to language barriers, and different skills such as the acquisition of literacy skills, mathematics, engineering, and vocational education skills are included in the research (Ahmad et al., 2013; Lindström et al., 2017; Drolia et al., 2022). In addition, in the integration of technology in the education of refugee children, the potential of technology in closing educational gaps, creating quality educational opportunities, and overcoming barriers related to accessibility and resources is emphasized (Taftaf & Williams, 2020). As a result of the research, it is seen that teachers prefer different contexts, methods, and tools in the educational processes of refugee children, but the use of communication tools, visuals, music, animations, games, and digital storytelling in the difficulties faced by children ensures that technology is adapted to the needs of children and comprehensive socio-cultural arrangements are made (Alain et al., 2018). Considering the developments in technology-education integration, it becomes important to use technology to meet the educational needs of refugee children by carefully planning, implementing, and evaluating educational processes. In this context, technology can be used to eliminate communication problems through the production of visual stimuli and materials and their use in the education process. Applications and software that aim to improve language skills can be developed.

It was observed that teachers demanded to work with qualified translation applications, electronic language cards, technology-based teaching tools such as smart boards and tablets, and innovative technology tools such as augmented reality and artificial intelligence in the education and adaptation processes of refugee children. More than half of the teachers stated that they made arrangements in the context of language and culture in the process of using technology with refugee children, such as extra explanation, using Arabic materials, and speaking English. Smart boards and tablets can facilitate the adaptation process of refugee children in educational environments by providing interactive and engaging ways to communicate language and cultural differences (Roxas & Fruja, 2019). In addition to language and cultural differences, digital storytelling and animations can be used as educational tools for refugee children to cope with trauma. These technologies can help children express themselves, understand their experiences, and provide a sense of belonging (Szente et al., 2006). Technology-supported arrangements for refugee children involve collaborative processes involving teachers, parents, and children. This collaboration ensures that digital tools and content are culturally sensitive and organized based on children's educational needs (Alain et al., 2018). Language applications can help improve language skills and cultural understanding by providing engaging and interactive learning experiences in addition to the learning experiences of refugee children in technology integration processes (Hong & Cai, 2023). It is also stated that there is a need for the use of technology appropriate to the developmental characteristics of refugee children and digital applications that can be used without being connected to the internet (Castaño-Muñoz et al., 2018; Lewis & Thacker, 2016). While the use of various digital tools such as tablets, smart boards, animations, games, and virtual reality in the education and adaptation processes of refugee children meet their learning needs, teachers' experiences related to these processes emphasize the potential of technology in the adaptation processes of refugee children, it also reveals the need to examine the difficulties arising from integration and language barriers.

In order to overcome the language and adaptation problems of refugee children, it may be more appropriate to plan in-class activities and family participation activities individually or in small groups, tailored to their needs. Integrating technology into this process can serve faster and more permanent learning by increasing learning motivation. For example, appropriate fictions can be prepared and presented to children through digital stories in order for children to acquire social rules and accepted behaviors in the society they are trying to adapt to. Overcoming the language barrier caused by teachers or other school personnel not speaking the same native language as the child, with artificial intelligence, and being able to work one-on-one with artificial intelligence during language acquisition processes can be an effective way to solve children's communication problems. Additionally, children's skills can be supported by using freely accessible digital games such as "Antura and Letters", which were developed to support early literacy skills. In this study, a teacher stated that she gave tasks to children and monitored their progress through an online platform. Technology can be used as an effective tool to support children in the home environment and to keep the process under the teacher's supervision.

In the experiences of the parents of refugee children regarding the use of technology in their participation in education, it was determined that most of the teachers used translation programs for communication. Apart from translation programs, it was determined that most of them used them for communication purposes. In the integration of technology in the education and participation of refugee children and the role of communication technologies, parents and teachers used various digital tools to overcome language barriers and encourage participation in the educational process. The use of translation programs and other communication tools by teachers and parents highlights the importance of technology in reducing language barriers and facilitating integration into new educational environments (Taftaf & Williams, 2020). Refugees' access to communication technology services is necessary for them to adapt to educational processes and to benefit from them for communication purposes (Leung, 2010). Consequently, the use of communication technologies by parents and teachers for communication purposes plays a critical role in the education and integration of refugee children. Educators can provide a more inclusive and effective learning environment for refugee children by making use of digital tools such as translation programs and interactive learning platforms. Providing access to these technologies and designing them in a way that meets the needs of refugee parents is very important in educational integration processes.

As a result of the research, it was determined that all of the teachers stated that the training on technology integration with refugee children was insufficient. In addition, when the results related to teachers' expectations from training on technology integration with refugee children were examined, it was determined that there are programs and applications suitable for use with refugee children, tools suitable for use with refugee children, presenting technology to refugee children, technology content approaches that can be used with refugee children, programs and applications to facilitate communication, programs, and applications to produce content and applications to be used for language education. At this point, it can be said that teachers need training on the use of digital tools in different subjects, such as facilitating communication about technology integration in classrooms with refugee children and using digital tools to produce content and language education. The integration of technology into the education of refugee children presents both opportunities and challenges for teachers and educational institutions. Although technology is a powerful tool to enhance learning, communication, and adaptation, teachers may face difficulties in effectively integrating technology into education and adaptation processes, especially in meeting the needs of refugee children.

Teachers need comprehensive training, including pedagogical strategies for using technology to support the learning and integration of refugee children. Training for teachers should include the integration of digital tools into language education, content creation, and the development of culturally sensitive materials that can assist in the integration process (Biasutti et al., 2019). The effectiveness of technology in refugee education can often be hampered by problems with access to appropriate hardware, software, and internet connectivity. Teachers also report the need for more support in identifying and using appropriate educational practices and programs that meet the needs of refugee children, as well as language training and content development tools (Rensburg & Son, 2010). Effective professional development programs are crucial for equipping teachers with the knowledge and skills necessary for technology integration. These programs should include hands-on training in the use of digital tools, the creation of inclusive and engaging content, and the application of technology in language teaching and cultural education. In addition, ongoing support and mentoring can help teachers overcome the challenges of using technology in diverse classrooms (Ertmer & Ottenbreit-Leftwich, 2010).

In conclusion, the quality integration of technology into refugee children's education requires a multifaceted approach that includes comprehensive teacher training, adequate resources, and collaborative design efforts. By addressing these needs, educators can more effectively utilize technology to support refugee children's learning, integration, and well-being.

REFERENCES

Ahmad, K. S., Armarego, J., & Sudweeks, F. (2013). Literature review on the feasibility of mobile-assisted language learning (MALL) in developing vocabulary skills among non-English speaking migrant and refugee women. In *2013 International Conference on Research and Innovation in Information Systems (ICRIIS)* (pp. 336-341). IEEE. 10.1109/ICRIIS.2013.6716732

Alain, G., Coughlan, T., Adams, A., & Yanacopulos, H. (2018). *A Process for Co-Designing Educational Technology Systems for Refugee Children*. Science Open. .10.14236/ewic/HCI2018.162

Albu, D. (2019). *UNHCR Global trends report: forced displacement in 2018*. Drepturile Omului, 114. https://www.unhcr.org/statistics/unhcrstats/5d08d7ee7/unhcr-global-trends-2018.html

Aman, A., & Shiratuddin, N. (2020). Virtual reality and augmented reality create fair education opportunities for refugee children in camps. *IACSIT International Journal of Engineering and Technology*, 9(3), 665. 10.14419/ijet.v9i3.31003

Amoako, I. (2023). Global migration crisis: Challenges and opportunities for migrants and refugees. *Journal of the Neurological Sciences*, 455, 455. 10.1016/j.jns.2023.122664

Barrett, N., & Berger, E. (2021). Teachers' experiences and recommendations to support refugee students exposed to trauma. *Social Psychology of Education*, 24(5), 1259–1280. 10.1007/s11218-021-09657-4

Baysar, Z., Çavuşoğlu, İ. E., & Günaydın, E. (2023). Sürdürülebilir kalkınma amaçları ve göç. *Türkiye İnsan Hakları Ve Eşitlik Kurumu Akademik Dergisi*, 6(10), 43–84. 10.59162/tihek.1217860

Biasutti, M., Concina, E., & Frate, S. (2019). Working in the classroom with migrant and refugee students: The practices and needs of Italian primary and middle school teachers. *Pedagogy, Culture & Society*, 28(1), 113–129. 10.1080/14681366.2019.1611626

Block, K., Cross, S., Riggs, E., & Gibbs, L. (2014). Supporting schools to create an inclusive environment for refugee students. *International Journal of Inclusive Education*, 18(12), 1337–1355. 10.1080/13603116.2014.899636

Buchmüller, T., Lembcke, H., Ialuna, F., Busch, J., & Leyendecker, B. (2020). Mental Health Needs of Refugee Children in Specialized Early Education and Care Programs in Germany. *Journal of Immigrant and Minority Health*, 22(1), 22–33. 10.1007/s10903-019-00896-431089910

Busch, J., Bihler, L. M., Lembcke, H., Buchmüller, T., Diers, K., & Leyendecker, B. (2018). Challenges and solutions perceived by educators in an early childcare program for refugee children. *Frontiers in Psychology*, 9, 378326. 10.3389/fpsyg.2018.0162130237777

Busch, J., Buchmüller, T., & Leyendecker, B. (2023). Implementation and quality of an early childhood education program for newly arrived refugee children in Germany: An observational study. *International Journal of Child Care and Education Policy*, 17(1), 3. 10.1186/s40723-023-00105-8

Busch, J., Cabrera, N., Ialuna, F., Buchmüller, T., & Leyendecker, B. (2022). Refugee Children's Early Development during Attendance of Specialized Preschool Programs and Transition into First Grade in Germany. *Early Education and Development*, 33(8), 1304–1325. 10.1080/10409289.2021.1970427

Busch, J., & Leyendecker, B. (2019). Socialization and Development of Refugee Children: Chances of Childcare. In Tulviste, T., Best, D., & Gibbons, J. (Eds.), *Children's Social Worlds in Cultural Context*. Springer. 10.1007/978-3-030-27033-9_14

Castaño-Muñoz, J., Colucci, E., & Smidt, H. (2018). Free digital learning for inclusion of migrants and refugees in Europe: A qualitative analysis of three types of learning purposes. *International Review of Research in Open and Distance Learning*, 19(2). 10.19173/irrodl.v19i2.3382

Cerna, L. (2019). *Refugee education: Integration models and practices in OECD countries*. OECD Education (Working Papers, 203), OECD Publishing.

Drolia, M., Papadakis, S., Sifaki, E., & Kalogiannakis, M. (2022). Mobile learning applications for refugees: A systematic literature review. *Education Sciences*, 12(2), 96. 10.3390/educsci12020096

Erdemir, E. (2022). Summer Preschools for Syrian Refugee and Host Community Children in Turkey: A Model of Contextually Sensitive Early Intervention. *Early Education and Development*, 33(5), 912–938. 10.1080/10409289.2021.1961426

Ergün, S., & Ulukuş, G. (2022). Göç ve mülteci olgusu: Kavramsal çerçeve. *International Journal of Disciplines in Economics & Administrative Sciences Studies*, 6(24), 1063–1074.

Ertmer, P., & Ottenbreit-Leftwich, A. (2010). Teacher Technology Change. *Journal of Research on Technology in Education*, 42(3), 255–284. 10.1080/15391523.2010.10782551

Euronews. (2020). *"Dünyada en fazla mülteciye ev sahipliği yapan ülke Türkiye, ilk 10'da Avrupa'dan sadece Almanya var"*. Euronews. https://tr.euronews.com/2020/02/28/dunyada-en-fazla-multeciye-ev-sahipligi-yapan-ulke-turkiye-ilk-10-da-avrupa-sadece-almanya

Fellmeth, G., Rose-Clarke, K., Zhao, C., Busert, L. K., Zheng, Y., Massazza, A., Sonmez, H., Eder, B., Blewitt, A., Lertgrai, W., Orcutt, M., Ricci, K., Mohamed-Ahmed, O., Burns, R., Knipe, D., Hargreaves, S., Hesketh, T., Opondo, C., & Devakumar, D. (2018). Health impacts of parental migration on left-behind children and adolescents: A systematic review and meta-analysis. *Lancet*, 392(10164), 2567–2582. 10.1016/S0140-6736(18)32558-330528471

Gall, M. D., Gall, J. P., & Borg, W. R. (2007). *Educational research: An introduction*. Allyn-Bacon.

Glesne, C. (2015). *Nitel araştırmaya giriş* (A. Ersoy & P. Yalçınoğlu, Çev. Ed.). Ankara: Anı Yayıncılık.

Güçer, M., Karaca, S., & Dinçer, O. B. (2013). *Sınırlar arasında yaşam savaşı Suriyeli mülteciler alan çalışması.* International Strategic Research Organization (USAK). https://ecec-care.org/fileadmin/careproject/Publications/reports/new_version_CARE_WP4_D4_1_Review_on_the_effects_of_ECEC.pdf https://www.un.org/development/desa/dspd/wp-content/uploads/sites/22/2020/02/World-Social-Report-2020-Chapter-5.pdf

Hong, H., & Cai, Q. (2023). Evidence-Based Educational Practices for Working With Refugee Children. *Journal of Research in Childhood Education*, 37(3), 405–422. 10.1080/02568543.2023.2211127

Hurley, J. J., Medici, A., Stewart, E., & Cohen, Z. (2011). Supporting Preschoolers and Their Families who are Recently Resettled Refugees. *Multicultural Perspectives*, 13(3), 160–166. 10.1080/15210960.2011.594400

Iakimova, G., Koval-Saifi, N., Wittmann, M., & Guardiola, E. (2022). A game to promote literacy and psychosocial well-being among syrian refugee children. 10.31219/osf.io/7u946

Kaplan, I., Stolk, Y., Valibhoy, M., Tucker, A., & Baker, J. (2016). Cognitive assessment of refugee children: Effects of trauma and new language acquisition. *Transcultural Psychiatry*, 53(1), 81–109. 10.1177/1363461515612933265638 91

Kardeş, S., & Akman, B. (2018). Suriyeli Mültecilerin Eğitimine Yönelik Öğretmen Görüşleri. *Ilkogretim Online, 17*(3).

Kendrick, M., Early, M., Michalovich, A., & Mangat, M. (2022). Digital storytelling with youth from refugee backgrounds: Possibilities for language and digital literacy learning. *TESOL Quarterly*, 56(3), 961–984. 10.1002/tesq.3146

Krakouer, J., Mitchell, P., Trevitt, J., Kochanoff, A., & Children, S. (2017). *Early years transitions : Supporting children and families at risk of experiencing vulnerability : Rapid literature review.* State of Victoria: Department of Education and Training. http://research.acer.edu.au/cgi/viewcontent.cgi?article=1015&context=early_childhood_misc

Leung, L. (2010). Telecommunications across borders: Refugees' technology use during displacement. *Telecommunications Journal of Australia*, 60(4), 58.1–58.13. 10.2104/tja10058

Lewis, K., & Thacker, S. (2016). ICT and the Education of Refugees: A Stocktaking of Innovative Approaches in the MENA Region. World Bank. 10.1596/26522

Lindström, N. B., Hashemi, S. S., Bartram, L., & Bradley, L. (2017). Mobile resources for integration: how availability meets the needs of newly arrived Arabic-speaking migrants in Sweden. *CALL in a climate of change: adapting to turbulent global conditions–short papers from EUROCALL*, 40-45.

Lonn, M. R., & Dantzler, J. Z. (2017). A Practical Approach to Counseling Refugees: Applying Maslow's Hierarchy of Needs. *Journal of Counselor Practice*, 8(2).

Merriam, S. B. (2013). *Nitel araştırma desen ve uygulama için bir rehber (S. Turan, Çev.).* Nobel Akademik Yayıncılık.

Moinolnolki, N., & Han, M. (2017). No Child Left Behind: What About Refugees? *Childhood Education*, 93(1), 1, 3–9. 10.1080/00094056.2017.1275231

Montgomery, M. A., Jackson, C. T., & Kelvin, E. A. (2014). Premigration harm and depression: Findings from the New Immigrant Survey, 2003. *Journal of Immigrant and Minority Health*, 16(5), 773–780. 10.1007/s10903-013-9810-z23504372

Murray, J. S. (2019). War and conflict: Addressing the psychosocial needs of child refugees. *Journal of Early Childhood Teacher Education*, 40(1), 3–18. 10.1080/10901027.2019.1569184

Nazzal, K. H., Forghany, M., Charis Geevarughese, M., Mahmoodi, V., & Wong, J. (2014). An innovative community-oriented approach to prevention and early intervention with refugees in the United States. *Psychological Services*, 11(4), 477–485. 10.1037/a003796425384000

Patton, M. Q. (2014). Nitel mülakat yapma. (M. Çakır & S. İrez, Çev.). M. Bütün & S. B. Demir (Çev. Ed.). *Nitel araştırma ve değerlendirme yöntemleri içinde* (s. 339-422). Ankara: Pegem Akademi.

Rensburg, H., & Son, J. (2010). Improving English Language and Computer Literacy Skills in an Adult Refugee Program. *International Journal of Pedagogies and Learning*, 6(1), 69–81. 10.5172/ijpl.6.1.69

Rice, M., & Cun, A. (2023). Leveraging digital literacies to support refugee youth and families' success in online learning: A theoretical perspective using a socio-ecological approach. *Online Learning : the Official Journal of the Online Learning Consortium*, 27(3). 10.24059/olj.v27i3.3628

Roxas, K., & Fruja, R. (2019). *Teacher Education and Refugee Students*. Oxford Research Encyclopedia of Education., 10.1093/acrefore/9780190264093.013.285

Samania, S. (2011). Family process and content model: A contextual model for family studies. *Procedia: Social and Behavioral Sciences*, 30, 2285–2292. 10.1016/j.sbspro.2011.10.446

Sirin, S. R., & Rogers-Sirin, L. (2015). *The Educational and Mental Health Needs of Syrian Refugee Children*. Research Gate. https://www.researchgate.net/profile/Selcuk_Sirin/publication/287998909_The_Educational_and_Mental_Health_Needs_of_Syrian_Refugee_Children/links/567ccd6c08ae19758384e4bf.pdf

Stevens, K. E., Siraj, I., & Kong, K. (2023). A critical review of the research evidence on early childhood education and care in refugee contexts in low- and middle-income countries. *International Journal of Child Care and Education Policy*, 17(1), 7. 10.1186/s40723-023-00109-4

Stolk, Y., Kaplan, I., & Szwarc, J. (2023). Majority language acquisition by children of refugee background: A review. *International Journal of Inclusive Education*, 1–24. 10.1080/13603116.2023.2210593

Szente, J., Hoot, J., & Taylor, D. (2006). Responding to the Special Needs of Refugee Children: Practical Ideas for Teachers. *Early Childhood Education Journal*, 34(1), 15–20. 10.1007/s10643-006-0082-2

Taftaf, R., & Williams, C. (2020). Supporting Refugee Distance Education: A Review of the Literature. *American Journal of Distance Education*, 34(1), 18–5. 10.1080/08923647.2020.1691411

Tunç, A. (2015). Mülteci davranışı ve toplumsal etkileri: Türkiye'deki Suriyelilere ilişkin bir değerlendirme. *Tesam akademi dergisi, 2*(2), 29-63.

Türkiye Cumhuriyeti İçişleri Bakanlığı Göç İdaresi Başkanlığı. (2024) https://www.goc.gov.tr/gecici-koruma5638

UNESCO. (2022). *Leveraging innovative technology in literacy and education programmes for refugees, migrants and internally displaced persons*. UNESCO. https://eric.ed.gov/?id=ED627597 Erişim 23.03

UNICEF. (2018). *Türkiye'de çocukların eğitim yoluyla korunması*. UNICEF. https://www.unicef.org/turkiye/hikayeler/t%C3%BCrkiyede-%C3%A7ocuklar%C4%B1n-e%C4%9Fitim-yoluyla-korunmas%C4%B1

Votruba-Drzal, E., Coley, R. L., Collins, M., & Miller, P. (2015). Center-based preschool and school readiness skills of children from immigrant families. *Early Education and Development*, 26(4), 549–573. 10.1080/10409289.2015.1000220

Wu, K. (2022). An exploration of the educational experiences of refugee children. *International Journal of Education and Humanities*, 5(2), 304–307. 10.54097/ijeh.v5i2.2194

Yurdakul, A., & Tok, T. N. (2018). Öğretmen Gözüyle Göçmen/Mülteci Öğrenci. *Adnan Menderes Üniversitesi Eğitim Fakültesi Eğitim Bilimleri Dergisi*, 9(2), 46–58.

Chapter 7
Leveling the Language Field:
A Qualitative Study of the Impact of AI on Learning English as a Foreign Language in Higher Education

Silvia María Bravo Palomares
University of Castilla-La Mancha, Spain

ABSTRACT

Nowadays, artificial intelligence (AI) has become a prevalent topic across the globe, particularly in academic institutions, as it has the potential to transform the teaching and learning process. Nonetheless, the emergence of AI also presents challenges that need to be addressed. This study delves into the role of AI in higher education, specifically in English as a foreign language (EFL) classrooms. The aim is to explore how AI tools affect learning experiences in this context. To that end, the research follows a qualitative approach, including semi-structured interviews and a questionnaire with students and teachers to gain insights into the influence of AI in EFL settings. Through a thematic analysis, the implications of AI in higher education were assessed. It is anticipated that the findings will provide new avenues for future research, shedding light on how the integration of AI could help level the language playing field.

DOI: 10.4018/979-8-3693-2591-9.ch007

INTRODUCTION

Artificial intelligence (AI) has gained traction in different societal contexts and as such, it offers the potential to revolutionize current methods of teaching and learning. Its prevalence in all aspects of human life has been steadily increasing, and recent years have witnessed a rise in AI's role in education (Hwang et al., 2020). In higher education, AI has gained rapid popularity over the last years, due to its potential to cater to different types of learners, deliver personalized feedback and enhance academic success (Verdú et al., 2017). However, despite the considerable interest in AI within higher education (Crompton & Burke, 2022), there is still a knowledge gap regarding its role and affordances in educational settings. In fact, as noted by Jiang (2022), in spite of studies on AI in English as Foreign Language (EFL) contexts, longitudinal research is needed to better understand the efficacy of AI. Along similar lines, teachers' perspectives ought to be explored as well to identify potential obstacles posed by AI. Other scholars have also highlighted that there is a lack of empirical studies on AI chatbots in EFL contexts, leaving unanswered questions about their implementation (Kim et al., 2019).

Thus, as AI technologies are integrated into EFL classrooms, it is of great importance to examine the pedagogical implications associated with their use. Along these lines, the concerns raised about their impact on teachers' roles, students' performance and the successful implementation of AI have become important issues in education that ought to be addressed as well. As Borenstein and Howard (2021) claim, it is crucial to prioritize the training of future members of the AI community and other relevant stakeholders so that they can critically consider how AI might affect people's lives, while also fulfilling their responsibility to maximize its benefits and minimize any adverse effects.

On this basis, this study aims to examine how AI tools can aid in the development of language skills, delving into the different ways in which they can shape language education and potentially enhance it. To achieve this, it draws on the data from semi-structured interviews and questionnaires among EFL teachers and students in undergraduate education, examining their perceptions of AI integration in their daily lives and the classroom. By addressing both students' and teachers' perspectives, higher education institutions can tap into the potential benefits of AI and improve teaching and learning outcomes. Therefore, this book chapter examines the current state, potential challenges and prospects of using AI in EFL settings for both teachers and students, suggesting areas of improvement and shedding light on how such tools can level the language playing field.

LITERATURE REVIEW

Understanding Artificial Intelligence

The term "AI" was first coined by John McCarthy, who is regarded as the founding figure of AI, in 1955. Since then, AI has grown into a field within computer science and has benefitted from contributions from biology, psychology, anthropology and linguistics. As a result, there are now multiple interpretations of what AI entails and, as posited by Alshumaimeri and Alshememry (2024), there is currently no unanimous agreement on a universal definition of AI, and even present-day definitions are prone to varying. This is partly due to the interdisciplinary nature of AI research and because of the continuous evolution of what constitutes AI. In the early stages of AI, it was possible to assess students' grammar (Bailin, 1987), provide feedback and process students' linguistic input (Nagata, 1996). Early research primarily focused on grammar; however, recent advancements in computer technologies demonstrate that AI has much more to offer (Sumakul et al., 2022), since using AI in language classrooms has been shown to benefit learners by facilitating meaningful communication and improving speaking and reading comprehension (Bailey et al., 2021).

AI's Educational Potential

In recent years, the application of AI in education and the importance of teaching AI, known as AI literacy, have garnered increased attention and become prominent topics in policy discussions. Within the field of education, AI-powered technologies offer unparalleled benefits, particularly in gathering and analyzing large amounts of data on students' academic progress (Pokrivcakova, 2019). This data is then used to tailor educational content and create personalized learning paths, allowing students to learn at their own pace. A further benefit of these technologies is also their ability to support learning by providing feedback and round-the-clock accessibility (Alshumaimeri & Alshememry, 2024), which assists students in identifying and correcting mistakes, and allows teachers to provide timely support. Moreover, teaching comprises a range of tasks, including lectures, exercises, examinations and tutoring. However, such tasks can be automated through AI technologies (Holmes & Tuomi, 2022), since one of their most promising prospects in education lies in tailored learning experiences. This approach ensures that students receive individualized attention and that teaching methods are adjusted to their specific needs.

The Role of AI in EFL Settings

Notwithstanding the fact that the integration of AI in education has gained momentum and has been studied in the last few decades, it is important to explore how AI technologies can support students and teachers. This is especially relevant in language learning, particularly in EFL, as students face unique challenges like language barriers, diverse educational backgrounds and cultural intricacies that can impact their learning outcomes. In this context, recent advancements in AI technology have disrupted the traditional roles of teachers (Sumakul et al., 2022). In fact, AI tools have been found to improve language acquisition outcomes by tailoring learning experiences to students, increasing engagement, as well as enhancing vocabulary and grammar (Hwang et al., 2012).

In a recent study conducted by Divekar et al. (2022), foreign language learning was combined with several AI tools, as well as with extended reality, so that students could engage in multimodal and collaborative interactions. The findings from their research showed that AI facilitated role-playing conversations in the target language (L2). In spite of this, some skepticism has been expressed regarding the usefulness of AI in language education. For instance, Wilson et al. (2021) have pointed out that the language produced by AI appears unnatural and decontextualized. Lastly, it is important to note that the scope of AI extends beyond EFL settings and encompasses different fields, including e-learning (Tang et al., 2021), mathematics (Hwang & Tu, 2021), medical education (Grunhut et al., 2022) and special education (Drigas & Ioannidou, 2012), among many others.

Controversies and Debates About AI in Education

Despite the potential of AI tools, not everyone views them favorably due to skepticism about their ability to encroach upon traditionally human domains. In the field of EFL, students may have varying perceptions of AI integration into their learning environments, ranging from feeling empowered to doubtful (DiGiacomo et al., 2023). With the rise of advanced technologies and AI, traditional teaching models may soon become obsolete, leading to an increased reliance on AI for learning and interaction. However, AI-powered technologies also pose challenges, including ethical issues concerning data privacy and the potential for exacerbating inequalities (Marzuki et al., 2023). Since the implementation of AI in education often entails gathering and scrutinizing substantial volumes of student data, this gives rise to concerns about the possible exposure of sensitive student information. Additionally, it is worth noting that not all students have equal access to cutting-edge technology and AI resources (Darwin et al., 2024), which can contribute to widening educational inequalities.

With this knowledge, a prominent fear regarding AI is its potential to alter and replace traditional roles, including those of teachers. Some argue that teachers will no longer be the primary sources of knowledge and will instead become guides and mentors, focused on facilitating learning, promoting critical thinking and encouraging independent research (Vairaperumal, 2023). As a response, those in the AI community who promote its use often argue that their goal is to assist and improve upon these roles, rather than replace them (Pinkwart, 2016). Despite the impact of AI on education, there is still a lack of consensus on its endorsement. The limited research available on how humans learn and benefit from being taught by AI has contributed to this issue, with some teachers admitting to having minimal or no knowledge of these technologies (Kim & Kim, 2017).

Ethical Considerations of AI Tools

One of the key issues with AI systems is the ethical challenges they pose. In fact, as Hrastinski et al. (2019) contend, algorithms can perpetuate the beliefs of their creators, who may occupy positions of influence. This leads to the development of data sets that reflect society's historical and systemic prejudices, resulting in algorithmic bias. This bias is largely due to the power dynamics and prejudices embedded in machine-learning models on AI platforms (Krutka et al., 2019).

In K-12 education, the ethical implications of AI implementation are of great importance, particularly regarding privacy concerns that impact both students and teachers (Regan & Jesse, 2019). To address this issue, AI systems request users' consent to access personal data. However, many individuals may give consent without fully understanding the extent of the information they are disclosing (Akgun & Greenhow, 2022). Scholars have also raised ethical questions about compelling students and parents to use AI as part of their education, even if they agree to relinquish privacy (Waller & Waller, 2020), highlighting a lack of choice for those in public school-mandated systems.

A further ethical issue stemming from the integration of AI in education is the implementation of surveillance and tracking systems, which collect information on the behaviors and preferences of students (Akgun & Greenhow, 2022). This does not only enable AI to monitor activities but also predict future preferences and actions (Regan & Jesse, 2019). With such capabilities, AI can anticipate students' academic performance and learning patterns. While some may view this as part of a teacher's duty or an educational strategy, others might consider it intrusive surveillance that compromises privacy.

Long-Term Impacts of AI

The potential impact of AI is vast and far-reaching, as it is a versatile technology with numerous applications that can stimulate complementary innovations and drive significant technical advancements (Clarke & Whittlestone, 2022). While human instructors will always be essential to effective teaching, interactive machine tutors are now being customized for students. If effectively integrated, AI is expected to significantly expand within both classroom settings and homes over the next fifteen years in an average North American city (Stone et al., 2022).

Furthermore, the concept of learner autonomy (LA), which encompasses the ability of learners to take charge of their learning process (Fenner & Newby, 2000), is a crucial aspect to consider when examining AI. Integrating LA in classroom settings has proven to be a challenge, as it requires approaches that encourage self-directed exploration and informed decision-making (Tahir & Tahir, 2023). In this regard, AI can improve self-regulation and reduce learning anxiety (Hsu et al., 2023). This is achieved by providing flexible instructions, smart tutoring systems and automated content generation (Hwang et al., 2020).

Additionally, trust and emotional discomfort play a key role in predicting changes in students' behavior toward AI, as they are linked to increased usage (Polyportis, 2020). These findings align with existing literature on technology acceptance that stresses the importance of user trust in the reliability and effectiveness of technology (Gefen et al., 2003), supporting the notion that enhanced trust is linked to positive changes in students' use of AI. Moreover, there is a potential for technology to de-skill students. As Rafner et al. (2021) argue, AI can result in a reduction of skills that can impact individuals, organizations and society. Deskilling poses a risk with AI, as it could diminish students' proficiency in academic skills, while also fostering dependency on technology for learning (Bali et al., 2024).

RESEARCH QUESTIONS

The research questions that this study attempts to address are the following:

Which types of AI tools are relevant in EFL settings?
How can AI tools be used more effectively and with academic integrity?
How do AI tools contribute to the development of English language skills?
What are the perceptions of teachers and students towards the role of AI in education?
Which challenges associated with AI in language education do teachers identify, and how do they impact the teaching and learning process?

To what extent does the use of AI tools contribute to leveraging existing inequalities among students' language proficiency levels?

OBJECTIVES

The research aims to achieve the following objectives:

To explore the impact of AI on English language proficiency.
To shed light on the perspectives of teachers and students on the integration of AI in EFL settings.
To clarify the advantages and concerns associated with AI in higher education.
To identify how AI can enhance student outcomes in this context.

METHODOLOGY

Research Design

The impact of AI tools in higher education was investigated using semi-structured interviews as a qualitative research method. This approach allows for greater focus on important issues (Rapley, 2001) and flexibility in seeking further details based on the participant's responses. The research tool was developed considering the objectives and literature review on AI in undergraduate education, which helped identify gaps and areas of interest. Interviews included main theme questions to ease into primary topics and follow-up questions to maintain focus. Initial questions focused on participants' knowledge of AI tools and their use in teaching and learning, while later questions addressed how these tools could support learning experiences in EFL settings and bridge proficiency gaps among students. Students were interviewed about their use of AI tools for learning English and how it supports their education. They discussed their preferred AI tools, and methods to improve language skills, and weighed the advantages and disadvantages of AI-powered technologies. Meanwhile, teachers' interviews centered on when and why they use AI tools in the classroom, and the pros and cons of using such tools in undergraduate education.

Qualitative data from interviews was complemented by questionnaires administered to teachers and students. When developing such questionnaires, questions were tailored to the research objectives and informed by existing literature. The questionnaire included close-ended questions on factors like age, attendance at a bilingual high school, English level or gender for students; and age, gender, years of teaching experience and English level for teachers. A Likert scale with options ranging from strongly agree to strongly disagree was used for responses.

Research Tools

Thus, the study relies on a qualitative approach, including semi-structured interviews with teachers and students, to understand the impact of AI on language education in higher education. Questionnaires were also used to supplement the insights gathered from the interviews. The rationale for combining both tools is that they serve to gather comprehensive data (Brookhart & Durkin, 2003), which subsequently underwent thematic analysis to identify common patterns and recurring themes.

Context and Participants

This research is conducted in first-year English classrooms as part of an Education degree program at a university in Central Spain, where English language learning is mandatory for all first-year students. Students have varying levels of English proficiency, so effective strategies are necessary to ensure that all learners benefit from the learning experience. As students have different levels of prior exposure and knowledge of English, their experiences at the tertiary level can provide valuable insights into how AI can help bridge the gap in their English language skills. As can be seen in Figure 1, more female students than male students participated in this research.

Figure 1. Gender variables within the chosen group

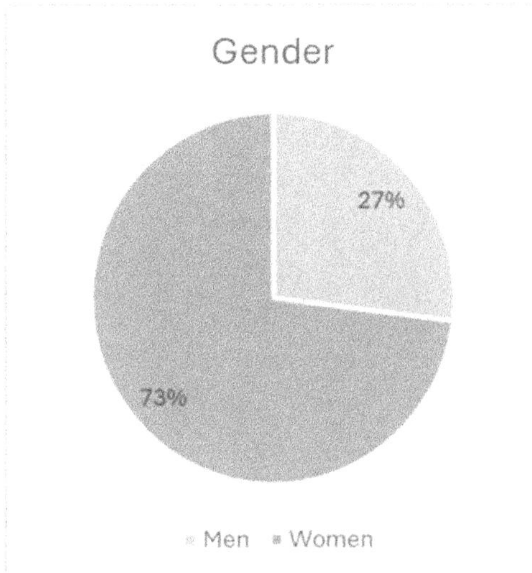

According to Figure 2, more than half of students attended bilingual education when they were in high school. However, 43% of students did not receive this type of education:

Figure 2. Prior attendance to bilingual education in high school

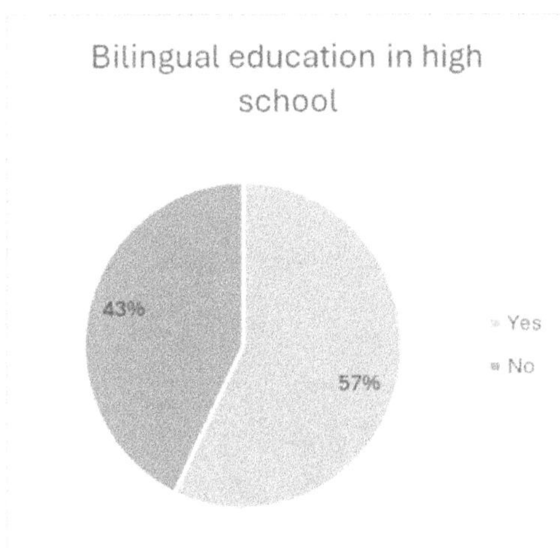

Students feel the need to improve listening, speaking and writing skills. Reading did not receive any ratings, showing that students are confident in this area:

Figure 3. Skills that students need to improve

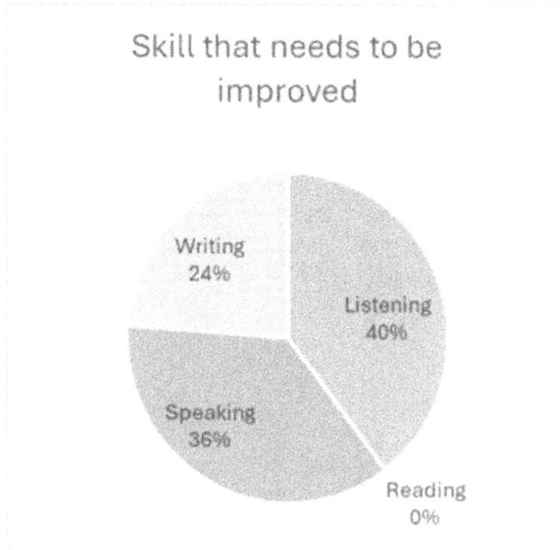

In the subject under examination, students are expected to achieve a B1 level according to the Common European Framework of Reference for Languages. However, there are disparities in English proficiency levels among students. Some have A2 proficiency while others have higher mastery such as B1, B2, and even C1 and C2. This presents a challenge for teachers who need to accommodate diverse learners within the same classroom.

Figure 4. Students' English proficiency level

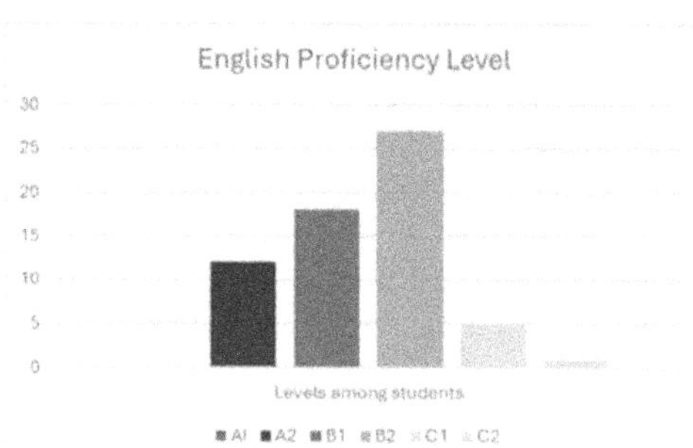

As Figure 5 illustrates, the most-used resources for learning English include songs, movies, TV series, translation tools and textbooks, while AI tools are used to a lesser extent:

Figure 5. Most used resources to learn English

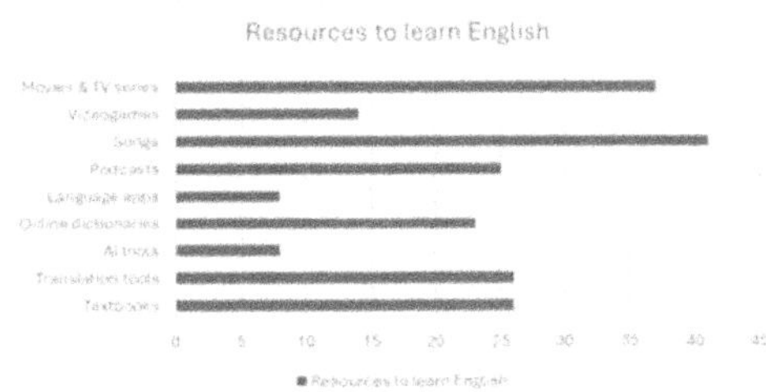

Thus, as exemplified by Figure 6, students use AI tools selectively to support the learning experience. For example, Jenni.AI is frequently used for paraphrasing and brainstorming (S1. "It allows me to progress with my work and achieve better results"), while Bardo helps with writer's block by generating ideas for essays (S29. "To help me brainstorm ideas on a topic").

Figure 6. Frequency of use of AI tools

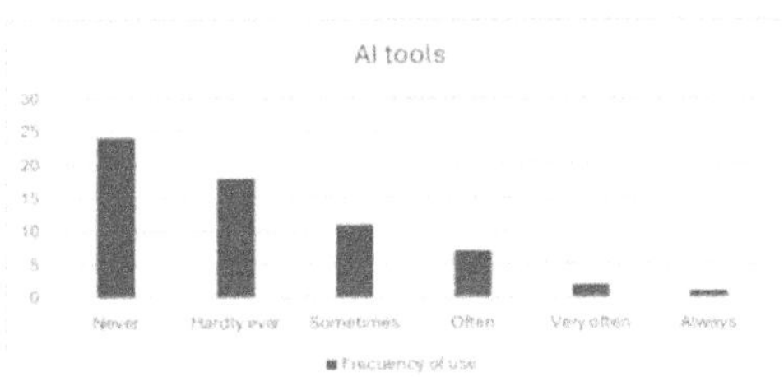

The research study also involves teachers at the university level, who play an integral role in providing a first-hand account of AI tools in their teaching practices and classroom settings. A selection process was undertaken to identify 13 teachers who were willing to participate and had the necessary practical experience, accessibility and expertise in EFL subjects. The teachers' demographic information is summarized in the next table:

Table 1. Demographic information of teachers

Demographic information					
Respondent	**Gender**	**Age**	**English level**	**L2 Languages known**	**Teaching experience (years)**
T1	F	44	C2	4	20
T2	M	32	C2	3	3
T3	M	42	C1	4	15
T4	M	37	C1	2	8
T5	M	29	B2	>4	1
T6	F	32	B2	4	14
T7	F	30	C1	2	2
T8	M	34	C1	2	3
T9	F	34	C2	3	10
T10	F	26	C2	2	1
T11	F	57	C2	4	32
T12	F	40	B1	3	4
T13	M	56	B2	3	32

To maintain confidentiality, participants were designated as "S1", "S2", "S3", etc., and "T1", "T2" and "T3", etc., for students and teachers, respectively. The recruitment process involved contacting potential participants and informing them about the study's purpose, data collection methods, their roles and their rights, including the option to withdraw without consequences.

FINDINGS

Students' Perspectives Toward the Impact of AI

The research findings on students' attitudes toward the impact of AI on EFL revealed the next key sub-themes: the use of AI tools for feedback and idea generation, and the potential to enhance language proficiency in writing, vocabulary and grammar. Students were given the option to respond in Spanish for their ease and comfort, which proved beneficial for those with limited English proficiency. For this paper, their responses have been translated into English.

AI's Role in Bridging Language Proficiency

Several perspectives were shared regarding the language skills necessary for students to pass the subject, including listening, speaking, reading and writing. S1, for instance, suggested that AI tools can be beneficial for improving English skills if they are used responsibly:

S1. "When used ethically and responsibly, and not for copying and pasting, I believe AI can help in learning English and other subjects."

This is in line with findings from other research studies, which demonstrated the potential of AI for enhancing speaking skills among learners (Rusmiyanto et al., 2023) and their linguistic proficiency (Qiao & Zhao, 2023). However, S5 and S10 do not believe that AI tools could improve English proficiency, noting that they are only useful for answering questions and do not always provide accurate answers. S10, for instance, argues that reading and listening to audio or videos are better options for enhancing English proficiency:

S5. "I don't really think they help improve English proficiency. They can be helpful in clearing up some doubts, but they aren't always accurate."

S10. "I don't think they help improve English proficiency. There are better options, like reading, watching videos, or listening to audios."

Regarding the statement made by S10, it is worth noting that research has shown a strong correlation between learners' motivation and the use of video materials in EFL classrooms. The use of authentic videos in English lessons enhances learners' engagement and understanding, as this medium offers a more interesting, attractive and effective experience compared to traditional book-based learning resources (Heffernan, 2005). When questioned about the usefulness of AI tools for practising grammar and vocabulary, several students noted that such tools can boost their confidence for exams by assisting with exercise checking and reinforcing classroom learning. Additionally, AI tools can introduce students to advanced and specific grammatical structures and vocabulary that may not have been covered in class:

S35. "To generate grammar exercises to practice before an exam."

S20. "You can learn a lot of advanced vocabulary, or words that you didn't know before."

Some students have found that AI tools can be useful for improving their language skills beyond just grammar and vocabulary. Specifically, they have reported benefits for pronunciation and listening. This is also consistent with other research, which reported the benefits of AI applications for listening and speaking (Divekar et al., 2022).

S12. "They can help me with pronunciation or listening."

S13. "It can help me improve my pronunciation."

S59. "To strengthen my listening skills."

As for speaking, S28 said that AI tools can help in this area, as students can ask questions that they are going to eventually answer in a real speaking exam ("AI tools can help to practice speaking instead of relying on real people"). AI tools, in fact, can serve to practise speaking by answering and asking questions to students, mimicking speaking tasks and aiding learners in this regard. Building upon this premise, such results are also supported by Junaidi (2020), who demonstrated that AI had a positive effect on learners' overall speaking abilities, such as fluency, grammatical correctness, vocabulary use and pronunciation. It has also been observed that AI tools serve a crucial role in providing valuable information for brainstorming, discovering new concepts and information in EFL and other subjects, facilitating learning and even improving creativity, as S38 and S43 claim. This is also in accordance with Oktradiksa et al. (2021), who concluded that the use of AI can enhance the creative skills needed to tackle opportunities and challenges today.

S38. "They can help correct superficial grammatical errors or give ideas to be more creative."

S43. "They make it easy to search for information or words that you can't find on your own."

Therefore, it can be contended that AI tools serve as a language "assistant" for most students, rather than a teacher. Notably, S7 highlighted that those who lack the financial means to hire a private tutor or attend English lessons outside of university could benefit from using AI:

S7. "AI could be a good alternative when you don't have enough money to pay for a private tutor."

Lastly, while AI tools can assist learners, S28 has emphasized that they cannot entirely replace a real teacher. Hence, this student perceives emotions as an essential element of the learning experience, which AI-powered technologies currently lack:

S28. "Artificial intelligence can help you with almost any problem you have, but having a real person to understand you and show emotions is always better."

AI Under Scrutiny: Perceived Advantages and Disadvantages

Upon examining students' responses, various benefits and drawbacks were found regarding the use of AI tools in the EFL classroom. The next table presents key advantages of AI tools, including mistake checking, self-correction, timesaving, their role as virtual assistants and their immediate response accessibility for student queries.

Table 2. Advantages of using AI tools within the EFL classroom

Main advantages		
Check mistakes	**S1**	**It can help save time, correct mistakes and have a virtual assistant.**
	S6	**You can correct your mistakes.**
Answer questions	S5	At a certain point in time, they can answer your questions.
Immediate answers	S59	They are available 24/7 and respond instantly to your queries.
	S60	They swiftly provide meanings and help in language learning.
Improvement of language skills	S13	You can improve your pronunciation and listening skills.
	S20	You can learn many new vocabulary words, grammar and know how to use them for writing tasks.
Brainstorm ideas	S27	It helps you find ideas on how to study/practice English.
Knowledge acquisition	S14	The acquisition of new concepts is an advantage.
	S4	They help us find much more elaborate information.

As shown below, students are aware of the limitations of AI, including concerns about lack of emotional support and the potential for overreliance on AI tools. There is also a risk of plagiarism and academic fraud associated with heavy reliance on AI.

Table 3. Disadvantages of using AI tools within the EFL classroom

Main disadvantages		
Lack of accuracy	**S4**	**They can make some mistakes.**
	S6	**It can have flaws.**
Lack of emotional connection	S15	There isn't someone physically present to help you.
	S59	There is no interaction with humans, so there is a limitation in interaction and context.
Overreliance	S22	You become reliant because you think it can do everything for you.
	S57	We might get used to it and not know how to do the activities on our own.
Plagiarism and academic fraud	S1	Plagiarism, academic fraud, people no longer trying because everything is given to them.

continued on following page

Table 3. Continued

Main disadvantages		
Lack of accuracy	**S4**	**They can make some mistakes.**
	S6	**It can have flaws.**
Lack of critical thinking skills and knowledge	S20	You don't always think; rather, everything is given to you.
	S60	You don't learn with them because they do things for you.

Critical Perspectives Towards its Use in EFL and Across the Board

Students were asked if teachers should allow the use of AI in EFL classrooms, as well as in other subjects. Some students agreed that it would be helpful, but the implementation of control measures and a responsible attitude would be needed to ensure that everyone can fully benefit from these tools. Furthermore, it was highlighted that AI can have positive implications for education and students' lives:

S1. "I think AI should be allowed in all subjects, but we must use it responsibly."

S19. "Teachers should allow it because they need to update and adapt to new technologies."

S20. "I believe so. It's like having a virtual teacher."

S46. "Technology advances as generations change, and prohibiting the use of AI when it's widely used outside of school seems like a mistake."

Other students remarked that AI tools can be used selectively in the teaching and learning process, rather than frequently. Therefore, to effectively use and incorporate AI in the classroom, it must serve an educational purpose. It is important for both teachers and students to be aware that AI may still err, and they need to have a critical mindset when using it:

S3. "I believe that it could be used for a specific activity, but I don't recommend using it frequently."

S11. "It should be allowed because it helps teachers, but with the awareness of possible mistakes it may make."

Some learners, however, argue that AI tools should be banned from classrooms due to concerns about control and the potential loss of human connections. Maintaining strong relationships between students and teachers, especially in EFL settings, is seen as crucial. While AI may have its benefits for certain educational tasks, human teachers are essential for their emotional intelligence and creativity (Manyika et al. 2017).

S14. "I think it would be very difficult to control how AI is used, so I'm not in favor of it."

S28. "Human relationships between students and teachers will be lost. In subjects like English, where communication is key, this is very important."

Teachers' Perspectives Toward the Impact of AI

Teachers' feedback on the effects of AI in EFL settings indicates promising potential for enhancing teaching and learning, a lack of teacher training and awareness of AI technologies, the importance of critically evaluating their implementation and observed benefits and drawbacks of AI integration.

Use of AI Tools to Improve the Teaching and Learning Process

T4 mentioned that AI tools could enhance the learning process by clarifying specific questions and improving efficiency, particularly in phonetics. This aligns with Senowarsito and Ardini (2023), who emphasize how the user-friendly features of AI applications allow students to practise correct English pronunciation at their own pace, without direct supervision from instructors.

T4. "It can be very useful to clarify specific doubts like vocabulary, without wasting a lot of time. It could be useful for phonetics, where one can connect their native language phonemes with those of a foreign language to better understand them."

Another teacher claimed that AI tools can alleviate teacher workload by swiftly locating information, but there is a concern about overdependence leading to complacency.

T2. "They [AI tools] are effective and fast, and can reduce your workload and even provide you with quick information that would otherwise take days to find, but only if used well. Using them can lead you to depend on them constantly and to learn less because you are less focused on what you are doing."

To mitigate this issue, T8 suggested assigning a final task for students to apply what they have learned, emphasizing the importance of clear guidelines and instructions. Additionally, T7 stressed the need for clearly defined boundaries when using AI tools:

T8. "It's okay to give learners a final task involving the use of certain tools, but it's important to provide them with clear guidelines on how to use them effectively."

T7. "I am in favor as long as their limits are clearly communicated to students."

When it comes to improving the learning process, T1 thinks that AI tools can enhance student engagement due to their novelty and appeal. Alongside these aspects, research suggests that AI plays a role in improving motivation by fostering active engagement during the language learning process (Chang, 2005).

T1. "They are appealing and innovative, and can inspire curiosity among students."

Moreover, AI tools offer students a sense of convenience by providing them with easy access to information such as definitions and other relevant materials. T7, for example, highlights the fact that this ease of use adds to students' engagement and motivation to incorporate AI tools into their learning process:

T7. "They use these resources because it's easier [...] and that can motivate them."

As a teacher, T13 highlights the usefulness of certain tools for summarizing and grasping key concepts from texts, as well as for accomplishing tasks and translating. In addition to relying on ChatGPT, this educator also favors Gemini, which offers the added benefit of free Internet access and a range of alternative response options:

T13. "I find it very useful to summarize and extract the main ideas from a text, for writing different types of assignments or even for translations. I also use Gemini, which I think is better than ChatGPT because its free version has internet access."

T7 suggests using AI tools alongside gamification and promoting cooperative work among students to maintain motivation and encourage critical thinking. According to Adadi and Berrada (2018), this is known as the "black box" dilemma of AI, which refers to the lack of understanding about how AI reaches its recommendation, leading to unquestioning trust and overreliance on these tools. This can prompt students to relinquish their agency and responsibility, accepting recommendations from AI tools without critical evaluation.

T7. "Nowadays, it is difficult to control it, so the best way to use these tools is through gamification, a methodology that involves students in the activity."

Perceived Advantages and Disadvantages

When considering the benefits of AI for students, teachers' responses highlighted academic support, time optimization, expanded learning opportunities, increased access to information, and enhanced creativity and motivation. Teachers also emphasized the importance of responsible and critical use of AI tools within an EFL learning environment:

Table 4. Advantages of AI according to EFL teachers

Main advantages		
Give support	**T1**	**It can be helpful to use AI as a support for lower levels in specific moments.**
	T2	**If the group is academically weak, AI can prevent students from being left behind.**
Timesaving	T5	If you have a special topic and related words, using AI can save a lot of time.
	T13	AI's speed and efficiency in carrying out tasks.
Provide learning opportunities	T4	They are closer to an authentic learning environment, where you gain more cultural insight, and get used to the sound and rhythm of the language.
	T6	They create situations that would otherwise not be possible.
Availability of information	T12	The vast amount of information available.
Improve creativity & motivation	T1	To create attractive materials.
	T3	It uses fairly good language and increases the creativity and versatility of the materials. It can be adapted to any learning situation with good results, motivating both teachers and students.

Concerning the disadvantages, a commonly cited issue is the overuse of AI tools, which may hinder students' autonomy and stifle creativity and critical thinking skills, as learners may become overly reliant on these tools for information:

Table 5. Disadvantages of AI according to EFL teachers

Main disadvantages		
Overreliance	**T2**	**One disadvantage is that students become less autonomous and are less used to oral comprehension.**
	T6	**They make students too used to working only with technology.**
Lack of critical thinking skills and creativity	T5	It can make you think less because it provides you with all the information.
	T12	The clear disadvantage is to let AI do the thinking process for the learner or teacher.

Furthermore, T7 expressed that AI tools can be a double-edged sword, both academically and personally, as they affect other life areas that are not necessarily related to education. As a result, students may rely too heavily on AI, becoming complacent and neglecting critical thinking skills. Therefore, it is important to regard AI as supplementary support, as suggested by T8:

T7. "It is a double-edged sword, both academically and personally, because it can make you lazier and more comfortable."

T8. "Tools like ChatGPT should serve as an aid and not replace our own work. They need to be used wisely and ethically."

Teacher Training and Knowledge about AI Tools

Teachers discussed implementing AI tools in EFL settings, acknowledging the need for training in AI. In fact, despite the increasing importance of AI, many school curricula and teacher training programs lack AI courses and well-defined implementation strategies (Karsenti, 2019).

T2. "I need to learn how to use these tools. I feel that students use them every day and I am concerned that they are unlearning instead of learning."

T5. "To be honest, I rarely use AI. I have only used ChatGPT very few times."

Conversely, T3 pointed out that AI could be used in a myriad of ways, as it depends on the imagination and creativity of each teacher. T5 believes that AI tools can streamline text organization and spark essay ideas in the classroom, but also acknowledges AI's limitations in grasping figurative language nuances, serving as a valuable reminder to students about independent thought and critical thinking skills.

T3. "It can be used in 1000 ways, depending on the creativity of the teacher, like creating activities, games, role-plays."

T5. "I would introduce it as an aid for organizing a text or giving ideas for an essay. Also, I would show that it sometimes fails to translate literally, such as metaphoric meanings."

Moreover, T9 uses AI tools to teach academic English and writing, enhancing the language skills of aspiring teachers. In this regard, AI can be helpful in educational contexts, streamlining the research paper process and improving work quality while saving time for teachers. Recent research conducted among faculty members has also shown that teachers are using AI to improve the quality of their work, saving time and enhancing accuracy in writing skills (Ahmed et al., 2024).

T9. "I use some tools for paraphrasing and improving academic English, especially for papers."

A Double-Edged Sword: Perspectives of the Future of AI

While AI tools are still developing, teachers' understanding and training in this area is limited. They acknowledge that AI has become an integral part of learners' lives, in both the classroom and everyday life. Therefore, it is crucial for teachers to become acquainted with how AI tools work. Most teachers are in favor of their use but recognize its potential as a double-edged sword. T4, for example, agreed that they should be used in a guided way in EFL classrooms, while T5 remarked that they can be beneficial if used to support learners.

T4. "In a guided and justified way, I don't see any problem. However, as a teacher, I would need more training to have a clear opinion."

T5. "I think each of us must reflect on how and how often we should use these tools. AI should be used as a help, not as a substitute."

Teachers are also hesitant since there is difficulty in controlling and regulating how students use AI. Both T4 and T6 agree that measures should be taken to use AI tools in very specific cases and with guidance, as students might become over-dependent on them.

T4. "In very sporadic and justified cases. If possible, it would be appropriate to minimize its use so that they don't become addicted to it."

T6. "Yes, but with control. We are becoming too dependent on technology."

Moreover, T11 stresses the importance of analyzing the educational potential of AI, rather than disregarding it altogether. Despite this, she knows that students might use these tools to cheat, particularly those who struggle academically. As T11 noted, this has become a growing concern in universities, where AI-generated dissertations are submitted as original works:

T11. "AI needs to be analyzed as a learning tool. Rather than turning our backs on it, we need to see how to take advantage of it in a win-win situation. Now, what we see the most is cheating. [...] At university, the vigilance is extreme because of the implications for dissertation projects."

DISCUSSION

The study examined the use of various AI tools in higher education EFL classrooms and their impact on English language skills. The findings indicate that while not widely used, these tools are considered beneficial by both students and teachers for providing linguistic support, saving time, offering immediate feedback and creating further learning opportunities. Additionally, AI tools can be customized for various scenarios to facilitate learning, boost motivation, produce additional exercises for continuous practice of pronunciation, listening and grammar skills, and help students feel more confident about their readiness for exams. This illustrates how AI tools can narrow the gap between students' initial proficiency and the level expected by the end of the academic year. Research on AI in EFL settings also underlines its benefits in enhancing language acquisition through support, brainstorming and L2 communication (Bailey et al., 2021).

The findings also suggest that learners use AI as a support strategy when they have difficulty understanding specific words or when they need additional practice. Hence, in this context, the use of AI tools hinges largely on students' English proficiency level and their individual backgrounds. This pertains to the issue of equity, as AI tools can provide students with access to personalized resources that support their learning process. The findings indicate that students rely on AI tools to seek activities and exercises for additional practice, as well as to improve their understanding of course content. In this way, AI could be seen as an after-school educational support system, which can reduce disparities in learning opportunities. This aligns with Chine et al. (2022), who posit that AI can positively impact learning outcomes, leading to reduced inequality and significant learning progress among under-achieving students; as well as with the results of Roshanaei et al. (2023), who highlight the potential of AI in tailoring learning and content to ensure that every student receives personalized instruction adapted to their individual needs.

Since AI is still a recent phenomenon, it is essential for teachers to familiarize themselves with these tools so that they can use them effectively to support and improve the learning process, as well as help students use them responsibly and thoughtfully. Walter (2024), for instance, emphasizes the importance of including real-life situations in digital literacy education to illustrate the intersection of AI theory and its practical applications. This approach aims to provide students and teachers with a holistic understanding of AI, advocating for its integration into various academic disciplines. By doing so, students would gain a foundational knowledge of AI tools, preparing them for an AI-driven professional landscape in the future.

Furthermore, the lack of teacher training and student knowledge of AI could be addressed by developing compulsory courses for both groups in higher education institutions. Combining traditional classroom knowledge with partnerships with AI experts and other educational institutions, as well as workshops on AI, would provide further insights and hands-on knowledge in this regard. As Walter (2024) contends, although regulating AI is an important initial measure, "creating ways for students and lecturers to engage more deeply with the topic would probably enhance these measures and might help to foster a respective culture" (p. 9).

As stated, teachers and students are aware of the potential benefits and challenges associated with AI, but its adoption is still not widespread among these participants. However, there is a growing realization of the importance of AI literacy, leading to its gradual incorporation into school curriculums and educational plans (Chiu, 2023). Given that AI integration is still in its early stages, the main challenge lies in teaching technical knowledge as well as developing a deeper understanding of its broader impact, whether on an ethical, social or economic level.

While AI can be helpful, teachers have raised concerns about over-reliance on these tools, which could limit students' creativity and critical thinking skills. Other scholars have similarly identified these concerns among students, emphasizing worries about the overreliance on AI, its impact on the quality of higher education, as well as issues related to precision, openness, privacy, innovation, critical thinking skills, development prospects and ethical considerations (Chan & Hu, 2023; Park et al., 2023; Peres et al., 2023).

In higher education institutions, research has highlighted the challenges posed by AI, including ethical issues, academic integrity and plagiarism (Chan & Hu, 2023). In fact, examining AI responses to academic writing prompts revealed relevant but largely original text output with inappropriate references and a lack of personal perspectives difficult for AI-powered technologies to generate (Kumar, 2023). For language learners, creating suitable prompts for AI is even more challenging due to the required level of linguistic proficiency. Hence, overreliance on AI tools in EFL settings may hinder students' efforts in developing their writing skills. Added to this, it is difficult for institutions to detect plagiarism and determine whether a piece of writing is an AI-generated text or a student's original work (Peres et al., 2023) — raising ethical concerns related to academic integrity.

In our modern era, technology has significantly influenced education, altering the interactions between teachers and students. Alongside this trend is the concept of "learnification", which views teachers primarily as facilitators of learning rather than experts with valuable knowledge to teach (Guilherme, 2019). This shift poses a challenge to the traditional notion that "teachers have something to teach and that students have something to learn from their teachers" (Biesta, 2013, p. 452). The devaluation of the teacher's role because of AI may have an adverse effect on relationships between teachers and students, as well as among students themselves (Guilherme, 2019). However, human relationships within education settings are pivotal in determining academic success, as they determine the development of students' self-worth, their ability to undertake new tasks and their learning motivation (Laura & Chapman, 2009).

In light of these findings, it is important to tailor AI applications for specific purposes and develop them to meet the needs of their users. This aligns with Park and Shin's (2017) results, which highlight the fact that AI technology should be used in specialized educational settings, with clear distinctions between AI tutors and human teachers. Hence, it is essential to support teachers in effectively integrating AI-based applications into their classrooms through appropriate guidance and management, as most of them did not receive any prior training. Likewise, as highlighted by Schmidt and Strasser (2022), "even in 2040, we will still have and need teachers: well-trained, data-literate teachers who are competent, critical, and reflective in their use of media and technology support" (p. 180).

CONCLUSION

The research found that AI tools are used to support the learning process and improve English language skills in higher education. Both teachers and students emphasized the importance of control measures and proper training for maximizing the benefits of AI. While AI tools are effective in improving student language proficiency, motivation and engagement, concerns were raised about overreliance on these tools potentially hindering critical thinking skills, creativity and knowledge acquisition.

Nonetheless, some limitations need to be addressed. A higher number of EFL teachers and students must be involved to gain further knowledge in this regard, providing a more diverse range of perspectives and offering new insights into their use and potential obstacles. In this study, it is important to note that most teachers do not actively use AI tools. To address this, future research studies should consider teachers who frequently use AI tools as well as those who are just beginning to incorporate them into their teaching practices. This will provide a more complete understanding of the impact of these tools on EFL education, including potential long-term effects on students' learning progress and any negative effects of overreliance.

Regarding equity, AI tools hold the promise of promoting personalized and accessible learning experiences, while also removing barriers that may hinder learning progress for students – on the condition that they are used strategically and ethically. However, it was shown that AI tools are still not widely used by the group of students involved in the study. To address this, human mentoring could encourage learners to responsibly engage with these resources and enrich their overall learning journey. Moreover, it can be argued that AI can improve learning experiences and reduce inequalities. Nonetheless, there is also a risk that AI could unintentionally amplify existing inequalities or create new ones. Issues such as algorithmic bias, ethical concerns, the potential deskilling of students, unequal access to AI technologies among learners and the lack of teacher training on AI could contribute to this problem. Therefore, to fully harness the potential of AI, it is essential to not only examine how these tools can address inequalities, but also how they might exacerbate them. This will lead to discussions about the necessary measures to ensure the positive progress of AI in education.

In light of the above, AI tools present a promising opportunity for teachers to improve language acquisition, boost student engagement and save valuable time and effort. To fully leverage their benefits, it is crucial to use them as a complementary resource to existing teaching approaches. In this regard, higher education institutions need to reassess their policies, curricula and teaching methods to adequately equip students and teachers for a future where AI tools may become integral. This could include promoting interdisciplinary education, highlighting the importance of critical thinking, and encouraging the development of digital literacy and ethical understanding of AI tools. Ultimately, to truly level the language playing field, teachers play a vital role in this effort, as they are the real agents that need to guide learners' use of AI and existing methodologies so that they can successfully navigate their learning journey and achieve their language learning goals.

REFERENCES

Adadi, A., & Berrada, M. (2018). Peeking inside the black-box: A survey on explainable artificial intelligence. *IEEE Access : Practical Innovations, Open Solutions*, 6(1), 52138–52160. 10.1109/ACCESS.2018.2870052

Ahmed, M., Siddique, M., & Tahira, Y. (2024). Impact of artificial intelligence-based writing assistant on the academic writing skills of University Faculty in Pakistan. *IJHS*, 4, 539–545.

Akgun, S., & Greenhow, C. (2022). Artificial intelligence in education: Addressing ethical challenges in K-12 settings. *AI and Ethics*, 2(3), 431–440. 10.1007/s43681-021-00096-734790956

Alshumaimeri, Y. A., & Alshememry, A. K. (2024). The extent of AI applications in EFL learning and teaching. *IEEE Transactions on Learning Technologies*, 17, 653–663. 10.1109/TLT.2023.3322128

Bailey, D., Southam, A., & Costley, J. (2021). Digital storytelling with chatbots: Mapping L2 participation and perception patterns. *Interactive Technology and Smart Education*, 18(1), 85–103. 10.1108/ITSE-08-2020-0170

Bailin, A. (1988). Artificial intelligence and computer-assisted language instruction: A perspective. *CALICO Journal*, 5(3), 25–45. https://www.jstor.org/stable/24147434. 10.1558/cj.v5i3.25-45

Bali, M., Compton, M., Davis, M., Draper, M., Grove, M., Jones-Devitt, S., McArthur, J., Peddie, C., & Webb, M. (2024). *Navigating the complexities of the artificial intelligence era in higher education*. The Quality Assurance Agency for Higher Education.

Biesta, G. J. J. (2013). Receiving the gift of teaching: From 'learning from' to 'being taught by'. *Studies in Philosophy and Education*, 32(5), 449–461. 10.1007/s11217-012-9312-9

Borenstein, J., & Howard, A. (2021). Emerging challenges in AI and the need for AI ethics education. *AI and Ethics*, 1(1), 61–65. 10.1007/s43681-020-00002-738624388

Brookhart, S. M., & Durkin, D. T. (2003). Classroom assessment, student motivation, and achievement in high school social studies classes. *Applied Measurement in Education*, 16(1), 27–54. 10.1207/S15324818AME1601_2

Chan, C. K. Y., & Hu, W. (2023). Students' voices on generative AI: Perceptions, benefits, and challenges in higher education. *International Journal of Educational Technology in Higher Education*, 20(1), 43. 10.1186/s41239-023-00411-8

Chang, M. M. (2005). Applying self-regulated learning strategies in a web-based instruction - An investigation of motivation perception. *Computer Assisted Language Learning*, 18(3), 217–230. 10.1080/09588220500178939

Chine, D. R., Brentley, C., Thomas-Browne, C., Richey, J. E., Gul, A., Carvalho, P. F., Branstetter, L., & Koedinger, K. R. (2022). Educational Equity Through Combined Human-AI Personalization: A Propensity Matching Evaluation. In Rodrigo, M. M., Matsuda, N., Cristea, A. I., & Dimitrova, V. (Eds.), *Artificial Intelligence in Education* (pp. 366–377). Springer International Publishing. 10.1007/978-3-031-11644-5_30

Chiu, T. K. F. (2023). The impact of Generative AI (GenAI) on practices, policies and research direction in education: A case of ChatGPT and Midjourney. *Interactive Learning Environments*, 1–17. 10.1080/10494820.2023.2253861

Clarke, S., & Whittlestone, J. (2022). A survey of the potential long-term impacts of AI. *2022 AAAI/ACM Conference on AI, Ethics and Society*, (pp. 192-202). ACM. 10.1145/3514094.3534131

Crompton, H., & Burke, D. (2022). Artificial intelligence in K-12 education. *SN Social Sciences*, 2(7), 113. 10.1007/s43545-022-00425-5

Divekar, R., Drozdal, J., Chabot, S., Zhou, Y., Su, H., Chen, Y., Zhu, H., Hendler, J., & Braasch, J. (2022). Foreign language acquisition via artificial intelligence and extended reality: Design and evaluation. *Computer Assisted Language Learning*, 35(9), 2332–2360. 10.1080/09588221.2021.1879162

Drigas, A. S., & Ioannidou, R. E. (2012). Artificial intelligence in special education: A decade review. *International Journal of Engineering Education*, 28(6), 1366–1372.

Fenner, A. B., & Newby, D. (2000). *Approaches to materials design in European textbooks: Implementing principles of authenticity, learner autonomy, cultural awareness*. Council of Europe Publishing.

Fitria, T. N. (2021). The use technology based on artificial intelligence in English teaching and learning. *ELT Echo*, 6(2), 213–223. 10.24235/eltecho.v6i2.9299

Gefen, D., Karahanna, E., & Straub, D. (2003). Inexperience and experience with online stores: The importance of TAM and Trust. *IEEE Transactions on Engineering Management*, 50(3), 307–321. 10.1109/TEM.2003.817277

Grunhut, J., Marques, O., & Wyatt, A. T. M. (2022). Needs, challenges, and applications of artificial intelligence in medical education curriculum. *JMIR Medical Education*, 8(2), 35587. 10.2196/3558735671077

Guilherme, A. (2019). AI and education: The importance of teacher and student relations. *AI & Society*, 34(1), 47–54. 10.1007/s00146-017-0693-8

Heffernan, N. (2005). Watching movie trailers in the ESL Class. *The Internet TESL Journal, 9*(3). https://bit.ly/3UW0sB5

Holmes, W., & Tuomi, I. (2022). State of the art and practice in AI in education. *European Journal of Education*, 57(4), 542–570. 10.1111/ejed.12533

Hrastinski, S., Olofsson, A. D., Arkenback, C., Ekström, S., Ericsson, E., Fransson, G., Jaldemark, J., Ryberg, T., Öberg, L. M., Fuentes, A., Gustafsson, U., Humble, N., Mozelius, P., Sundgren, M., & Utterberg, M. (2019). Critical imaginaries and reflections on artificial intelligence and robots in postdigital K-12 education. *Postdigital Science and Education*, 1(2), 427–445. 10.1007/s42438-019-00046-x

Hsu, T. C., Chang, C., & Jen, T. H. (2023). Artificial Intelligence image recognition using self-regulation learning strategies: Effects on vocabulary acquisition, learning anxiety, and learning behaviours of English language learners. *Interactive Learning Environments*, 1–19. 10.1080/10494820.2023.2165508

Hwang, G. J., Sung, H. Y., Hung, C. M., Huang, I., & Tsai, C. C. (2012). Development of a personalized educational computer game based on students' learning styles. *Educational Technology Research and Development*, 60(4), 623–638. 10.1007/s11423-012-9241-x

Hwang, G. J., & Tu, Y. F. (2021). Roles and research trends of artificial intelligence in mathematics education: A bibliometric mapping analysis and systematic review. *Mathematics*, 9(6), 584. 10.3390/math9060584

Hwang, G. J., Xie, H., Wah, B., & Gasevic, D. (2020). Vision, challenges, roles and research issues of artificial intelligence in education. *Computers and Education: Artificial Intelligence*, 1(13), 1–5. 10.1016/j.caeai.2020.100001

Junaidi, J. (2020). Artificial intelligence in EFL context: Rising students' speaking performance with Lyra virtual assistance. *International Journal of Advanced Science and Technology Rehabilitation*, 29(5), 6735–6741.

Karsenti, T. (2019). Artificial intelligence in education: The urgent need to prepare teachers for tomorrow's schools. *Formation et Profession*, 27(1), 105–111. 10.18162/fp.2019.a166

Kim, H. S., & Kim, H. (2017). A study of Korean English teachers' future readiness for the fourth industrial revolution. *Multimedia-Assisted Language Learning*, 20(3), 179–205.

Kim, N. Y., Cha, Y., & Kim, H. S. (2019). Future English learning: Chatbots and artificial intelligence. *Multimedia-Assisted Language Learning*, 22(3), 32–53.

Krutka, D., Manca, S., Galvin, S., Greenhow, C., Koehler, M., & Askari, E. (2019). Teaching «against» social media: Confronting problems of profit in the curriculum. *Teachers College Record*, 121(14), 1–19. 10.1177/016146811912101410

Kumar, A. H. S. (2023). Analysis of ChatGPT tool to assess the potential of its utility for academic writing in biomedical domain. *BEMS Reports*, 9(1), 24–30. 10.5530/bems.9.1.5

Laura, R. S., & Chapman, A. (2009). The technologisation of education: Philosophical reflections on being too plugged in. *International Journal of Children's Spirituality*, 14(3), 289–298. 10.1080/13644360903086554

Manyika, J., Chui, M., Miremadi, M., Bughin, J., George, K., Willmott, P., & Dewhurst, M. (2017). *A future that works: Automation, employment, and productivity*. McKinsey Global Institute.

Marzuki, W., Widiati, U., Rusdin, D., Darwin, , & Indrawati, I. (2023). The impact of AI writing tools on the content and organization of students' writing: EFL teachers' perspective. *Cogent Education*, 10(2), 1–17. 10.1080/2331186X.2023.2236469

Nagata, N. (1996). Computer vs. workbook instruction in second language acquisition. *CALICO Journal*, 14(1), 53–75. 10.1558/cj.v14i1.53-75

Oktradiksa, A., Bhakti, C. P., Kurniawan, S. J., Rahman, F. A., & Ani, . (2021). Utilization artificial intelligence to improve creativity skills in society 5.0. *Journal of Physics: Conference Series*, 1760(1), 012032. 10.1088/1742-6596/1760/1/012032

Park, J. H., & Shin, N. M. (2017). Students' perceptions of artificial intelligence technology and artificial intelligence teachers. *The Journal of Korean Teacher Education*, 34(2), 169–192.

Peres, R., Schreier, M., Schweidel, D., & Sorescu, A. (2023). On ChatGPT and beyond: How generative artificial intelligence may affect research, teaching, and practice. *International Journal of Research in Marketing*, 40(2), 269–275. 10.1016/j.ijresmar.2023.03.001

Pinkwart, N. (2016). Another 25 years of AIED? Challenges and opportunities for intelligent educational technologies of the future. *International Journal of Artificial Intelligence in Education*, 26(2), 771–783. 10.1007/s40593-016-0099-7

Pokrivcakova, S. (2019). Preparing teachers for the application of AI-powered technologies in foreign language education. *Journal of Language and Cultural Education*, 7(3), 135–153. 10.2478/jolace-2019-0025

Polyportis, A. (2024). A longitudinal study on artificial intelligence adoption: Understanding the drivers of ChatGPT usage behavior change in higher education. *Frontiers in Artificial Intelligence*, 6, 1–10. 10.3389/frai.2023.132439838249792

Qiao, H., & Zhao, A. (2023). Artificial intelligence-based language learning: Illuminating the impact on speaking skills and self-regulation in Chinese EFL context. *Frontiers in Psychology*, 14, 1255594. 10.3389/fpsyg.2023.125559438022973

Rafner, J., Dellermann, D., Hjorth, A., Verasztо, D., Kampf, C., Mackay, W., & Sherson, J. (2021). Deskilling, upskilling, and reskilling: A case for hybrid intelligence. *Morals & Machines*, 1(2), 24–39. 10.5771/2747-5174-2021-2-24

Rapley, T. J. (2001). The art(fulness) of open-ended interviewing: Some considerations on analysing interviews. *Qualitative Research*, 1(3), 303–323. 10.1177/146879410100100303

Regan, P. M., & Jesse, J. (2019). Ethical challenges of edtech, big data and personalized learning: Twenty-first century student sorting and tracking. *Ethics and Information Technology*, 21(3), 167–179. 10.1007/s10676-018-9492-2

Roshanaei, M., Olivares, H., & Lopez, R. R. (2023). Harnessing AI to Foster Equity in Education: Opportunities, Challenges, and Emerging Strategies. *Journal of Intelligent Learning Systems and Applications*, 15(4), 123–143. 10.4236/jilsa.2023.154009

Rusmiyanto, R., Huriati, N., Fitriani, N., Tyas, N., Rofi'i, A., & Sari, M. (2023). The role of artificial intelligence (AI) in developing English language learner's communication skills. *Journal of Education*, 6(1), 750–757. 10.31004/joe.v6i1.2990

Schmidt, T., & Strasser, T. (2022). Artificial intelligence in foreign language learning and teaching: A CALL for intelligent practice. *Anglistik*, 33(1), 165–184. 10.33675/ANGL/2022/1/14

Senowarsito, S., & Ardini, S. N. (2023). The use of artificial intelligence to promote autonomous pronunciation learning: Segmental and suprasegmental features perspective. *IJELTAL*, 8(2), 133–147. 10.21093/ijeltal.v8i2.1452

Stone, P., Brooks, R., Brynjolfsson, E., Calo, R., Etzioni, O., Hager, G., Hirschberg, J., Kalyanakrishnan, S., Kamar, E., Kraus, S., Leyton-Brown, K., Parkes, D., Press, W., Saxenian, A., Shah, J., Tambe, M., & Teller, A. (2022). *Artificial intelligence and life in 2030: The one hundred year study on artificial intelligence*. Standford University.

Sumakul, D. T. Y. G., Hamied, F. A., & Sukyadi, D. (2022). Artificial Intelligence in EFL classrooms: Friend or foe? *LEARN Journal*, 15(1), 232–256.

Tahir, A., & Tahir, A. (2023). AI-driven advancements in ESL learner autonomy: Investigating student attitudes towards virtual assistant usability. *Linguistic Forum -. Journal of Linguistics*, 5(2), 50–56. 10.53057/linfo/2023.5.2.8

Tang, K. Y., Chang, C. Y., & Hwang, G. J. (2023). Trends in artificial intelligence-supported e-learning: A systematic review and co-citation network analysis (1998–2019). *Interactive Learning Environments*, 31(4), 2134–2152. 10.1080/10494820.2021.1875001

Vairaperumal, V. (2023, December 15). *AI in Education: Reimagining the Role of Teachers*. Integra. https://bit.ly/4byG3Ze

Verdú, E., Regueras, L. M., Gal, E., de Castro, J. P., Verdú, M. J., & Kohen-Vacs, D. (2017). Integration of an intelligent tutoring system in a course of computer network design. *Educational Technology Research and Development*, 65(3), 653–677. 10.1007/s11423-016-9503-0

Waller, M., & Waller, P. (2020). *Why predictive algorithms are so risky for public sector bodies*. Social Science Research Network. 10.2139/ssrn.3716166

Walter, Y. (2024). Embracing the future of artificial intelligence in the classroom: The relevance of AI literacy, prompt engineering, and critical thinking in modern education. *International Journal of Educational Technology in Higher Education*, 21(1), 15. 10.1186/s41239-024-00448-3

Wilson, J., Ahrendt, C., Fudge, E. A., Raiche, A., Beard, G., & MacArthur, C. (2021). Elementary teachers' perceptions of automated feedback and automated scoring: Transforming the teaching and learning of writing using automated writing evaluation. *Computers & Education*, 168, 104208. 10.1016/j.compedu.2021.104208

ADDITIONAL READING

Baum, H. (2023). *Introduction to artificial intelligence*. A G Printing & Publishing.

Boyatzis, R. E. (1998). Transforming qualitative information: Thematic analysis and code development. *Sage (Atlanta, Ga.).*

Braunschweig, B., & Ghallab, M. (2021). *Reflections on artificial intelligence for humanity*. Springer Nature. 10.1007/978-3-030-69128-8

Dimitrova, V. (2009). *Artificial intelligence in education*. IOS Press.

Dornyei, Z., & Ryan, S. (2015). *The Psychology of the Language Learner Revisited*. Routledge. 10.4324/9781315779553

Fang, P. (2024). *AI in language teaching, learning, and assessment*. IGI Global.

Galip, K. (2023). *Transforming the language teaching experience in the age of AI*. IGI Global.

Knox, J., Wang, Y., & Gallagher, M. (2019). *Artificial intelligence and inclusive education: speculative futures and emerging practices*. Springer. 10.1007/978-981-13-8161-4

Nilsson, N. J. (2009). *The quest for artificial intelligence*. Cambridge University Press. 10.1017/CBO9780511819346

Yu, S., & Lu, Y. (2021). *An introduction to artificial intelligence in education*. Springer Nature. 10.1007/978-981-16-2770-5

KEY TERMS AND DEFINITIONS

Affective Factors: They encompass the psychological and emotional aspects that can have an impact on learning, behavior and attitudes in educational settings, such as motivation and self-esteem.

Artificial Intelligence: It refers to computer systems simulating human cognitive processes, which carry out a wide variety of tasks like problem-solving or reasoning.

English as a Foreign Language (EFL): It involves using English in a non-primary spoken language context, often in countries where English is not the dominant language.

Language Outcomes: The observable accomplishments related to language acquisition, which may range from proficiency levels and communicative skills development to fluency and language improvement.

Linguistic Input: The linguistic information individuals receive through listening or reading, contributing to their language learning and growth.

Natural Language Processing: It entails computer-human interaction using natural language, focusing on enabling computers to understand, interpret and produce human language.

Qualitative Approach: A research approach that gathers information through non-numerical data such as interviews, observations and textual analysis.

Thematic Analysis: A qualitative research technique used to recognize patterns within textual data, which are subsequently categorized to reveal underlying themes.

Chapter 8

The Deployment of Blended Learning for English Vocabulary Enhancement:
Voice of Vietnamese L2 Students

Thao Quoc Tran
https://orcid.org/0000-0001-8063-8853
HUTECH University, Vietnam

Thao Phuong Nguyen
Van Lang University, Vietnam

ABSTRACT

Blending learning (BL) has emerged as one of the effective teaching and learning approaches in education, and research on the deployment of BL has been extensively conducted. This book chapter sets to present a mixed-methods study exploring Vietnamese L2 students' perceptions of the effects of BL on their English vocabulary enhancement. A cohort of 300 L2 students studying general English (GE) at a Ho Chi Minh City-based university in Vietnam took part in answering a questionnaire, and 15 of them participated in semi-structured interviews. Statistical analysis and content analysis were employed for quantitative and qualitative data analysis, respectively, and the sociolinguistic perspective was adopted for interpreting the results. The findings unraveled that Vietnamese L2 students perceived the effects of the deployment of BL in GE courses on their vocabulary enhancement as they could remember a wide range of vocabulary, recognize vocabulary meaning in context, and apply vocabulary in writing and speaking effectively.

DOI: 10.4018/979-8-3693-2591-9.ch008

INTRODUCTION

In the education landscape, blended learning (BL) is developed as a connection between face-to-face and online learning in an attempt to leverage the traditional learning modality (Sharma, 2010), and it is believed to optimize learners' success and reduce costs (Garrison & Vaughan, 2007). Additionally, the BL approach with the assistance of technology is an enabling tool that helps educational institutions offer solutions. The implementation of BL allows educators to manage large classes, extend students' learning outside the classrooms, and allow students to have thoughtful reflection through personalized learning that is believed to suit a wider range of learning styles (Qinda, 2018). Nevertheless, although acknowledging these benefits of the BL approach in education, several higher educational institutions in different countries are still resistant or slowly adopt this learning approach due to many challenges as well as requirements, namely financial investment in technologies, time investment in building E-learning materials and designing accessible and affordable communication systems or equipping lecturers with new methodologies (Badawi, 2009).

In the realm of language education in general and English language teaching in specific, research that the BL approach in English language education is effective in enhancing students' English language proficiency (Ebadi, 2018; Khodabandeh & Mombini, 2024; Mohammed Nuri et all, 2023; Saswandi & Ningsih, 2023). Furthermore, the deployment of blended learning in English courses is proven to be effective in many ways. BL allows students to have learning opportunities at any time and anywhere thanks to a flexible learning platform that encourages learners to practice inside and outside classrooms, and this contributes to solving the problem of time constraints in lessons and allows teachers to design more collaborative and student-oriented activities in lessons; BL also supports students' motivation through authentic language learning practices and leads to better academic achievement (Qinda, 2018). Students can engage with the course content at their own pace and revisit digital materials as needed so that they can foster deeper understanding and mastery of the target language, which can lead to their improvement of linguistic competence and academic.

Like other many developing countries, Vietnam has recognized the need for educational transformation and has developed comprehensive plans to modernize its system (Government of Vietnam, 2021), and e-learning has been identified as one of the chief factors in leveraging the quality of education (e.g., Duong & Tran, 2023; Duong et al., 2021; Tran, 2016; Tran et al., 2023; Tran & Nguyen, 2023). E-learning development sheds light on the emergence of BL in education in general and English language teaching in specific. Higher education institutions are encouraged to design training courses using the BL modality. Regarding this research context, which is a multidisciplinary university in Ho Chi Minh City, Vietnam, the BL approach has been applied officially to offer general English courses. Nevertheless, the BL-based English course focuses primarily on teaching vocabulary for the try-out phase. Over the course of implementing this BL course, one educators and researchers noticed that many students have shown positive attitudes towards the deployment of BL in learning English vocabulary as they are well adapted to the BL approach. Alternatively, some students still encounter difficulties, such as a lack of self-regulated language learning, computer literacy, and time management, when first being exposed to the BL-based English course. More critically, the BL-based English courses' deployment effects have not been supported. To address this void, this research sets to delve into how L2 students perceive the effects of BL on their English vocabulary enhancement in the context of a Ho Chi Minh City-based university in Vietnam. It addresses the research question below:

- How do Vietnamese L2 students perceive the effects of BL on their English vocabulary enhancement?

Theoretically, this study is expected to contribute its part to the existing theories in terms of BL by giving an in-depth discussion of L2 students' perceptions of the effects of BL on vocabulary enhancement. Regarding practical contributions, the study findings should provide a preliminary understanding of the deployment of BL in a specific EFL context, which can serve as a reference for stakeholders (e.g., teachers, material designers, administrators) in different similar ambiences to assist students' English language learning via BL platform.

LITERATURE REVIEW

Blended Learning

BL is variously defined. Sharma (2010) delineated that BL is referred to as the traditional learning integrated with web-based online learning. Similarly, Bath and Bourke (2010) viewed BL as an approach to strategically and systematically apply technological resources to face-to-face learning. Likewise, Watson (2008) defined BL as an innovative combination of face-to-face and online learning to enhance learning experience and learning quality. Within this study, BL is understood as a learning platform that features an integrated combination of online learning and in-class learning.

BL has four levels including activity level, course level, program level, and institutional level; the nature of BL is determined by the designer, instructor, or learner (Graham, 2006). Regarding BL at the activity level, the learning activity consists of both face-to-face and online modalities. Learners can participate in the in-class lesson and be required to complete follow-up assignments online or vice versa. In addition, technology can be integrated to bring instruction or virtual instruction into the learning process by simulating a face-to-face online learning experience. In this aspect, technological equipment can be used to make learning activities more authentic by embedding high-quality audio and video resources which can enable students to engage with authentic language materials. As for BL at the course level, some BL systems segregate the time blocks to maintain chronological sequencing and avoid overlapping, others engage learners in various but supportive face-to-face and online activities that overlap in time (Graham, 2006). With respect to BL at the program level, BL often occurs at the degree program level and has two models. The first model requires learners to choose a mixture of face-to-face delivery in the first half of the course and online delivery in the rest of the course or vice versa. The second educational model offers learners a combination of the two delivery modes throughout the course length. As regards BL at the institutional level, this type of BL allows face-to-face instruction at the start and conclusion of the course and online activities in between. Learners may occasionally be required to attend an online course in addition to campus-based or in-person courses (Graham, 2006). Within the context of this research, BL at the activity level is designed since students are required to attend face-to-face classroom lessons and complete online assignments as well as predetermined activities.

BL in English Language Learning

BL can offer educators a more student-centered approach to English language instruction and learning. Garrison and Vaughan (2007) highlighted that through BL strategy, student-centered learning is promoted highly thanks to collaborative tasks, and teachers can redesign learning activities to be more student-oriented. Additionally, BL with the utilization of web-based communication technology optimizes students' engagement by integrating online and face-to-face learning, enhancing students' engagement after class-contact hours, and replacing a number of class-contact hours with new components of pedagogy to help students analyze, construct, and confirm knowledge through personal responsibility and choice.

An important trend in 21st-century education is that the BL approach in English language teaching and learning can enable students to learn whenever and wherever they want by using a flexible learning platform. As a result, the BL strategy promotes language practice among language students, especially ESL students, both within and outside of the classroom. Zhang and Zhu (2018) argued that although it is challenging to create an effective learning environment for all EFL students, the BL strategy can provide an adaptable, engaging, motivating, and inspirational teaching and learning environment. Therefore, BL substitutes technologically integrated language teaching mindsets for conventional techniques in the future of education, especially in English language education (Graham, 2006).

Previous Studies

Research on the application of BL in English language education has been conducted in various contexts. Regarding the international context, Dastjerdi's (2011) study investigated how traditional and BL teaching impact EFL learners' vocabulary learning. Sixty Iranian high school students were recruited and divided into a control group and an experimental group. Students from two groups took a vocabulary test, and the results showed that students from the experimental group outperformed those from a traditional group in terms of recalling and recognizing the vocabulary. In Russia, Vasbieva et al., (2016) conducted a study to enhance students' vocabulary through the BL approach. The participants were university students, and the research instrument was pre-test and post-test. The findings concluded that participants were satisfied with the BL strategy to learn vocabulary, and they could improve their vocabulary through the BL strategy. Another study was conducted in Iran by Ebadi and Ghuchi (2018) who investigated EFL students' perspectives on the effects of the BL approach on vocabulary enhancement. Two groups of students, viz. the control group and the experimental group did the pre-test and post-test, and those from the experimental group partook in semi-structured interviews. Ebadi and Ghuchi's (2018) results presented that experimental students learned vocabulary better than the traditional ones.

Within the context of Vietnam, a number of studies on different aspects of BL have been found. Pham (2019) studied the advantages and challenges in taking BL English courses faced by English majors at a university in Vietnam. The questionnaire and semi-structured interview were research instruments. It was found out that students' learning was hindered due to the inappropriate application of the BL approach and inadequate practice experience. Similarly, Phuong et al.'s (2019) study investigated impressions of BL from a group of 165 students at a university in the

South Vietnam. The findings were that BL offered a good learning environment and many benefits to students. Ho et al. (2021) surveyed 1500 students' opinions on the application of BL in learning English. The results indicated that BL helped students improve their speaking skills and promoted communication, teamwork, and critical thinking skills.

It is noticed that different aspects of BL have been investigated in both international and local contexts. Many international studies on English vocabulary enhancement via the BL approach have been found; however, it seems that there is still a scarcity of studies delving into an in-depth investigation into vocabulary enhancement through the BL in higher education in Vietnam. Research on teachers' and students' attitudes and perceptions of the application of BL in Vietnam at the university level focused on a wide range of aspects of teaching and learning, such as motivation, materials, autonomy, engagement level, advantages, challenges or needs for support rather than giving an insight into any specific language skills or features of the language like vocabulary. Hence, the present research aims to investigate L2 students' perceptions of the effects of BL on their vocabulary enhancement in the context of a Ho Chi Minh City based university in Vietnam to partially fulfill this void.

RESEARCH METHODOLOGY

Research Design, Site, and Participants

This research employed the convergent mixed methods design, and it adopted a pragmatic worldview (Creswell & Creswell, 2018) to explore L2 students' perceptions of the effects of BL on their vocabulary enhancement. A questionnaire was designed for quantitative data collection from L2 students' perceptions of the effects of BL on their vocabulary enhancement, and semi-structured interviews were utilized to gather qualitative data from participants' further elaboration of opinions which give more insights for data interpretation.

The research site was a university located in Ho Chi Minh City, Vietnam. This institution is a multidisciplinary university. General English (GE) is one of the compulsory courses that students must take. There are seven levels (English 1 to English 7) of GE ranging from basic level to upper-intermediate one (English 1: Foundation; English 2: Elementary; English 3: pre-intermediate; English 4-5: Intermediate; English 6-7: Pre-intermediate). Upon the completion of these GE courses, students are supposed to achieve B2 level - upper-intermediate level in reference to the Common European Framework of Reference (CEFR) to be eligible for graduation. Since 2022, BL has been deployed for teaching English vocabulary for GE courses. The purpose of implementing BL in GE courses is to provide more flexibility for students' English learning and promote higher independence in students' learning attitudes. Besides traditional classroom instruction, the students are required to study English online outside the classroom. The main section that students are responsible for studying online outside the classroom is vocabulary. Students watch videos that feature instruction on vocabulary and then complete a number of controlled practice activities on E-learning to check if they have understood the vocabulary being instructed in the videos. The video instructions of vocabulary are designed and filmed by the University lecturers as in-house materials. The vocabulary items selected in the videos are taken from the student's textbooks used in the GE courses. The format of the videos, including images, illustrations, pacing, and structure of scripts, is consulted by academic specialists and approved by the academic leaders. Before class, students can study online by themselves through videos and complete certain exercises after watching the videos to make sure they have acquired the knowledge; then, they can be more confident when coming to class and more willing to participate in practice activities in classrooms. During class time, students can have more collaborative practice activities in class such as group discussions, presentations, writing under time limitations, reading at speed, and so on. After the lesson in class, students are required to continue to review and practice what they have learned online and in class.

A cohort of 300 GE students was conveniently sampled, and they were from different fields of study and had experience studying GE via the BL approach. They were from different levels of academic study. One hundred and one (43.7%) students were freshmen; 86 (28.7%) students were sophomores; and 83 (27.7%) students were juniors. Therefore, their English language proficiency also varied. Among 300 participants answering the questionnaire, fifteen students were voluntarily invited for semi-structured interviews. They were from different levels of academic study.

Data Collection Instruments

The questionnaire and semi-structured interview were deployed for data generation. The first research instrument is a closed-ended questionnaire which consists of two main parts: Part I gathers participants' background information (four items); Part II (the main questionnaire content) seeks for participants' perceptions of the effects of BL on vocabulary enhancement (20 items). The questionnaire items were divided into four categories: remembering a wide range of vocabulary (five items), recognizing vocabulary in context (five items), applying vocabulary in writing (five items), and applying vocabulary in speaking (fived items). These 20 questionnaire items were adapted from previous studies (Somjai & Pamararat, 2014; Vasbieva et al., 2016; Al Zumor et al., 2013) and were in the form of a five-point Likert scale (from *Strongly disagree* to *Strongly agree*). The questionnaire was in English, and it was then converted into the respondent's first language to avoid misunderstanding in relation to language. Additionally, the questionnaire was double-checked by two experts in the field of English language studies and piloted with a group of five intended students to ensure the validity of the questionnaire. Besides, the level of reliability of the questionnaire was measured at 7.88, i.e., the questionnaire was acceptably reliable.

As for the second research instrument, it was designed based on the research aim and questionnaire since it seeks in-depth information from respondents in order to triangulate and support the gained data from the questionnaire. Five main interview questions in English were designed and translated into the respondent's first language. So as to valid the interview questions, two experts were invited to double-check the interview questions in relation to the research aim, and a group of five students were invited to partake in the pilot interview.

Steps for Data Collection and Analysis

The data generation was conducted within major steps. The first step is that the questionnaire in the Microsoft Form was directly administered to students via their email. Students could complete the questionnaire with ease by using their smartphone, laptop, iPad, or computer. They spent approximately 15 – 20 minutes completing the questionnaire. The reception of the responses to the questionnaire was open within one week. All the collected responses were screened and double-checked for their validity. The number of received responses was 343, but that of accepted responses was 300. When it came to the second step, fifteen students were voluntarily invited to participate in the semi-structured interviews conducted in groups of five students, and all students were informed of the interview purpose and given a consent form. Each interview lasted roughly 30-35 minutes. All interviews were audio-recorded with the interviewee's agreement.

In terms of data analysis steps, this study adopted the sociolinguistic perspective to interpret the research results in relation to different features of society (e.g., cultural & linguistic characteristics) (Meyerhoff, 2011). Both quantitative and qualitative types of data were obtained from this study. The first type of data was from the questionnaire and processed in terms of descriptive statistics (M = Mean; SD = Standard Deviation) with the assistance of the SPSS software (version 24) (Mackey & Gass, 2005). The five-point Likert scale was interpreted in an interval of .80, i.e., 100-1.800: Strongly disagree; 1.81-2.60: Disagree; 2.61-3.40: Neutral; 3.41-4.20: Agree; and 4.21-5.00: Strongly agree (Kan, 2009). The second one was from semi-structured interviews and analyzed using the content analysis approach (Curtis et al. 2000). Firstly, all interview recordings were transcribed in textual forms and translated into English. Secondly, three major transcripts were coded as T1, T2, and T3, and fifteen interviewees were given anonymous names as S1, S2 to S15 for confidential purposes. Next, all the transcripts were read and reread many times. Finally, deductive analysis was employed to generate the categories and themes. The preliminary results were sent back to the interviewees for content double-checking to ensure that their ideas were not misunderstood. Apart from that, the intra-rating technique was carried out to ensure the reliability of the qualitative data analysis.

RESULTS AND DISCUSSION

Results

Vietnamese L2 Students' Perceptions of the Effects of BL on Their Vocabulary Enhancement

The constructs of Vietnamese L2 students' perceptions of the effects of BL on their vocabulary enhancement include four components, namely remembering a wide range of vocabulary (five items), recognizing vocabulary in context (five items), applying vocabulary in writing (five items), and applying vocabulary in speaking (five items). As can be seen in Table one, the average mean score of Vietnamese L2 students' perceptions of the effects of BL on their vocabulary enhancement was rather high (M = 3.66; SD = .77). Regarding the mean score of each component, it was noticed that participants considered the use of BL could promote their remembering a wide range of vocabulary (M = 3.72; SD = .79) and recognize the vocabulary meaning in context (M = 3.65; SD = .81). Furthermore, participants also believed that the application of BL could help them and apply vocabulary in writing effectively (M = 3.66; SD = .80) and in speaking effectively (M = 3.61; SD = .82). Such results mean that the research participants perceived that the deployment of BL in GE courses could have positive effects on their vocabulary enhancement.

Table 1. Vietnamese L2 students' perceptions of the effects of BL on their vocabulary enhancement

No.	Components	N = 300	
		M	SD
1	Remembering a wide range of vocabulary	3.72	.79
2	Recognizing vocabulary meaning in context	3.65	.81
3	Applying vocabulary in writing effectively	3.66	.80
4	Applying vocabulary in speaking effectively	3.61	.82

continued on following page

Table 1. Continued

No.	Components	N = 300	
		M	**SD**
Everage		**3.66**	**.77**

Vietnamese L2 Students' Perceptions of the Effects of BL on Remembering a Wide Range of Vocabulary

As for Vietnamese L2 students' perceptions of the effects of BL on remembering a wide range of vocabulary, five items as displayed in Table two indicate that respondents supposed that BL-based GE courses could help them remember "complicated words" (item one: M = 3.89; SD = .92 and "word collocations" (item five: M = 3.72; SD = .89) they had learned in the course. Additionally, they admitted that they could remember "idiomatic expressions" (item two: M = 3.68; SD = .91), "antonyms of the words" (item three: M = 3.58; SD = .93) and "word family of the words" (item four: M = 3.75; SD = .88) they had learned in the course thanks to the deployment of BL in GE courses. In brief, participants believed in the positive effects of BL on remembering a wide range of vocabulary.

Table 2. Vietnamese L2 students' perceptions of the effects of BL on remembering a wide range of vocabulary

No.	The deployment of BL in GE courses can help me remember...	N = 300	
		M	**SD**
1	complicated words I have learned in the course.	3.89	.92
2	idiomatic expressions I have learned in the course.	3.68	.91
3	antonyms of the words I have learned in the course.	3.58	.93
4	word family of the words I have learned in the course.	3.75	.88
5	word collocations I have learned in the course.	3.72	.89

The qualitative results were seen to support the quantitative ones. It was found out that most of the interviewees agreed that the BL approach was effective in enhancing their vocabulary as they could remember most of the words learned in the course and they could identify the word family effectively. Some significant extracts are:

In my opinion, the BL approach was effective in helping my friends and me learn and remember the vocabulary because we had appropriate time to learn the vocabulary through videos on E-learning at home and then spent more time practicing the vocabulary in exercises, discussion, presentation, sentence formation and so on in the classroom under the lecturer's instruction. The videos of vocabulary lessons were also delivered in English and motivated us to guess the meaning of new words by relating to words of similar meanings. (S1)

...BL can help me remember new words and learn the word family effectively thanks to the design of assignments on E-learning.... In the videos of vocabulary introduction, the teaching of vocabulary was always accompanied by word family, which motivated me to learn new words together with their word family. (S3)

Vietnamese L2 Students' Perceptions of the Effects of BL on Recognizing Vocabulary Meaning in Context

In terms of recognizing the vocabulary meaning in context, there are five items as illustrated in Table three. It was observed that thanks to the application of BL in GE courses, participants could recognize a word's "denotative meanings" (item six: M = 3.74; SD = .90) and "connotative meanings" (item eight: M = 3.67; SD = .91), and "similar meanings of different words" (item nine: M = 3.64; SD = .90) based on the context. Additionally, through the BL approach, participants could recognize "different meanings of a word in different contexts" (item seven: M = 3.65; SD = .94) and "different meanings of different words with similar spelling based on the context" (item 10: M = 3.56; SD = .92). In short, participants in this research advocated the positive effects of BL on their recognizing vocabulary meaning in context.

Table 3. Vietnamese L2 students' perceptions of the effects of BL on recognizing vocabulary meaning in context

No.	The deployment of BL in GE courses can help me recognize...	N = 300	
		M	SD
6	a word's denotative meanings based on the context.	3.74	.90
7	a word's connotative meanings based on the context.	3.65	.94
8	different meanings of a word in different contexts.	3.67	.91
9	similar meanings of different words based on the context.	3.64	.90
10	different meanings of different words with similar spelling based on the context.	3.56	.92

In respect of the qualitative results, similar results were found. Interviewed participants shared about the positive effects of BL on their ability to recognize the meaning of vocabulary in context. They said:

During the course, I learned vocabulary by watching video clips online at home and did 2 -3 follow-up vocabulary exercises; hence, I could remember the vocabulary quite clearly before going to class. Thus, when I came up with the new words in the reading passages in class, I could quickly identify the meaning of the words in the context or based on the learned words to predict the meanings of the words around. (S6)

I did not have many difficulties in recognizing the meaning of the new words in the context, especially in reading assignments in class, because I had to complete many exercises of vocabulary before going to class, and it was compulsory for me to learn and finish vocabulary exercises at home. (S11)

Vietnamese L2 Students' Perceptions of the Effects of BL on Applying Vocabulary in Writing Effectively

As shown in Table four, there were five items to measure L2 students' perceptions of the effects of BL on applying vocabulary in writing effectively. Participants agreed that the BL-based GE courses could help them use words "with correct meanings" (item 14: M = 3.82; SD = .97) and "with an appropriate formality" (item 15: M = 3.65; SD = .90) in writing. Besides, they also thought that they could use words with correct "connotative meanings (item 12: M = 3.70; SD = .87), "denotative meanings" (item 11: M = 3.62; SD = .89), and "collocations" (item 13: M = 3.53; SD = .90) in writing upon the completion of the BL-based GE course. To summarize, the deployment of BL in GE courses affected research participants' ability to apply vocabulary in writing.

Table 4. Vietnamese L2 students' perceptions of the effects of BL on applying vocabulary in writing effectively

No.	The deployment of BL in GE courses can help me use words...	N = 300	
		M	SD
11	with correct denotative meanings in writing.	3.62	.89
12	with correct connotative meanings in writing.	3.70	.87
13	with correct collocations in writing.	3.53	.90
14	with correct meanings in writing.	3.82	.97
15	with an appropriate formality in writing.	3.65	.90

The interview data revealed that the qualitative results supported the quantitative ones as interviewees showed positive feedback on the application of BL in GE courses. As they could remember and recognize a wide range of vocabulary, they could use vocabulary in their writing more proficiently.

With the BL approach, I have more time to practice vocabulary in class. My practice time for vocabulary increased as I had to complete the online vocabulary modules at home. I can remember new words and use them in my writing better. (S3)

"Thanks to the online vocabulary modules, I feel more confident in writing activities in class and handle writing tasks in comfort...." (S4)

Vietnamese L2 Students' Perceptions of the Effects of BL on Applying Vocabulary in Speaking Effectively

Table five presents the five items measuring L2 students' perceptions of the effects of BL on applying vocabulary in speaking. It was seen that participants reckoned that they could use words with "correct meanings" (item 19: M = 3.70; SD = .93), "correct denotative meanings" (item 16: M = 3.65; SD = .90), and "correct connotative meanings" (item 17: M = 3.62; SD = .90) in speaking after taking the BL-based GE courses. They could also use words with "correct pronunciation" (item 18: M = 3.63; SD = .94) and "an appropriate formality (item 20: M = 3.46; SD = .92) in speaking. In brief, participants could use vocabulary in speaking effectively thanks to the deployment of BL in GE courses.

Table 5. Vietnamese L2 students' perceptions of the effects of BL on applying vocabulary in speaking effectively

No.	The deployment of BL in GE courses can help me use words....	N = 300	
		M	SD
16	with correct denotative meanings in speaking.	3.65	.90
17	with correct connotative meanings in speaking.	3.62	.90
18	with correct pronunciation in speaking.	3.63	.94
19	with correct meanings in speaking.	3.70	.93
20	with an appropriate formality in speaking.	3.46	.92

Concerning the qualitative data collected from the interviews, it was found out that participants thought that BL-based GE courses were helpful for them as they could use vocabulary in speaking appropriately. They could speak English with correct pronunciation and meanings. They shared:

I can practice my pronunciation at home when I watch the video clips about vocabulary. Thus, I feel more comfortable when using the words in speaking activities in class. In addition, the vocabulary modules are accompanied by supplementary sessions of pronunciation practice in which I can practice basic vowels or consonants with audio and phonetic illustration.... (S5)

...I can practice and remember new words before the lessons. By doing different exercises about vocabulary, I understand the denotative and connotative meanings of the words. Moreover, I can practice using vocabulary in different speaking activities in class, so I can use vocabulary in speaking effectively. (S7)

DISCUSSION

This study explored Vietnamese L2 students' perceptions of the effects of BL on their vocabulary enhancement, and it revealed that research participants believed BL-based GE courses were effective in enhancing their vocabulary. Firstly, the BL approach could have positive effects on L2 students' ability to remember a wide range of vocabulary. One of the plausible reasons is the nature of the BL model. It is theoretically asserted that BL can replace classroom hours with components of pedagogy to provide more academic activities outside the classroom so that students can have more opportunities to engage in EFL tasks as well as construct meaningful understanding (Garrison & Vaughan, 2007). This theoretical foundation is applicable in the context of the research site where materials, curriculum, and technology applications were designed to adapt to students' weekly workload, review demands, assessment requirements, and user convenience in order that the students could enrich as many lexical resources as possible. In this research context, students were asked to learn and practice vocabulary before and after the in-class lessons on the E-learning platform, which provides interactive video instruction and requires students to understand the word's meaning through synonymous expressions, synonyms, and antonyms; hence, they could learn and remember vocabulary. This finding was supported by the study carried by Vasbieva et al. (2016) who concluded that the BL-learning approach with appropriate design of tools, materials, and technology applications according to the students' needs and interests could increase the number of the learned vocabulary.

Secondly, the study indicated that BL-based GE courses could enhance L2 students' ability to recognize the vocabulary meaning in contexts. This can be explained by the fact that BL promotes a student-centered approach and student-oriented education, allowing students to reflect more during their learning process to effectively confirm their knowledge (Garrison & Vaughan, 2007). The acquisition and practice of vocabulary meaning is one part of this process. This finding resonates with the finding from the previous study carried out by Ono and Ishihara (2012) who claimed that as long as students increased their consciousness and motivation in language learning, they could create their own strategies in vocabulary learning, which could lead to a better ability to recall and recognize the vocabulary in context. Within this study, the before-class lessons on E-learning were designed to well-equip students with the vocabulary knowledge (part of speech, forms, meanings, and examples) before they practiced the new words in reading, writing, and speaking activities in the in-class lessons; thus, this could contribute to the results that students found the BL approach effective in helping them to recognize vocabulary in context.

Thirdly, BL-based GE courses were believed to have positive effects on L2 students' ability to use vocabulary in their writing and speaking. This finding may be due to the fact that students were required to do various vocabulary exercises before class, during class and after class. Thanks to this instruction modality, students could gain a better ability to carry out meaningful communication in speaking and writing (Vasbieva et al., 2016). This finding was aligned with that from Ebadi and Ghuchi's (2018) study which unraveled that the application of the BL approach in EFL courses could provide students with in-class and online instructions to enhance their capacity to remember new words and apply them to speak and write effectively.

CONCLUSION

This research has gained the conclusion that Vietnamese L2 students perceived the positive effects of the deployment of BL on their vocabulary enhancement as they believed that BL-based GE courses could help them remember a wide range of vocabulary, recognize vocabulary meaning in context, and apply vocabulary in writing and speaking effectively. Accordingly, pedagogical implications are drawn. Firstly, as found that BL was effective in vocabulary enhancement, the deployment of BL in English language education should be extensively encouraged. The BL approach should be embedded in different online platforms (e.g., Moodle, LMS) to promote flexible, interactive, and collaborative learning, and the learning and teaching experience become more engaging, encouraging, and inspiring. Additionally, the BL approach can make English language education more student-centered and student-oriented so that students are intrinsically motivated to develop self-autonomy, self-discipline, and self-regulated learning strategies to construct meaningful understanding and critical reflection for knowledge.

Secondly, both teachers and students should be equipped with the necessary skills to exploit the benefits of BL for English language education fully. Being equipped with a profound understanding of BL and skills to design lesson plans, assignments, activities, and assessment forms suitable for the BL approach, teachers can make the fullest use of the in-class instruction to optimize students' application of knowledge, strengthen productive skills, and develop their critical thinking, creativity, and confidence in English. Training for teachers is fundamental because teachers play a crucial part in facilitating students' learning process by helping them to combine the knowledge from online lessons and the practice tasks in physical classrooms and in real-life situations (Shivam & Singh, 2015). As for students, it is also important to train them in basic comprehension of the BL approach, 21st-century soft skills, and self-regulated language learning strategies before the implementation of the BL model (Lalima & Dangwal, 2017). In order to carry out this process, workshops should be organized to introduce to students the characteristics and benefits of the BL approach for their learning outcomes. As long as the students understand the purposes of implementing blended learning methods in EFL courses, they will be more cooperative and active in the implementation process. Furthermore, students should be well-informed about the functions of web-based online lessons, guidelines for using online materials, studying with videos, and the utility of platforms, namely, LMS, E-learning, or Moodles.

Some limitations in this study can be acknowledged. The first limitation is that this study only delved into students' perceptions by using a survey questionnaire and semi-structured interview for data generation. Although valuable insights into participants' perspectives can be collected by these instruments, various biases cannot be avoided. Another limitation is the research focus on vocabulary enhancement, which may not provide a general picture of the effect of BL on other language skills, such as grammar, reading, speaking, listening, speaking Last but not least, the research site and participants were narrowed to a research context; therefore, the findings may not be generalized to a larger EFL students in the context of Vietnam. Therefore, it is recommended that further research should be designed with an experimental design using pre-test and post-test, and it should involve more research variables, i.e., micro language skills (grammar, pronunciation) and macro language skills (listening, speaking, reading, writing).

ACKNOWLEDGMENT

The authors would like to appreciate all the unwavering support from administrators, lecturers, and experts so that this study could be smoothly conducted. They also thank the anonymous participants for their willingness to partake in this study.

REFERENCES

Al Zumor, A. W. Q., Al Refaai, I. K., Eddin, E. A. B., & Al-Rahman, F. H. A. (2013). EFL students' perceptions of a blended learning environment: Advantages, limitations and suggestions for improvement. *English Language Teaching*, 6(10), 95–110. 10.5539/elt.v6n10p95

Badawi, M. P. (2009). *Using language learning for enhancing EFL prospective teachers' pedagogical knowledge and performance*. Learning & Language - The Spirit of the Age, Ain Shams University Guest House, Cairo, Egypt.

Bath, D., & Bourke, J. (2010). *Getting started with blended learning*. Griffth University Press.

Creswell, J. W., & Creswell, J. D. (2018). *Research design: qualitative, quantitative, and mixed methods approaches* (5th ed.). SAGE Publications, Inc.

Curtis, S., Gesler, W., Smith, G., & Washburn, S. (2000). Approaches to sampling and case selection in qualitative research: Examples in the geography of health. *Social Science & Medicine*, 50(7-8), 1001–1014. 10.1016/S0277-9536(99)00350-010714922

Dastjerdi, H. V. (2011). An investigation into the impact of traditional vs. blended teaching on EFL learners' vocabulary acquisition: M-learning in focus. *International Journal of Humanities and Social Science*, 1(15), 202–207.

Duong, T. M., & Tran, T. Q. (2023). Facebook-based language learning: Vietnamese university EFL students' attitudes and practices. In Bui, H. P., & Kumar, R. K. (Eds.), *Multidisciplinary applications of computer-mediated communication*. IGI Global. 10.4018/978-1-6684-7034-3.ch007

Duong, T. M., Tran, T. Q., & Nguyen, T. T. P. (2021). Non-English majored students' use of English vocabulary learning strategies with technology-enhanced language learning tools. [AJUE]. *Asian Journal of University Education*, 17(4), 455–463. 10.24191/ajue.v17i4.16252

Ebadi, S., & Ghuchi, K. D. (2018). Investigating the effects of blended learning approach on vocabulary enhancement from EFL learners' perspectives. *Journal on English Language Teaching*, 8(2), 57–68. 10.26634/jelt.8.2.13981

Garrison, D. R., & Vaughan, N. D. (2007). *Blended learning in higher education: Framework, principles and guidelines*. John Wiley and Sons. 10.1002/9781118269558

Government of Vietnam. (2021). *National Education Development Strategy 2021-2030*. Government of Vietnam. https://shorturl.at/g3sO5

Graham, C. (2006). Blended learning systems. Definitions, current trends and future directions. In Bonk, C., & Graham, C. (Eds.), *The handbook of blended learning: Global perspectives, local designs*. John Wiley and Sons.

Kan, A. (2009). *Statistical procedures on measurement results. In the H. Atilgan. Assessment and evaluation in education*. Ani Publications.

Khodabandeh, F., & Mombini, A. (2024). Exploring the effect of augmented reality technology on high school students' vocabulary learning, personality traits, and self-efficacy in flipped and blended classes. *Education and Information Technologies*, 1–24. 10.1007/s10639-024-12486-5

Mackey, A., & Gass, M. S. (2005). *Second language research: Methodology and design*. Lawrence Erlbaum Associates.

Meyerhoff, M. (2011). *Introducing Sociolinguistics*. Taylor & Francis.

Mohammed Nuri, H. S., Azeez, N., & Mustafa, A. (2023). The effectiveness of blended learning in improving the vocabulary range of postgraduate students. *Journal of Garmian University*, 10(2), 1015–1022. 10.24271/garmian.2023.10281

Nguyen, H. T. T., Sivapalan, S., Hiep, P. H., Van Anh, P. T., & Lan, N. T. M. (2021). Teaching English as a second language in Vietnam: Transitioning from the traditional learning approach to the blended learning approach. In *SHS Web of Conferences* (*Vol. 124*, p. 01003). EDP Sciences.

Ono, Y., & Ishihara, M. (2012). Integrating mobile-based individual activities into the Japanese EFL classroom. *International Journal of Mobile Learning and Organisation*, 6(2), 116. 10.1504/IJMLO.2012.047597

Pham, T. T. H. (2019). Applying blended learning method in teaching English at the University of Da Nang, Vietnam. *Educational Review*, 1, 1–5. 10.26855/er.2019.01.002

Phuong, H. Y., Huynh, M. H., & Huynh, C. M. H. (2019). Students' perceptions of a blended learning environment for English training at a university in Vietnam. *Can Tho University Journal of Science*, 11(3), 57–64. 10.22144/ctu.jen.2019.039

Qinda, S. (2018). The Effects of blended learning on EFL students' usage of grammar in context. *The Eurasia Proceedings of Educational & Social Sciences (EPESS), 10*(2587 – 1753), 11-22.

Saswandi, T., & Ningsih, P. E. A. (2023). The effect of using blended learning strategy toward the students' vocabulary mastery at tenth grade of SMKN 2 *Sungai Penuh.Jurnal Ilmiah Wahana Pendidikan*, 9(2), 633–643.

Sharma, P. (2010). Blended Learning. *ELT Journal*, 64(4), 456–458. 10.1093/elt/ccq043

Srimongkontip, S., & Wiriyakarun, P. (2014). Measuring vocabulary size and vocabulary depth of secondary education students in a Thai-English bilingual school. *Art journal Abulratchathani University, 10*(2), 181-209.

Tran, N. K. N. (2016). The adoption of blended e-learning technology in Vietnam using a revision of the Technology Acceptance Model. *Journal of Information Technology Education*, 15, 253–282. 10.28945/3522

Tran, T. Q., Duong, T. M., & Nguyen, D. T. H. (2023). The use of Edtech Apps in English language learning: EFL learners' perspectives. *Theory and Practice in Language Studies*, 13(5), 1115–1123. 10.17507/tpls.1305.04

Tran, T. Q., & Nguyen, V. L. T. (2023). Insights into Vietnamese bilingual students' Quizlet-based English vocabulary learning. *Journal of Language Teaching and Research*, 14(3), 682–688. 10.17507/jltr.1403.15

Vasbieva, D. G., Klimova, I. I., Agibalova, E. L., Karzhanova, N. V., & Bírová, J. (2016). Enhancement of students' vocabulary learning through a blended learning approach. *International Electronic Journal of Mathematics Education*, 11(5), 1195–1203.

Watson, J. (2008). *Blended learning: The convergence of Online and face to face education*. North American Council for Online Learning. https://files.eric.ed.gov/fulltext/ED509636.pdf

Zhang, W., & Zhu, C. (2018). Comparing learning outcomes of blended learning and traditional face-to-face learning of university students in ESL courses. *International Journal on E-Learning*, 17(2), 251–273. https://www.learntechlib.org/primary/p/171512/

KEY TERMS AND DEFINITIONS

Blended Learning: A learning platform which features an integrated combination of online learning and in-class learning.

Perception: This refers to students' beliefs and opinions about the effects of blending learning on their English vocabulary enhancement.

Vocabulary Enhancement: This refers to the ability to remember a wide range of vocabulary, recognize vocabulary meaning in context, and apply vocabulary in writing and speaking effectively.

Chapter 9
Using Digital Tools to Innovate in Higher Education:
From Icebreakers to Various Skills Development

Véronique Delplancq
https://orcid.org/0000-0002-5456-3832
CIDEI, Polytechnic Institute of Viseu, Portugal

Ana Maria Costa
https://orcid.org/0000-0002-8373-4223
CIDEI, Polytechnic Institute of Viseu, Portugal

José Pereira
CIDEI, Polytechnic Institute of Viseu, Portugal

Romain Gillain
https://orcid.org/0000-0003-1933-1072
CIDEI, Polytechnic Institute of Leiria, Portugal

Susana Fidalgo
CIDEI, Polytechnic Institute of Viseu, Portugal

ABSTRACT

This chapter explores the evolving role of pedagogical innovation in foreign language (FL) classes for media studies undergraduates at the School of Education (ESEV) of the Polytechnic Institute of Viseu (Portugal). It highlights the transformation of digital tools, initially seen as "icebreakers," into powerful aids for active methodol-

DOI: 10.4018/979-8-3693-2591-9.ch009

ogies, fostering both hard and soft skills essential for contemporary society and the job market. Teachers commonly integrate online applications, online platforms, and social networks to enhance FL learning. The narrative delves into challenges faced by teachers and students amid constant societal changes. The text emphasizes skills development, improvements over traditional methods, encountered difficulties, and the dynamics within the teaching-learning process. One relies upon gamification as a tool in FL classes, so as to look into its potential to contribute to the systematic exploration of successful educational innovations supported by digital tools in higher education, providing a foundation for future research.

INTRODUCTION

The rapid evolution of the labour market in the Industry 4.0 panorama has brought about new economic and social challenges (Belchior-Rocha et al., 2022). When recruiting, it is not just hard skills that are sought after, but also soft skills and, recently, mad skills. The aim of these skills games is to discover profiles that are increasingly differentiated and suited to the jobs in question. The various stages of teaching and learning must prepare all students, without exception, to become responsible citizens and quality professionals. To achieve this, the methodologies adopted must ensure that each student feels comfortable and satisfied with their course while working with the community.

The impact of globalization and the marked evolution of digital accessibility is very significant on practices at the level of Higher Education (HE). Recent years have seen an acceleration in the need for teachers to update their teaching skills, namely digital competences (Mirete et al., 2020) and a diversification of the areas of knowledge they need to master, which are often far removed from their academic training. Pedagogical innovation implies a clear improvement in teaching and learning practices, compared with the so-called traditional methods.

In the specific case of HE, other factors come into play, notably the introduction of active and up-to-date methodologies, the consequences of which are the development of students' knowledge and skills, in close correlation with changes in society and in the labour market. A multi-disciplinary perspective, the focus on students aiming at more effective learning, autonomy, motivation, individualized pathways in a collaborative environment are all guarantees of integration, success and of discouraging academic drop-out. This involves reviewing teaching practices, acquiring new skills for teachers and rethinking the whole teaching-learning process.

This chapter aims to highlight the path followed by teachers in the School of Education (ESEV) of the Polytechnic Institute of Viseu (IPV) (Portugal) over several years in order to adapt the teaching-learning of foreign languages (FL) in curricular units of the 1st cycle of studies in Media Studies at ESEV to the students' profiles (their needs, but also their well-being and expectations, overcoming difficulties in learning and adapting), career paths and the demands of the current labour market. Thanks to the first project (LEE), we were able to gain a better understanding of the demands posed by the job market including the needs in terms of FL. This allowed for a reflection on our teaching practices pertaining to the skills to be developed with our students, the methodologies and strategies to be adopted to better achieve these objectives and the content to be covered. This reflection has been complemented by the need to innovate to keep pace with technological developments and the realities of the day-to-day digital environment within which our students and society in general interacts. The JASM project has enabled us to work on a range of skills with students, including linguistic, cultural and intercultural skills, using digital tools, in particular the Korsakow platform. This work allowed us to understand that students greatly appreciate the implementation of activities associated with active pedagogies (especially project-based pedagogy) involving digital tools, which helped them to realise where their weaknesses lay in terms of creativity, critical thinking, effective management of their learning autonomy, and so on. These reflections led us to diversify the use of digital tools, to intensify interdisciplinarity, to give students even more autonomy in the choice of projects per group, the production of documents, their disclosure, etc. Gamification (APSASeG) has naturally emerged as an effective strategy for updating practices and strengthening the environment to ensure more equitable and sustainable learning.

After presenting the key competences of the 21st century and recalling the relationship between digital tools and educational innovation, we will see what the challenges of using active methodologies and digital technologies are, from the point of view of the different actors in the learning process. We will look into their trajectory as they deepen the various competences to be worked on with the students, who are intended to be highly motivated, no matter if the path is experimental and made possible by the implementation over time of different projects inside and outside the classroom, designed and developed by international and multidisciplinary teams. In brief, objectives, methodology and conclusions of each project are as mentioned below.

From our point of view, sharing FL learning teaching experiences in HE contributes to a critical enquiry into the evolution of possible and effective strategies in the digital age, the needs of students and the labour market, and the practices of teachers. The conclusions show that the difficulties are numerous, ranging from the time invested by teachers in training and creating their material, to their availability, to their need for flexibility and rapid readjustment in the face of new situations, not to mention the constant monitoring of students' progress and the consequent reorientation of strategies to ensure effective teaching. In terms of benefits, it is undeniable that students are much more motivated, attentive and creative, which favours the acquisition of knowledge and skills related to FL.

The Starting Point: Key Competences of the 21st Century

In 2019 the European Commission defined a set of eight key competences for education and lifelong learning. These include namely multilingual competence, digital competence, personal, social and learning to learn competence, citizenship competence, and cultural awareness and expression competence:

- Multilingual competence covers the development of positive attitudes and intercultural communication (European Commission, 2019).
- Digital skills range from the search for information to its use, including its processing. Van Laar et al. (2020) propose as 21st century digital skills, six categories: information digital skills (searching, evaluating and organizing information); communication digital skills (communication at a distance); collaboration digital skills (sharing information in online collaborative platforms); critical thinking digital skills (critical reflection to combat fake news); creative digital skills (new digital environments enable the creation of creative content); problem-solving digital skills (figuring out how to solve the problem effectively).
- Acquired in formal education or not, the social and learning to learn competence is essential to become responsible, critical citizens, actors in their learning and their professional career (Sala et al., 2020). The European Framework (LifeComp) for this competence is divided into three subgroups, due to its global competence nature: personal (self-regulation, flexibility, wellbeing), social (empathy, communication, collaboration) and learning to learn (growth mindset, critical thinking, managing learning). Communicative competence involves cognitive skills combined with emotional and behavioural skills (Qobilovna, 2023).
- The citizen competence, crossed with multilingual and intercultural competence, makes it possible to train responsible intercultural, critical, and democratic citizens. It is essential for reviewing the performance of our social representations, questioning these representations, and working for change (Byram & Golubeva, 2020).
- In the complex context of diversity, the cultural awareness and expression competence contributes to positive cultural responses. It must be supplemented or championed by the cultural humility (Nguyen et al., 2021).

According to a report by the World Economic Forum (Schwab & Zahidi, 2020), the job market will require twelve soft skills from its employees by 2025. Skills in problem solving, creativity and originality, teamwork, critical thinking, communication, adaptability and flexibility are all examples of these competences. New skills have emerged due to extremely rapid technological advancements, especially in the field of artificial intelligence (Conceição, 2022).

It is extremely important to take all of these skills into consideration throughout the learning process, to set or propose guidelines for the teachers' work, but also the students. The real challenge is to integrate them into the teaching-learning of a subject, in a form adapted to the students' profile, their expectations and their needs, with the adequate modern technologies. For this purpose, teachers must also demonstrate these skills.

In FL classes in HE, students develop a wide range of skills that go beyond simple language acquisition: linguistic, intercultural, communication (including intercultural mediation and cultural sensibility), cognitive, digital, social and collaborative skills. We will show in the project part how these skills were integrated into the work with the students in the FL classroom, thanks to the implementation of projects which followed one another with the same objectives, with a view to improvement.

Digital Tools and Pedagogical Innovation

The simple use of digital tools is not enough to define educational innovation, but today they are essential and valuable aids in the implementation of new dynamic strategies for working with generation Z, for greater openness to the real world and the competitiveness of the professional sectors associated with student training, to guarantee sustainable development and a more democratic education (Ovcharuk et al., 2020). Digital tools are seen as an invaluable help to facilitate innovation by the entire academic community from a perspective of efficiency, equal opportunities and pedagogical challenges (Remond et al., 2021). Digital tools are helping to meet the United Nations' requirements for quality, inclusive and equitable lifelong education (Arora & Mishra, 2019). Technology is intended to enhance learning, regardless of the context and method chosen (Cowling et al., 2022).

The real benefits of digital pedagogy are much discussed, but it is undeniable that it plays a vital role for sustainable learning, collaborative and networked work. The study by Nanjundaswamy et al. (2021) describes the evolution of learning platforms and the concerns, particularly in terms of employability, underlying their design in multidisciplinary teams. The conclusions are that digital collaboration contributes to sustainable learning and the implementation of active methodologies such as collaborative learning, blended learning, and flipped learning. These tools use technology to improve the teaching and learning experience. Learning becomes more interactive, engaging and effective, among other contributions, such as:

- Adaptive and personalized learning: the active learner can choose their path in relevant activities geared to learner's interests and needs and frequently aided by technologies (Cleave, 2020);
- Collaborative environment: beyond the walls of the classroom, students can collaborate on projects, exchange ideas, and have debates. This facilitates group problem-solving and builds a sense of community (Sawant, 2021);
- Interactivity: digital platforms can easily integrate multimedia content and interactive simulations, which helps to make learning more dynamic, while varying the visuals, for example (Clark & Mayer, 2023).

The navigation structure is an essential condition for any digital platform that has a playful or utilitarian intention. To corroborate this same idea, Brenda Laurel (2013) suggests that we think of computers as a theatrical experience. This premise will guide her work in the field of games, stimulating analysis practices, from a behavioral perspective, laying the foundations for usability tests and the way in which interactive systems are evaluated.The interactive potential of platforms does not arise only due to their attractive and stimulating capabilities of joining various media into a perfect and harmonious organizational information platform, but also through a 'friendly contact surface' which, through a given iconography, allows the user to interpret signs that guide navigation, making greater or lesser intellectual effort as the result of the quality of the interactive model and its communication interface.

The growing democratization of computer systems, aimed at globalized use, has placed issues related to interaction and interface at the center of concerns. Nicholas Negroponte (1996) developed this idea, pointing out a somewhat radical solution that seems worthy of some attention: "When it comes to the interface, my dream is to see computers resemble men. (...) What today is called 'character-oriented interface' will become the dominant way in which people talk to machines" (pp. 129-130). This prediction is not only reflected in the new uses of artificial intelligence, together with a general sense of fascination with the potential of using emerging technologies, but also in the creation of bold interfaces that generate an unprecedented level of interest by incorporating perspectives that challenge forms of thinking, teaching and learning.

Learning management systems (LMS) are platforms designed to manage, distribute and track online educational content. Many LMS options are available. For choosing the right platform, it is important to consider factors such as scalability, ease of use, mobile compatibility, collaboration features and the specific needs of the target audience. Also, worthy of being kept in mind is that the landscape of LMS platforms may evolve over time, and new options may emerge.The best-known of these platforms are Moodle, Canva, Blackboard, and Google Classroom.

Other platforms not originally designed for education can be used with and by students to make content more attractive and interactive. These include the Korsakow platform. This platform was developed as an editing system for creating interactive multilinear films for the web, intended for use by journalists, filmmakers, artists, and others engaged in creative jobs. According to its author, Florian Thalhofer, the Korsakow platform was based on a study of Korsakoff's syndrome among university students, whose most frequent symptom, roughly speaking, is the expression of discontinuous and disconcerting thinking, common to individuals who overindulge in alcohol. In this sense, the platform dismisses the archetype of hierarchical arborescent thinking, sharing Deleuze and Guattari's (2007) rhizome thesis and supporting Korsakow's structural multiplicity, which favours horizontality and a great potential for derivation through the suggestion of different evolutions. A distinctive feature of k-film narratives is the non-linear foundation and the idea of parallel possibilities that radically question the traditional conventions of the organization of information to reflect associations and multiplicities. In this regard, Lev Manovich (2001) points to non-sequentiality as the most significant contrast of the new media when compared to their predecessors, i.e. we have moved from a static order of presentation to interactive flexibility. Thus, the architecture of the Korsakow platform provides a favorable spatial dimension for the development of the storytelling process in interactive navigable spaces and with evolution flows of narratives that are perpetuated indefinitely, reconfiguring the k-film dimension.

Its fundamental design makes it possible to arrange text, images, audio, and video from a database and follow dynamically changing visualization sequences based on the choices made by the user or spectator. As a result, the creative process of a K-film necessitates a non-hierarchical mindset that supports an open branching scheme, where the story develops and various outcomes are accepted. It is a potent instrument for writing stories for the 21st century. It is based on the logic of computers, which is their capacity to blend different media, languages, and narrative components to produce a unique, adaptable, and imaginative story. However, it is highly recommendable that the usability of the Korsakow platform categorically rejects preconceived conventions, as Lopes (2010) warns us with the question "Old wine in new bottles?", or Favilla (2007) says in the essay "New technologies, old ideas: notes for a genealogy of computational art", i.e. to oppose the tendency to create projects that work with emerging technologies in the conceptual moulds and with the formal qualities of their old references.

Genially is a web-based tool to create visual materials, appealing interactive presentations, infographics, posters, quizzes, etc., providing resources for the development of interactive multimedia content without requiring sophisticated design or programming knowledge. It allows interactivity, variety of templates, real-time collaboration, integration of multimedia elements, gamification, adaptation to mobile device, among others.

Mobile assisted language learning (MALL) or Mobile-learning (M-learning) can include various forms, such as apps, videos, podcasts, and interactive simulations, using mobile devices, such as smartphones and tablets. The use of mobile devices in the classroom is becoming more and more common (Bernacki et al., 2020). M-learning and its adaptability to busy lives and flexibility have made it increasingly popular in educational environments offering new opportunities for education. Several factors affect the use of M-learning, such as appropriate equipment, teacher training, etc. (Qashou, 2021). Social media is very important in today's classroom (Galvin & Greenhow, 2020). Students and teachers can collaborate, communicate, and share resources on websites like Facebook, Instagram, Youtube, Twitter, etc. They can help students and teachers feel more connected to facilitate group conversations, cooperative projects and exchange of instructional materials, but also to share their production with the communities, encouraging the student to be more active and engaged.

The teachers have opportunities to create a more engaging and inclusive learning environment, incorporating all of these digital tools and M-learning into the classroom for more interativity and dynamism. Project-based learning, problem-based learning, flipped classroom approach, etc. are alternatives to the traditional methodology. Combined with digital tools and other strategies such as gamification (icebreaker games, serious games, among others), virtual and augmented reality, M-learning, etc., these methodologies constitute a real pedagogical activation for forthcoming professionals whose training is not FL oriented (Delplancq et al., 2021). Careful preparation and continuous professional development for teachers are necessary for integrating these digital technologies into the classroom. The intention is to provide a setting where technology supports efficient pedagogy rather than subsumes it, resulting in a more individualized and captivating learning experience for students.

To achieve perfect harmony among skills development, active, equitable and inclusive teaching methods and digital tools, many obstacles must be identified and overcome.

The Challenges

Based on the constructivist paradigm (Bada, 2015), which focuses on how students construct knowledge and give meaning to their experiences, autonomous work should be encouraged and carried out in a collaborative way (cooperative learning), which allows for the development of critical and participatory skills. With demonstrated benefits for language learning, enhancing the experience of leadership and autonomy that favours intellectual maturity and confidence, and stimulating creativity and cooperation, this paradigm calls for combining various active learning methodologies in a holistic approach, such as embodied learning, multiliteracies, project-based learning, and inquiry-based learning (Panigua & Istance, 2018; Sinnayah et al., 2019). By incorporating these approaches into the classroom, teachers hope to establish a dynamic learning environment that accommodates a range of learning preferences and promotes the development of critical thinking, creativity, communication, teamwork, digital literacy, and other vital life skills in addition to academic success.

The goal of multiliteracies is to foster competence in a variety of communication media, such as digital, visual, and conventional literacy (reading and writing), as well as other forms of expression relevant for modern-day societies. The field of neurodidactics has made significant contributions to the understanding of the neuro-communicative component of students, emphasizing its importance in helping them communicate critically in a social context (Carrillo-Garcia & Martínez-Ezquerro, 2018). Of particular importance is the affective component, which allows for the formation of the student's emotional maturity, as well as their linguistic and cultural knowledge, creativity, and aesthetic experience.

In this confluence between pedagogical activation and the use of digital technologies, in the perspective of equity and inclusion learning by crossing with digital literacy, the various actors in the learning process have set work and find themselves faced with some major problems.

With regard to teachers (Biletska et al., 2021), these include, for example, equitable access to digital resources for students, rapid and dazzling improvement/adaptability in managing technological devices and advances, the existence of a large number of easily accessible digital tools on the Internet, which must be mastered and managed correctly without falling into the trap of 'all digital' at all costs; the keen choice of these tools according to the audience, its objectives and expectations; the investment of time and energy; the identification of new problems and their rapid resolution; the redefinition of relationships between stakeholders and their respective roles; the renewal of creativity in productions; rapid adaptation; proactive strategies; sense of community; constant flexibility; the choice of methodologies to be adopted, particularly in terms of evaluation (assessment and feedback, adaptive assessments), etc.

With respect to students in the Portuguese context of HE, the challenge lies more in their acceptance of new working methodologies, including assessment strategies and development of interpersonal relationships, the use of digital tools and technologies in an academic context instead of a private one, the development of their critical thinking and creativity, and making the most of their autonomy (Delplancq et al., 2023). The students can go beyond their difficulties with the introduction of scaffolding, feedback and reflections to maximize their potential learning.

Especially in FL teaching, a regular monitoring and a special attention are necessary to secure the effectiveness of learning organized with digital technologies and active pedagogy (Karsenti et al., 2020).

FL Projects and Development of Competences

Learning a FL for a specific purpose at HE level is very useful because it allows for the focus on acquiring vocabulary, grammar, and various skills that match the student's goals (professional outings, career opportunities, personal interests) (Grynyuk, 2016). The use of resources such as online platforms and other digital tools for immersion experiences guided by the teacher are a powerful aid for implementing active methodologies. The following projects developed in Portuguese HE show how FL learning practices are evolving, both at teacher level and in terms of interaction with students, not only to keep pace with changes in technology, society and the job market, but also with a view to ensuring that students are proactive and feel good, combating drop-out and promoting success for all.

All these projects have in common the fact that they promote FL learning for specific purposes in HE, which necessarily involves developing diversified skills linked to changes in the labour market and in society in general, increasing student motivation and challenging teaching practices. Undeniably, issues such as the monitoring of the work of students and that of teachers, the reflections arising therefrom and thereafter shared with other researchers have enabled our practices to evolve.

The LEE (FL and Employability) Project

For several years now, a few European recommendations have highlighted the importance of forthcoming professionals to develop skills in FL and their underlying cultures. Research has also been carried out in this area, as shown in several studies, like, for example, those of Grasmane & Grasmane (2011) or Tight (2023).

The goal of the LEE project (PROJ/CI&DETS/CGD/0016; 2017-19) was to highlight the needs of the private sector in the Viseu region (Portugal) in terms of the FL skills of its professionals. This study aimed at understanding the importance of FL for enterprises (to clarify how these businesses would handle their first hiring procedures with regard to the value they would place on FL competence and the kind of revenue these abilities may generate for the business), but also for workers' development and how and to what extent companies value and develop such skills. The underlying research question was: which is companies and workers' perception concerning the importance of FL for their economic development?

Methodology

The LEE research project team was made up of teachers and researchers who are experts in FL and entrepreneurship and who worked at the different HE units within the Viseu Polytechnic at the start of the project in 2017. The goal of this form of collaboration was to better understand the interests and concerns of several work settings, be they more general or more specific, to become more familiar with these multiple realities, and to come across individuals with a variety of professional experiences.

Following a comprehensive analysis of the body of research on the topic, a questionnaire was created. Its primary goal was to gather information about the characteristics of businesses situated in the Viseu region, the value that FL skills have in the hiring process, and the necessity for businesses to appoint workers with strong FL expertise. The supplied data was treated with the utmost confidentiality and was solely utilized for statistical analysis. For access to its database, the research team asked the Associação Empresarial da Região de Viseu, the business association of the Viseu area, for cooperation. 495 entrepreneurs had access to the survey online.

By analyzing the job offers that were available in Viseu and the surrounding area, we could determine the relationships among the jobs that were offered (in terms of function, tasks, requirements, professional experience required, hiring conditions, etc.), the FL competences that were demanded and their corresponding levels, the required level of education, the working hours, the pay, and the opportunities for career advancement. Over the course of thirty weeks, 180 job offers that were advertised on various websites (such as Indeed, Net-jobs, Trovit, etc.) were examined. Certain employment offers can show up on multiple websites and for multiple weeks at a time, thus extra care was taken to make sure the identical offers wouldn't be considered more than once. The purpose of conducting semi-structured interviews with employers in the Viseu region was to provide clarity on how language skills and the labour market can establish a genuine and effective connection. This objective would be accomplished by analysing the information gathered from selected job offers. The topics discussed during these interviews were focused on the correlation between FL skills and recruitment competitions, career advancement, and business strategies. Additionally, the added value that such skills can bring to businesses was also explored. It is important to note that the project envisaged primarily to highlight the demands of the preliminary phase of the recruitment process. Simultaneously, activities focused on dissemination and raising awareness were carried out to target various audiences. These activities aimed to highlight the role that FL can play as a potential catalyst for growth, aiding to the successful development of professionals and enhancing people's understanding of the significance of FL in diverse professional fields.

Conclusion

In line with the studies mentioned above and the ELA (European Labour Authority) recommendations (2023), in Viseu and its surrounding area, FL proficiency and employability are strongly intertwined. These FL abilities appear to be a catalyst for increased job prospects, offering an additional advantage when individuals seek employment and a favourable aspect for career advancement. They facilitate a smoother entry into positions that demand a certain level of accountability. When candidates possess similar skills and abilities, their proficiency in a FL often sets them apart. While English is the most commonly sought-after FL, other languages such as French, German, Dutch, and Italian are also highly valued. Having mastery in two or more FL can be greatly appreciated. Additionally, some companies view international experiences as an added advantage: FL skills are most often required in management, the company's board, consultancy services, commercial sectors, and back-office sectors. The level of FL requirements increases with qualifications and experience. Both written and oral FL competences are necessary. Employers can infer other competences, such as adjustment capacity, curiosity, empathy, and the ability to develop the business image, effectiveness, and competitiveness, based on their employees' language skills.

The difficulties encountered were to collect a relevant number of surveys from local companies which, while recognizing the importance of FL, misunderstood the immediate connection between a more theoretical academic approach and the experiential labour market. Nevertheless, the development of this project showed that the mastery of several FL was recognized during recruitment and favoured career progression (Costa Lopes et al., 2018). Consequently, it is essential to strengthen the impact that academic work has upon life in society and professional development.

On the strength of these conclusions, the FL teachers at ESEV have decided to continue their research with the aim of providing students, forthcoming media professionals, with the best possible help in working with FL and developing skills that are vital for the job market.

Learning Context

As a follow-up to the LEE project described above, other projects were implemented with students from the Bachelor's Degree in Media Studies (2nd year) at ESEV. The study plan of this particular course is developed along three years (180 ECTS), now comprising one compulsory FL curricular unit (which includes English and French; 4 ECTS each) and three optional ones (4 ECTS each). It also includes curricular units within the fields of photography, digital art and journalism. This course intends to train media professionals (journalism, audio-visual production and direction and communication consultancy) and develops research in these areas.

The JASM (Open Window onto the World: Foreign Languages, Multimodal Creativity, and Pedagogical Innovation in Higher Education) Project

Today, globalization in HE is a reality associated with multilingualism and multiculturalism (Karpava, 2022). Implementing methodologies based on a constructivist perspective, requires the development of strategies likely to improve the quality of teaching, in line with the objectives of training courses and the needs of the labour market (Rubtsova et al., 2019). Numerous experiments around the world rely on digital tools to work on FL skills for specific purposes with HE students. Examples include the work of Zhang and Zou (2020) or Alzhanova and Chaklikova (2022).

The JASM project (PROJ/IPV/ID&I/030) implemented during the years from 2019-2021, allowed for the acquisition of multilingual and multicultural skills, upon which rests multilingual awareness (Costa Lopes et al., 2023) in the perspective of flipped classroom, project-based learning and multidisciplinarity. The cognitive, aesthetic and emotional dimensions of language were explored. The two FL used were English and French.

Methodology

The teaching team was made up of FL teachers, as well as experts in digital art, educational innovation and migrant integration.

The project was presented to the students. Twenty students volunteered to join the project team. These students and their classmates were given an initial language level test. The test was based on the CEFR levels for written and oral comprehension and written and oral production, and was inspired by the DELF, DALF and TOEFL tests. Response times were checked for each skill block. The average level for English was B2 and for French was between A2 for speaking and B2 for writing.

Five groups of four students were formed. Each group chose a nationality from among those present (Pordata, https://www.pordata.pt/db/municipios/ambiente+de+consulta/tabela/5839568) in the city of Viseu. The nationalities chosen were Angolan, Belarusian, Indian, Italian and Ukrainian. Each group dealt with a different nationality from the other groups and then carried out a study of the country and the stereotypes associated with the respective nationalities/cultures, illustrating the cultural and linguistic diversity in question. This research was presented in the classroom, in the two FL, to all the students in the same year of the course and was one of the elements of continuous assessment for the semester. A seminar on photography was offered to them, in addition to the classes, to emphasize particular aspects of the context in which their photographs were taken.

The groups then had to go and meet a migrant living in the town. Social networks were used to exchange information among students and teachers and the Local Support Centre for the Integration of Migrants facilitated certain contacts. The aim of the first meeting was to present the project and conduct an interview, so that the students could write the story (in both FL) of the migrants' lives. Permission was sought to publish the story and the photos. Through subtitled photographs, in English and French, students tried to show important aspects of the life journey of the chosen migrant families and to highlight relevant unique personality traits. These assignments were also presented and commented on in FL classes, in both languages, and served as the basis for the mid-year assessment. The cross-curricular skills acquired in the FL class and in other technical courses were thus mobilized, giving a clearly practical dimension and an orientation in relation to the objectives of the training and the future professional.

A second evaluation was carried out, based on a conversation with the project students and their colleagues, to take stock of the situation and understand their perception of the work and their feelings about their progress. The results were extremely positive.

Using a migrant object or tradition as a starting point, the students created a story and wrote a storyboard, which formed the basis of an animation that was worked on using the Korsakow multilinear storytelling platform, in both languages (exploration of material culture and digital scenography). The productions were published on social networks, exhibited, screened at events and published in an e-book.

The final assessment also involved an interview with the students, due to health restrictions caused by COVID-19. The learners continued to show great satisfaction and enthusiasm with the methodology followed and the knowledge and skills acquired in a real-life context, while having built on skills worked on in other curricular units.

Conclusion

Digital tools make it easier for students to get involved in the learning process, particularly by activating the emotional component of FL (Bedenlier et al., 2020). The JASM project considered the social and interactive dimension of FL, encouraging communication from a variety of angles, collaboration, and the experience of participation in authentic contexts and in direct relation to the objectives of the course being followed. Linguistic knowledge was combined with cultural and social knowledge as part of the project-based learning pathway. As well as being a learner in the academic context, the student was also a social actor, capable of carrying out tasks other than those rigorously described in the curricula of the teaching units, using interdisciplinary skills associated with the course of study followed. Interdisciplinarity in the work of the specialized FL helped learners to grasp the reality of their future profession. Organized activities were based on the specific theme defined in the project. These various aspects, combined with productions published in different formats, helped to motivate students.

Students were subject to a rigorous work plan. They felt very interested and touched by the people they met and their stories. They recognized that this strategy motivates them more in the acquisition of knowledge and skills. They appreciated collaborative work and shared tasks effectively and naturally, without conflict. They acknowledged that project-based learning makes them work harder and keeps them busier.

The constant sharing of knowledge, good practices and difficulties and the evaluation of progress enabled the development of students' curiosity, motivation, enthusiasm, creativity and autonomy, allowing for language improvement, multiculturality, intercultural communication, autonomous learning and the acquisition of collaborative, as well as transversal skills, particularly digital, namely with the online platform Korsakow, and other professional ones. Students even suggested replicating the work but leaving them free to choose the general themes.

The conclusions of the two FL teachers directly involved were that the students made more autonomous progress, that they made suggestions for improving the work and presenting it, and that they spontaneously intervened in class to point out weaknesses they had come across, and the extent to which they had been able to overcome them, detail which data they had collected and the problems they had encountered. In terms of participation, students' guidelines and outlines were open to suggestions and all productions were corrected, both orally and in writing. The teachers felt motivated and pleased, in a mentor's role, taking on other attitudes and concerns and showing greater availability and flexibility. They had to acquire digital skills and to work with colleagues from other scientific fields. The real difficulties arose with self-training in the use of digital tools, both for teachers and students, as highlighted by a number of studies (for example, Zhang & Zou, 2020).

Considering the strengths and weaknesses of previous experiences, FL teachers felt the need to implement a new project, with the aim of continuing to update classroom practices in order to develop FL skills that would come closer to the needs of today's society and the job market. The active citizenship of future professionals of excellence, for example, is one of the areas of interest.

Project-based learning and Mobile assisted language learning (MALL) or Mobile-learning (M-learning) for a more Engaging, Equitable and Inclusive Learning Environment

In 2021-2022 another project-based learning experience was developed, using digital tools that are easily available in the classroom (Delplancq et al., 2023). With the inclusion of MALL or M-learning (android devices, tablets and laptops) (Hoi, 2020), the mobility in the classroom to recreate other workspaces in class, but also the mobility in and out of the university are guaranteed. The whole process followed strict organisational criteria from the outset, essentially with regard to the pace of work, the timetable and assessment, establishing a culture of sharing, constructive critical self-assessment and autonomy in terms of research and carrying out tasks. More autonomy was given to the students, who were able to choose the project theme, their working methodologies and strategies, as well as the digital formats for presentation and sharing (Criollo-C et al., 2021).

Methodology

Small, heterogeneous groups of students were created. The themes of the projects were chosen by the students, with the only condition that they be socially relevant, to encourage reflection, criticism and debate. Another indication was that the productions, in English and French, had to be presented in a variety of digital formats, in original and creative ways, for publication on social networks and presentations to colleagues.

The project proposals had to follow a well-defined structure and were shared in class with the aim of improving the proposals through collaborative work and constructive criticism. A class Facebook account was created, with the necessary security and privacy settings, and invitations were sent out to form the group of friends. Other social networks (Instagram, Youtube) were chosen by some groups to complement their Facebook publications. The students also shared the material with each other via a class WhatsApp group. The Moodle platform, managed by the two teachers, was used to share support documents, announcements in the forum, and so on and proved to be an essential tool for the exchange of information and work.

After theoretical research on the themes, also presented in class, the students began their interviews and their photographic and video reports. They worked on their productions to give them rhythm and dynamism, using the Canva platform and image and video editors in particular (Photoshop, Adobe Premiere, etc.). A digital art expert delivered a session on photography mid-way.

All the students' assignments were posted on social media accounts and presented in the classroom. The work was formally assessed by the teachers on a regular basis during the course of the semester. The results were systematically discussed in class.

Among other benefits, the students appreciated their autonomy and the opportunity to write job-oriented FL assignments, mobilizing their already acquired skills in the field. Because this type of support is more demanding and thorough than preparing lessons using traditional methods, it is also more valuable in terms of the learning environment, both inside and outside the classroom.

Conclusion

The use of online social networking platforms is commonplace in FL learning (see for example Andujar & Çakmak, 2023). We consider them a way of sharing student productions, and therefore appropriate for presenting FL content in a creative, animated and reduced format, likely to appeal to the audience.

It was noted that all the students' FL level increased by one grade, both in writing and speaking. With regard to the monitoring of the activities and the qualitative assessment carried out throughout and at the end of the semester, through conversations based on free questions and comments, it can be said that the students appreciated the freedom to choose the theme of the project and the design of the course. They recognised that they had gained autonomy and were more comfortable communicating in FL. The session on photography offered by an expert was considered beneficial and the teachers' suggestions for follow-up, reorientation and correction were seen as very useful. However, they admitted that they found it difficult to rely on all the benefits of autonomy, even considering the collaborative nature of the work, due to a lack of innovative ideas and creativity at the various stages of the process, particularly to make the result more attractive.

Assuming the role of a supervisor implied that the teachers needed to acquire proficiency in the mastery of new technologies (specifically employing digital tools), possess a commendable understanding of the subject matter and its attributes, exhibit flexibility, adaptability on the spot, enhanced accessibility even beyond the confines of the classroom walls, provide guidance in challenging scenarios, and offer diverse forms of assistance that extend beyond language boundaries. Given that this form of support is considerably more demanding and rigorous than preparing lessons using conventional methods, it also proves to be highly gratifying in terms of fostering a conducive learning atmosphere within and beyond the classroom. Maintaining the pace of work during the different sessions and the balance of material produced among the groups are other difficulties that should be highlighted.

Many skills have been developed, far beyond the traditional skills in the FL class. To continue the introduction of new digital tools and to further increase the interactivity and motivation of the students, as well as a certain curiosity, a new project has been launched, within the framework of the gamification of learning, a new challenge for both teachers and learners.

The APSASeG (Opening the Classroom Doors: Serious Games – The Impact of Gamification on the Teaching/ Learning of FL in Higher Education) Project

As the subtitle announces, a new project is underway (PROJ/I&DI/CI&DEI/009), focusing on the gamification within FL classes at the same level of teaching. Its main objective is to assess the impact of the use of serious games on FL learning and skills development, for a differentiated and diversified learning approach, based on classroom learning experiences (in line with experiments carried out around the world, as can be seen, for example, in Laura-De La Cruz et al., 2023).

A serious game merges the educational nature of a pedagogical scenario with the entertaining elements of a video game (Alvarez, 2007). Presently, serious games have experienced significant growth in various fields, aiming to enhance awareness, education, and training without any limitations of space or time. To effectively facilitate learning, the game should align with the training environment and the students' characteristics, encompassing well-defined objectives and instructions, while fostering skill acquisition for the user (Vermeulen, 2018).

Methodology

The methodologies applied, within a collaborative and constructive learning environment, are project-based learning, mobile learning, flipped learning, gamification and peer assessment. A work plan has been designed with dashboard panel and KPI (Key Performance Indicator) defined with the SMART (specific, measurable, achievable, relevant, and time-bound) method. The platform Genially was found to be the most useful, for creating escape games, in English and in French, around specific themes pertaining to media studies. In addition to this platform, one plans to use Canva or Gamma.app (mind map, presentations, etc.), Pinterest (Mood board), Google Doc (joint work on documents), Moodle and social networks for sharing materials and productions and Kahoot, Flippizz, LearningApps and Mendimeter for evaluation.

At the start of the semester, students took language level tests (in French and English, at the written and oral level, both in terms of reception/understanding and production). Students will be required to do another language level test at the end of the semester. Throughout the sessions, regular monitoring made it possible to reinforce or redirect the work in progress. The chosen evaluation process is of a continuous nature, involving assignments submitted through the Moodle platform and presented to the class, in each of the FLs. Obvious challenges arise when choosing the platforms and activities created which must correspond to the level of the students, their professional areas and avoid routine and also the wow effect.

DISCUSSION AND PERSPECTIVES

The primary aim of this experimental pathway is to help systematize the relationship between FL learning in HE, for specific purposes, the needs of the job market alongside personal development and the need to update practices. Even though the activities undertaken by students within the FL curricular units enable them to develop a substantial set of skills that go well beyond linguistic competence, FL are often seen as complementary to curricular units that are considered core training units. It should, thus, be said that practice with the various well-known skills in FL learning (linguistic, cultural, and intercultural) in a joint way with transversal skills, namely digital and social ones, is essential for the training of responsible citizens and competitive professionals, able to meet the demands of the labour market according to the key competences of the 21st century presented above (multilingual competence, digital skills searching, evaluating and organizing information, communication, collaboration, critical thinking, creative digital skills, problem-solving digital skills, social and learning to learn competence, citizen competence, cultural awareness and expression competence).

These reflections were the trigger for the creation of a multidisciplinary team and the development of projects with a common objective: the teaching-learning of FL for specific purposes, at a higher level, in a more dynamic way, more and more centered on the student. While aiming at collaboration and interaction, the main target is obviously focused on increasing students' opportunities of progress in a friendly environment, regardless of their different interests and heterogeneous FL levels, and on intensifying the dialogue with these learners to better guide them in their learning process providing proper training pertaining to their forthcoming professional field. This way, through relevant and constant interactions, even outside the classroom, discriminatory processes make no sense. Persistent dialogue and monitoring also make it possible to create a trustworthy environment, which promotes the emotional component of the language. The fatigue caused by certain activities and time spent by students creating productions using digital platforms should be considered too. The fact that teachers are involved in students' learning progress and not just in quantitative evaluation has also contributed greatly to student motivation, that is to say to our general objective, which is that of revalidation of FL learning in HE.

Bearing in mind the scientific literature outlined, the fact that the projects developed has led to similar outcomes shows that the benefit of the use of active learning methods centered on the student, in collaborative work environments facilitates interactive processes among the various participants, increases student interest and motivation and makes knowledge acquisition easier compared to traditional strategies, language knowledge and skills. Students struggle with autonomy, creativity, a more focused work process and critical thinking. The difficulties in implementing new methodologies in the classroom lie in the preparation time required from teachers, their necessary training (often self-training) the management of working time, the need to ensure a balanced participation of all actors, so as to maintain the enthusiasm often shown by students in the classroom, fostering flexibility and creativity on their part with respect to the preparation of activities, followed by the required and expected evaluation of what has actually been learnt. At student level, we note a very easy adaptation, an obvious willingness to collaborate, even though they sometimes show some difficulty in distinguishing purely playful from educational gamification and also in terms of the fulfilment of all the tasks in a thorough, in-depth manner.

We can also deduce that the role of the teacher has very clearly changed. Student's development is reflected in his/her enthusiasm, his motivation, the quality of his/her interactions with other students and the teaching staff, his/her general satisfaction and well-being, in addition to the acquisition of new knowledge and the development of many skills. The teacher must, therefore, search self-training inasmuch as concerns the use of new, constantly evolving digital tools, creating his/her own material adequate to the specific objectives pursued, but also acquire flexibility to respond immediately to students' queries and fluidly redirect activities in case of emerging difficulties. This coaching role involves much more availability and knowledge than the ones inherent to traditional FL learning. The methodology followed, including evaluation, has to be very clearly stated in a work plan negotiated with the students. The activities need to be clearly explained and all steps justified and framed within this plan and its objectives. Constant dialogue with students is fundamental to ensure that they feel well integrated and aware of their progress and difficulties, which they should be able to express easily and quickly. All students' difficulties have to be carefully observed and accounted for, once overcoming such difficulties is also the key to success. Let us consider, for example, the difficulty encountered by some in taking full advantage of the autonomy offered them. This may arise from the fact that, for these students, the task instructions (for instance in an escape game) were not clear enough, or that they feel less comfortable with certain digital tools. This challenge is extremely motivating in terms of teaching practices, allowing students to become more and better involved in their learning.

As digital skills have become increasingly important, these results also highlight the fact that such skills should absolutely be integrated into the teaching practice, regardless of the subject area. In this context, gamification poses new challenges and offers great prospects, although there is still much work to be done in the area. During the monitoring process and the self- and hetero-evaluation phases, students clearly expressed both the positive aspects and the difficulties that were described above, but they also made suggestions, such as an increasing motivation due to the competitiveness that is naturally felt in a multiplayer game. In agreement with the World Economic Forum report (Schwab & Zahidi, 2020), these methodologies, together with digital tools, enable the development of soft skills that are in demand in the labour market: communication, flexibility, adaptability, critical thinking, teamwork, active learning strategies, creativity and originality, and problem-solving skills. With the rapid advancement of technology, especially in the field of artificial intelligence, new capabilities are constantly emerging.

Future research must continue to be concerned with meeting the new challenges of society, as well as integrating the new tools that artificial intelligence offers us, in a reasoned and effective manner, in the respect for the well-being of the student and the satisfaction of the teachers. Special attention must be paid to the real benefits of the application of active pedagogies supported by the use of digital tools, in terms of skills discussed throughout this chapter as well as to the evolution of the evaluative model. It seems obvious that one of the complexities of this work is that each audience has its characteristics and that there are no miraculous recipes that can be applied over time and in any context. Another major problem is the extremely rapid evolution of these digital tools not only in terms of quality but also in terms of quantities.

ACKNOWLEDGMENT

This work is funded by National Funds through the FCT - Foundation for Science and Technology, I.P., within the scope of the project Ref[a] UIDB/05507/2020. Furthermore, we would like to thank the Centre for Studies in Education and Innovation (CI&DEI) and the Polytechnic Institute of Viseu for their support.

REFERENCES

Alvarez, J. (2007). *Du jeu vidéo au serious game: Approches culturelle, pragmatique et formelle*. [Thesis, Université de Toulouse].

Alzhanova, A., & Chaklikova, A. (2022). Multilingual education: Development of professional foreign language communicative competence of students in a digital environment. [IJWLTT]. *International Journal of Web-Based Learning and Teaching Technologies*, 17(1), 1–13. 10.4018/IJWLTT.294572

Andujar, A., & Çakmak, F. (2023). Foreign language learning through instagram: A flipped learning approach. In I. *Management Association (Ed.), Research Anthology on Applying Social Networking Strategies to Classrooms and Libraries* (pp. 278-299). IGI Global.

Arora, N. K., & Mishra, I. (2019). United Nations sustainable development goals 2030 and environmental sustainability: Race against time. *Environmental Sustainability*, 2(4), 339–342. 10.1007/s42398-019-00092-y

Bada, S. O., & Olusegun, S. (2015). Constructivism learning theory. *Journal of Research & Method in Education*, 5(6), 66–70.

Bedenlier, S., Bond, M., Buntins, K., Zawacki-Richter, O., & Kerres, M. (2020). Facilitating student engagement through educational technology in higher education: A systematic review in the field of arts and humanities. *Australasian Journal of Educational Technology*, 36(4), 126–150. 10.14742/ajet.5477

Belchior-Rocha, H., Casquilho-Martins, I., & Simões, E. (2022). Transversal competencies for employability: From higher education to the labour market. *Education Sciences*, 12(4), 255. 10.3390/educsci12040255

Bernacki, M. L., Greene, J. A., & Crompton, H. (2020). Mobile technology, learning, and achievement: Advances in understanding and measuring the role of mobile technology in education. *Contemporary Educational Psychology*, 60, 101827. 10.1016/j.cedpsych.2019.101827

Biletska, I. O., Paladieva, A. F., Avchinnikova, H. D., & Kazak, Y. Y. (2021). The use of modern technologies by foreign language teachers: Developing digital skills. *Linguistics and Culture Review*, 5(S2), 16–27. 10.21744/lingcure.v5nS2.1327

Byram, M., & Golubeva, I. (2020). Conceptualising intercultural (communicative) competence and intercultural citizenship. In *The Routledge handbook of language and intercultural communication* (pp. 70–85). Routledge. 10.4324/9781003036210-6

Carillo-García, M. E., & Martínez-Ezquerro, A. (2018). Neurodidáctica de la lengua y la literatura. *Revista Iberoamericana de Educación*, 78(1), 149–164. 10.35362/rie7813243

Clark, R. C., & Mayer, R. E. (2016). *E-learning and the science of instruction: Proven guidelines for consumers and designers of multimedia learning*. John Wiley & Sons. 10.1002/9781119239086

Cleave, J. (2020). *Hats off to adaptive learning: Tailoring corporate training for each learner*. SweetRush.

Commission Européenne. (2007). *Compétences clés pour l'éducation et la formation au long de la vie. Un cadre de référence européen*. Office des Publications Officielles des Communautés Européennes.

Costa Lopes, A. M., Costa, C. A., Coutinho, E., Oliveira, I., Pereira, J., Gillain, R., Amante, S., Fidalgo, S., Relvas, S., & Delplancq, V. (2023). Looking into foreign languages and multimodal creativity as a tool for pedagogical innovation in higher education: The JASM Project – Open window onto the world. In Carrillo, M. E., & Garcés-Manzanera, A. (Eds.), *New approaches to the investigation of language teaching and literature* (pp. 141–153). IGI Publishing. 10.4018/978-1-6684-6020-7.ch008

Costa Lopes, A. M., Oliveira, A., Amante, F., Oliveira, I., Abrantes, J., Jesus Pato, M. L., Amaral, O., Relvas, S., Fidalgo, S., & Delplancq, V. (2018). Foreign languages and employability: A complex relationship: Case study in the region of Viseu (Portugal). *Proceedings of EDULEARN18*. IEEE. 10.21125/edulearn.2018.0246

Cowling, M. A., Crawford, J., Vallis, C., Middleton, R., & Sim, K. N. (2022). The EdTech difference: Digitalisation, digital pedagogy, and technology-enhanced learning. *Journal of University Teaching & Learning Practice*, 19(2), 1–13. 10.53761/1.19.2.1

Criollo-C, S., Guerrero-Arias, A., Jaramillo-Alcázar, A., & Luján-Mora, S. (2021). Mobile learning technologies for education: Benefits and pending issues. *Applied Sciences (Basel, Switzerland)*, 11(9), 4111. 10.3390/app11094111 da Conceição, L. C. (2022). *As principais competências para um contexto profissional de alto desempenho – "Future of Work"*. [Dissertação de Mestrado, Instituto Universitário de Lisboa]. Repositório Iscte. http://hdl.handle.net/10071/26691

Deleuze, G., & Guattari, F. (2007). *Mil planaltos: capitalismo e esquizofrenia 2*. Assírio & Alvim.

Delplancq, V., Costa Lopes, A. M., Pereira, J., & Fidalgo, S. (2023). Active foreign language learning practices in higher education: The perspectives of actors. In Carmo, M. (Ed.), *Education Applications & Developments VIII* (pp. 208–217). In Science Press.

European Commission, Directorate-General for Education, Youth, Sport and Culture. (2019). *Key competences for lifelong learning*. Publications Office.

European Labour Authority. (2023). *Unlock the power of a multilingual workforce*. ELA. https://eures.europa.eu/unlock-power-multilingual-workforce-2023-06-30_en

Favilla, A. (2007). Novas tecnologias, velhas ideias: Notas para uma genealogia da arte computacional. Revista Nada. *Instituto Português do Livro e das Bibliotecas*, 9(2), 31–43.

Galvin, S., & Greenhow, C. (2020). Writing on social media: A review of research in the high school classroom. *TechTrends*, 64(1), 57–69. 10.1007/s11528-019-00428-9

Grasmane, D., & Grasmane, S. (2011). Foreign language skills for employability in the EU labour market. *European Journal of Higher Education*, 1(2-3), 192–201. 10.1080/21568235.2011.629487

Grynyuk, S. (2016). Foreign language teaching for specific purposes: Basic aspects. *ScienceRise.*, 3/5(20), 18–23. 10.15587/2313-8416.2016.64803

Hoi, V. N. (2020). Understanding higher education learners' acceptance and use of mobile devices for language learning: A rasch-based path modeling approach. *Computers & Education*, 146, 146. 10.1016/j.compedu.2019.103761

Karpava, S. (Ed.). (2022). *Handbook of research on multilingual and multicultural perspectives on higher education and implications for teaching*. IGI Global. 10.4018/978-1-7998-8888-8

Karsenti, T., Kozarenko, O. M., & Skakunova, V. A. (2020). Digital technologies in teaching and learning foreign languages: Pedagogical strategies and teachers' professional competence. *Education and Self Development*, 15(3), 76–88. 10.26907/esd15.3.07

Laura-De La Cruz, K., Noa-Copaja, S., Turpo-Gebera, O., Montesinos-Valencia, C., Bazán-Velasquez, S., & Pérez-Postigo, G. (2023). Use of gamification in English learning in higher education: A systematic review. *Journal of Technology and Science Education*, 13(2), 480–497. 10.3926/jotse.1740

Laurel, B. (2013). *Computers as theatre*. Addison-Wesley.

Lopes, D. M. (2010). *A Philosophy of Computer Art*. Routledge.

Manovich, L. (2001). *The Language of New Media*. MIT Press.

Mirete, A. B., Maquilón, J. J., Mirete, L., & Rodríguez, R. A. (2020). Digital competence and university teachers' conceptions about teaching. A structural causal model. *Sustainability (Basel)*, 12(12), 4842. 10.3390/su12124842

Nanjundaswamy, C., Baskaran, S., & Leela, M. H. (2021). Digital pedagogy for sustainable learning. *Shanlax International Journal of Education*, 9(3), 179–185. 10.34293/education.v9i3.3881

Negroponte, N. (1996). *Ser Digital*. Editorial Caminho.

Nguyen, P. V., Naleppa, M., & Lopez, Y. (2021). Cultural competence and cultural humility: A complete practice. *Journal of Ethnic & Cultural Diversity in Social Work*, 30(3), 273–281. 10.1080/15313204.2020.1753617

Ovcharuk, O., Ivaniuk, I., Soroko, N., Gritsenchuk, O., & Kravchyna, O. (2020). The use of digital learning tools in the teachers' professional activities to ensure sustainable development and democratization of education in European countries. *E3S Web of Conferences, 166*(10019).

Paniagua, A., & Istance, D. (2018). *Teachers as designers of learning environments. The importance of innovative pedagogies. Educational Research and Innovation.* OECD Publishing.

Pordata, Base de Dados Portugal Contemporâneo. (n.d.). *Fundação Francisco Manuel dos Santos*. Pordata. https://www.pordata.pt/db/municipios/ambiente+de+consulta/tabela/5839568

Qashou, A. (2021). Influencing factors in M-learning adoption in higher education. *Education and Information Technologies*, 26(2), 1755–1785. 10.1007/s10639-020-10323-z

Qobilovna, A. M. (2023). Communicative competence as a factor of teacher's professional competency. *American Journal of Social Sciences and Humanity Research*, 3(09), 32–44.

Remond, E., Massou, L., & Bonfils, P. E. H. (2021). Enseignement supérieur et numérique. Mondialisation, mobilités. In *Colloque international Pédagogie et numérique: l'enseignement supérieur au défi de la mondialisation?* Presses universitaires de Nancy-Éditions universitaires de Lorraine.

Rubtsova, A., Almazova, N., Bylieva, D., & Krylova, E. (2019). Constructive model of multilingual education management in higher school. *IOP Conference Series. Materials Science and Engineering*, 940(1), 012132. 10.1088/1757-899X/940/1/012132

Sala, A., Punie, Y., & Garkov, V. (2020). *LifeComp: The European framework for personal, social and learning to learn key competence. EUR 30246 EN.* Publications Office of the European Union.

Sawant, S. (2021). Online collaborative learning tools and types: Their key role in managing classrooms without walls. In *Human-computer interaction and technology integration in modern society* (pp. 12–41). IGI Global. 10.4018/978-1-7998-5849-2.ch002

Schwab, K., & Zahidi, S. (2020). *The future of jobs report 2020.* World Economic Forum.

Sinnayah, P., Rathner, J. A., Loton, D., Klein, R., & Hartley, P. (2019). A combination of active learning strategies improves student academic outcomes in first-year paramedic bioscience. *Advances in Physiology Education*, 43(2), 233–240. 10.1152/advan.00199.201831088160

Tight, M. (2023). Employability: A core role of higher education? *Research in Post-Compulsory Education*, 28(4), 551–571. 10.1080/13596748.2023.2253649

van Laar, E., van Deursen, A. J. A. M., van Dijk, J. A. G. M., & de Haan, J. (2020). Determinants of 21st-century skills and 21st-century digital skills for workers: A systematic literature review. *SAGE Open*, 10(1), 1–14. 10.1177/2158244019900176

Vermeulen, M. (2018). *Une approche meta-design des learning games pour développer leur usage* [PhD final thesis]. Université de la Sorbonne.

Zhang, R., & Zou, D. (2020). Types, purposes, and effectiveness of state-of-the-art technologies for second and foreign language learning. *Computer Assisted Language Learning*, 35(4), 696–742. 10.1080/09588221.2020.1744666

Chapter 10
Exploring Students' Perceptions of Online EAP Writing Courses in the EMI Context in Mainland China

Luyue Wang
Science and Technology City Campus of the First High School of Suzhou Hi-Tech Zone, Jiangsu Province, China

Bin Zou
https://orcid.org/0000-0002-4863-0998
Xi'an Jiaotong-Liverpool University, China

Chenghao Wang
https://orcid.org/0009-0009-5655-3740
Xi'an Jiaotong-Liverpool University, China

ABSTRACT

Proficiency in writing is vital for EAP education. The COVID-19 pandemic prompted a shift from traditional classrooms to online platforms, leading higher education institutions to adapt their EAP courses accordingly. As students' perceptions and attitudes towards learning methods can significantly affect their effectiveness in acquiring knowledge, it is imperative to understand their perceptions of online EAP writing courses. This study, using surveys and interviews, revealed varied student reactions to online EAP courses. While online learning offers flexibility, it faces challenges including diminished motivation, lack of engagement, and limited

DOI: 10.4018/979-8-3693-2591-9.ch010

interaction. Student satisfaction was linked to factors such as engagement, learning environment, instructor presence, and technology use. Moreover, structured online forums were found useful in enhancing critical thinking. Finally, the study offered three recommendations for the future development of online EAP instruction.

INTRODUCTION

Background of the Study

In recent years, many Chinese students have pursued higher education abroad in English-speaking countries. Transnational programs, which enroll students from different countries, often use English as the medium of instruction (EMI) (Yung & Fong, 2019). Second language learners in these programs typically take English for Academic Purpose (EAP) courses to improve their English skills, academic vocabulary, and writing proficiency (Evans & Morrison, 2011). These courses help them adapt to the English-medium environment. And most universities offering EMI often provide effective English support to learners, as developing academic language skills helps students meet new academic expectations.

Academic writing is crucial for successful learning in universities as it encompasses complex vocabulary, sophisticated grammar, and a formal style (Babcock & Thonus, 2018). It involves presenting academic knowledge in an appropriate format for interpreting texts (Hinkel, 2003). Universities emphasize the importance of writing skills for academic success, as evidenced by the requirement of writing courses for both second language learners and native English speakers (Christison and Krahnke, 1986). Thus, good writing skills are necessary to achieve and demonstrate academic achievement.

EAP courses, including online academic writing instruction, have gained popularity globally (Kohnke & Jarvis, 2021). Many scholars have pointed out the positive elements of online writing instruction. To begin with, online technology enhances immediacy, active engagement, and dynamic feedback (Séror, 2012; Slavkov, 2015). Morever, it teaches authentic tasks like email writing (Jarvis, 2001) and develops online literacy, enabling students to assess source credibility (Stapleton, 2003). Additionally, technology-mediated instruction fosters participatory online learning environments, promoting autonomy and 21st-century communication skills (Dede, 2010; Hockly & Dudeney, 2018). Furthermore, digital literacy is crucial for students entering higher education to effectively learn, think critically, solve problems, communicate, innovate, and collaborate (Dede, 2010). These studies validate the value of online learning in L2 EAP writing classes.

However, the COVID-19 pandemic had drastically affected global education, forcing higher education institutions to close their physical campuses and adopt emergency distance learning (Davies et al., 2020; Kohnke & Jarvis, 2021). This abrupt transition posed challenges for EAP practitioners, who had limited time to design and integrate course materials specifically for online learning (Kohnke & Jarvis, 2021). Courses offered during this emergency period lack focus on high-quality course design and instruction, as they are primarily aimed at maintaining the academic calendar during the crisis (Hodges et al., 2020). The pandemic highlighted the need for intentional online course development and instructional support in EAP during emergency situations (Bozkurt & Sharma, 2020).

The shift to fully online courses has presented opportunities and challenges for instructors (Kohnke & Jarvis, 2021). While it has fostered innovation and collaborative learning, instructors have faced difficulties in communication and monitoring student progress. Davies et al. (2020) found that some students were engaged and managed well, while others were less active and submitted tasks late. This affected the quality of online discussions and made it challenging for teachers to grasp students' learning process clearly.

Significance of the Study

During the COVID-19 pandemic, Chinese institutions quickly transitioned to online education without prior guidance or good practice models. However, Chinese universities remain at risk of switching to online teaching at any moment, which increase the importance of investigating online academic writing courses at an EMI university in China. Hu and Lei (2014) state that many students in Asia lack the language proficiency for effective learning in EMI settings. Thus, writing plays a crucial role in academic success, as it allows students to construct subject knowledge and demonstrate their abilities (Nesi & Gardner, 2012). However, most studies on EAP courses during the pandemic focused on teachers' perspectives, with limited research on students' perceptions, specifically in online academic writing courses. This study aims to explore students' general perceptions, technology acceptance, and perceived learning outcomes, particularly critical thinking skills, in a fully online EAP writing course under an EMI context. This study engages with the following research questions:

Research question 1: What are the factors that influence students' satisfaction with online EAP writing courses?

Research question 2: Do students perceive online EAP writing courses as effective in helping students acquire greater critical thinking skills in written works?

LITERATURE REVIEW

EAP in China

EAP has evolved from a marginal branch of English for Specific Purposes (ESP) to a major force in English language teaching and research (Hyland, 2006). English's status as the lingua franca in international academic communication has made it prevalent in Chinese higher education, leading universities to offer academic English courses (Gao & Bartlett, 2014). However, most mainland Chinese universities focus on "College English" courses, prioritizing grammar practice over academic writing (Zhang & Luo, 2004). Students' low academic writing ability can be attributed to factors like large class sizes, the disconnect between classroom instruction and College English Test (CET), and test-driven learning styles (You, 2004).

In China, there are two major models of EAP courses: EMI and hybrid EAP. EMI is common in collaborative programs at universities like Xi'an Jiaotong-Liverpool University and the University of Nottingham Ningbo. Hybrid EAP is used in state-owned elite universities such as Fudan University and Tsinghua University (Gao & Bartlett, 2014). In EMI setting, fluency in academic writing is crucial for non-native speakers to understand their disciplines and excel academically (Hyland, 2013; Kuiken & Vedder, 2021). However, Chinese students face challenges in academic writing, including a lack of critical thinking, difficulty in selecting suitable materials (Yu, Xu & Bai, 2011; Al Badi, 2015), reviewing previous research and creating research gaps (Cai, 2017). These challenges require students to have a certain level of critical thinking skills to address.

Critical Thinking Skills in EAP Writing

Critical thinking plays a crucial role in academic writing (Loo, 2020). Various definitions of critical thinking emphasize skills like reasoning, analyzing, judging, and reflecting (Chance, 1986; Ennis, 1962). Kuhn (1991) adds that critical thinking involves distinguishing one's own theory from supporting evidence, presenting credible evidence, proposing alternative theories, refuting alternatives with evidence, and weighing the evidence. These definitions highlight the cognitive and logical aspects of academic writing, emphasizing the need for critical thinking skills in organizing and expressing ideas (Al Fadda, 2012; Abu-Ghararah & Hamzah, 1998).

Critical thinking skills are also crucial for students to solve problems effectively and succeed academically (Snyder & Snyder, 2008). Studies have shown the benefits of critical thinking in student learning. For example, Pally (1997) found that discussing literary texts enhanced both language and critical thinking skills. While in online courses, online discussions have been advocated to promote critical thinking (Bai,

2009; Richardson & Ice, 2010) and cognitive skills (Darabi et al., 2011; Sauter, 2007). Research by Schumm et al. (2006) and Derry et al. (2006) demonstrated that online discussions increased critical thinking and enhanced higher-order thinking skills.

Research on Online Writing Courses

Online writing instruction offers unique opportunities for students to develop their writing skills. In online courses, the volume of written communication between students and instructors is high, providing ample opportunities for writing (Warnock, 2009). Students engage in ongoing reading and writing practice, creating a "classroom textualization" that privileges writing (Harrington et al., 2000). As the online format requires students to use writing as a means of interaction, fostering better composition skills (Warnock, 2009). Moreover, online writing courses create a continuous writing environment where students can learn through their own work in a guided setting (Grego and Thompson, 1996).

During the pandemic, online learning particularly gained significant popularity with implications for the education sector. Previous studies have explored students' perceptions of online learning. Sharpe and Benfield (2005) studied the online learning experience of students at Oxford Brookes University. They identified common themes and made recommendations, including addressing the emotional aspect of the student experience and emphasizing time and schedule management. Additionally, Fedynich et al. (2015) found that interactions between students and faculty significantly influenced student satisfaction, while learner support and instructional design were identified as challenges. Agung et al. (2020) reported mixed perceptions of online learning during the COVID-19 pandemic, with some students facing difficulties adapting to the new format. Sujarwo et al. (2020) found that students were interested in flexible online learning during the pandemic. Xu (2021) found that students had positive attitudes toward online writing courses during COVID-19, appreciating the availability of tutorials and feedback. Overall, online learning offers an alternative when offline classes are not feasible, but challenges and varying perceptions exist among students and teachers.

While online writing courses offer advantages, they also present challenges. Some studies indicate that not all students find online writing courses more effective. Challenges include slow uptake of educational technology by teachers (Lawrence et.al., 2014; Shebansky, 2018), higher dropout rates (Harker & Koutsantoni, 2005), lack of student motivation (Karkar-Esperat, 2018), and a perceived sense of isolation (Starr-Glass, 2014). While instructors face difficulties in providing timely feedback, as online assessments and feedback take longer compared to face-to-face settings (Woodrich & Fan, 2017). The process of checking writing assignments can be time-consuming, limiting the number of assignments instructors can review in a day (Putri et al., 2020). Online learning requires adjustments in feedback practices, particularly in writing instruction .

The Interaction in the Online Discussion Forum

Students' active participation in online platform interactions is essential to improve their cognitive and academic writing skills. As Michinov et al. (2011) stated that lack of engagement with online platforms is similar to passive participation in a physical classroom setting (Hysaj et al.,2019). As interactive learning is very important in online academic courses, and most of the venues for productive interaction, whether teacher-student or student-student interaction, are discussion forums. From a sociocultural perspective and based on Vygotsky's view, knowledge is co-constructed when individuals work with others to achieve a common goal (Wells, 2000). Online discussion boards provide a useful tool to extend learners' existing knowledge (scaffolding) and encourage them to actively engage in dialogue with other students and teachers (reciprocal teaching), rather than simply asking them to answer questions. In this way, discussion boards support the social constructivist paradigm (Stacey, 2002). Daugherty and Funke (1998: 8) found that more than half of the graduate and undergraduate students in their study valued online courses in large part because of "the level and quality of communication among classmates and with instructors when participating in online activities". This study demonstrates the importance of student interaction in online writing classes.

Boyd (2008) also argued that one of the greatest potential benefits of online education is that students have new and unique opportunities to interact with the instructor, their peers, and the course content. Meyer (2003: 62) found that threaded discussions led students to spend more time on their coursework and to spend more time interacting with their peers, thus giving themselves "more time to think about the material, ask questions, and participate more in class discussions". In addition, Swan (2003) found in a study of 369 online students at Imperial College that there was a significant correlation between students' satisfaction with the course and their sense of learning, and their level of participation in the online discussion forum.

In multiple studies, students commented on several benefits of online discussions. For example, students emphasized the importance of reading their peers' posts in a non-hostile environment where all viewpoints could be presented and thus considered (Boyd, 2008). In Bullen's (1998: 9) study, it was indicated by some students that they appreciated the potential offered when multiple people interacted. Because of the availability of other student's ideas and opinions in multi-person discussions and the opportunity for everyone to speak, as well as the importance of feedback and interaction from peers and teachers were cited by students as positive influences". In addition, students perceived that they contributed better to online classroom discussions because they had more time to develop their ideas before posting them to online discussions. Meyer (2003: 61) found that students in her study reported that "threaded discussions were generally more 'thoughtful' and more justified because students could obtain evidence from other sources (e.g., other peers or research related to the discussion) ". However, to realize these potentials, instructors must pay careful attention to the structure of their assignments, their feedback to students, and the instructor/student and student/student interactions.

TAM Model

When studying students' perception of online education, it is important to consider their technology acceptance behaviors. The Technology Acceptance Model (TAM) proposed by Davis (1985, 1989, 1993) explores the impact of technology on user behavior. According to TAM, user acceptance and usage are crucial for the success of a system. The model focuses on perceived usefulness and perceived ease of use as key factors influencing individuals' intention to use technology. Perceived usefulness refers to the belief that technology improves performance, while perceived ease of use pertains to the belief that using technology is effortless. External variables, like computer self-efficacy, can influence these perceptions. Acceptance and adoption by users are essential for the effectiveness of new technologies. Therefore, designing a successful online learning environment should consider user acceptance, perceived utility, and usability.

TAM has been used to study learners' acceptance of e-learning systems. In Tsai's (2015) quasi-experimental study, it indicated that most students displayed positive learning outcomes, suggesting that the instructional model using the CMS could contribute to the effectiveness of learning English writing. The TAM, which focuses on perceived usefulness and perceived ease of use, provided general information about the acceptance of the CMS technology.

Moreover, Alfadda and Mahdi (2021) applied TAM to understand students' reactions to Zoom for language learning. The study involved undergraduate students from Saudi universities who used Zoom and BlackBoard during the COVID-19 university closure. Findings showed a strong positive correlation between actual Zoom use and students' attitudes and behavioral intentions. Computer self-efficacy also correlated positively with other variables. However, limitations include a small sample size and limited generalizability due to a homogeneous cultural and linguistic background. Future studies should consider including observational data to validate findings and address the reliance on self-reported data.

METHOD

Study Context

This study was conducted at a mainland Chinese university where the majority of students are local Chinese students. The university provides an intensive EAP program for all students in the first two academic years to prepare them for English-medium instruction. The program includes EAP courses, academic skills courses, lectures, and tutorials. Lectures aim to familiarize students with academic listening, while tutorials focus on face-to-face interaction with tutors. Formative assessments, such as group projects, essays, and presentations, are used to evaluate student performance.

Participants

The participants were purposively selected from students who had experienced the switch to online courses during the pandemic. The sample consisted of 111 participants from various disciplines, including economics, architecture, biology, and TESOL. These students were chosen based on their enrollment in the emergency transfer online EAP writing course and their need to learn academic writing for their studies and careers.

Instruments

This study used a mixed-method approach to examine students' experiences of online academic writing courses during COVID-19. Questionnaires and interviews were employed to gather data on students' perceptions. The questionnaire covered areas such as student interaction, learning environment, technology acceptance, and critical thinking skills. Semi-structured interviews provided additional insights. Participants were informed about the study's purpose and their voluntary participation. Questionnaires were administered online, and online surveys mainly relied on the Internet for collecting data as they offered several advantages to most researchers (Wright, 2005). Meanwhile, interviews were conducted offline and face-to-face. Participants were assured that their responses would not impact their current studies or work.

Data Collection and Analysis

Quantitative Data

Quantitative data were collected through a questionnaire in the first semester of 2022-2023. Participants were selected using a purposive sampling approach to provide information-rich cases. The questionnaire was distributed to sophomore undergraduates who had recently experienced the emergency switch to online mode in the previous semester due to the pandemic. Additionally, questionnaires were sent to other students who had also experienced the switch to online courses. Participants were required to indicate if they had attended an online course before, and only valid responses were considered. A total of 111 valid questionnaires were collected at the end of the data collection stage.

Questionnaire was chosen to gather quantitative data on students' perceptions and attitudes toward online writing course. The online survey on the learning environment was adapted from Fortune et al. (2011) to evaluate students' online learning perceptions, while the section on interactions in online courses was adapted from Gray and DiLoreto (2016) as the authors had piloted the questionnaire and optimized it based on the results. The section on technology acceptance was adapted from the TAM model which was previously validated (Davis, 1989; Venkatesh and Davis, 1996). In order to measure students' self-perceived mastery of critical thinking skills, Castle's (2006) questionnaire was adapted because students in Castle's (2006) experiment were asked to self-report how they thought the course had developed their critical thinking skills. The questionnaire used multiple-choice for demographic characteristics and a 5-point Likert scale for the other sections to measure student's perceptions. The validity and reliability of the data were analyzed using SPSS software, with a Cronbach alpha of .892, indicating good reliability. Descriptive statistics, frequencies, and Pearson correlation tests were used for data analysis. The results were presented in tables and figures to illustrate students' perceptions of interactions, learning environment, and learning outcomes in online academic writing during the pandemic.

Qualitative Data

Semi-structured interviews were conducted with 10 participants at the conclusion of the questionnaire phase, facilitating the inclusion of follow-up questions and the exploration of unplanned areas of inquiry. The interview questions were deliberately designed to have a general scope to mitigate the risk of overlooking any unforeseen but crucial aspects pertaining to the overall course. Each interview, lasting between 30 and 45 minutes, was audio recorded and transcribed using Xunfei software. The interviews were conducted in Chinese, the interviewees' mother tongue, to facilitate more precise and thorough expression of their views (Dörnyei, 2007). The interviewees were coded as Student 1, Student 2, Student 3, and so on.

Thematic analysis (Boyatzis, 1998) was employed to analyze the qualitative data. This method aims to identify salient themes in participants' perceptions of the fully online academic writing course and its impact on their critical thinking skills. The analysis followed an open-ended thematic coding approach (Liu & Sadler, 2003), where the transcribed interviews were coded to identify core variables. These variables were then examined for interrelationships and organized through axial coding. Each cluster was given a label representing common themes within that cluster. The identification and categorization of core variables followed an iterative, bottom-up approach.

FINDINGS

This section explores students' responses to the choices made in the questionnaire and provided in the interviews where they were asked about their online EAP learning experiences during the pandemic. A mix of questionnaires and group interviews was used to engage with a large number of participants. Their responses were collated into key themes, which were identified after careful analysis of the learners' responses and the results of a comprehensive literature review of the question.

Overall Satisfaction

Student engagement results indicate that most students are satisfied and actively engaged in online learning. However, this doesn't necessarily mean they are enthusiastic. Over 60% of students were satisfied with the online academic writing course, citing convenience and time-saving as positive aspects. However, around 40% of students remained dissatisfied, with only 21% preferring the online delivery mode. Further analysis using the Pearson Correlation Test and group interviews will uncover factors influencing student satisfaction and gather more detailed perceptions.

Learner Interaction and Engagement

To investigate whether there is a significant correlation between students' satisfaction with the online EAP writing course and students' interaction and engagement in the online classroom, Pearson correlations were calculated. As shown in Table 1, the calculated Pearson statistics (correlation values) were: $r(111) = 0.241$ ($p = 0.011$, $p < 0.05$) and 0.266 ($p = 0.005$, $p < 0.01$), respectively (for each category).

These results indicate that student perceptions of satisfaction with online EAP writing courses are significantly related to items in both the student interaction and engagement categories. The direction of the correlation was positive, meaning that the more students interacted and engaged in their online courses, the more satisfied they were with their online courses. This indicates that student satisfaction with online courses increases when there are more interactions and high student engagement in online courses.

Table 1. Correlation between students' satisfaction and their interactions and engagement during the online courses

	student satisfaction	**learner interaction**	**student engagement**
student satisfaction	**1**		
learner interaction	.241*	1	
student engagement	.266**	.278**	1

***. Correlation is significant at the 0.05 level (2-tailed).**
**. Correlation is significant at the 0.01 level (2-tailed).

Similar results could be found in the interview. Two interviewees addressed this factor.

Student 2: Online classes have similar content to offline classes, but there is less interaction. I may feel reluctant to participate and embarrassed when asked to answer questions or engage in discussions.

Student 5: If my classmates are very active and interactive, the class experience is very good. But if people don't want to interact, the whole class will be dull and even the teacher will interact less often.

The interviewees believed that when everyone is actively interacting in the online course, the class becomes interesting and their own engagement level rises. However, because their peer participation was low, this led to a reluctance to interact with them as well.

Instructor Presence

The correlation coefficient between student satisfaction and teacher presence was 0.258 at a significant level of $p < 0.01$ ($p = 0.006$), indicating a significant positive relationship between the two variables (see table 2). This indicates that teacher presence in the online classroom has a positive effect on students' satisfaction with the online EAP writing courses.

Table 2. Correlation between students' satisfaction and their instructor presence

	student satisfaction	instructor presence
student satisfaction	**1**	
instructor presence	.258**	1

**. Correlation is significant at the 0.01 level (2-tailed).

The students who participated in the interviews similarly confirmed the importance of the instructor's presence in online courses.

Student 2: I prefer the interaction with the teacher because the teacher can give more constructive comments and answers than my peers.

Student 1: I think everything is boring because my teacher is just trying to finish a lesson. It is especially difficult to communicate with foreign teachers because I don't always understand everything and there is very little peer support.

The teacher's presence in online courses is essential as a provider of knowledge. It is especially useful for students when they can provide some feedback to them. The teacher's presence is important in online courses during emergency periods when students are alone in class without peer support and discussion. However, as Student 1 said when the teacher treats the online course as a task to be completed, the student experience is severely diminished.

Learning Environment

At a significant level of $p < 0.05$ ($p = 0.042$), the correlation coefficient between student satisfaction and learning environment was 0.193, indicating a significant positive relationship between the two variables (see table 3). This means that a good and comfortable learning environment can increase students' satisfaction with the online EAP writing course.

Table 3. Correlation between students' satisfaction and learning environment

	student satisfaction	learning environment
Student satisfaction	**1**	
Learning environment	.193*	1

*. Correlation is significant at the 0.05 level (2-tailed).

More information can be obtained in the student interviews.

Student 3: *In online classes, I can comfortably share my answers and ideas in the discussion forum, providing a relaxed environment for participation.*

Student 4: *Although there are often quiet situations in offline classes where no students answer the teacher's questions. But in online classes, everyone hides behind the screen, which makes it easier for us to avoid interaction.*

The online environment makes it easier for introverted students to express themselves because they can type their ideas. However, the online environment also provides a great way for students to escape when they are distracted or do not want to participate in the interaction. In addition, when the teacher is the only one talking in an online class and no other students are participating, the class can become very dull and students are more likely to be distracted.

TAM

The results of the Pearson correlation test mentioned below (Table 4) showed that TAM factors were associated with students' satisfaction with the online EAP writing course ($p = 0.006$, $p < 0.01$). The effect size related to TAM was 0.258. This indicates that student satisfaction with online EAP writing courses is significantly associated with the use and acceptance of technology.

Table 4. Correlation between students' satisfaction and TAM factors

	Student satisfaction	technology
student satisfaction	**1**	
TAM	.258**	1

**. Correlation is significant at the 0.01 level (2-tailed).

Although the correlation coefficient values were not high, students in the interviews provided possible reasons for this.

Student 8: *I am familiar with the technology and equipment needed for online courses and using these is not difficult for me. I just occasionally experience network lag during classes.*

Student 9: *I have also been taking my computer with me and using these techniques in offline classes, the only difference being that I am at home instead of at school.*

This shows that most of the students have no problem using technology and they can use various tools available on the internet proficiently. Therefore, when they master the use of these technologies, they are more satisfied with the online courses.

Critical Thinking Skills

Table 5 shows a significant positive relationship ($p < 0.05$ and $p < 0.01$) between critical thinking skills and student interaction, engagement, and learning environment. This suggests that these factors have a positive impact on the development of critical thinking. Student interviews revealed that critical thinking skills often develop in small group discussions, requiring a high level of peer cooperation for successful progress.

Table 5. Correlation between students' critical thinking skills and learner interaction, engagement and learning environment

		Critical thinking	learner interaction	Student engagement	Learning environment
Critical thinking		**1**			
Learner interaction		.206	1		
	Sig. (2-tailed)	.030			
Student engagement		.336	.278	1	
	Sig. (2-tailed)	.000	.003		
Learning environment		.374	.225	.279	1
	Sig. (2-tailed)	.000	.018	.003	

*. Correlation is significant at the 0.05 level (2-tailed).
**. Correlation is significant at the 0.01 level (2-tailed).

Similar results could be found in the interview.

Student 5: *The teacher will give a topic for us to debate, but it's hard to get this activity going when your partner doesn't talk.*

In addition, when the teacher organizes a group discussion, the instructor gives a proposition for students to debate and think about both sides. However, when the topic is not interesting to the students or has become outdated, the student's participation is also significantly low.

Student 2: *The choice of topic can greatly impact student engagement and willingness to participate. If the topic is fresh or related to current affairs, I would be more likely to be motivated to think and actively participate in discussions.*

From the interviews, it was observed that when it comes to critical thinking activities in online courses, students are often less motivated to participate and less willing to interact thus making the activities ineffective. This requires appropriate activity tasks, prompts from the instructor, and guidelines to facilitate higher-order thinking.

The implementation of critical thinking in the discussion forum

In traditional classroom settings, the constraints of limited time and large student numbers often pose significant challenges to engaging effectively in discussions that promote critical thinking. Online discussions provide a solution, as students can type their opinions in the chat section and have their views displayed on the screen. This allows everyone to have a fair chance to express themselves without being ignored or overshadowed by dominant voices.

Student 4: *During a group discussion, we communicated through typing, which I found beneficial. Though it took more time than speaking, I could think more deeply while expressing my ideas in text. This allowed me to weigh my words and make my arguments more convincing. Additionally, in the discussion forum, everyone's views were visually presented, preventing me from forgetting what others had said, which sometimes happens when speaking directly.*

In preparing their arguments, students first systematically thought about a plausible answer and use online tools to find more compelling evidence to support their views. Then looked for and considered in depth the voices that countered their ideas. The online delivery model gives students the time and space to search for their own information when conducting critical thinking activities, allowing them to use their own learning strategies to engage in the activities.

Student 10: *During critical thinking activities, sometimes I can only think of a simple and general idea, and in that case, I immediately go to the Internet to search for relevant information. There are also moments when I think of something I have seen before that is relevant to the topic, but I can't express it precisely, and I immediately go looking for it.*

Students who regularly participated in online discussions mentioned that the opportunity to explore, reflect, and share was a positive part of posting online.

Student 8: *I personally found the online text discussions annoying at first, but as the semester progressed, more interesting thoughts and examples were posted in the chat section, so I found myself replying to more of my peers' ideas, which felt like chatting with a friend, except the content was related to academic issues.*

Students also expressed positive attitudes when asked if online courses were helpful in developing critical thinking skills.

Student 10: *When I see an argument, I usually have a general idea, but I need some evidence to support my opinion. Especially when I am faced with a topic I am not familiar with, I will immediately go online and search for information. But if it's an offline class, I probably won't do that and I'll discuss it with my peers.*

In an online course, because everything is done in an online format, students are more inclined to search for evidence and information to support their ideas and opinions through the internet when faced with a problem.

Application of Critical Thinking in Academic Life

In interviews, three students felt that they had never been exposed to critical thinking in their previous academic careers, but now felt it was necessary for academic studies. In discussing what cognitive skills EAP students bring to the classroom, Student 3 explained that in his past studies he was taught to think in one way and not consider other points of view. However, now he believes that critical thinking is universal and necessary and can be used by anyone for their own purposes. He did not have critical thinking in his past schooling, but he can now use it for his own benefit.

Student 3: *This class provided me with an opportunity to learn about critical thinking, which I now understand is crucial for college. I believe that using critical thinking can also enhance my English skills, possibly because it was taught in English. Whenever I think about critical thinking, I naturally associate it with thinking in English.*

Similar to student 3's belief that international students wishing to study in the UK need to think critically. Student 4 described the need for critical thinking to complete a business administration essay while studying at XJTLU, despite having no formal training in her past Chinese school.

Student 4: *When I began writing my academic paper, I struggled due to a lack of critical thinking skills. I couldn't effectively analyze the given topic, resulting in a low score. My teachers' explanations were unclear, suggesting I reread the topic and discuss it with classmates. They also recommended seeking assistance from a writing center for grammar and spelling. Unfortunately, this didn't make sense to me as I still couldn't grasp the requirements. Hence, I believe that critical thinking is crucial for college students when writing research papers.*

Student 4 mentioned the need for higher-level thinking skills to meet the requirements of university study in the UK. Whether her difficulties stemmed from critical thinking skills or language skills, she did not receive explicit guidance or assistance. She believes that critical thinking is important in EAP writing courses. Her experience shows that EAP courses that include critical thinking skills are needed to prepare students for their future studies.

DISCUSSION

Research question 1 aimed to identify the factors influencing students' satisfaction with the online EAP writing course. Findings from the questionnaires and interviews indicated that students generally expressed satisfaction with the online course, particularly regarding course content, instructor guidance and interaction, and the convenience of online learning. These findings align with previous studies by Fedynich et al. (2015), which emphasized the positive impact of student-teacher interaction on satisfaction and the preference for flexibility offered by distance education. However, when asked about their preferred mode of delivery, most students still favored offline or blended modes, which is consistent with Agung et al.'s (2020) findings that some students were more satisfied with face-to-face courses. During the interviews, students in this study mentioned feeling bored and easily distracted when studying alone at home, especially when the classroom atmosphere was not engaging. These findings are in line with Starr-Glass's (2014) study, which reported that students grew tired of studying at home after a couple of weeks.

The study highlighted the challenge of fostering a sense of community in online education. The pandemic forced students to attend classes independently at home, hindering the establishment of physical connections with teachers and peers. This lack of connection can lead to feelings of loneliness and isolation. To address this, previous studies emphasized the importance of promoting social presence, communication, and cooperation, as well as the emotional nature of the student experience (Sharpe & Benfield, 2005). Both learners and instructors must actively engage in building interaction and collaboration among themselves and with peers to create an effective online learning community. In the interviews, students expressed that their peers lacked willingness to communicate and interact, resulting in difficulties during classroom activities and group discussions, and diminishing their own sense of participation. This aligns with Xu's (2021) findings on the limited effectiveness of peer interaction due to low peer writing and willingness to provide feedback. Swan (2003) also found a significant correlation between students' satisfaction and their level of participation in online discussion forums.

Online writing courses provide ample opportunities for written communication between students and instructors, surpassing what most traditional courses can offer (Warnock, 2009). This study supported this notion, as interviewees mentioned that the online course environment was less psychologically stressful for introverted students. They could express themselves through typing in discussion boards, which also served as writing exercises. When assigned group discussions, most students chose to communicate through writing. In this context, all members' opinions were displayed on the screen, allowing for reflection and consideration. Boyd (2008) suggests that reading others' posts in a non-hostile environment facilitates the presentation of ideas. Similarly, Meyer (2003) argues that discussions that can be read are often more thoughtful and reasonable, as students can gain insights from their peers or relevant research.

The study found that transitioning to the online platform was generally smooth for students, particularly in academic writing classes. Both students and teachers were able to utilize the various features of the online platform without difficulties. As Davis (1989) emphasizes, user acceptance and usage are crucial factors for system success, and effectiveness can only be achieved when the system is accepted, supported, and used by consumers. Furthermore, higher computer self-efficacy is positively correlated with perceived usefulness and perceived ease of use (Venkatesh and Davis, 1996). However, specific measures and procedures should be taken to ensure a successful learning experience. This study underscores the importance of instructors creating a supportive and communicative environment on the online platform, as it significantly influences how a subject is taught, assessed, and perceived by students. The sense of isolation in online teaching can be greatly reduced when both teachers and students actively engage in online activities and interactions.

Consistent with previous literature findings (Fedynich et al., 2015), the questionnaire responses in this study highlighted the importance of teachers providing feedback and comments. Hyland (2006) also emphasizes the positive impact of feedback on the development of second-language writing skills and learner motivation. Warnock (2009) suggests considering teacher personality, as the immediacy and social presence of teachers and peers are key factors in student achievement. Therefore, online EAP courses should include a balanced feedback mechanism that encompasses classroom interactions, oral presentations, and written assignments. Warnock (2009) argues that migrating materials online does not mean teachers should lose their teaching personalities, but rather find new ways to express themselves, just as they ask students to do in the written environment. In the interviews, students expressed a preference for interacting with and receiving feedback from instructors, as they provide effective information and assistance. Xu's (2021) study also revealed that students in online courses prefer tutorials and feedback from instructors as they can review them repeatedly.

Research question 2 focused on the development of critical thinking skills in an online EAP writing course. The online course model was found to be supportive of critical thinking by providing tools that encourage independent language learning strategies, such as finding online resources and managing learning progress. The use of typed communication in online discussions allowed for more evidence-based arguments, as students had more time to think and consult sources before responding. This format facilitated reflection, idea construction, and the use of evidence to support arguments. Online discussions also fostered thoughtful responses and arguments, aligning with Kuhn's (1991) assertion that critical thinking involves forming independent opinions and supporting them with credible evidence. While face-to-face discussions may involve more interaction, online discourse still involved students responding to each other's ideas, expressing agreement or disagreement in their messages.

The students' accounts confirmed the value of critical thinking in their academic lives. Similar to previous study (Yang & Gamble, 2013), these students expressed positive views about the value of online EAP writing courses and the development of critical thinking skills. They found critical, analytical, and in-depth thinking about academic writing in English to be challenging yet valuable for their language development. Despite the difficulty, they recognized that critical thinking skills improved the quality of their writing and prepared them for academic work in college. However, the data also highlighted a common issue in second language writing: teaching writing through basic structures may not adequately prepare EAP students for the scholarly writing they aspire to (Hinkel, 2015). Students acknowledged that high-quality thinking is essential for high-quality writing and felt better equipped for academic tasks as their writing skills improved.

When it comes to practical implementation, teachers should view critical thinking as a practical cognitive tool, not a superior concept. They should use pragmatic curricula and instructional materials to implement critical thinking skills effectively in EAP writing courses. Lesson plans should incorporate powerful dialectical thinking to account for complex belief systems and perceptions. Developing critical thinking skills in EAP writing can improve student writing and education quality. Further research is needed to explore effects on motivation and language development, supporting findings of previous studies. A deeper understanding of foreign language thinking in online EAP writing courses would inform best practices for teaching and learning.

When implementing critical thinking activities, students may find it difficult to engage if the discussion topics are outdated or lack relevance. To maintain meaningful discussions, critical thinking activities should continually assess themselves. Teachers should not position critical thinking as superior, but as a cognitive tool for understanding complex issues. Academic writing is a product of thought, and by exposing beliefs and assumptions, students can discuss and validate different perspectives.

CONCLUSION

Online education has rapidly evolved, driven by connectivity, technology, and market demand. From 19th-century correspondence programs to modern institutional online offerings, it has become a mainstream alternative to traditional higher education. The pandemic further highlighted its flexibility, accessibility, and affordability for those facing physical distance or time conflicts. Online education will continue to grow, reinvent, refine, and reshape higher education.

The shift from physical classrooms to online learning was necessitated by the COVID-19 pandemic and elicited both positive and negative perceptions from students. Factors like learning environment, student interaction, instructor presence, and technology use influenced student satisfaction. Availability of devices, stable internet access, and diverse online learning media are important for engaging students. Online courses provide convenience and autonomy in scheduling learning time, while typed communication benefits introverted students. However, some students find the online classroom atmosphere dull, leading to reluctance to communicate and limited interactive opportunities. Overall, students were receptive and satisfied with the online EAP writing course transition.

This study offers valuable insights for EAP practitioners. To enhance social engagement, it is recommended that instructors incorporate student response systems and interactive features into their teaching methods. Additionally, collaborative learning can be effectively supported by using shared documents and providing timely feedback to students. For fostering critical thinking, it is crucial to design practical curricula centered around topics that are relevant and engaging to students. Such approaches are likely to increase student engagement and significantly improve their critical thinking skills.

REFERENCES

Abu-Ghararah, A. H. (1998). *Teaching English as a foreign language: Procedures, techniques and activities*. Tawbah Library.

Agung, A. S. N., Surtikanti, M. W., & Quinones, C. A. (2020). Students' perception of online learning during COVID-19 pandemic: A case study on the English students of STKIP Pamane Talino. *SOSHUM: Jurnal Sosial Dan Humaniora*, 10(2), 225–235. 10.31940/soshum.v10i2.1316

Al Fadda, H. (2012). Difficulties in academic writing: From the perspective of King Saud university postgraduate students. *English Language Teaching*, 5(3), 123–130. 10.5539/elt.v5n3p123

Alfadda, H. A., & Mahdi, H. S. (2021). Measuring students' use of zoom application in language course based on the technology acceptance model (TAM). *Journal of Psycholinguistic Research*, 50(4), 883–900. 10.1007/s10936-020-09752-133398606

Babcock, R. D., & Thonus, T. (2018). *Researching the Writing Center: Towards an Evidence-Based Practice* (Revised Edition). Peter Lang International Academic Publishers.

Bai, H. (2009). Facilitating Students' Critical Thinking in Online Discussion: An Instructor's Experience. *Journal of Interactive Online Learning*, 8(2).

Boyatzis, R. E. (1998). *Transforming qualitative information: Thematic analysis and code development*. Sage.

Boyd, P. W. (2008). Analyzing students' perceptions of their learning in online and hybrid first-year composition courses. *Computers and Composition*, 25(2), 224–243. 10.1016/j.compcom.2008.01.002

Bozkurt, A., & Sharma, R. C. (2020). Emergency remote teaching in a time of global crisis due to CoronaVirus pandemic. *Asian journal of distance education, 15*(1), i-vi.

Bullen, M. (1998). Participation and critical thinking in online university distance education. *Journal of Distance Education*, 13, 1–32.

Cai, L. J. (2017). Students' perceptions of academic writing: A needs analysis of EAP in China. *Asian-focused ELT research and practice: Voices from the far edge*, 127-151.

Castle, A. (2006). Assessment of the critical thinking skills of student radiographers. *Radiography*, 12(2), 88–95. 10.1016/j.radi.2005.03.004

Chance, P. (1986). *Thinking in the Classroom: A Survey of Programs*. Teachers College Press.

Christison, M. A., & Krahnke, K. J. (1986). Student perceptions of academic language study. *TESOL Quarterly*, 20(1), 61–81. 10.2307/3586389

Darabi, A., Arrastia, M. C., Nelson, D. W., Cornille, T., & Liang, X. (2011). Cognitive presence in asynchronous online learning: A comparison of four discussion strategies. *Journal of Computer Assisted Learning*, 27(3), 216–227. 10.1111/j.1365-2729.2010.00392.x

Daugherty, M., & Funke, B. L. (1998). University faculty and student perceptions of Web-based instruction. *Journal of Distance Education*, 13(1).

Davies, J. A., Davies, L. J., Conlon, B., Emerson, J., Hainsworth, H., & McDonough, H. G. (2020). Responding to COVID-19 in EAP contexts: A comparison of courses at four Sino-foreign universities. *International Journal of TESOL Studies*, 2(2), 32–51.

Davis, F. D. (1985). *A technology acceptance model for empirically testing new end-user information systems: Theory and results* [Doctoral dissertation, Massachusetts Institute of Technology].

Davis, F. D. (1989). Perceived usefulness, perceived ease of use, and user acceptance of information technology. *Management Information Systems Quarterly*, 13(3), 319–340. 10.2307/249008

Davis, F. D. (1993). User acceptance of information technology: System characteristics, user perceptions and behavioral impacts. *International Journal of Man-Machine Studies*, 38(3), 475–487. 10.1006/imms.1993.1022

Dede, C. (2010). Comparing frameworks for 21st century skills. *21st century skills: Rethinking how students learn, 20*, 51-76.

Derry, S. J., Hmelo-Silver, C. E., Nagarajan, A., Chernobilsky, E., & Beitzel, B. D. (2006). Cognitive transfer revisited: Can we exploit new media to solve old problems on a large scale? *Journal of Educational Computing Research*, 35(2), 145–162. 10.2190/0576-R724-T149-5432

Dörnyei, Z. (2007). *Research methods in applied linguistics*.

Ennis, R. H. (1962). A concept of critical thinking. *Harvard Educational Review*.

Evans, S., & Morrison, B. (2011). The student experience of English-medium higher education in Hong Kong. *Language and Education*, 25(2), 147–162. 10.1080/09500782.2011.553287

Fedynich, L., Bradley, K. S., & Bradley, J. (2015). Graduate Students' Perceptions of Online Learning. *Research in Higher Education*, 27.

Fortune, M. F., Spielman, M., & Pangelinan, D. T. (2011). Students' perceptions of online or face-to-face learning and social media in hospitality, recreation and tourism. *Journal of Online Learning and Teaching*, 7(1).

Gao, Y., & Bartlett, B. (2014). Opportunities and challenges for negotiating appropriate EAP practices in China. In *English for academic purposes (EAP) in Asia* (pp. 13-31). Brill Sense. 10.1007/978-94-6209-752-0_2

Gray, J. A., & DiLoreto, M. (2016). The effects of student engagement, student satisfaction, and perceived learning in online learning environments. *The International Journal of Educational Leadership Preparation*, 11(1), n1.

Grego, R., & Thompson, N. (1996). Repositioning remediation: Renegotiating composition's work in the academy. *College Composition and Communication*, 47(1), 62–84.

Harker, M., & Koutsantoni, D. (2005). Can it be as effective? Distance versus blended learning in a web-based EAP programme. *ReCALL*, 17(2), 197–216. 10.1017/S095834400500042X

Harrington, S., Day, M., Rickly, R., & Bowen, B. (2000). *The online writing classroom*. Hampton Press.

Hinkel, E. (2003). *Teaching academic ESL writing: Practical techniques in vocabulary and grammar*. Routledge. 10.4324/9781410609427

Hockly, N., & Dudeney, G. (2018). Current and future digital trends in ELT. *RELC Journal*, 49(2), 164–178. 10.1177/0033688218777318

Hodges, C. B., Moore, S., Lockee, B. B., Trust, T., & Bond, M. A. (2020). *The difference between emergency remote teaching and online learning*.

Hu, G., & Lei, J. (2014). English-medium instruction in Chinese higher education: A case study. *Higher Education*, 67(5), 551–567. 10.1007/s10734-013-9661-5

Hyland, K. (2006). *English for academic purposes: An advanced resource book*. Routledge. 10.4324/9780203006603

Hysaj, A., Elkhouly, A., Qureshi, A. W., & Abdulaziz, N. A. (2019). Study of the impact of tutor's support and undergraduate student's academic satisfaction. *Am. J. Hum. Soc. Sci. Res*, 3(12), 70–77.

Jarvis, H. (2001). Internet usage of English for academic purposes courses. *ReCALL*, 13(2), 206–212. 10.1017/S0958344001000623a

Kohnke, L., & Jarvis, A. (2021). Coping with English for academic purposes provision during COVID-19. *Sustainability (Basel)*, 13(15), 8642. 10.3390/su13158642

Kuhn, D. (1991). *The skills of argument*. Cambridge University Press. 10.1017/CBO9780511571350

Kuiken, F., & Vedder, I. (2021). The interplay between academic writing abilities of Dutch undergraduate students, a remedial writing programme, and academic achievement. *International Journal of Bilingual Education and Bilingualism*, 24(10), 1474–1485. 10.1080/13670050.2020.1726280

Lawrence, G., Haque, E., King, J., & Rajabi, S. (2014). Exploring the feasibility of e-learning in Ontario ESL programs. *Contact (Thousand Oaks, Ventura County, Calif.)*.

Liu, J., & Sadler, R. W. (2003). The effect and affect of peer review in electronic versus traditional modes on L2 writing. *Journal of English for Academic Purposes*, 2(3), 193–227. 10.1016/S1475-1585(03)00025-0

Loo, D. B. (2020). Integrating critical thinking in online language tasks: Considerations for an academic writing class. *International Journal of TESOL Studies*, 2(2), 52–61.

Meyer, K. A. (2003). Face-to-face versus threaded discussions: The role of time and higher-order thinking. *Journal of Asynchronous Learning Networks*, 7(3), 55–65.

Michinov, N., Brunot, S., Le Bohec, O., Juhel, J., & Delaval, M. (2011). Procrastination, participation, and performance in online learning environments. *Computers & Education*, 56(1), 243–252. 10.1016/j.compedu.2010.07.025

Nesi, H., & Gardner, S. (2012). *Genres across the disciplines: Student writing in higher education*. Cambridge University Press. 10.1017/9781009030199

Pally, M. (1997). Critical thinking in ESL: An argument for sustained content. *Journal of Second Language Writing*, 6(3), 293–311. 10.1016/S1060-3743(97)90016-3

Putri, R. S., Purwanto, A., Pramono, R., Asbari, M., Wijayanti, L. M., & Hyun, C. C. (2020). Impact of the COVID-19 pandemic on online home learning: An explorative study of primary schools in Indonesia. *International Journal of Advanced Science and Technology*, 29(5), 4809–4818.

Richardson, J. C., & Ice, P. (2010). Investigating students' level of critical thinking across instructional strategies in online discussions. *The Internet and Higher Education*, 13(1-2), 52–59. 10.1016/j.iheduc.2009.10.009

Schumm, W. R., Webb, F. J., Turek, D. E., Jones, K. D., & Ballard, G. E. (2006). A comparison of methods for teaching critical thinking skills for US Army officers. *American Journal of Distance Education*, 20(1), 39–50. 10.1207/s15389286ajde2001_4

Séror, J. (2012). Show me! Enhanced feedback through screencasting technology. *TESL Canada Journal*, •••, 104–104.

Sharpe, R., & Benfield, G. (2005). The student experience of e-learning in higher education. *Brookes eJournal of Learning and Teaching, 1*(3), 1-9.

Shebansky, W. J. (2018). Blended learning adoption in an ESL context: Obstacles and guidelines. *TESL Canada Journal*, 35(1), 52–77. 10.18806/tesl.v35i1.1284

Slavkov, N. (2015). Sociocultural Theory, the L2 Writing Process, and Google Drive: Strange Bedfellows? *TESL Canada Journal*, 32(2), 80–94. 10.18806/tesl.v32i2.1209

Snyder, L. G., & Snyder, M. J. (2008). Teaching critical thinking and problem solving skills. *The Journal of Research in Business Education*, 50(2), 90.

Stacey, E. (2002, January). Learning links online: Establishing constructivist and collaborative learning environments. In *Proceedings of the International Education & Technology Conference: Untangling the web-establishing learning links* (pp. 1-6). ASET.

Stapleton, P. (2003). Assessing the quality and bias of web-based sources: Implications for academic writing. *Journal of English for Academic Purposes*, 2(3), 229–245. 10.1016/S1475-1585(03)00026-2

Starr-Glass, D. (2014). Internalizing cross-cultural sensitivity: Reflective journals of migrant students. *Journal of International Education in Business.*

Sujarwo, S., Sukmawati, S., Akhiruddin, A., Ridwan, R., & Siradjuddin, S. S. S. (2020). An analysis of university students' perspective on online learning in the midst of covid-19 pandemic. *Jurnal Pendidikan Dan Pengajaran*, 53(2), 125–137. 10.23887/jpp.v53i2.24964

Swan, K. (2003). Learning effectiveness online: What the research tells us. *Elements of quality online education, practice and direction, 4*(1), 13-47.

Tsai, Y. R. (2015). Applying the Technology Acceptance Model (TAM) to explore the effects of a Course Management System (CMS)-Assisted EFL writing instruction. *CALICO Journal*, 32(1), 153–171. 10.1558/calico.v32i1.25961

Venkatesh, V., & Davis, F. D. (1996). A model of the antecedents of perceived ease of use: Development and test. *Decision Sciences*, 27(3), 451–481. 10.1111/j.1540-5915.1996.tb01822.x

Warnock, S. (2009). *Teaching writing online: How and why*. National Council of Teachers of English.

Wells, G. (2000). Dialogic inquiry in education. *Vygotskian perspectives on literacy research*, 51-85.

Woodrich, M. P., & Fan, Y. (2017). Google Docs as a tool for collaborative writing in the middle school classroom. *Journal of Information Technology Education*, 16, 391–410. 10.28945/3870

Wright, K. B. (2005). Researching Internet-based populations: Advantages and disadvantages of online survey research, online questionnaire authoring software packages, and web survey services. *Journal of Computer-Mediated Communication*, 10(3), JCMC1034. 10.1111/j.1083-6101.2005.tb00259.x

Xu, J. (2021). Chinese university students' L2 writing feedback orientation and self-regulated learning writing strategies in online teaching during COVID-19. *The Asia-Pacific Education Researcher*, 30(6), 563–574. 10.1007/s40299-021-00586-6

You, X. (2004). New directions in EFL writing: A report from China. *Journal of Second Language Writing*, 13(4), 253–256. 10.1016/j.jslw.2004.09.002

Yu, J., Xu, G., & Bai, F. (2011). Exploring the problems and countermeasures of Chinese students' English academic writing. [ ]. *Teaching Research*, 6, 41–44.

Yung, K. W. H., & Fong, N. (2019). Learning EAP at university: Perceptions of high-achieving first-year ESL undergraduates. *ELT Journal*, 73(3), 306–315. 10.1093/elt/ccz019

Zhang, W., & Luo, L. (2004). Some thoughts on the development and current situation of college English teaching in China. *Foreign Language World*, 3, 2–7.

Section 3
Practical Applications and Resources for Educators: Activities, Assignments, Syllabi, and Course Design

Chapter 11
Pedagogical Strategies for Developing Digital Literacy

Amina Parveen
https://orcid.org/0000-0002-5092-0011
University of Kashmir, India

Fazila Bashir
University of Kashmir, India

Aamir Nazir
University of Kashmir, India

Phayaola Zimik
University of Kashmir, India

Shazia Jan
https://orcid.org/0000-0003-2849-4463
University of Kashmir, India

ABSTRACT

In a technologically advanced world, it is crucial to equip pupils who possess the understanding and skills they must use the digital world responsibly. This chapter examines a holistic approach for cultivating digital literacy skills in students by employing innovative pedagogical strategies. The proposed strategies include practical applications, an interactive learning platform, critical thinking development, cyber security awareness, multimedia integration, continuous assessment, adaptive learning paths, global perspectives, ethical considerations, professional development for educators, and involvement from the community. By addressing these issues,

DOI: 10.4018/979-8-3693-2591-9.ch011

educators can create an environment for learning that prepares preparing pupils for the digital age presents both opportunities and challenges, stresses the significance of developing not only technical proficiency, but also ethical responsibility, critical evaluation, and a global viewpoint in the pursuit of knowledge of digital media.

INTRODUCTION

Digital proficiency is increasingly appreciated these days, both among students and in educational institutions. Massive technology advancements have brought about substantial changes one of which enables us to strive toward becoming digital citizens in our day-to-day lives. The expanding global network has a more profound effect on society and people's daily lives. The 21st century's arrival of new media technologies resulting in conventional knowledge of electronic devices. The importance of digital literacy in the classroom is being examined by an increasing number of researchers and educators. Technical, procedural, cognitive, and emotional intelligence are all seen as components of digital literacy. For instance, using a computer program necessitates applying procedural and cognitive skills, such as data processing, visual picture editing, and the capacity to "read" or decode visual signals inherent in graphical interfaces for users. It is believed that being digitally literate is a "survival skill," a vital talent that makes possible to effectively execute challenging digital activities, in view of the increasing reliance on digital work and learning environments. Students' personal habitats are greatly enhanced and unity is promoted when they are able to use media and technologies freely to interact with their surroundings. They obtain the necessary knowledge by studying, researching, and producing their own digital works using contemporary, reasonably priced technologies. Within the framework of online education, this broadens knowledge to encourage learning throughout life.

In today's rapidly evolving digital landscape, the capacity to use digital technology to navigate, assess, and create information has become essential. Digital proficiency encompasses a broad set of skills and competencies that go beyond traditional literacy, incorporating the effective Usage of electronic devices and resources. As educators, giving pupils the tools they need to succeed is essential in this digital era.

The section on instructional tactics for digital literacy aims to explore and elucidate the various methods and approaches educators can employ to foster digital literacy in learners. With the ubiquity of digital devices and the internet, students are constantly exposed to a vast array of information. However, being able to access information is not synonymous with being digitally literate. True digital literacy involves Critical thinking abilities, abilities to solve issues, and the capacity for efficient communication and teamwork in digital environments.

This chapter discusses

- ✓ The notion of computer literacy and its importance in contemporary education.
- ✓ The evolution of digital literacy across history.
- ✓ The impact of digital learning on pedagogy.
- ✓ Practical strategies for integrating digital literacy into various subjects and grade levels. This includes leveraging technology to enhance traditional teaching methods, using digital tools to support student learning, and creating digital literacy-specific curricula.

DIGITAL LITERACY

Proficiency with the Internet and ICT have evolved into digital literacy, a novel reading style. Mayes and Fowler (2006, p. 27) describe literacy in e-learning pedagogy as the capacity to use various forms of technology. Excel abilities with worksheets and word processing abilities (Reed, Doty, & May, 2005); software applications and programming (Wilson, 2003), software and the internet (Hackbarth (2002); databases, web browsing, and aesthetic applications Nokelainen & associates (2002); hardware as well as security (Schaumburg, 2001) are all included in the knowledge of computers. Digital literacy is defined as the use of using technology as a tool for issue resolution, research, management, and interaction (Eisenberg & Johnson, 2002). Digital literacy encompasses cognitive, emotional-social, and procedural technical abilities. For instance, utilizing a computer requires cognitive skills like intuitively comprehending graphic user interfaces and procedural skills like file management (Aviram & Eshet-Alkalai, 2006).

People who are not digitally literate will not be able to fully engage in society or acquire the knowledge and abilities needed to prosper in the twenty-first century. Digitally proficient individuals are rapidly becoming fundamental need for inventiveness, originality, and business acumen.

An expanding corpus of research has been conducted regarding the common ways in which individuals utilize the Internet (Wellman & Haythornthwaite, 2002; Howard & Jones, 2003; Fallows, 2004), with a focus regarding the disparities in Internet usage amongst various demographic groups (DiMaggio, et al., 2004). To function effectively in digital contexts, users must possess a wide range of complex intellectual, physiological, societal, and emotional abilities, all of which are part of knowledge of digital media. It goes beyond simply knowing how to use software or handle electronic devices. Due to digital technology is developing so quickly, people in digital environment need to be capable to perform activities. The consequences of the nearly all-pervasive digital technologies on identity of a person can be both positive and disastrous. Digital tools enable people to produce and disseminate statements through many means such as blogging, personal websites, online forums, emailing, texting, presenting curriculum vitae. some of the negative factors of digital divide are as

- ✓ **Information Overload:** People who have constant access to large amounts of information may become overwhelmed, which can cause stress and make it harder for them to discern between true and irrelevant information.
- ✓ **Digital Divide:** Improved digital literacy has the potential to worsen existing disparities in educational and economic chances between people with and without the necessary skills and access to technology. Privacy and Security Risks people who use the internet more frequently run the danger of experiencing identity theft, cyberattacks, and privacy violations—especially if they lack basic cybersecurity knowledge.
- ✓ **Mental Health Issues** a combination of decreasing in-person interactions, cyberbullying, and social comparison, together with excessive use of digital devices and social media, can Addressing mental health conditions such depression, anxiety, and other mental health disorders. Reduced attention span is the constant barrage of digital information can impair learning and productivity by shortening attention spans and making it harder to focus on longer tasks. Addiction digital platforms, especially social media and gaming, can be addictive, leading to excessive screen time and neglect of other activities, including physical exercise and in-person socializing. Misinformation and Fake News higher digital literacy does not always equate to better discernment of information, potentially leading to the spread of misinformation and fake news, with serious social and political consequences.

Addressing these challenges requires a balanced approach to digital literacy, emphasizing critical thinking, responsible use, and continuous learning to mitigate negative effects.

The Evolution of Digital Literacy Across History

Among the authors Bawden (2001), Bawden & Robinson (2002), Kope (2006), Martin (2006a, 2006b), & Williams & Minnian (2007) have all attempted to interpret digital literacy. In addition to finding a place among concepts that reject the idea of "literacy," such as informacy and information fluency, the concept of digital literacy needs to be contrasted to terms like computer proficiency, ICT proficiency, e-literacy, network literacy, and media competence. In reality, there are times when it's best to avoid talking about knowledge or anything like, especially at work. circumstances such as "smart working," "Internet savvy," or "basic skills" (Robinson., Et al 2005). The idea of the "digital gap" has changed from its early manifestations in the 21st century, when it was primarily associated with the availability and accessibility of technology. These days, most people agree that this phenomenon, which is typical of modern civilizations, is multidimensional and multilevel (Gorski, 2005; Van Deursen et al., 2017).

This is due to the disparity between those who have access to ICT and the resources needed for its effective usage and those who do not. Numerous factors, such as motivation, educational achievement, and digital skill levels, impact these variances. The scientific community that investigates the digital gap takes a multilayered and multifaceted view, as well as an endemic approach, which holds that the Internet amplifies existing inequality (Zhao, 2006). Consequently, as social inequality increases, the Internet tends to reinforce it (DiMaggio and Garip, 2012). In the same-titled book, Paul Gilster established the notion of the contemporary definition of digital literacy (Gilster, 1997). Gilster did not originate the phrase "digital literacy," as other writers had previously used it in the 1990s to describe a concept that was essentially the same— the capacity to read and understand material in the then-emerging hypertext or multimedia formats (Bawden, 2001). It is evident from Gilster's 1997 book that the statement "digital literacy is about mastering ideas, not keystrokes" sets his method apart based on the more restrictive meaning of "technical skills. Martin (2006b) actually argues that the terms "E-literacy" and "digital literacy" are interchangeable terms. Kope (2006) examines the idea and makes the case that it should be seen as having components of learning styles, the integration and interpretation of previous writers, and "academic literacy," which is comparable to "research literacy.

DATA FROM EMPIRICAL STUDIES ON DIGITAL LITERACY

Case Study One

Digital literacy and procedural knowledge — digital storytelling . According to Hartley and McWilliam (2009), "ordinary" people are trained in the art of "digital storytelling," which involves using digital technologies to create brief, typically autobiographical movies or "digital stories," in small workshops held by organizations. Digital storytelling was created in California in the early 1990s, ten years before the most well-known social networking sites of today—Facebook and MySpace—launched in the same year. As such, among the first meaningful fusions of user- and expert-led creativity in the context of digital media is digital storytelling. Thus, digital storytelling serves as a helpful foundation for our three case studies in many ways. Despite being widely used in education today, especially in North America, digital storytelling did not originate there (for more on this, see McWilliam, 2009). — In workshops or unofficial seminars, an expert instructs a less experienced or inexperienced person on how to produce original media content. Despite this, the basis of it is adults or community-based approaches.

On the other hand, the teaching approach involves active participation. Instead of being strictly institutionalized and lectured to, participants are guided and consulted. This differs

Compared to our second and third case studies' more collaborative and self-directed methods,as well as formal education. Flickr is the online a community and photo-sharing website) and Fury, an MMOG (massively multiplayer online game). In other words, digital storytelling represents a kind of compromise between the top-down, expert-centered formal education system and the bottom-up, user-driven open innovation platforms found in our remaining case studies. This essay makes the case against continuing with this tactic. Digital storytelling, on the other hand, usually uses "top-down participation," a hybrid approach where specialists supervise interactive workshops. For more details on " participation from the highest position down," see the studies of Tacchi (2009) and Tacchi et al. (2009).

For at least two reasons, digital storytelling has become more and more popular as a middle ground between expert- and user-led communication tactics. To begin with, digital storytelling was around far before Flickr and Fury. Workshops held the first conferences in digital storytelling in 1993 over ten years before Flickr and Fury were launched in 2004 and 2007, respectively hence coming before a large portion of the current trend toward systems of open innovation. The second explanation is that in comparison to the previous instances, digital storytelling depends far more on institutions. Two distinct ways in which this institutional reliance is evident are: 1. Logistically, digital storytelling depends on an organization providing a physical location for the workshops that are the center of the program, tools for participants to use, and instructors to lead the workshops. 2. The workshop model, which is central to digital storytelling ideology, implies an additional reliance on the "modernist space of enclosure" that is the classroom and schools in general, along with the expert-led information transfer that goes along with it (Lankshear, 2002). The most important place in Australia for digital storytelling, The Australian Centre for the Moving Image (ACMI) (2006, n.p.) is one institution that describes itself as the "national center for Digital Storytelling" and sees the development of a digital tale as the end rather than the beginning of a learning process. For instance, ACMI's "production" includes its core digital storytelling projects. As a result of specialized knowledge and skill instruction, digital storytelling becomes a propositional understanding pedagogy in this setting, as demonstrated by the measurable output of a completed digital story.

Case Study Two: The Skillful Navigator — Fur

Player vs Player in October 2007, Fury (www.unleashthefury.com)—a competitive versus-player (PvP) massively multiplayer online game—was released. That year, Banks worked with Brisbane-based Auran Games, an Australian firm, to perform an ethnographic study that followed Fury's development to its end. He looked into how testers and gamers, who provided Auran with a lot of design and input, interacted with the company's in-house engineers.

In addition to characterizing emergent co-creator relationships, the study also involved in their formulation and negotiation. When Banks encountered Auran, she observed his online community management strategies for Fury on social media. Before Fury's October 2007 commercial launch, many of the game's seasoned players devoted hundreds of hours to playtesting it, providing the Auran development team with candid and perceptive feedback.

The testers found weak game aspects that needed to be updated and fixed in addition to looking for little issues. Through lengthy posts they successfully and convincingly petitioned the professional devs for these on the Fury forum and through direct communications improvements. The creators updated and changed the game significantly in response to this input. Even in the last few weeks leading up to the retail debut in early October, Auran revealed more changes to the essential elements of the design that were focused on consistency. As a result of these experienced gamers' persistent requests, Auran revealed additional changes to the fundamental design elements. Following the commercial release, many of these modifications were made available for download, and the ongoing collaborative effort between the creators and players Persisted in shaping and altering Fury's design. Clearly, this is not a top-down sector that objectsifies its clientele. The "market in which the consumer is an agent, able to make a deal," is one that is currently developing and as such, it is still undefined and frequently chaotic (Hartley, 2008).

The Impact of Digital Literacy on Pedagogy

As an instance, in order to create technology-enhanced learning materials that are both engaging and effective, educators and students must be proficient in digital literacy. They also need to understand how to apply traditional " guidelines" for navigating non-linear hypermedia, interpersonal interactions in cyberspace, and collaborative papers, and assess the reliability along with caliber of information found online (Eshet, Citation 2012; Ferrari, 2013; Hwang and colleagues, 2015).

Nowadays, acquiring these digital abilities are necessary for lifetime education in the workplace and for educators as well as students (Kurbanoglu et al., 2015). The discourse in education emphasizes the significance of acquiring digital skills by discussing how to enhance staff training and development in institutions (like the OECD, EU, and UNESCO; Coughlan, et al., 2015) and the way to incorporate new pedagogy in educational settings (e.g., Sharples et al., 2015). Teachers' ideas and lesson plans and their behavior in a classroom with plenty of technology are related, according to research on how technology is used and integrated into learning environments (Cuban, 1986; Park & Ertmer, 2008; Erdmer & Ottenbreit-Leftwich, 2010).

Significance of Digital Literacy in Pedagogy

The communication landscape has evolved due to globalization and digitization, which has had a significant impact on instruction in language and literacy in addition to how and with whom we communicate.Digitaliteracy is increasingly significant in today's world for several key reasons as it provides various eonomic oportunities that are very essential in the modern economy. Many jobs require digital skills, and those proficient in these skills have better employment prospects and potential for higher earnings.It enhences literacy access to educational resources and tools. It enables students to engage in e-learning, access vast information repositories, and develop new skills through online courses.

- ✓ **Access to Information**: It allows individuals to efficiently find, evaluate, and use information. This capability is crucial for making informed decisions in personal, professional, and civic life.
- ✓ **Civic Engagement:** Digital literacy promotes active citizenship by enabling people to participate in digital forums, engage in political discussions, and access government services online.
- ✓ **Social Connectivity:** It facilitates communication and connection with others through social media, email, and other digital platforms, helping maintain personal relationships and build professional networks.
- ✓ **Innovation and Creativity:** Digital literacy fosters innovation by providing tools and platforms for creative expression, such as digital art, video production, coding, and content creation.
- ✓ **Health and Well-being:** Access to digital health resources allows individuals to seek medical information, book appointments, and use health tracking apps, contributing to better health management.

Overall, digital literacy is foundational for thriving in a technology-driven world, equipping individuals with the skills needed to navigate and succeed in various aspects of life.

Relevance of Digital Technology in Current Scenario

The communication styles that are common in today's digitally and multimedia-rich society are reflected in multimodal literacy. Through interacting utilizing a range of discourse formats and media, students gain the abilities necessary to navigate and take part in modern communication environments.

All things considered, the opportunities for teaching and learning are increased when multimodality is incorporated into literacy training. This gives students the tools they need to interact with texts in meaningful ways, communicate clearly, and navigate a complex, interconnected world. The New London Group proposed including six design elements in the "'what' of literacy pedagogy" (p. 65) principles in their 1996 manifesto, which presented the idea of multiliteracies aspects verbal, visual, auditory, gestural, and spatial meaning, as well as multimodal interaction, all play a role in the process of creating meaning. But the early multiliteracies When considering the static Web 1.0 era, there were dynamic, participatory elements regarding Web 2.0. Research on Since then, there has been an explosion in the study of multimodal literacies from a number of angles: The New London Group proposed including six design elements in the "'what' of literacy pedagogy" (p. 65) The visual aspect of comprehension (Cummins, 2006; Dagenais, Toohey, & Day, 2006; Gutierrez, 2008; Kenner, Lotherington, 2008, 2009, 2011; Lotherington, Sotoudeh, Holland, & Zentena, 2008; Martin-Jones & Saxena, 2003; Al-Az); videogaming (Beavis, 2002; de Castell & Jenson, 2009 Gee, 2003; Peterson, 2010; Zheng, Wagner, Young, & Brewer, 2009); and though not all theories and practitioners use digital mediation, most do. Multimodality was described by Kress using the term " area of study "(2009b), p. 54. Highlighting the range of modalities that are available across media, including the capacity to integrate linguistic, gestural, visual, aural, and spatial modes to communicate ideas with depth. Kress (2010) provided evidence of the profound transformations that even the traditional textbooks have undergone changes in terms of appearance and content. It has moved from a linear to a a more adaptable framework for design and has become more image-centered. In their discussion of how reading varies by technology, Cope and Kalantzis (2009a) noted that people read websites more like graphics than like text. Children are knowledge producers who require space for digital play, according to Sinclair's (2010) view of modern education. The core three Rs of contemporary education are reading, writing, and math—were updated by Sinclair for the digital age to become the 4 Rs, which are basically collaborative and ludic: remix (combine), redistribute (share), reuse (backup), and revise (adapt). Since information is seen as recombinant, these techniques are essential to the creation of multimodal texts employing digital media. In line with Sinclair (2010).

Various Pedagogical Approaches Useful for Practitioners and Help Promote Digital Literacy

In relation to the use of contemporary methods such as ChatGPT, AI, flipped classrooms, mind mapping, E- Portfolio, active learning, experiential learning, UDL, collaborative learning, and the traditional realms of reading and writing, One aspect of digital literacy is the capacity for navigate online spaces, critically evaluate information accuracy, and participate responsibly in digital communication. The instructional approaches outlined in this document are intended to bridging the gap between the changing demands of the digital world and traditional educational paradigms. By incorporating practical applications, interactive learning platforms, and a focus on critical thinking, educators can provide with the abilities required to with the capacity required to thrive in an constantly evolving technological ecosystem. Furthermore, the emphasis on cyber security awareness, multimedia integration, and ethical considerations highlights the significance of overall digital literacy. As learners are encouraged to become content creators and contributors, they must also be nurtured with a sense of responsibility, ensuring that their digital footprint is ethically sound. This proposal acknowledged the symbiotic relationship between educators' ongoing professional growth and effective digital literacy instruction. Educators can help students become responsible and discerning digital contributors by creating a learning environment that adapts to new technologies. Furthermore, the following sections provide a detailed plan for implementing these pedagogical strategies. By incorporating these approaches into educational frameworks, we can help the next generation navigate the world of digital technology with confidence, critical thinking, and ethical awareness. By integrating these strategies into schooling and achievement frameworks, we can help the next generation navigate the digital landscape with self-assurance, critical thinking, and ethical awareness.

Table 1.

Title	Summary
Engaged Education Description	is a method of teaching that centers on the needs of the students and incorporates them in the learning process. Teachers serve as facilitators, encouraging communication, participation, and reflection from their students. Active learning has been researched, discussed, and used for many years. According to Grunert (1997), students who employ active learning tactics and approaches are more likely to be involved in their schoolwork, comprehend the content more deeply, and be able to solve problems more effectively. Quick comprehension tests to evaluate students' capacity to retrieve material or ascertain prior knowledge, case-based learning, mind mapping, gamification, and other features are all included in Kahoot.
Authentic assessments	Authentic assessments assess student learning by requiring students to complete duties in the actual world or use information or abilities in significant ways. Usually, these take the shape of a project or a finished good.
ChatGPT and Artifical Intelligence	It is our responsibility as educators to arm ourselves with the knowledge and abilities required to respond to inquiries in an appropriate manner, recognize the potential benefits, uses, and abuses of artificial intelligence systems, and understand how to take full advantage of accessible technology and instructional design strategies to both embrace the opportunities that artificial intelligence brings and lessen its misuse and abuse to speed up student work. Late in 2022, popularity took off. As of March 2023, Google Bard has been made available and is presently waiting list only.
E-Portfolio	All that is an e-Portfolio is a website on which students keep electronic records of their education. With e-Portfolios, be used by educators to assess students' progress.
Case-based and experiential learning	Group learning is facilitated by case-based teaching approaches, which make use of real-world experiences. Students may find it difficult to communicate in real-world situations. These circumstances provide a collective "experience" for kids where they can solve problems together, make decisions, and use critical thinking.
Changing the way that we teach	The phrase "flipping the classroom" describes a teaching approach that employs a mixed learning paradigm to achieve what the name suggests: "flipping" the conventional educational paradigm. In a flipped classroom, which follows a different format, students are introduced to schoolwork outside of the classroom through online video lectures or readings.
Diversity and Inclusion	Making substantial gains towards diversity and inclusion in your course starts with a commitment to analyzing your course and its material through a culturally aware lens and acknowledging the need to develop a curriculum that supports inclusion.
Learning using Universal Design	A set of guidelines for your teaching style is provided by Learning with Universal Design (UDL).
Collaboration & teamwork	Students engage in cooperation and teamwork as part of active learning strategies, collaborating in small groups to achieve common objectives. It is thought that cooperative learning and effective teamwork are crucial to students' academic success.

Over one billion people, or 70% of the country's population, reside in villages. The World Bank (2003) reports that in 2002, the adult literacy rate was approximately 58.8%, while the female literacy rate was approximately 47.3%. Studies have indicated that there is a strong correlation between schooling and the digital divide. Furthermore, just one of the sample articles has addressed the digital divide at the company level. The findings also suggest that a new form of internet access as well, two potential additional layers of the digital divide—data inequalities and algorithmic awareness—have been identified in the current study. The disparity in access to information and communication technology (ICT) between those who have good access and those who have limited or no access is referred to as the "digital divide" (Soomro et al., 2020). Some scholars claim that one of the biggest challenges to social justice in the twenty-first century is the digital gap (Rogers, 2016). In certain cases, this condition has even been referred to as "digital poverty" (Manduna, 2016; Setthasuravich and Kato, 2020). It's true to argue that since not everyone has the same opportunities, social inequality is being caused by the growing digital revolution (Bartikowski et al., 2018).

Additionally, ICT is regarded as one of the most useful tools for accomplishing the UN-started Sustainable Development Goals (SDGs). Its effective use has been emphasized as a means of supporting the SDGs' objectives, particularly Goal 10: "Reduced Inequalities" (United Nations, 2015, 2020). In the middle of the epidemic, the UN Secretary-General stated that "the digital divide is now a matter of life and death" (UN, 2020). The epidemic has forced people to significantly alter their everyday digital routines (Iivari et al., 2020). Because of the digital revolution, not everyone has the same chances (Bartikowski et al., 2018).

Digital Gap

The "digital divide" and related ideas empirical analyses of its constituent pieces have been the subject of extensive discussion and controversy (Chen & Wellman, 2004; Companies, 20014 ; Cooper, 2002; Dewan & Riggins, 2005; Norris, 2001; Nohan, 2000). The term "digital divide" gained prominence in the 1990s when it was discovered that some people and organizations were not adopting broadband or going online. The concept of a "digital divide" between technical "haves" and "have-nots" has proven useful in efforts to give better, more equitable access to powerful new knowledge and prospects for growth. communication technologies, like the Internet.

"Digital Inequality" describes situations in which there is a market divide in the population's ability to utilize ICT devices, as demonstrated, for example, by the number of internet connections, mobile users, or fixed line phones per resident. According to the OECD (2001), the phrase "digital difference" describes the differences in access to and use of information and communication technologies (ICTs) and the Internet that exist for individuals, families, companies, and geographic areas at different socioeconomic levels. It exhibits differences across and among countries." This definition only covers the national and international levels. The digital divide does exist on other levels, though, such as the industry, community, and individual levels.

Digital divide can be categorized as:

Global digital divide: This is the first divide: only 6% of people on the planet utilize the Internet, and 85% of them live in industrialized nations, which are home to 90% of Internet hosts;
Regional digital divide: In Asia, 50% of South Korea and 1% of Indonesia are predicted to be online by 2004. Between these two will be India; and
National digital divide: States in India with higher levels of digital literacy than Bihar and Uttar Pradesh include Andhra Pradesh, Tamil Nadu, Karnataka, and Maharashtra. The variations are even more noticeable when considering population proportion. There are also digital disparities between urban and rural communities, as well as between literate and illiterate urban residents and wealthy and impoverished educated residents.There are worries about racial and gender disparities even in developed nations. Actually, the global economic and social divisions are amplified by the digital divide. The digital gap must be transformed into a digital dividend in order to reduce the existing economic and social disparities.The digital gap must be transformed into a digital dividend in order to reduce the existing economic and social disparities.

Initiatives to Close the Digital Divide Recent Works on Digital Literacy

Digital literacy encompasses a broad variety of complex cognitive, physical, sociological, and emotional skills that people need in order to function well in digital environments. It involves more than just being able to use software or a digital device.The following are synopses of a few significant projects that helped close the digital divide in India.

Table 2. Platforms for online education

Coursera	**provides courses on a variety of digital skills, such as coding, data science, and digital marketing, from universities and businesses.**
EdX	offers both paid and free courses on a variety of digital literacy topics from prestigious colleges and institutions.
Udacity	focuses on courses and nanodegree programs related to technology, especially those in programming, data science, and artificial intelligence.

Smartphone applications

Khan Academy	**provides a mobile app with lessons and activities covering a variety of topics, such as computer science and internet fundamentals.**
Duolingo	Although Duolingo is primarily an app for language learning, its platform design also teaches interactive learning skills and digital navigation.
Grasshopper	A Google mobile app that uses interactive puzzles to teach the principles of coding.

Digital inclusion accessibility tools

Assistive Technologies	**Accessible keyboards and screen readers such as JAWS, NVDA, and SPEECH RECOGNITION SOFTWARE facilitate the efficient use of digital devices by people with disabilities.**
Be My Eyes	a smartphone software that arranges live video calls between blind or low-vision individuals and sighted volunteers to provide visual aid.
Microsoft Accessibility Tools	offers a variety of features and capabilities in office and Windows products to assist people with impairments.

It will never be possible to close the digital gap in isolation; instead, a multifaceted and multipronged approach is required. One of the tools that can help close the digital gap is ICTs. The development of ICT content and infrastructure is fundamental, and promoting technological advancement in a deliberate way will help close the technology divide. Although the digital divide has garnered attention recently, the technology difference has been for much longer. Enhancing literacy (common people's access to basic, functional technology and computer education) is one way to make technology and information revolutions more widely beneficial. Another is to create IT tools that are appropriate for the tasks at hand, like Simputer (http://www.simputer.org/), which uses audio/visual input/output without the need for special training. to possess literacy; inexpensive data and phone communication (VOIP, WiFi, and CorDECT, among other wireless technologies).

Some Practical Suggestions That Educators Can Use in Classroom

Teachers can use these to provide meaningful feedback that encourages continuous progress and greater engagement with digital literacy abilities by concentrating on the factors discussed below.

Table 3. Tools for meaningful feedback

Specificity	**Teachers should provide students with detailed comments on both their areas of strength and growth.**
Actionable suggestions	Feedback ought to offer doable, practical actions that students can take to get better. Try using Google's sophisticated search methods, for example, to locate more pertinent content.
Positive Reinforcement	Highlighting the excellent work that students have completed accurately might help them feel more confident and motivated to keep working hard. It can be inspiring to hear remarks like "your use of digital tools to create a multimedia presentation was excellent."
Timeliness	Giving feedback promptly after the assignment aids in students' comprehension and application of the recommendations right away, enhancing learning while the experience is still new.
Encouraging critical thinking	Students should be prompted to consider their digital habits critically by their feedback. For example, "Consider the ethical implications of using images that are protected by copyright without permission." How about searching for and using properly acknowledged or open-source photos in their place?
Personalized Feedback	Feedback is more pertinent and useful when it is customized to meet the requirements and skill levels of each individual student. A instructor might see, for instance, that you had trouble setting up the digital presentation. Together, let's go over the steps again.
Resource recommendations	Students' digital literacy can be improved by suggesting new materials or tools. for instance, "This online tutorial on spreadsheet functionality might be useful for your projects."
Encouraging Exploration	Encouraging pupils to experiment with new digital tools and platforms can help them develop a borderline skill set. Remarks such as "Have you tried using (certain tool or software)? It might make your workflow more efficient.

CONCLUSION

Pedagogical strategies have a significance in digital literacy as they guide how educators teach learners to interact with digital technologies. Effective instructional methods ensure that instruction in digital literacy extends beyond technical knowledge to include analytical thinking, problem-solving, and responsible digital citizenship. By considering effective pedagogical approaches, the teachers are able to encourage an in-depth comprehension of technological resources and advocate meaningful educational opportunities in the digital age. It is the need of the hour to make provision of some basic courses regarding computers, to bridge this this gap of digital divide so that marginalized sections also benefit from it. In the 21st century, it is critical that all educators, instructors, learners, students, and pupils learn about digital proficiency to reduce the electronic divide. Digital reading comprehension, also known as proficiency with computers, is simply the capacity for Utilize of this knowledge skillfully while also understanding computer features, capabilities, and applications. Because of the COVID-19 epidemic, pedagogy has shifted from traditional to nontraditional, with novel ideas emerging such as e-learning and mobile learning. However, we will never be able to replace the teacher because in-person interaction is essential and takes place in classrooms. The rapid transition of the entire educational system from offline to online has culminated in significant changes in instructional approaches. To fill in the knowledge gaps, we should be able to learn and re-learn essential material. Teachers must be available to offer assistance and guidance to their students, whether they are learning via internet.

REFERENCES

Alkali, Y. E., & Amichai-Hamburger, Y. (2004). Experiments in digital literacy. *Cyberpsychology & Behavior*, 7(4), 421–429. 10.1089/cpb.2004.7.42115331029

Anthonysamy, L., Koo, A. C., & Hew, S. H. (2020). Self-regulated learning strategies in higher education: Fostering digital literacy for sustainable lifelong learning. *Education and Information Technologies*, 25(4), 2393–2414. 10.1007/s10639-020-10201-8

Aviram, A., & Eshet-Alkalai, Y. (2006). Towards a theory of digital literacy: Three scenarios for the next steps. *European Journal of Open, Distance and E-Learning, 9*(1).

Barrantes, R. (2007). Analysis of ICT demand: What is digital poverty and how to measure it. *Digital poverty: Latin American and Caribbean perspectives*, 29-53.

Bawden, D. (2008). Origins and concepts of digital literacy. *Digital literacies: Concepts, policies and practices, 30*(2008), 17-32.

Carlsen, L., & Bruggemann, R. (2022). The 17 United Nations' sustainable development goals: A status by 2020. *International Journal of Sustainable Development and World Ecology*, 29(3), 219–229. 10.1080/13504509.2021.1948456

Chetty, K., Qigui, L., Gcora, N., Josie, J., Wenwei, L., & Fang, C. (2018). Bridging the digital divide: Measuring digital literacy. *Economics*, 12(1), 20180023. 10.5018/economics-ejournal.ja.2018-23

Choshanov, M. A. (2013). E-didactics: New view on education theory in digital technology era. Educational technologies and society. *Journal of Educational Technology & Society*, 16(3), 684–696.

Correia, A. P. (2020). Healing the digital divide during the COVID-19 pandemic. *Quarterly Review of Distance Education*, 21(1).

Dasgupta, S., Lall, S., & Wheeler, D. (2005). Policy reform, economic growth and the digital divide. *Oxford Development Studies*, 33(2), 229–243. 10.1080/13600810500137889

English, J. A. (2016). *A digital literacy initiative in honors: Perceptions of students and instructors about its impact on learning and pedagogy.*

Eshet, Y. (2004). Digital literacy: A conceptual framework for survival skills in the digital era. *Journal of Educational Multimedia and Hypermedia*, 13(1), 93–106.

Eshet, Y. (2004). Digital literacy: A conceptual framework for survival skills in the digital era. *Journal of Educational Multimedia and Hypermedia*, 13(1), 93–106.

Hargittai, E. (2005). Survey measures of web-oriented digital literacy. *Social Science Computer Review*, 23(3), 371–379. 10.1177/0894439305275911

Hartley, J., McWilliam, K., Burgess, J., & Banks, J. (2008). The uses of multimedia: Three digital literacy case studies. *Media International Australia, Incorporating Culture & Policy*, 128(1), 59–72. 10.1177/1329878X0812800108

Iivari, N., Sharma, S., & Ventä-Olkkonen, L. (2020). Digital transformation of everyday life–How COVID-19 pandemic transformed the basic education of the young generation and why information management research should care? *International Journal of Information Management*, 55, 102183. 10.1016/j.ijinfomgt.2020.10218332836640

Joseph, N., Kar, A. K., & Ilavarasan, P. V. (2017, October). A model for prioritization and prediction of impact of digital literacy training Programmes and validation. In *Conference on e-Business, e-Services and e-Society* (pp. 227-238). Cham: Springer International Publishing. 10.1007/978-3-319-68557-1_21

Kasperski, R., Blau, I., & Ben-Yehudah, G. (2022). Teaching digital literacy: Are teachers' perspectives consistent with actual pedagogy? *Technology, Pedagogy and Education*, 31(5), 615–635. 10.1080/1475939X.2022.2091015

Krumsvik, R. J. (2008). Situated learning and teachers' digital competence. *Education and Information Technologies, 13*(4), 279-290. 10.1007/s10639-008-9069-5

Liu, Z. J., Tretyakova, N., Fedorov, V., & Kharakhordina, M. (2020). Digital literacy and digital didactics as the basis for new learning models development. [iJET]. *International Journal of Emerging Technologies in Learning*, 15(14), 4–18. 10.3991/ijet.v15i14.14669

Lotherington, H., & Jenson, J. (2011). Teaching multimodal and digital literacy in L2 settings: New literacies, new basics, new pedagogies. *Annual Review of Applied Linguistics*, 31, 226–246. 10.1017/S0267190511000110

Lythreatis, S., Singh, S. K., & El-Kassar, A. N. (2022). The digital divide: A review and future research agenda. *Technological Forecasting and Social Change*, 175, 121359. 10.1016/j.techfore.2021.121359

Marín, V. I., & Castaneda, L. (2023). Developing digital literacy for teaching and learning. In *Handbook of open, distance and digital education* (pp. 1089–1108). Springer Nature Singapore. 10.1007/978-981-19-2080-6_64

Martin, A. (2008). Digital literacy and the “digital society”. *Digital literacies: Concepts, policies and practices, 30*(2008), 151-176.

Martin, A., & Grudziecki, J. (2006). DigEuLit: Concepts and tools for digital literacy development. *Innovation in teaching and learning in information and computer sciences, 5*(4), 249 -267.
Martin, A., & Grudziecki, J. (2006). DigEuLit: Concepts and tools for digital literacy development. *Innovation in teaching and learning in information and computer sciences, 5*(4), 249-267.
Milton, M., & Vozzo, L. (2013). Digital literacy and digital pedagogies for teaching literacy: Pre- service teachers' experience on teaching rounds. *The Journal of Literacy and Technology*, 14(1), 72–97.

Nawaz, A., & Kundi, G. M. (2010). Digital literacy: An analysis of the contemporary paradigms. *Journal of Science and Technology Education Research*, 1(2), 19–29.

Ryberg, T., & Georgsen, M. (2010). Enabling Digital Literacy. *Nordic Journal of Digital Literacy*, 5(2), 88–100. 10.18261/ISSN1891-943X-2010-02-02

Singh, S. (2010). Digital divide in India: Measurement, determinants and policy for addressing the challenges in bridging the digital divide. [IJIDE]. *International Journal of Innovation in the Digital Economy*, 1(2), 1–24. 10.4018/jide.2010040101
Singh, S. (2010). Digital divide in India: Measurement, determinants and policy for addressing the challenges in bridging the digital divide. [IJIDE]. *International Journal of Innovation in the Digital Economy*, 1(2), 1–24. 10.4018/jide.2010040101
Suraci, C., Pizzi, S., Montori, F., Di Felice, M., & Araniti, G. (2022). 6G to take the digital divide by storm: Key technologies and trends to bridge the gap. *Future Internet*, 14(6), 189. 10.3390/fi14060189

Wadmany, R., & Kliachko, S. (2014). The Significance of Digital Pedagogy: Teachers' Perceptions and the Factors Influencing Their Abilities as Digital Pedagogues. *Journal of Educational Technology*, 11(3), 22–33.

Chapter 12
The Last Frontier(s): Teaching Archive-Based, Historical Texts in a Digital Context

José Manuel Correoso-Rodenas
https://orcid.org/0000-0002-8732-9970
Universidad Complutense de Madrid, Spain

ABSTRACT

The main purpose of this chapter is to offer a case-study about the educational exploration of some pieces of archival material related to the Spanish exploration of Northwestern America. The particular feature of my contribution focuses on the technical difficulties this process my encompass. Having access to the discussed documents, and a proper scenario for remote teaching are only some of the challenges that the students may encounter. In consequence, the following pages will try to offer a solution (via an academic teaching-learning experience) to the different difficulties that may appear. Concepts such as digital gap, digital literacy, or urban-rural duality will be discussed, and how these can affect our students will be addressed.

GENERAL INTRODUCTION

To enter that place where the past lives, where ink on parchment can be made to speak, remains still the social historian's dream, of bringing to life those who do not for the main part exist (Steedman, 1998, p. 69)

DOI: 10.4018/979-8-3693-2591-9.ch012

The Classical Era, in which Humanity faced an evolutionary intellectual stage halfway between the mythical and the rational, was a period in which many cultural notions that would shape the future of Europe were coined. Among other, more practical notions such as "λόγος," ancient natural philosophers developed the conception of entities that would also have such a long journey. One of them was that of Thule, first proposed by Pytheas of Massalia (*ca.* 350 BC-*ca.* 320/306 BC) in his lost work, *Τ περ το κεανο* (referenced in Polybius' -*ca.* 200 BC-*ca.* 118 BC- *στορίαι Historíai*), as a "factual" recreation of mythical Hyperborea. Although this paradise among ice never manifested as a reality and was finally discarded after the contemporary exploration of the Arctic and Antarctic regions, it triggered the imagination of Europeans for centuries, having inspired narrations such as that of Brendan of Clonfert (*ca.* 484-*ca.* 577), the *Navigatio Sancti Brendani Abbatis*, or Miguel de Cervantes' (1547-1616) novel *Los trabajos de Persiles y Sigismunda* (1617), just to pinpoint two examples.

The early exploration of the Americas, as known, shared a great deal of influence from the aforementioned cultural notions, that were employed by explorers, conquistadores, etc., as a source of inspiration to understand, and to (re)name the different territories that were newly opened for European eyes. Among others, we can mention the Seven Cities of Cibola[2] or the Fountain of Youth.[3] As for the topic here discussed, probably the most transcendental notion was that of California, first proposed by Garci Rodríguez de Montalvo (*ca.* 1450-*ca.* 1505) in his chivarly novel *Las sergas de Esplandián* (1510): "Sabed que a la diestra mano de las Indias ovo una isla llamada California mucho llegada a la parte del Paraíso terrenal, la cual fue poblada de mugeres negras sin que algún varón entre ellas oviesse, que casi como las amazonas era su estilo de bivir [...]" (2003, p. 727). Within this context of fiction-reality conundrum, the end of the eighteenth century witnessed one of the most picturesque historical circumstances that the European presence in the North American territories would offer for modern historians: the presence of a Spanish expedition taking possession of what today is Alaska in the name of the Spanish king Charles IV. That territory received the quasi-legendary denomination of San Francisco del Mar Ártico and,[4] later on known as San Lorenzo de Nutca:

Figure 1. Spanish territorial claims in Northwestern America, with the main foundations and present-day names. Source: Wikimedia Commons

That day, June 3rd, 1790, would mark a culmination for the Spanish expansionist aspirations in the Northwest of the American continent. Departing from Alta California, the last quarter of the century had hosted several independent expeditions to the unknown north,[5] towards the search of the (also quasi-legendary) Strait of Anián.[6] These milestones in the exploration of Northwest America will produce, as a result, along with a rosary of demonyms along the coast, a vast and interesting amount of documents which included the narration of these journeys.[7] To this day, most of this documents are still preserved in institutions such as the General Archive of the Indies (Seville, Spain),[8] the archives of the Museo de América (Madrid, Spain),[9] or the archives of the Naval Museum of Madrid,[10] among other cultural institutions.[11] Although these entities are public, official agencies devoted to the promotion of science, and although they have made a great effort in working towards the achievement of this goal, the truth is that access to these (or similar) documents (very valuable for the researcher) still remains limited and paper-limited. Archives are particular institutions that deserve a particular theoretical consideration. In the words of Carolyn Steedman, archives are crucial for the reconstruction of the memory, a theoretical implication that traverses all disciplines:[12] "There is a common desire - this has been so since at least the end of the last century - to use the Archive as metaphor or analogy, when memory is discussed" (1998, p. 66). As Umberto Eco (1932-2016) claimed for the role of libraries, something similar can be stated for archives. That attraction that the Italian academician exposed in his collection of essays *La memoria vegetale e altri scritti di bibliofilia* (2006) can also refer to the ineludible attraction that archives show for the researcher of the early modern period. As it will be seen below, this fascination can be stopped due to technical reasons, a circumstance that may suffocate the potential fascination experienced by students, as well.

As American Studies scholars, on several occasions we need to deal with these documents and resources referring to the colonial or early modern periods of the continent, for which the digital age is still only a partial reality. It is true that several first-rate Spanish (and international) archival institutions have made a great effort offering some of the aforementioned tools available for every interested researcher, but several others still remain behind in this necessary process. When dealing with the necessity of teaching the textual production related to the socio-historical and cultural contexts we devote our research to, we (and many of our colleagues) usually have to search for innovative and creative solutions to complete our educational mission. Following again some of the semiotic postulates of Umberto Eco, the archival researcher becomes the *lector in fabula* proposed by the Italian. As the collaborative reading is necessary (and undeniable) when dealing with Literature, the discussion of historical documents, whose information is displayed in the form of pre-literary narrations, also needs of the concourse of this collective intellectual exercise. Under normal circumstances, this collectivity of thoughts is composed in the classroom with the quasi-scholastic discussion with students. However, when digital means collide with archive-stored documents, the focus of the discussion may be blurred. The *lector in fabula* sees his actions burdened by external factors towards which intellectuality has to struggle. As probably guessed, this is specially emphasized when we have to do so in a digital context. The problem of how to transfer all this to the (digital) classroom will be the main topic discussed in the following pages, in order to fix the possible situations of inequality that the duality digital-analogic world may produce.

INTRODUCTION TO THE TEXTS (AND RESEARCH JUSTIFICATION)

For this chapter, we have decided to focus on a collection of historical texts that share a communal interest for the researcher and the student, for all of them are deposited in Spanish archival institutions (both public and private) and all of them deal with textual production related to the Spanish exploration of the North-Westernmost regions of the North American continent (more or less, encompassing present day Alaska and British Columbia) during the second half of the eighteenth century, as stated in the previous paragraphs. As it has also been mentioned, the topic remains only partially explored. As for March 2024, the most promising ongoing research is that authored by Diana Ramos Milla at the Universidad de Alcalá.

In 2021, Juan Francisco Maura published the volume Españoles y portugueses en Canadá en tiempos de Cristóbal Colón; to this day it is one of the most complete and valuable sources for exploring the Spanish presence in present-day Canada. However, Maura does only adhere to the Atlantic coast of the continent, leaving the vast interior territories and the western coast unexplored. The documents are as follows:[13]

1) *Diario que yo Fray Juan Crespi, Misionero del Apostólico Colegio de Propaganda Fide de Sn. Fernando de México, formo del viaje de la Fragata de Su magestad nombrada Santiago, alias la Nueva Galicia, mandada por su Capitán y Alférez de Fragata D. Juan Pérez... (Misión de San Carlos de Monterrey 5 octubre)*, by Juan Crespi (1721-1782), held at the General Archive of the Indies (ref. AGI: Estado 43, n.º 10).
2) *Relación de la expedición de la fragata la "Nueva Galicia" en el año 1774 al descubrimiento de la costa del norte, cuyo capitán era el primer piloto D. Juan Pérez... Copia de lo particular que vio la expedicion de mar en las costas del Norte, sacado del Diario original, que se formo abordo de la Fragata por los P.P. Fr. Juan Crespi, y Fr. Tomas de la Peña, que iban en la dicha expedición*, by Francisco Palou (*ca.* 1722-1789),[14] held at the archives of the Naval Museum of Madrid (ref. M. N. Ms. 335, doc. 40, f. 99-105).[15]
3) *Continuación del diario que formó el Alferez graduado de Fragata Dn. Juan Perez, Primer Piloto del Departamento de Sn. Blas, con la titulada Santiago, alias la Nueva Galicia de su mando, que comprehende su salida de Monterrey á explorar la Costa Septentrional, y su regreso á este propio Puerto en 26 de Agosto de este año de 1774*, by Juan José Pérez Hernández (*ca.* 1725-1775),[16] held at the General Archive of the Indies (ref. AGI: Estado 38A, n.º 3). Thus, through the different experiences presented below, we will be able to explore the different levels of accessibility to historical sources that are possibly found in the Spanish (and European) context and, on the other hand, how teaching these resources sometimes becomes a challenge both for the professor and the student, confronting each of them their own personal circumstances when accessing the digital universe. Then, a dual exploration of the digital literacy will be offered,[17] for I will deal with the pre-teaching digital literacy needed to access the very raw materials to compose my classes and my research, and I will also deal with the digital literacy of the students that have to deal with my classes, again at two different levels (accessing the document and having dissimilar possibilities of accessing the digital context in which it is taught).

As a result, both the researcher and the student can clearly benefit from the information that is progressively included.

THE STUDENTS WE ARE DEALING WITH

Traditionally, the gap between native and non-native digital learners has been the subject of fruitful and interesting research pieces.[18] Scholars such as Isabel María Gómez Trigueros and Cristina Yáñez de Aldecoa go even a step further in the categorization of this gap, offering three different stages in the expansion of this gap (2022, p. 40), each of them affecting particular groups within the general population or having particular manifestation in the intellectual and educational evolution of students. It has shown how different generation (or students with different capabilities/possibilities in having access to digital means) react and interact with the teaching-learning process. As known, differences such as those of social class, urban-rural origins, stereotyped gender, or the impact of racialization have had a strong a massive (and, sometimes, pervasive) effect in the evolution of the academic trajectory of students across the world. This has led to a debatable situation in which certain communities, of community segments, are progressively left behind as the digitalization of educational contexts becomes a common-day reality. In the particular case of Spain, this has become a specially relevant social class marker. Despite the efforts made by official agencies and private institutions, it is still visible how students with traditionally less developed backgrounds are more highly challenge when to adapt to modern-day educational systems.[19] This last vicissitude, added to the gender gap, can lead to what Judith Mariscal, Gloria Mayne, Urvashi Aneja, and Alina Sorgner have proposed in their essay "Bridging the Gender Digital Gap:" Existing gender gaps in digital inclusion, if not properly addressed, are likely to lead to gender inequalities in many other areas, including inequalities in labour markets and less financial inclusion of women. The main reason behind this is that digital technologies are omnipresent, and digitization affects all areas of our lives. Therefore, digitally excluded women will be left out from more attractive and lucrative employment opportunities, because they lack digital literacy, which is one of the most demanded skills in the present digital age. This exclusion, in turn will also prevent them from finding a fairly paid job. The job search markets are becoming increasingly digital and many employers prefer to hire their employees on online platforms. Women without access to such platforms run the risk of receiving significantly lower wages for their work than current market wages. Therefore, the inability to access and use digital technologies is likely to lead to an even wider gender pay gap (2019, p. 2).

Our essay is dealing with higher, tertiary education, a stage in life that will have a direct impact in the social and economic future of students. In consequence, the existence of the problematic gap the authors of the precedent quotation explain can lead to actual social inequality, based on a dissimilitude in the access to digital resources, tools, or literacy. Understood as a chain of consequences, the challenges we face in the college classroom towards digitalization will have a direct reflection in how the citizens of the forthcoming years can integrate in society. In the particular case of Spain, the different challenges that will be explored in the following paragraphs can manifest in the perpetuation of inequality situations that threat to become a burden for the evolutionary perspectives of the country.

In the previous paragraph, we have mentioned the duality existent in the rural and urban regions as one of the fundamental sources of inequality, partially derived from a dissimilar access to digital means. In Spain, this particular circumstance is crucial to understand how the situations that are going to exposed below have come to and can find a solution. Although a great deal of the Spanish population is concentrated in urban and suburban areas, and most universities are also located in these regions, the reality proves that many students have the rural world as their immediate background. Having to daily commute or to move from their original locations to bigger places can be one of the first challenges for students in order to face higher education, for the monetary implications this may mean for the family can surpass their possibilities. Applied to the access to digital technologies, this is even highlighted. It is an undeniable truth that in the most recent years, especially since the COVID-19 pandemic and the subsequent lockdown imposed by the Spanish authorities, many technology companies have worked to offer better connections, high-speed internet, etc., even in the remotest areas of the country, propitiating distance-learning and remote working. However, when dealing with certain services, such as archive access, these measures may not be enough. For instance, some of the aforementioned archival institutions require researchers to offer digital identification just to make a petition. Even if connection is possible, several rural regions in the country lack the conditions for these identifications to be properly implemented, having the student or the intellectual to travel to nearest medium-sized town to obtain this access granted by authorities, in consonance with what Angela Pearce states:

For far too long, rural and impoverished communities have been overlooked and underserved regarding information communication technologies (ICTs) accessibility and broadband connectivity. Individuals in impecunious situations continue to face barriers and inequities. Being denied internet access and opportunities to available resources and services due to low economic wealth only adds fuel to the uneven digital landscapes (2020, p. 2015).

In consequence, although a specific national circumstance, rurality remains as one of the main focuses of inequality, making that students belonging to (or living in) rural areas, can be technologically handicapped in comparison to their peers. Angela Pearce also discusses how educational institutions fail in granting these (on many occasions) necessary devices to students:

Respectively, some academic institutions lack proper administrative and technical support, funding, and resources, assets needed to acquire and maintain digital pieces of machinery to use pedagogical instructions. These academic establishments also fall short academically compared to education institutions that can afford emerging and innovative technologies. Affording primary stakeholders, e.g., students and teachers, with essential and versatile instruments, tools, contexts, and control for the betterment of academic, socialization, and collaboration, it can augment teacher-student presence and dyadic relationships. Aside from this, it can interject successful devotion to educational experiences, upward academic achievement, and productivity. Providing stable and equitable broadband connectivity and access to available resources can heighten students' and teachers' motivation, collaboration, culpability, and increased engagement. The digital divide has unmistakably found its place in various life genres, whether generational, academically, professionally, or personally. When it comes to educational attainment, some institutions are not well-equipped, as the disadvantages of integrating technology into their curriculum outweigh the advantages. Individuals residing rural communities need to be. More proactive in taking action to access available resources and appropriate broadband connections. Doing this can yield an equitable spread among resources and networking links so that all students and teachers and individuals are provided with similar opportunities as others, which will aid in bridging the digital gap (2020, p. 221).

The propositions that will be offered below will try to bear all these particular circumstances in mind, applying the individual cases to the various conditions that can be found withing the Spanish university system.

However, the aim of this chapter is not to focus on students as a subject (as hundreds of other researchers have offered more valuable results that we could provide myself, as seen in the previous paragraphs). The aforementioned gap does not only affect the different agents involved in the teaching-learning process, but also the materials that have become the object to be studied. This is especially relevant when we deal with areas or fields related to the Humanities, in which many of the raw materials have historically been created in a physical, pre-digital format. In consequence, the access and interpretation of many of these has become an additional challenge for the student and the researcher, who have to not only deal with a dissimilar position towards technology but also with a dissimilar (and, sometimes, discouraging) level of access to materials that, on several occasions, are crucial for a positive fulfilment of the current research. It is an undeniable truth that, in the most recent years, technology has showed as an allied in this process, for new techniques and tools have been developed to allow interested intellectuals (and citizens in general) a more accessible version of the materials to be checked.[20] However, still today, many of these documents are only partially accessible online, and the researcher still has to deal with the handicap of physicality to complete a full exploration of the topic. When we add that these documents need to be taught, all the aforementioned problems (digital gap, in both senses) come to imbricate in a more and more complicated educational context.

THE EXPERIENCE

So, back to the central question of this chapter: how do we teach the materials associated with the Spanish exploration of British Columbia and Alaska in a digital context, bearing in mind all the aforementioned challenges, and trying not to leave anyone behind?[21] The second part of this chapter, in consequence, will turn around the proposition of different possibilities that have proved valuable, along with others whose implementation is still ongoing, and whose results can only be partially extracted.

Premises and Preliminary Questions

Let's start with those propositions whose value has already been proved with our students. As mentioned before, the specific documents included in this chapter are not necessarily displayed in the electronic tools the Spanish cultural authorities have created for the promotion of historical and philological research. This means that our students need to further navigate the Spanish archival system in order to get the information they need to complete the different activities that have been proposed in class. These activities encompass questions (or exercises) such as:

1) Place the geographical location of the events that are narrated in the documents. To do so, you may help yourselves with the aid of both printed maps or elctronic cartographical devices (i.e. Google Earth).

2) Search the information the Spanish National Library hosts about the events whose narration is included in the documents. To do so, please proceed with a (re)evaluation of the digital tool "Relaciones de Sucesos."
3) Once you have done so, state the "status" of the documents that are being evaluated. Are they included in the "Relaciones"? If so, to which extent? Does the Spanish National Library provide direct online access to the contents of the document? In case this is not granted, does the device offer alternative ways of accessing the document (i.e. contacting the archive, signature of the document, etc.)?

As seen, these questions (only showing a selection of those we usually utilize in class) are directed in order to show the "digital status" of our students. Through these questions, and through the different responses the students propose for them, we are able to see how the digital gap (or the different levels of digital literacy) can mean a challenge for the future completion of the activities. As a preliminary result, what the solution to these questions usually shows is that several of our students are burdened by certain circumstances that make their advancement more difficult.

Rural/Urban Access to Information

As it has been explored in some of the precedent paragraphs, the duality rural/urban world has proved, from our own perspective, one of the most relevant circumstances to condition the happy conclusion of the educational process. We teach in one of the urban areas of Spain, around the city of Madrid, in which several of the problems that are presented are inexistent. However, as suggested before, many of our students have their residences either at family homes or at their own living environments but, in both cases, far from the plain urban area. Day to day teaching is a different issue that will not be covered here, but we have to bear in mind that commuting or driving to the university is not unusual. Some of the reasons may be the high rent prices in Madrid, that makes it impossible to reside in the city for many students, or a better work (study)-life balance that is usually associated in Spain with life in non-urban areas. Although basic services are totally covered, when we reach the necessity of non-essential services, things tend to be different. What the aforementioned questions prove is that many of these students have to daily fight with poor or limited connection, and with an unequal level of knowledge about how to use digital tools (something that is not our competence but that we still try to solve). The access to "Relaciones de sucesos" is usually non-problematic, but the further connection to archives, or the identification through these can be, as partially shown in the following screenshot:

Figure 2. Access systems required by Spanish official institutions. Screenshot

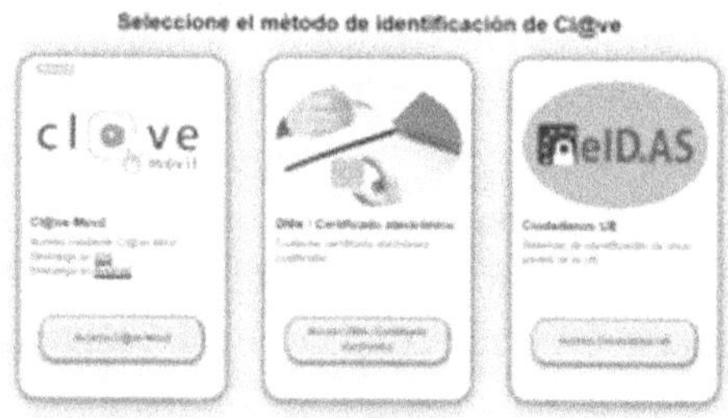

As seen, there are three main ways to access the interesting parts of the archival institutions we have to work with, where the visualization of (some of) the documents is possible. Focusing on the first and second, it is possible to appreciate that they rely on the utilization of digital identification systems (either *via* smartphone or *via* digital ID). This is when the real problems for our students begin. Obtaining a smartphone access key ("Cl@ve") is not necessarily challenging, for the only things that are needed are an operating smartphone and internet access. However, when trying to do this we face that the levels of digital literacy appear, and that operating the application for the downloading of the key is not an easy task for many (at first, it can be difficult for almost everyone). Secondly, the added difficulties of living in a rural area appear, for trying to connect through "Cl@ve" requires high-speed internet, an updated computer, and an updated graphics card. Although this is not necessarily a marker of the rural/urban gap, the reality is that students living in rural areas have more problems to have all this together and, in consequence, to obtain the access required to work with the documents we are exploring. Not only for this, for both "Cl@ve" and the digital ID are progressively needed for more and more official procedures within the context of the European Union.

Obtaining a digital ID, although a much more secure procedure (and with a wider scope of digital access, for example, granting access to restricted areas of official webpages), can be even more challenging. In order to get one of these, citizens (independently or their status or their profession) need to go to a delegation of the Spanish Ministry of Finance. There, after the validation of your physical ID or passport by a public servant, you are granted a four-year digital ID (it must be renewed afterwards following the same process). Again, living in a rural area is an added difficulty to all this, for our students need to travel to the nearest medium-size town in order to get the appointment. For workers of official institutions (i.e. universities) this is operated internally, and we do not need to visit the Ministry of Finance. Besides being a source of discrimination for our rural students, it may also turn in a marker of the social class or the economic possibilities of each student, for not all of them can financially face a journey towards the nearest town (in some occasions, especially in empty shires of Spain, this town may be eighty miles apart). And we have not approached the archive yet… If none of these measures works, the only option is to visit the archive, leading to new problems for students who live far or who cannot easily afford a journey.

Students *vs.* Information

Once again, let's imagine all this works and our students can access the digital tools that we have proposed to them in order to answer the first series of questions that have been included before. Then, the second part of the problems discussed in this chapter appears. Considering as a possibility that our students can properly see the documents that we are using for the activity, now they are required to work with them. In order to decently do this, a new stage in digital literacy is displayed, for our students need to be well versed in word processors, digital languages, and metatextuality, among other areas that are useful for the task. In addition, lest we forget that we are dealing with documents produced in the 18th century and, on many occasions, lacking a modern-day transcription. In consequence, the paleographic skills that would be required to analyze the original document are also needed when dealing with a scanned version. Although Paleography is a discipline usually studies in Spanish universities (for degrees related to the Humanities), all the other aforementioned skills can fall within the digital gap, for they can (and usually do) show the class and origin differences between the students that compose our classroom. Better computers, with more modern (or updated) software make these tasks easier, and they even facilitate the labor of paleographic interpretation (usually the hardest among our students). If all this goes smoothly enough, students are offered a second round of questions to prove their skills (again facing the possibility of subjecting our students to the problems derived from the digital gap):

1) After having checked the document, which the main paleographic challenges that you would highlight? Are you emphasized due to the fact of dealing with a digital version of the document? Does this circumstance make the reading and comprehension process easier?
2) Once you have proceeded with the reading of the document, how do word processors (both commercial and professional) help with the interpretation? Is it necessary to apply a digital language processor? If so, are you facing problems in order to do so?
3) Are tools like "Relaciones de sucesos" compatible with these word processors and/or digital languages?

As seen, these questions are directed towards a better comprehension of how our students can deal with the documents they have to work with for the completion of the activity. Usually, this part of the exercise is the least acclaimed by our students, for it does not really allow them to proceed with the expansion of their knowledge of the Spanish exploration of Northwestern America. There is a powerful reason for this to be: these questions usually have the purpose of showing us which kind of students we have in front of us, and how well (or unwell) they can manage with materials that are usually very sensitive and, on some occasions, very obscure. Remember, again, Umberto Eco's notion of the *lector in fabula*, for it is perfectly applicable to the reading process that is compulsorily necessary towards the comprehension of the documents we are dealing with.

As for now, we have already covered the experiences that have been fully developed in our classroom. Due to the fact that we are American Studies scholars, our results are more qualitative than quantitative. To summarize thing up, the success that our students show towards the completion of these exercises usually approaches 100% (which shows the level of compromise they tend to express, and the commitment to become hardworking students when given the appropriate tools; although this completion rate is excellent, the level of success could be higher the whole process being easier: less effort to reach the same goals). However, as mentioned and detailly explained in the previous paragraphs, the difficulties that our students can encounter in order to teach this point vary significantly from case to case. Broadly speaking, we can conclude that those students who live in rural areas generally experience bigger technological problems that their peers. However, as shown below, when discussing about interpretation of comprehension of the documents, figures usually equal. The digital gap (and the subsequent dissimilitude in digital literacy) are a burden when discussing technical issues, but the level of academic formation of our students usually contributes to surpass this lack when actually completing the teaching-learning process.

Students Apud Information

As mentioned, we are now discussing those parts of the experience that have not been fully implemented yet, and that are still either under construction or under total evaluation. As the reader may have deduced, these have to do with the actual work related to the narration included in the documents. To complete this part of the exercise, devices like the aforementioned "Relaciones de sucesos" will be crucial, for they provide background and context to the texts our students have to confront. Just a brief reminder, the documents that have been selected for the particular case of this chapter are related to the 1774 expedition towards present-day Alaska (taking place between January and November) promoted by the Viceroy of New Spain

Antonio María de Bucareli (1717-1779). The purposes of this expedition were the limitation of the Russian presence in the region with the foundation of Spanish settlements, leading to the confrontation between Spain and the Russian Empire in Alaska by the end of the 18th century (Martínez Láinez and Canales Torres, 2009, pp. 357-358). and the contact with the Natives who populated the American coasts. Although it is probable that more contacts were made effective, only two are recorded in the documents we are working with: the trade established with the Haida in Haida Gwaii, and the trade established with the Tlingit in what today is Southeastern Alaska. In none of these cases, the Spanish explorers landed on the American territory, but the interchanges of goods were performed aboard small boats. During these months, the explorers visited what today is known as Haida Gwaii (formerly known as Queen Charlotte Islands), belonging to present-day Canadian province of British Columbia. After visiting Alexander Archipelago (in present-day Alaska), Juan José Pérez Hernández decided to return to present-day Mexico. Bearing this in mind, the questions that are usually proposed have to do with these historical circumstances, in order to seek our students' comprehension of the archival material we are dealing with. Some examples are:

1) After having read the documents, try to map the route followed by the Spanish expedition using present-day locations. Which locations are distinguishable? Which are not?
2) How are the descriptions of the ecosystem included in the chronicles you are dealing with? Do the Spanish chroniclers show any special emotion or reaction towards the landscapes, the fauna, the flora, etc.? What are the impressions of the chroniclers, do they describe Alaskan territory in positive terms or not?
3) When discussing about the Natives, which different nations are mentioned, both in the terms of the chroniclers and in present-day terms? Which aspects of the culture, trade, lifestyle, etc., of these nations are highlighted? How is the cultural/imperial approach of the Spanish explorers to the Natives?

As it can be deduced, these questions do not try to emphasize the technological aspects of the archival activity. On the contrary, they aim to trigger the reflection and the imagination of our students. As many of them are enrolled in BAs and MAs in English or in Spanish (we usually also have majors in History attending our courses), the consideration of the narrative material is crucial for the complete formation of their academic careers. In consequence, our aim is for them to explore and to try to establish an independent narration of the events that are being explored. That is one of the reasons why this part of the experience is still underdeveloped, for it requires of a large timespan to complete. As mentioned above, the results shown by these questions are usually slightly different from those shown through the previously stated ones: in this case, students with a rural background, or living in rural areas tend to be more accurate in their reflection, showing a more carefully composed discussion of the topics, and a better organized presentation of the conclusions. A more direct contact with the territory, and a deeper understanding of what identity means can be some of the reasons to explain this. A partial conclusion that can deduced of this aspect of the research is that, once the technical issues have been surpassed, intellectual activity can be perfectly displayed, and the most satisfying results can be obtained.

The Role of the Professor

As professors, we may be wondering what our role in the whole aforementioned process is, beyond the slight support we can provide towards the solution of technical problems. Some of the questions that arise (and that should be taken into consideration) are: Do we as educators have an obligation to offer these materials in-class rather than online to circumvent these equity issues? Should we provide more tech support for these students? Or is there another solution? What should we take from all of this? Although they trigger interesting aspects of the teaching-learning experience, we have usually faced this experience as a guidance for the students to explore their capabilities, more than a traditional class scenario (that is why the question of the digital/territorial inequality is especially relevant). In consequence, as always, the role of the professor is ambivalent, for we need to be there in support of the process our students are going through but, at the same time, we cannot interfere too much in order to aim and motivate their freedom and curiosity. Thus, bringing the previously discussed materials to class could lead to a less enhancing pedagogical situation. As mentioned above, many of our students are English, Spanish, or History majors, who will have to deal with textuality (and the materiality it encompasses) along their professional careers (even if they do not follow an active research path), so the direct contact with primary sources is crucial (something applicable to historical documents, as the previous pages tend to explore, and to literary texts).

The digital context is an ongoing, quasi-biological, dynamic reality unfamiliar to most of us. In consequence, it requires our constant effort for expanding our comprehension and for updating our skills. However, teaching these materials, with all the digital implications that have been shown, proves that the collaborative concourse of the professor and the student can lead to the completion of an implausible task: 18th century materials produced as manuscripts on the Alaskan shores, kept for centuries stored in an archive, revived thanks to the participation of the most modern technology. If we add "Relaciones de sucesos" to que equation, we get a bigger (and better) picture, for we appreciate how technology also provides with the interpretative tools that are necessary for the ineludible creation of a context, among other crucial aspects.

In addition to all this, professors are also in charge of triggering a further methodological action that can prove as extremely beneficial for students: aiming and encouraging their mutual collaboration. As seen, distance and (relative) isolation can be a challenge for the aforementioned experience to be fully implemented (although technology means a great source of help). Mutual collaboration can algo mean a great difference to complete the formation of these students. First, we can propose the implementation of mutual support networks, such as forums, chatlines, etc., where our students can share their doubts and difficulties (i.e. when accessing the digital ID). The existence of these networks can also help students from the most remote areas physically access the information they are dealing with, if necessary. For instance, students can plan their potential trips to the archival institutions in order to travel together, enhancing personal interrelations and the flow of information. After this, we can also encourage our students to collaborate when completing the different tasks they are proposed. Although the evaluation remains individual,[22] our students can collaborate when reflecting about the questions or when examining the materials. This is something we can do little about, for the Spanish university system does not recognize (by law) group evaluation. Several attempts have been made to modify this, but none has fructified so far. As more eyes see more, conclusions reached can be richer and more thoughtful. This collaboration can be done under the supervision of the professor, independently, or both.

CONCLUSION

In conclusion, although a long seems to have been travelled since Classical Antiquity to metatextuality and digital IDs, it has been proved that what is presented in this chapter is a reliable reflection of that evolutive process. Technology, created and developed in order to make our lives easier, can turn, under certain circumstances, into a tool which can produce discrimination, which can show the undesirable truth about our reality. The existence of digital gaps, and the dualities they produce is one of these circumstances. As stated in the precedent paragraphs, students who have a poorer literacy (of any kind) towards digital systems tend to lie a step behind their peers. This can lead to situations o inequality that our labor as academicians should try to abolish or, at least, to reduce. Although this may be applicable to any discipline, the exploration of archival material is specially dependent on these facts. Unlike in other areas of science, we are working with materiality (along with the abstract entities History and narrations mean), so we need that our students can have the necessary material contact with the documents: we do not only deal with texts, but with the physical objects those texts are written on. Otherwise, the teaching-learning process is impossible. As shown above, many actions have been developed in order to fix the different problems that have appeared, and that still appear (one of them being "Relaciones de sucesos"). Particular situations such as the residence in a rural area can burden or delay the observation of the documents that are needed. A well-stablished, well-organized preparation of classes is crucial for not leaving anyone behind, independently of their family or geographic realities. It is true that the age of exploration ended a long time ago, but the digital era that lies before us can mean a Thule similar to that of ancient times. Our students (ourselves, too) may feel, sometimes, like the navigators towards San Francisco del Mar Ártico, with a cold, unexplored panorama ahead of them. Like them, we have to rely on the technological compasses we have, hoping for them to properly work and not provoke our loss among the (digital) fog.

REFERENCES

Atwood, M. (2004). *Strange Things. The Malevolent North in Canadian Literature*. Virago.

Bartoli, T. (1970). Presencia hispánica en la costa noroeste de América (siglo XVIII). In Carlos H. Magis (Dir.), *Actas del Tercer Congreso Internacional de Hispanistas* (pp. 105-115). El Colegio de México.

Black, L. T. (2004). *Russians in Alaska, 1732–1867*. University of Alaska Press.

Bruhn, J., López-Varela, A., & de Paiva Vieira, M. (Eds.). (2023). *The Palgrave Handbook of Intermediality*. Palgrave Macmillan. 10.1007/978-3-030-91263-5

Brunner, B. (2019). *Die Erfindung des Nordens. Kulturgeschichte einer Himmelsrichtung*. Verlag Galiani Berlin bei Kiepenheuer und Witsch.

Caeners, T. (2015). Memory and Memory Work. In Julian Wolfreys (Ed.), *Introducing Criticism in the 21st Century* (pp. 282-307). Edinburgh University Press.

Crespi, J. (1774). *Diario que yo Fray Juan Crespi, Misionero del Apostólico Colegio de Propaganda Fide de Sn. Fernando de México, formo del viaje de la Fragata de Su magestad nombrada Santiago, alias la Nueva Galicia, mandada por su Capitán y Alférez de Fragata D. Juan Pérez... (Misión de San Carlos de Monterrey 5 octubre)*. Archivo General de Indias (ref. AGI: Estado 43, n.º 10).

de Cervantes, M. (2004). *Los trabajos de Persiles y Sigismunda*. Cátedra.

de Mendoza, T. Luis (Ed.). (1866). *Colección de documentos inéditos, relativos al descubrimiento, conquista, y organización de las antiguas posesiones españolas en América y Oceanía, sacados de los Archivos del Reino, y muy especialmente del de Indias*. Imprenta de Frías y compañía.

de Montalvo, R. Garci (2003). *Sergas de Esplandián*. Castalia.

Domingos, M., Cláudia, A., Vieira, C., Viviane, É., de Paiva Vieira, M., de Figueiredo, P., & Augusta, C. (2023). Intermediality, Teaching, and Literacy. In Bruhn, J., López-Varela, A., & Miriam de Paiva, V. (Eds.), *The Palgrave Handbook of Intermediality* (pp. 2–18). Palgrave Macmillan. 10.1007/978-3-030-91263-5_21-2

Eco, U. (1979). *Lector in fabula. La cooperazione interpretativa nei testi narrativi*. Bompiani.

Eco, U. (2006). *La memoria vegetale e altri scritti di bibliofilia*. Rovello.

Hawthorne, N. (1987 [2013]). *Nathaniel Hawthorne's Tales*. W. W. Norton & Company.

Hernández, P., & José, H. (1774). *Continuación del diario que formó el Alferez graduado de Fragata Dn. Juan Perez, Primer Piloto del Departamento de Sn. Blas, con la titulada Santiago, alias la Nueva Galicia de su mando, que comprehende su salida de Monterrey á explorar la Costa Septentrional, y su regreso á este propio Puerto en 26 de Agosto de este año de 1774*. Archivo General de Indias (ref. AGI: Estado 38A, n.º 3).

Láinez, M. (2009). *Banderas lejanas. La exploración, conquista y defensa por España del territorio de los actuales Estados Unidos*. Crónicas de la Historia.

Leibrandt, I. M. (2019). Postmodern Literacy. Multimodal, Hypertextual, Intertextual Reading. In Romero, E. D., Bobkina, J., & Stefanova, S. (Eds.), *Teaching Literature and Language Through Multimodal Texts* (pp. 258–276). IGI Global. 10.4018/978-1-5225-5796-8.ch014

Longoria, A.-I., Inés, B.-B., Rogelio, R.-M., Soledad, M., & Molina, A. (2022). Systematic Mapping of Digital Gap and Gender, Age, Ethnicity, or Disability. *Sustainability (Basel)*, 14(3), 1–20. 10.3390/su14031297

Magis, C. H. (Dir.). (1970). *Actas del Tercer Congreso Internacional de Hispanistas*. El Colegio de México.

Mariscal, J., Mayne, G., Aneja, U., & Sorgner, A. (2019). Bridging the Gender Digital Gap. *Economics*, 13(1), 2–12. 10.5018/economics-ejournal.ja.2019-9

Maura, J. (2022). Gestación del mito de las "Siete Ciudades" en Naufragios de Alvar Núñez Cabeza de Vaca. *Lemir*, (26), 405-420.

Maura, J. F. (2016). Sobre el origen hispánico del nombre "Canadá.". *Lemir*, (20), 17–52.

Maura, J. F. (2021). *Españoles y portugueses en Canadá en tiempos de Cristóbal Colón*. Universitat de València.

McDowell, J. (1998). *José Narváez: The Forgotten Explorer*. The Arthur H. Clark Company.

Moreno, D. (2019). *Teaching Literature and Language Through Multimodal Texts*. IGI Global.

O'Connor, F. (1971). *The Complete Stories*. Farrar, Straus and Giroux.

Palou, F. (1774). *Relación de la expedición de la fragata la "Nueva Galicia" en el año 1774 al descubrimiento de la costa del norte, cuyo capitán era el primer piloto D. Juan Pérez... Copia de lo particular que vio la expedicion de mar en las costas del Norte, sacado del Diario original, que se formo abordo de la Fragata por los P.P. Fr. Juan Crespi, y Fr. Tomas de la Peña, que iban en la dicha expedición*. Museo Naval de Madrid (ref. M. N. Ms. 335, doc. 40, f. 99-105).

Palou, F. (1787). *Relación histórica de la vida y apostólicas tareas del Venerable Padre Fray Junípero Serra, y de las misiones que fundó en California septentrional, y nuevos establecimientos de Monterrey*. Imprenta de Don Felipe Zúniga.

Pearce, A. (2020). The Digital Gap Still Exists, Generationally, Rurally, and Academically. In *ICETC '20: Proceedings of the 12th International Conference on Education Technology and Computers* (pp. 215-222). Association for Computing Machinery. 10.1145/3436756.3437048

Pethick, D. (1976). *First Approaches to the Northwest Coast*. J.J. Douglas.

Polybius, . (2010). *The Histories*. Oxford University Press.

Rodríguez-Sala, M. L. (Ed.). (2006). *De San Blas hasta la Alta California. Los viajes y diarios de Juan Joseph Pérez Hernández*. Universidad Nacional Autónoma de México.

SánchezR, ,. (2021). Lorenzo Ferrer Maldonado: El almeriense que descubrió el Estrecho de Bering. *REAL.Revista de Estudios Almerienses*, (1), 6–52.

Sanchez-Prieto, J., Trujillo-Torres, J. M., Gómez-García, M., & Gómez-García, G. (2020). The Generational Digital Gap within Dual Vocational Education and Training Teachers. *European Journal of Educational Research*, 9(4), 1557–1567. 10.12973/eu-jer.9.4.1557

Steedman, C. (1998). The Place of Memory: In an Archive. *History of the Human Sciences*, 11(4), 65–83. 10.1177/095269519801100405

Tovell, F. M. (2008). *At the Far Reaches of Empire: The Life of Juan Francisco De La Bodega Y Quadra*. University of British Columbia Press. 10.59962/9780774855952

Trigueros, Gómez, María, Isabel, & de Aldecoa, Yáñez, Cristina. (2022). La brecha digital en el contexto educativo: Formación y aprendizaje de la ciudadanía digital. *REALIA.Research in Education and Learning Innovation Archives*, (30), 39–45.

Wolfreys, J. (Ed.). (2002). *Introducing Criticism in the 21st Century*. Edinburgh University Press.

ENDNOTES

1 https://www.cultura.gob.es/cultura/areas/archivos/mc/archivos/agi/portada.html. https://www.cultura.gob.es/museodeamerica/portada.html. https://armada.defensa.gob.es/ArmadaPortal/page/Portal/ArmadaEspannola/cienciaorgano/prefLang-es/01cienciamuseo. https://www.boe.es/buscar/doc.php?id=BOE-A-2020-3692. https://www.google.com/maps/d/u/0/viewer?mid=1MoHZ33dxXE0U73ZmjEQ3SNJqqLpBYJqc&ll=34.74234614488728%2C-31.047040336422057&z=5-https://erasmus-plus.ec.europa.eu/

2 See Juan Maura (2022).

3 Arguably located in Florida and whose influx would last until the 19th and 20*th* centuries, being included by Nathaniel Hawthorne (1804-1864) in his short story "Dr. Heidegger's Experiment" (1837), and by Flannery O'Connor (1925-1964) in her "A Stroke of Good Fortune" (1949).

4 Concerning denominations, Juan Francisco Maura states that the term Canada would have had a Spanish origin: "Todo indica e invita a pensar que la etimología de 'Canada', equivalente a 'cañada,' es mucho más plausible, tanto en castellano como en portugués antiguo que la de 'Kanatta,' como villa o pueblo. 'Canada' no es un nombre aislado dentro de la toponimia ibérica en Norteamérica. Sin duda, los recientes descubrimientos arqueológicos, tanto en mar como en tierra, así lo demuestran. La historia de Norteamérica y, en este caso particular de Canadá, tiene una afinidad con la península Ibérica mucho más fuerte y profunda de lo que hasta la fecha se había creído. Desde la Tierra del Labrador hasta la Florida, la inmensa mayoría de los topónimos que nos encontramos en la cartografía temprana del siglo XVI están escritos en español o portugués, y 'Canadá' no es una excepción" (2016, p. 42).

5 Participating in the cultural connotations the this geographical term implies, as recently stated by Bernd Brunner (born in 1964) in his essay *Die Erfindung des Nordens. Kulturgeschichte einer Himmelsrichtung* (2019). Canadian writer Margaret Atwood (born in 1939), in the lectures delivered at the University of Oxford in 1991 (later collected under the *title Strange Things. The Malevolent North in Canadian Literature*) explains that "Until you get to the North Pole, 'North,' being a direction, is relative. 'The North' is thought of as a place, but it's a place with shifting boundaries. It's also a state of mind. It can mean 'wilderness' or 'frontier.' But we know -or we think we know- what sorts of things go on there" (1995 [2004], p. 10).

6 In 1588, Lorenzo Ferrer Maldonado (1557-1625) would offer the first documental mention to this geographic entity (see Luis Torres de Mendoza, 1866, pp. 424-433). For more information about this explorer, see Valeriano Sánchez Ramos and Alfonso Viciana Martínez-Lage (2021). Contemporary, scientific explorations of these areas will lead to the search for the Northwest Passage, giving as a cultural result the literary and historical reconstruction of events such as those of Franklin's lost expedition.

7 Lest we forget that these explorations are only a partially known reality, as stated below. In the words of Fernando Martínez Láinez and Carlos Canales Torres: "Si hay una parte desconocida de la presencia española en el Norte de América, sin duda son los intentos de colonización del Noroeste, en la ignorada costa que se extendía desde San Francisco hasta el Mar Ártico. Un territorio inmenso e inexplorado que interesaba a varias potencias europeas, en el que las exploraciones españolas fueron mucho más intensas de lo que se cree y dejaron huellas que no han sido borradas" (2009, p. 335). So, discussing and studying them more highly emphasizes what Carolyn Steedman aims to express in the quotation that opens this chapter: "To enter that place where the past lives, where ink on parchment can be made to speak, remains still the social historian's dream, of bringing to life those who do not for the main part exist [...]" (1998, p. 69).

8 See https://www.cultura.gob.es/cultura/areas/archivos/mc/archivos/agi/portada.html.

9 See https://www.cultura.gob.es/museodeamerica/portada.html.

10 See https://armada.defensa.gob.es/ArmadaPortal/page/Portal/ArmadaEspannola/cienciaorgano/prefLang-es/01cienciamuseo.

11 The participation of institutions in the educational processes that are going to be discussed in the following pages will receive a wider attention below. However, it is interesting to see how scholars such as Gómez Trigueros and Yáñez de Aldecoa discuss how institutional implication is crucial in order to reduce digital inequality, the preamble of social inequality: "En este sentido, las instituciones encargadas de la formación de profesorado deben luchar contra el riesgo de aumentar la 'brecha digital', en cualquiera de sus modalidades, generada por las tecnologías, aprovechando precisamente las bondades que estas herramientas poseen. Para ello, no sólo se debe contar con currículos educativos, que fomenten la alfabetización digital del alumnado, sino también con un profesorado formado en y con tecnologías, que proporcione un sustento formativo inclusivo a partir de tales recursos digitales. Es aquí donde mod-

elos de enseñanza y aprendizaje como el modelo TPACK puede generar esas sinergias, que potencien un uso inclusivo de las tecnologías y que planteen una nueva perspectiva social de las TIC, formando a los futuros docentes para eliminar las brechas digitales del siglo XXI" (2022, p. 43).

12 Memory, and the academic research of the implications it has, has recently developed interesting theoretical approaches. One of them is that of the so called "School of Memory," led by, among others, Torsten Caeners. When working with archival materials about the past, these implications become specially relevant, for we are not only facing contents regarding past moments, but also formats or materialities that do not belong (at least in similar terms) to our historical moment. As Caeners states: "Where does one begin with memory? With memory works? Involuntarily, with the past, my past, our past, a past the pastness of which is always already effaced, effaces itself constantly into the present, presents its absence, inscribes itself in the endless succession of the now, the temporality of the Cartesian *cogito*, the Freudian consciousness, the Platonic thought, the *logos*" (2015, p. 282).

13 This is only a selection that has been gathered for the purposes of this chapter due to their chronological proximity. The exploration of these regions encompassed many other expeditions that produced several other narrations. For a more accurate description of the process, with detailed references to the remaining documents see, for instance, Tomás Bartoli (1970), Derek Pethick (1976), Jim McDowell (1998), Freeman M. Tovell (2008), or Fernando Martínez Láinez and Carlos Canales Torres (2009, pp. 335-349).

14 Specially renown as the first biographer of Junípero Serra (1713-1784).

15 In a research project we had developed earlier, we had the opportunity of proving that the reference included in the archives of the Naval Museum of Madrid was incorrect (a forthcoming publication will acknowledge this). While exploring some of the documents held by the Naval Museum of Madrid, we realized that the correct reference was M. N. Ms. 335, doc. 40, f. 99-105. We shared this with the curators of the archive but, as far as we have been able to check for the completion of this document, it has not been fixed. That is why we have decided to maintain the reference included in the digital databases of the Museum.

16 Born Joan Perés. For more information about this explorer, see María Luisa Rodríguez-Sala (2006).

17 The concept of digital literacy is closely linked to that of "postmodern literacy." Although we are not discussing this topic here due to space limitations, the concept may be the object of further research. For more information, see Isabella Monika Leibrandt (2019).

18 Even affecting professionals of education, such as teachers, as stated by Sanchez-Prieto, Trujillo-Torres, Gómez-García, and Gómez García: "The results found in the descriptive analysis made it clear that teachers do not consider themselves deep digitally literate in practically any of the dimensions of digital competence. These results are similar to previous studies carried out at an international level (Amhag et al., 2019; Chandrasena, 2019; Li et al., 2019), which conclude by advocating the need for ongoing training for teachers, which would provide practical skills and abilities in digital matters to a teaching staff that increasingly needs to make frequent use of these tools and that, currently, does not see the teaching opportunities that these resources offer" (2020, p. 1564).

19 Traditionally, in Spain this has become problematic when dealing with social groups such as those of Romani descent (the "vulnerable population" of Alvarez-Icaza Longoria, Bustamante-Bello, Ramírez-Montoya, and Molina -2022, p. 14-). Within this groups, even primary education levels are much lower for the rest of the population. When dealing with women, whose roles in Romani groups have been traditionally attached to the family and the house, this situation even increases. As Mariscal, Mayne, Aneja, and Sorgner state: "Socio-cultural factors are a key impediment to access for many women" (2019, p. 6). Something further explored by Jesús Sánchez-Prieto, Juan Manuel Trujillo-Torres, Melchor Gómez-García, and Gerardo Gómez-García: "[...] the Spanish National Institute of Educational Technologies and Teacher Training (Instituto Nacional de Tecnologias Educativas y Formacion del Profesorado [INTEF]), which belongs to the Ministry of Education and Vocational Training, is the one responsible for the integration of ICTs and teacher training in the non-university educational stages. This agency proposed in 2017 within the "Digital Teaching Framework" five areas or dimensions that make up the Digital Competence of Teachers (Table 1). Having this knowledge, as indicated by institutions such as the European Commission, the World Bank or the Organization for Economic Co-operation and Development (OECD), is a strategic requirement for the economic and social development of any country" (2020, p. 1558).

20 One of these is "Relaciones de Sucesos" (available at https://www.google.com/maps/d/u/0/viewer?mid=1MoHZ33dxXE0U73ZmjEQ3SNJqqLpBYJqc&ll=34.74234614488728%2C-31.047040336422057&z=5-). Created by the Spanish National Library (in consequence, with an undeniable academic validity) is actively shows the different worldwide locations of historical texts created during the early modern period in the Lusophone and Spanish contexts. Still under completion (for instance, the documents we are dealing with in the chapter are only partially included -hoping this chapter to be a stimulus fill this gap-), it is an organic-like software that allows the academic community a series of valuable resources when having to deal with archival documents.

21 A question that, in itself, leads to subsequent questions related to the intermedial nature of archival documents and their teaching: "Regarding teaching, all the proposals presented end up leading us to the same questions: What is a medium? How to define media and mediality? What is intermediality about? These seem to be questions that are repeated in works that relate intermediality and literacy" (Munari Domingos, Costa Vieira, de Paiva Vieira, and Pires de Figueiredo: 2023, 12).

Chapter 13
Scaffolded Literacy Instruction for English Language Learners: Using Technology to Transform the Playing Field

Héctor Manuel Serna Dimas
Universidad Ean, Colombia

ABSTRACT

This chapter describes a teaching sequence in a course of English for English language learners. The participants developed a literacy project whose foundations integrated some of the principles of the educational model at Universidad Ean in Bogotá, Colombia. The guiding concepts that the instructor used to shape the instructional design were digital literacy, technology, and inclusion. These elements took precedence as students worked on each one of the phases of the class project. The chapter makes a claim for literacy instructors to work with a more comprehensive understanding of literacy instruction in classrooms.

INTRODUCTION

"If we write and teach (reading and) writing, we have a theory of literacy by definition." (Zebroski, 1986, p.57)

DOI: 10.4018/979-8-3693-2591-9.ch013

This chapter describes and reflects on the intersection between literacy, technology, and inclusion. These elements are present in the planning and implementation of a digital literacy teaching sequence based upon the educational tenets and the pedagogical principles of Ean University in Bogotá, Colombia.

The literacy perspective follows the genre-based pedagogy that considers reading and writing as complementary processes, which means that what a person can do in reading, he or she must be able to do in writing. For example, if a person can summarise the main ideas of a text by determining the topic sentences in the various paragraphs, this person can produce a written text that is guided by the presence of topic sentences in each one of the paragraphs. Moreover, genre-based pedagogy promotes the idea that reading is an exercise in deconstructing meaning to achieve comprehension, and writing is the process of constructing meaning to elaborate and communicate a message.

The students enrolled in the Upper-Intermediate English course develop a literacy project that follows the 'Sydney School' Literacy Cycle (Martin & Rose, 2007), which works in a series of interrelated steps, namely context setting, text deconstruction, joint construction, and independent (text) construction. Each one of these phases is supported by technology and class opportunities for students to collaborate and work around their writing.

Technology is one of the key drivers of student engagement these days. These students are given the chance to use the technological resources at their disposal, such as laptops, tablets, and smartphones, to conduct their literacy work. These resources are enriched by the use of learning platforms such as Bookwidgets®, Nearpod®, Pear Deck®, and Wooclap®, to name a few. As a result, students can work both synchronically and asynchronically since course work and assignments can be accessed online at different times.

Inclusion happens when teachers provide scaffolds, so students have equal chances to develop their literacy skills regardless of the readiness stage for an assignment or project. Scaffolding as a teaching strategy works towards levelling the playing field so that students are given the same opportunities in terms of their cognitive development and goal achievement. Consequently, students are not either gifted or at risk; they receive the same help to develop their projects. Another element of inclusion has to do with the idea of collaborative activities where students can measure their levels of achievement and work ethics accordingly. When students are given the chance to read exemplars of the work they are to develop in their class activities, they will have a better idea of how to write projects that match those exemplars. Writing is not a task that students write for their teacher to comply with a class assignment, obtain a grade, and continue with their lives. It is, in fact, an opportunity to use literacy as an artefact where the reader or writer can explore the horizons and limits of their literacy.

This chapter begins with a brief context about Ean University, followed by a characterization of sociocultural theory as one of the key drivers of the university's pedagogical model. Once this context is provided, the text presents the rationale for genre-based pedagogy, particularly the 'Sydney School' cycle to approach literacy. This cycle is then exemplified by the planning and implementation of a teaching sequence in an Upper-Intermediate English class with students in the Modern Languages Program. The text continues with some reflections about the digital literacy exercise, the use of technology, and the opportunities for inclusion along the teaching sequences. The document ends with some motivations and limitations around genre-based pedagogy and some conclusions.

The Context of the Chapter

Universidad Ean is a Colombian university that offers undergraduate and graduate programmes in humanities and social sciences, engineering, finance, and administration faculties. The Modern Languages Program belongs to the faculty of humanities and is intended to educate professionals in modern languages who may major in either business and legal translation or organizational communication and digital communication.

Sociocultural Theory at Universidad Ean

The teaching and learning processes at Universidad Ean are founded on a sociocultural perspective, which means that these processes are socially constructed. Thus, individuals interact with the reality around them by using systems of symbols in order to know about the world. Language and literacy are tokens of such interaction that happens due to the mediation that occurs in language teaching and learning practices. Lantolf and Thorne (2006) conceptualized mediation as "the process through which humans deploy culturally constructed artifacts, concepts, and activities to regulate (i.e., gain voluntary control over and transform) the material world" (p.79).

Another important feature of mediation is the idea of regulation, where learners are subordinated to the supervision of tutors or teachers, and progressively, as they develop control over the systems of symbols, they will not require the presence or supervision of others; these learners see themselves as self-regulated, which also means that these learners already internalized or learned the concepts they were taught.

The ideas by Lantolf and Thorne (2006) can be extrapolated to literacy processes where language is used in terms of both gaining control and transforming the material world. Literacy processes are ignited by the idea of producing texts, which are the result of controlling and transforming thinking through the use of a system of symbols (written language). For example, literacy processes have been characterized as the completion of several steps such as pre-writing, drafting, revising, editing, proofreading, and publishing.

Thus, every teacher's attempt to plan, teach, and evaluate literacy practices must consider how learners display their language and literacy abilities through a progression from teacher-led activities to student-assisted practice, and finally the student's free or creative practice that does not require the tutor's supervision.

Genre-Based Pedagogy

The concept of pedagogy has had a long history that has been marked by changes in the education of individuals. It was considered the art of leading children that evolved into the art of changing the individual. Not (2013) defined it more recently as a field that organizes different means to serve an end, which in essence is to transform individuals by developing learning situations (p. 13).

Literacy is one of those fields where the instructor uses the means at their disposal so that individuals are able to use their knowledge of letters to create messages and communicate them to a community. Johns (1997) characterizes text writing as the interaction of several factors that are both external and internal to text production. External factors are those related to the aspects that motivated the writing of the text, such as the context, the writing situation, and the idea of an audience as a community. The internal factors are those aspects related to the actual writing where writers condense their knowledge of aspects such as the content, the form, and the register. Both internal and external factors are combined in the writing of specific texts that need to revolve around a communicative intention.

Thus, text creation becomes part of the learner's schemata that the learner may reproduce when a situation requires the writing of a new text whose general structure is recognized by the writer, so he can proceed to actualize it in a new product or project. Johns (1997) considers that these texts have a prototypicality that allows for their recognition as a short story, a poem, or the quintessential five-paragraph essay.

This knowledge that a reader or writer needs to understand a text or produce one is known as genre knowledge. Swales (1990) defines genre as a 'class of communicative events' (p. 45); Martin (2007) conceptualizes genre as a 'staged goal-oriented social process through which social subjects in a given culture live their lives' (p. 13); and Nesi and Gardner (2012) view genre as an abstraction on how to proceed about text reading and/or writing. However, Johns (1997) regards genre as a framework where text writing is a multi-layered process where the writer, the text, and the context of writing itself converge as a socioliterate perspective on literacy since the above elements are motivated by a communicative purpose and the expectations of an audience and a community. This socioliterate perspective determines that "literacies are acquired principally through exposure to discourses from a variety of social contexts. Through this exposure, individuals gradually develop theories of genre" (Johns, 1997, p. 14).

The 'Sydney School' Literacy Cycle

The 'Sydney School' of literacy instruction was born as an attempt for the Australian educational authorities to offer education to the newly arrived immigrants and underprivileged populations in the country. The educational effort was oriented towards giving these learners literacy instruction using authentic materials that were part of their everyday lives, so they could transition more easily into demands of education and the workforce. The instructional approach was based on the use of genre knowledge, which was implemented in the school curricula.

The 'Sydney School' literacy instruction is described as a cycle that is comprised of four stages: the first moment of context and content building, followed by a deconstruction of a text, where instructors indicate students to pay attention to the text features that characterize the text structure and determine the reading comprehension of the text. By doing this, the instructor is providing students with anticipated information that they will retrieve for the writing assignment. Then the instructor continues with a collaborative activity where students construct a text in groups or with the instructor's guidance. Students reflect upon the exercise to draw the elements they use in the writing process. The cycle ends when students work on an autonomous writing task.

The following section will present the Modern Languages Program at Ean university, the Upper-Intermediate English Course, and the application of the 'Sydney School' literacy cycle in a class project intended to write a product review.

The Modern Languages Program at Ean University

The Modern Languages Program has several key areas of instruction namely Spanish literacy and linguistics, English as the second language of the program, and two other language options among Italian, French, German, and Portuguese. Students enrolled in the program study five semesters of English from basic to advanced. In the last three semesters of the program, students pursue content areas that are taught in English. It is estimated that students in fifth semester already possess a language proficiency that allows them to study courses such as International Culture, English Culture, and Business Speech, which are the last in the program.

The Modern Languages Program adheres to the Common European Framework of Reference for Languages, (2020), CEFR from now on. The CEFR is a descriptive scale of language levels ranging from A1 (beginner) to C2 (proficient). The framework aims to provide learners with a description of statements that declare what they can do with the language as a result of their work and the collaborative interactions with both their instructor and peers.

The CEFR has had several updates from its original publication in 2001; one of the most recent concepts added to the latest version is the idea of mediation which is introduced in Section 2.1.3 as follows:

In both the receptive and productive modes, the written and/or oral activities of mediation make communication possible between persons who are unable, for whatever reason, to communicate with each other directly. Translation or interpretation, a paraphrase, summary, or record, provides for a third-party a (re)formulation of a source text to which this third party does not have direct access. Mediation language activities – (re)processing an existing text – occupy an important place in the normal linguistic functioning of our societies. (p.34)

Mediation of language activities is one of the key concepts that this chapter is based upon since language or languages make it possible for people to communicate among themselves. It is the learner who has to solve the communicative challenges that circumstances will impose on them. In regard to these circumstances, North & Piccardo (2016)) assert that "the learner finds him/herself confronted with a text or situation that requires some form of mediation to become accessible: linguistic, social or cultural mediation – or a combination of the three" (p.10).

North and Piccardo (2016) also address mediation from the pedagogic perspective, and they define it as a tripartite component namely scaffolded, collaborative, and relational. The first one is related to providing access to knowledge so that people are prompted to develop their ideas. The second one is related to the concept of co-construction, and the last one encompasses the provision of spaces for creativity. (p.11)

Upper-Intermediate English

The English component of the Modern Languages Program has five semesters of English: Basic English I, Basic English II, Intermediate English, Upper-Intermediate English, and Advanced English. The first four courses are taught with the book *Language Leader*, Pearson®. The Advanced level is a course aimed at preparing students to take the IELTS academic exam and also uses a preparation book by Pearson Education®.

Students enrolled in the Upper-Intermediate course have already studied four semesters of English with an estimated of 90 hours in 18 weeks and 150 hours of independent work for each semester as stated in the course syllabus. The students in this course have had at least 360 hours of direct instruction, and they must be at the B1 exit level of proficiency according to the CEFR.

The course covers six units of the *Language LeaderIntermediate* book (Cotton, Falvey, Kent, 2014); each unit has a topic that is developed following the four modes of communication: reception, production, interaction, and mediation, which correspond to the language skills of listening, reading, writing, and speaking.

Unit 7 entitled "Design" is intended to describe products, and it addresses aspects such as product functionality, target consumers, and selling points. The unit begins with short readings about the history of design in the twentieth century and has a short video in which a design expert discusses her job as a designer. The unit progresses into some speaking activities where students select a product and present it in class using the criteria mentioned above. The book unit also addresses vocabulary and grammar items intended to work on the vocabulary related to design and the use of modals accordingly.

Description of the Class Literacy Cycle

The students are presented with a literacy (reading/writing) project where they have to work on products that characterize the idea of design in several realms. The purpose of the project is for students to write a product review. The next section of the chapter establishes de class objectives together with the lesson development.

Objectives

Students **W**ill **B**e **A**ble **T**o...

- **SWBAT** identify key vocabulary from a reading passage
- **SWBAT** scan the key elements of a reading passage
- **SWBAT** summarise the content of a reading passage
- **SWBAT** discuss the criteria for writing an effective product review
- **SWBAT** use their knowledge of product reviews to write their texts

The course sessions for this particular project were divided into setting the context and content building, text deconstruction, joint text construction, text writing moderation, and independent text writing.

Setting the Context and Building the Content

This stage took place as preparation for students to determine their prior knowledge and vocabulary about commercial products and their descriptions as it is illustrated in Figure 1.

Figure 1. Product description

PRODUCTS

Read the adjectives and complete the chart with the words that best describe the product.

ADJECTIVES	PRODUCT		
attractive, comfortable, economical, efficient, light, expensive, fashionable, thin, popular, practical, pure, reliable, safe, athletic	CAR	SPORT SHOES	TABLET

Look at the following products and describe them using the adjectives from the chart above.

The purpose of the activity was to engage students in product description by giving them the vocabulary to use for three products. Once they categorized the word, they were asked if the words could be used to describe three products or one in particular. The end product of this activity was to describe the product students could describe in detail.

The Upper-Intermediate activities are supported by the tool Bookwidgets®, which is a learning platform that promotes interactive activities. The platform offers a variety of resources such as games, pictures, videos, and handouts that can be customized to work with languages or even numbers since some of these resources can be used with mathematics. The platform also allows users to embed resources from outside sources such as videos, webpages, or PDF files (see Figure 2).

Bookwidgets works in a variety of digital learning environments such as Google Classroom and TEAMS. It also works very well on smartphones which are used extensively in the Upper-Intermediate English classes.

Figure 2. Bookwidgets interface

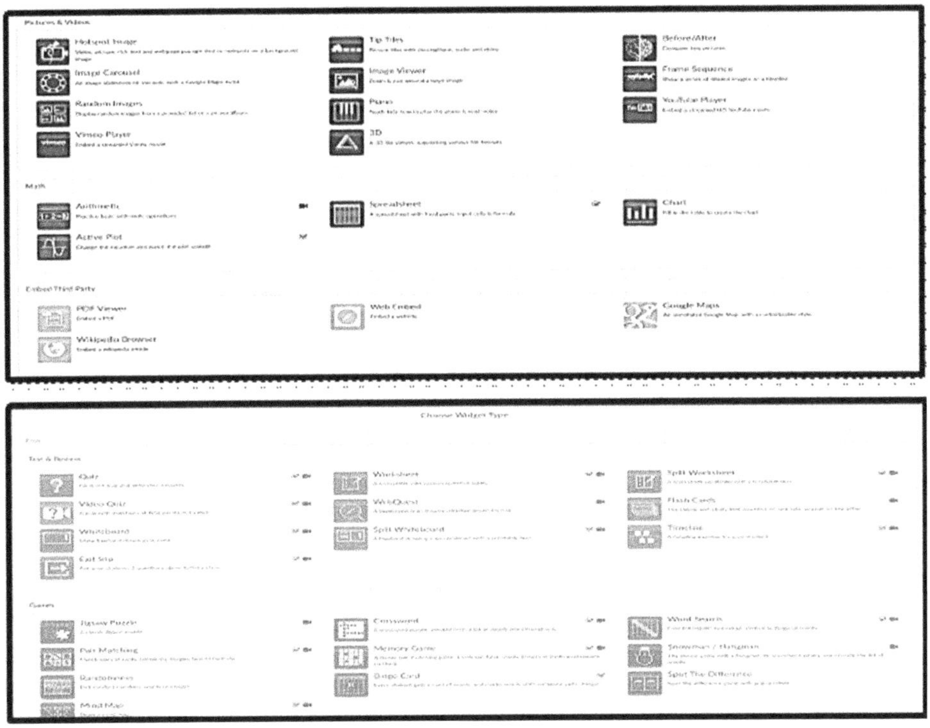

For the reading activity, students were provided with a split worksheet (Bookwidgets) where they had the reading and the comprehension questions aimed at working on their scanning skills for reading.

Text Deconstruction

The first handout students obtained on their smartphones or tablets was a split worksheet where they scanned for specific information so that they knew the main elements to cover in a product review. The product that they were given to review was an application that delivered food to people. These food deliveries were customized according to the customers' dietary preferences (see Figure 3).

Students read the product review and paid close attention to the criteria that were used to determine the quality of the product and its benefits. Students were encouraged to look at specific information regarding consumers' ratings, product quality, shipping, customer service, and some comments by application users. Once they were familiar with the product, they answered the questions that followed (see Figure 3).

Figure 3. Product review: Scanning for information

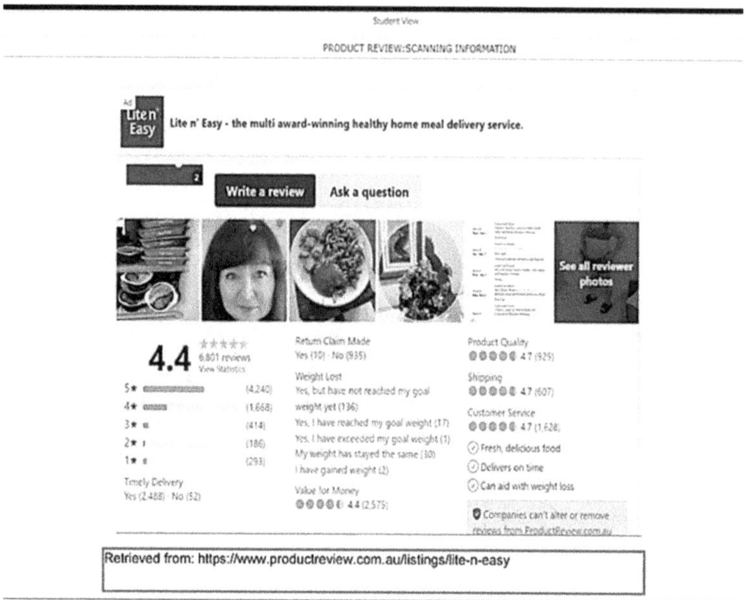

The Upper-Intermediate course had twenty students enrolled, and the work of two students was selected to illustrate the ideas of digital literacy, technology, and inclusion. These students are identified as Student_1 and Student_2, and their work will be the subject of analysis and further reflections.

Figure 4. Product Review: Comprehension questions

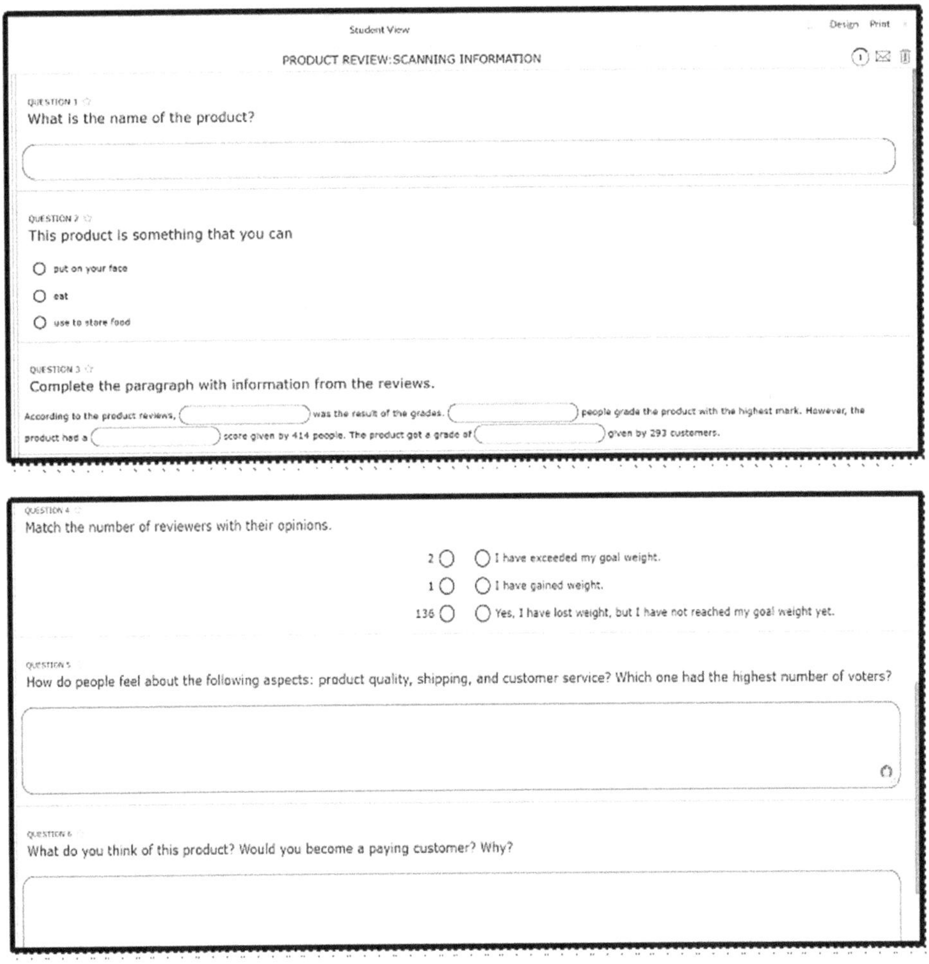

Students had to be able to extract from the original text the relevant information that could give them the constituents of the review. Then they had to be able to discuss in class the criteria to have a comprehensive understanding of the product. Additionally, they had to give their personal opinions as though they were potential customers (see Figures 5 and 6).

Figure 5. Student_1 reading answer sheet

PRODUCT REVIEW:SCANNING INFORMATION 8 / 11

Aug 14, 2023, 7:35 AM

Student 1

1. What is the name of the product? / 1 ✗

Lite n' Easy

2. This product is something that you can 1 / 1 ✓

- ○ put on your face
- ● eat ✓
- ○ use to store food

3. Complete the paragraph with information from the reviews. 4 / 4 ✓

According to the product reviews, 4.4 ✓ was the result of the grades. 4,240 ✓ people grade the product with the highest mark. However, the product had a 3 ✓ score given by 414 people. The product got a grade of 1 ✓ given by 293 customers.

4. Match the number of reviewers with their opinions. 3 / 3 ✓

136 → Yes, I have lost weight, but I have not reached my goal weight yet. ✓

2 → I have gained weight. ✓

1 → I have exceeded my goal weight. ✓

5. How do people feel about the following aspects: product quality, shipping, and customer service? Which one had the highest number of voters? / 1 ✗

They feel really good about the different 3 aspects because all of them have positive opinions of 4.7 stars.

The field with the highest number of voters is "customer service"

6. What do you think of this product? Would you become a paying customer? Why? / 1 ✗

Personally, I would not pay for this service because I consider I don't need to loose weight, but I think it can be a great option for people who would like to do it.

Figure 6. Student_2 reading answer sheet

PRODUCT REVIEW:SCANNING INFORMATION 8 / 11

Aug 14, 2023, 7:38 AM

Student 2

1. What is the name of the product? / 1 ✗

Lite n' easy

2. This product is something that you can 1 / 1 ✓

- put on your face
- eat ✓
- use to store food

3. Complete the paragraph with information from the reviews. 4 / 4 ✓

According to the product reviews, 4.4 ✓ was the result of the grades. 4,240 ✓ people grade the product with the highest mark. However, the product had a 3 ✓ score given by 414 people. The product got a grade of 1 ✓ given by 293 customers.

4. Match the number of reviewers with their opinions. 3 / 3 ✓

2 → I have gained weight. ✓

1 → I have exceeded my goal weight. ✓

136 → Yes, I have lost weight, but I have not reached my goal weight yet. ✓

5. How do people feel about the following aspects: product quality, shipping, and customer service? Which one had the highest number of voters? / 1 ✗

As we can see people approve the product. For instance, (925)people enjoyed the product quality, (607)feel comfortable with the shipping and then with the highest number of voters (1,628) they thought a good costumer service.

6. What do you think of this product? Would you become a paying customer? Why? / 1 ✗

I'm not really sure about that but it could be a possibility. Just for know why people like this.

The students' completion of this handout allowed them to deconstruct the text; they also had the chance to work on a paragraph exercise whose accomplishment combined sentences and numbers. This type of exercise was meant to work as a scaffold so students became familiar with the paragraph structure to review a product.

Joint Text Construction

Students were then presented with another split worksheet (Bookwidgets). This time they had to write a review of a product, but they had to examine the text *The Ten Commandments for Product Review* (see Figure 7). This text also worked as a scaffold for students to make sure their text covered the key points for an effective review. Product reviews cannot be lengthy since people do not spend a lot of time or consideration in buying a product, so they needed precise information that engaged customers in buying a product or service.

Figure 7. The ten commandments for product review

THE TEN COMMANDMENTS FOR PRODUCT REVIEW

1. **Straight To The Point Intro** builds trust, shows readers you tested the product, and shares some key conclusions so that readers start getting value from the post right away.
2. **How You Tested** methodology/summary to build trust.
3. **Quick Scan Ratings / Summary** for "Give me the facts".
4. **In-Depth Details** for "Tell me everything".
5. **Highlight Real Use Cases** to show how it solves actual relevant points.
6. **Present Pros and Cons** to verify authenticity.
7. **Show Who It Is For, and Who It Is Not For** to help people make the right decision.
8. **Include Product Photos or Screenshots** that you personally took to verify authenticity.
9. **Highlight Important Purchase Details for More Complex Products** such as pricing plans, licensing terms, and so on.
10. **Summary / Recap with Calls To Action (CTAs)** to purchase this product as well as the recommended alternatives.

Retrieve from: https://wordpress.com/go/content-blogging/product-review-template/

The structure of the *Ten Commandments* helps to direct students' attention to what they had to focus when they had to structure their review. They did not have to comply with them all; however, some of the elements had to be present based on their particular approach to the task. In general terms, many of them addressed "*commandments*" 4, 7, and 9.

Students 1 and 2 (Figures 8 and 9) writing samples are provided here to determine how well they complied with the task. Both students complied with the task although there is more elaboration on the piece presented by student_1.

Figure 8. Students' writing samples: Student_1 product review

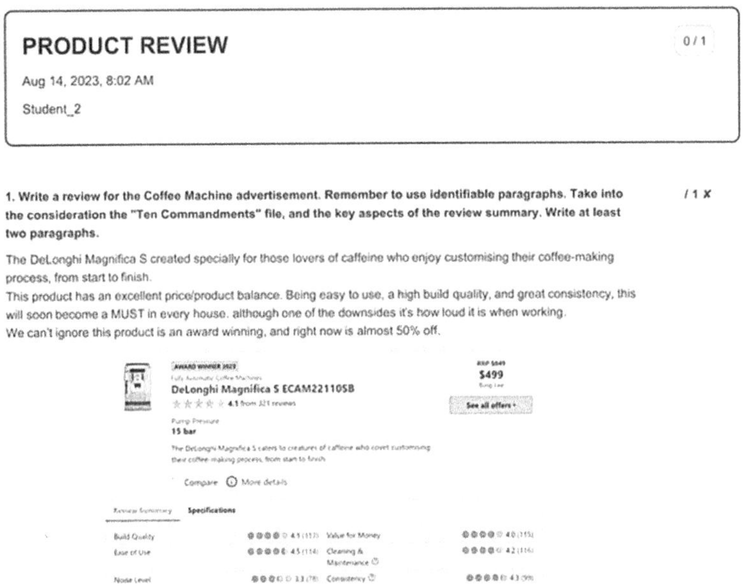

Student_1 used a narrative of how he searched for the product in his first paragraph. The second paragraph was more about the practicality of the coffee machine and some details about the purchase.

Figure 9. Students' writing samples: Student_2 product review

PRODUCT REVIEW 0 / 1

Aug 14, 2023, 7:59 AM

Student_1

1. Write a review for the Coffee Machine advertisement. Remember to use identifiable paragraphs. Take into the consideration the "Ten Commandments" file, and the key aspects of the review summary. Write at least two paragraphs. / 1 ✗

Last week I decided to buy the amazing DeLonghi Magnifica because I really needed it, I spent months searching the perfect coffee machine and I finally found it, it serves coffee of all kinds, even cold coffee drinkings, this machine actually achieved solving all my problems when making coffee.

It is really easy to use, you just have to press the button with the coffee you want and in just 1 minute it is ready to drink and enjoy, this product is great for anyone who loves coffee, if you don't really like this drink, even though the price is amazing and accessible, I advice you to spend your money in something else.

Student_2 had a more reduced version of the review. This student made a general statement about the product and continued with some details that were meant to persuade the readers to buy the appliance. The students complied with the assignment; however, the review had to be analyzed against the criteria of the *ten commandments* list.

Text Writing Moderation

Students worked on their assignments and submitted them for their revision. This revision was done individually first and then as a group assignment. For this particular assignment, students were given a handout where they could read some of the reviews done by their classmates as it can be seen in Figure 10. These product reviews were anonymous, and they were chosen at random.

Figure 10. Product review: Moderation activity

PRODUCT REVIEWS

RUBRIC

Read the product reviews and then fill out the rubric. The criteria are Yes (Y) or (No) if the student complies with the criteria for the assignment.

REVIEW 1

DeLonghi Magnifica S ECAM22110SB

"It is a coffee machine that each person who want to have a great cup of coffee at all time. It is easy to use so that makes it comfortable for all people who wants coffee without having complications. Probably it is a bit irritating the noise that makes but it is something tolerable.

In the other hand, it has a discount of almost the 41.3% so it costs $499, if it were a little cheaper, it could cover the fact that the noise is annoying. But It has a cleaning and maintenance service that is absolutely an advantage because many products doesn't have it. Finally it is made of very good materials, which are resistant and have a very great build quality."

		TEN COMMANDMENTS FOR PRODUCT REVIEW									
Two paragraphs	Review summary	1	2	3	4	5	6	7	8	9	10

REVIEW 2

"As to coffe machines the DeLonghi Magnifica S is the best one you can buy it. This machine allows you to customise the making process of your coffe, from start to finish. It was awarded this year. Now, it's in discount so, you can save some money buying this machine.

In depth details, based on the reviews, ease of use, consistency, cleaning and maintenance are the best qualified aspects that you can find in this machine."

		TEN COMMANDMENTS FOR PRODUCT REVIEW									
Two paragraphs	Review summary	1	2	3	4	5	6	7	8	9	10

REVIEW 3

"this coffee machine is a great way to get more time to do other things. it has a easy system to be use, the materials are good and they don't change the texture and flavor of the coffe. you can have a great experience and relaxing time drinking your coffe. it's price is very nice because it is not expensive but it offers a lot of advantages for your live, before you start working at your job, also you can carry it very easy."

		TEN COMMANDMENTS FOR PRODUCT REVIEW									
Two paragraphs	Review summary	1	2	3	4	5	6	7	8	9	10

Students worked individually in rating the three reviews. Then they worked in small groups to share their ratings and their ideas on the best review according to the criteria given to them. At this point, students were confronted with their work, so they could judge how close or far they were from producing a review that integrated the 10 *commandments* for a product review.

As a result, all class groups concurred that the first review matched most of the criteria set for the task. For example, it had at least two paragraphs; it also complied with criteria 1 (going straight to the point), 4 (in-depth details), and 6 (presented pros and cons). This exercise was important since the activity allowed their genre knowledge to emerge. Students had criteria to analyze their work and determine their strengths and weaknesses for the writing of this particular assignment.

The Upper-Intermediate course has several moments for evaluation. One moment is classwork since students' handouts are collected and archived so that the professor assigns a grade for classwork. Another moment of class evaluation is the speaking activities where students present a product to their classmates. The product reviews are also part of the evaluation of their writing skills. Finally, students are given a test at the end of the term.

Independent Text Construction

The end of the term exam is based on the topic of "Design", and it has listening, reading, and writing sections. The task in the writing section of the exam is to write a product review characterized in Table 1.

Table 1. Upper-intermediate: Writing section

<table>
<tr><th colspan="6">WRITING (60 points)</th></tr>
<tr><td colspan="6">Write a product review of about 250 words. You can write a review of a product that you bought recently.</td></tr>
<tr><td colspan="6">Consider the following contents:
1. Say what the product does
2. Say what you consider is good about the product
3. Say what you consider is not so good about the product
4. Give recommendations</td></tr>
<tr><td colspan="6">Consider the following layout:
1. Introduction
2. Discuss good points
3. Discuss bad points
4. Give recommendations
5. Conclusion</td></tr>
<tr><th colspan="6">Evaluation criteria</th></tr>
<tr><td>Content
/12</td><td>Communicative achievement /12</td><td>Organization
/12</td><td>Grammar
/12</td><td>Vocabulary
/12</td><td>Total</td></tr>
</table>

Figures 11 and 12 shows the sample answers of Student_1 and Student_2. They had to select a product and write a review according to the above criteria. Student_1 decided to write a new version of the iPad and Student_2 went for a recording gadget to help students record their lessons.

Figure 11. Students' exam reviews: Student_1 exam answer

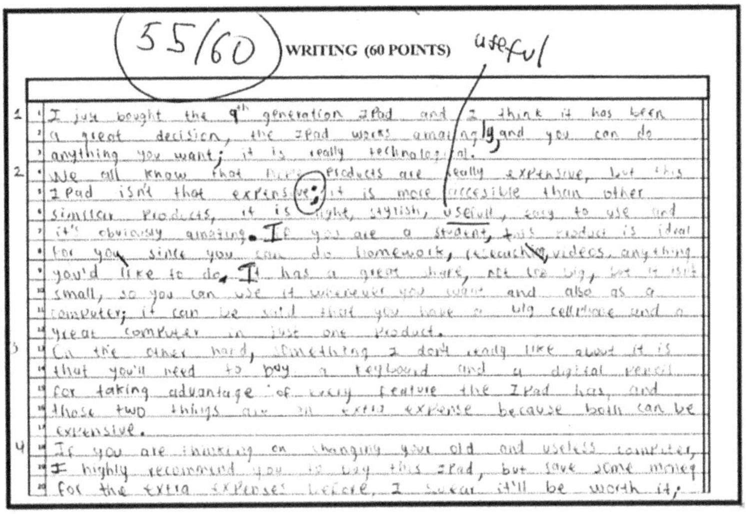
55/60 WRITING (60 POINTS) useful

1 I just bought the 9th generation IPad and I think it has been a great decision, the IPad works amazingly, and you can do anything you want; it is really technological.

2 We all know that [illegible] products are really expensive, but this IPad isn't that expensive; it is more accessible than other similar products, it is light, stylish, usefull, easy to use and it's obviously amazing. If you are a student, this product is ideal for you since you can do homework, research, videos, anything you'd like to do. It has a great [illegible], not too big, but it isn't small, so you can use it wherever you want and also as a computer; it can be said that you have a big cellphone and a great computer in just one product.

3 On the other hand, something I don't really like about it is that you'll need to buy a keyboard and a digital pencil for taking advantage of every feature the IPad has, and those two things are an extra expense because both can be expensive.

4 If you are thinking on changing your old and useless computer, I highly recommend you to buy this IPad, but save some money for the extra expenses before. I swear it'll be worth it.

Student_1 wrote four paragraphs as he diligently numbered them in his piece of writing. The first paragraph was the introduction to her review. The second paragraph described the positive elements of the new product. Paragraph three was about some disadvantages of the product. The text concluded with a recommendation to the reader.

This piece of writing has some relevant aspects to discuss against the rationale of the literacy cycle. First, the student knew how to introduce the purchase. Next, the second paragraph was used to mention some conditions the product could fulfill. Paragraph three was about possible disadvantages, which worked towards the authenticity of the piece. The review ended in a positive note about the convenience of the product.

Figure 12. Students' exam reviews: Student_2 exam answer

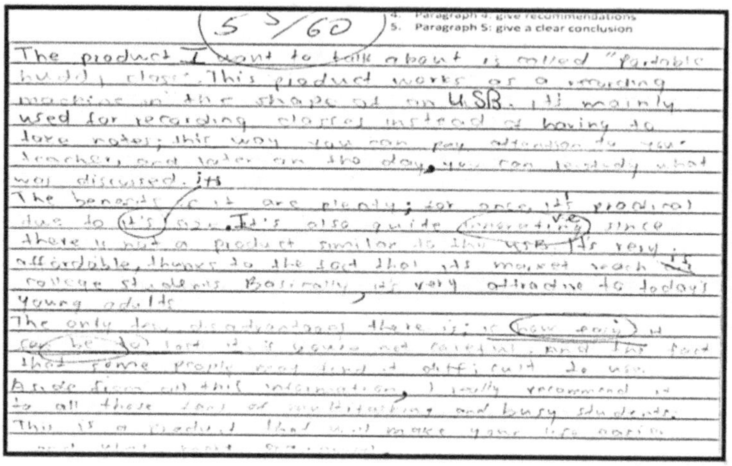

Student_2, on the other hand, writes three paragraphs. The first one is a general presentation of the product. The second paragraph shows the positive elements of the product, and the last paragraph is about the disadvantages of the product and a conclusion.

The last section of the present chapter resumes some of the key concepts that guided the instructional design for the literacy project in an English course. The concepts to review are mediation, genre-based knowledge, technology and digital expression, scaffolding, and both the motivations and limitations of genre-based pedagogy.

Language and Literacy as Mediated Activities

The chapter began with the idea of mediation, and the quote from the CEFR defines mediation as instances of text reformulation by the learners so that their production begins to exist as they attempt to express their ideas by using the linguistic symbol at their disposal while attending a new communicative event.

The design of the teaching sequence proposed that students write a product review and included the reading of an exemplar (authentic) text that students analyzed and deconstructed to make sense of the product review components. Then, the sequence allowed students to write their own texts, which were later confronted by a collaborative activity projected to give students feedback on their pieces. By having students evaluate two writing samples, the instructor provided feedback to students as they could compare their own pieces with what two of their classmates did. Finally, students had a second moment where they could write a product review based on criteria that were well-known to all of them. This second moment took place as part of the end-of-quarter test in which students were asked to write a product review.

Genre-Based Projects as Artifacts for Students to Expand Their Literacy Thinking

The term constructionism was first used in mathematics by Papert (1972) as he studied the approaches people used to teach mathematics to children. He argued that children had to be taught mathematics as mathematicians. That is, they had to be given opportunities to use materials "artifacts", so their mathematical thinking would flourish. Moreover, he considered that working with these artifacts and promoting people's mathematical thinking would be the heuristics required to learn and theorize the mathematical world. In a very similar way, genre-based pedagogy and the 'Sydney School' literacy cycle provide teachers and students with steps where the latter can explore the horizons and limits of their literacy thinking. Literacy projects that place reading and writing face-to-face will help both teachers and students to have a common map where they can explore their territory; they will probably start on the same ground, but the nature of their exploration and their journeys will take them to different territories.

Technology and Digital Expression as Drivers of Dynamic Literacy Learning Processes

The use of technological resources created a plethora of spaces and opportunities for students to develop and share their work. Multimodality has been the subject of research that studies the relationship between technology and literacy. Walsh (2010) presents an account of such research with the advent of scenarios such as social media, and virtual reality. She discusses how communication is a combination of different media. Moreover, she defines multimodal literacy as the "meaning-making that occurs through the reading, viewing, understanding, responding to and producing and interacting with multimedia and digital texts" (p.213).

Walsh (2010) also discusses the theory of multimodality (Kress & van Leeuwen, 2001; Kress, 2003), which conceptualizes reading and writing on screen as reciprocal processes where these two modes of communication live on each other to integrate what has been termed as digital literacy.

Both technology and digital expression are pivotal elements in the meaning-making processes that literacy is to enact in classrooms these days. The classroom experience in the present chapter is attuned to Walsh's already-quoted definition of multimodality, as students were engaged in processes of reading, analyzing, responding, and eventually writing by making use of technological resources that were made available by the instructor.

Scaffolded Literacy Teaching to Promote Learner's Inclusion

Teachers and instructors are required to become familiar with their territory so that the literacy maps they provide their learners are conducive to the same point. This safe arrival at an agreed destination is due to a great deal in the way there were scaffolds for students to overcome the literacy project obstacles.

Genre-Based Pedagogy: Motivations and Limitations

On the one hand, writing practices need to be oriented towards students' literacy experiences in various academic contexts. Genre offers constant ways for people to integrate their writing into different tasks not only in the academic world but also in their lives outside of school. Another aspect associated with the students' needs is the possibility of genres acting as frameworks that can be scaffolded to match the students' abilities. As a result, literacy practices based on genre provide students with both a supportive and empowering environment. On the one hand, the focus of many lessons is to familiarize students with the texts and the genre features so that they gain control over these elements. On the other hand, the students' initiation in particular genres allows them to develop ownership of the genre as their writing will be identified with particular text types. Hyland (2004) considers this aspect to be important since "genre approaches are committed to a redistribution of literacy resources to help learners gain admission to particular discourse communities" (14). Genre pedagogy is also critical in the sense that the production of texts is motivated and conditioned by contexts. These contexts are populated by people and organizations with ideology and power. Therefore, membership in communities of practice entitles their participants to challenge the discourse practices within the community so that they are able to reshape the text construction practices and standards.

On the other hand, genre approaches have also received criticism from other writing perspectives. Genre has been challenged by the situated learning perspective, the critical pedagogy, and the process approaches. The situated learning perspective argues that genre is extraneous to the artificial environment of the classroom. The critical theorists contend that genre approaches maintain the *status quo* and do not criticize power inequalities established by a dominant culture. As the process approaches, believers claim that genre displaces the importance of both writing and the writer by giving prominence to the form. They also maintain that such an approach toward literacy is oriented towards prescriptivism (Hyland, 2004).

CONCLUSION

This chapter addressed the intersection of literacy, technology, and inclusion in a class with English language learners in higher education. The teaching sequence of a literacy project, propelled for the most part by the use of technological resources, imprinted a particular dynamic that allowed learners to understand, analyze, respond, and write their own projects based on the criteria provided by the instructor, but more importantly, by criteria that emerged as students worked with their materials and shared insights with both their teacher and classmates.

Classrooms are still pervaded by activism that promotes ideas of standardized education or high-stakes testing embedded in set-in-stone curricula. However, language and literacy instructors must be prepared to address the complexities of literacy teaching with criteria much more comprehensive than the technicalities of teaching how to read and write.

REFERENCES

Cotton, D., Falvey, D., & Kent, S. (2014). *Language Leader Intermediate*. Pearson Education.

Council of Europe. (2020). *Common European Framework of Reference for Languages: Learning, teaching, assessment.* Council of Europe Publishing, Strasbourg. www.coe.int/lang-cefr

Hyland, K. (2004). Genre and Second Language Writing. Diane Belcher and Jun Liu Series (Eds.), *Michigan Series on Teaching Multilingual Writers*. The University of Michigan Press. 10.3998/mpub.23927

Johns, M. A. (1997). *Text, Role and Context: Developing Academic Literacies*. Cambridge University Press. 10.1017/CBO9781139524650

Kress, G. (2003). *Literacy in the New Media Age*. Routledge.

Kress, G., & van Leeuwen, T. (2001). *Multimodal Discourse*. Routledge.

Lantolf, J. P., & Thorne, S. L. (2006). *Sociocultural Theory and the Genesis of Second Language Development*. Oxford University Press.

Martin, J. R., & Rose, D. (2007). *Genre Relations*. Equinox.

Nesi, H., & Gardner, S. (2012). *Genres across the Disciplines: Student writing in higher education*. Cambridge University Press. 10.1017/9781009030199

North, B., & Piccardo, E. (2016). *Developing illustrative descriptors of aspects of mediation for the CEFR*. Education Policy Division, Council of Europe.

Not, L. (2013). *Las pedagogías del conocimiento[The pedagogies of knowledge]*. (Sergio, R. M. B., Trans.). Fondo de Cultura Económica de México.

Papert, S. (1972). Teaching Children to be Mathematicians Versus Teaching About Mathematics. *International Journal of Mathematical Education in Science and Technology*, 31(3), 249–262. 10.1080/0020739700030306

Swales, J. (1990) Genre Analysis: English in academic and research settings. (Cambridge Applied Linguistics) Cambridge: Cambridge University Press.

Walsh, M. (2010). Multimodal literacy: What does it mean for classroom practice? *Australian Journal of Language and Literacy*, 33(3), 211–239. 10.1007/BF03651836

Zebroski, J. T. (1986). The uses of theory: A Vygostkyan approach to composition. *Writing Instructor*, 5, 57–67.

Chapter 14
Authentic Presentation Experiences as a Tool to Develop Transferable Skills

Jennifer Schneider
Community College of Philadelphia, USA

ABSTRACT

Despite the widely recognized and acknowledged importance of communication, written, and presentation skills, students often struggle in this area, especially in connection with digital literacy. A noted disconnect between current skill sets, including digital literacy, and workplace needs supports an inquiry into how best to address this challenge in equitable and inclusive ways so as to strengthen both student awareness of the importance of transferable skills and the associated development of digital literacy and soft skills across disciplines. This chapter describes a course-long project that is grounded in principles of feminist digital pedagogy digital literacy, inclusive instruction, and equity and designed to support the development and transfer of written, presentation, and soft skills in a legal technology course developed at a two-year community college located in a large urban area and with a student population comprised primarily of minority and first-generation students. The project emphasizes equitable and inclusive reliance upon technology in all steps and components.

DOI: 10.4018/979-8-3693-2591-9.ch014

INTRODUCTION

Oral and written communication, presentation skills, and so-called soft skills are a critical component of workplace and professional success (Rios et al., 2020; Sethi, 2016). Literature consistently emphasizes the importance of strong communication skills on success in business, legal, and other careers (Camacho, 2015; Clark & DeSanctis, 2013; Hampton, 2019; Vekaric & Jelic, 2013). However, despite the widely recognized and acknowledged importance of communication, written, and presentation skills, students often struggle in this area. Nolop (2013) describes a lack of strong writing skills as one of the most significant gaps in terms of workplace readiness, while Leef (2015) writes of persistent and widespread awareness regarding challenges on the part of educational systems and programs to successfully ensure students acquire strong and transferable written communication skills. Relatedly, Sethi (2016) discusses challenges students face in connection with soft skills and oral presentations. According to Plant, Barac & Sarens (2019), tensions regarding the varying roles and related obligations of both educators and employers in connection with the development of such skills exist and persist, as well.

The noted disconnect between current skill sets and workplace needs supports an inquiry into how best to address this challenge in equitable ways so as to strengthen both student awareness of the importance of transferable skills and the associated development of transferable and soft skills across disciplines. This chapter describes a course-long project (a "Teach Me a Tech Tool Project" or the "Project") that is grounded in principles of feminist digital pedagogy digital literary, and equity and is designed to support the development and transfer of written, presentation, and soft skills in a legal technology course developed for paralegal studies students at a two-year community college located in a large urban area in the United States and with a culturally diverse student population comprised primarily of minority and first-generation students. The project emphasizes equitable reliance upon technology in all steps and components.

This chapter includes a review of related literature, an overview of the Project, student reflections on the learning experience, and a variety of ways audience and authentic presentation experiences can support both student self-efficacy and the ongoing development of transferable skills across disciplines. Throughout the course-long Project, emphasis is placed on the equitable use of technology, digital literacy, and inclusion as well as the related development of student awareness of the importance of a wide range of soft skills, including written and oral communication, peer feedback, listening, and time management, among others, including student self-efficacy in connection with technological, written, and oral presentation skills.

CHALLENGES AND CONTEXT

The Project was designed specifically to support attainment and mastery of both technical course learning outcomes as well as broader, transferable soft skills alongside the development of digital literacy in an inclusive learning community. This section provides an overview of the challenges that the Project sought, in part, to address.

Soft and Transferable Skills

In general, soft skills refer to "non-technical 'people' skills—sometimes called '21st century skills'—that help people secure and keep a job" (Foster, Wiczer, & Eberhardt, 2019, p. 54). Soft skills include "skills related to professionalism, communication, a positive attitude and politeness, teamwork, problem-solving and critical thinking, and networking" (Foster, Wiczer, & Eberhardt, 2019, p. 54). While the importance of soft skills in the workplace is widely understood (Majid et al., 2019), the question of how to define and interpret the term is subject to some debate (Fioravanti, Sena, & Barbosa, 2020).

Fioravanti et. al. (2020) notes that "[w]hile there are common features among definitions in the literature, there is little consensus on a definition of the list of soft skills. In most cases, they are understood primarily in opposition to technical or hard, i.e., the non-domain-specific skills that help individuals thrive in a professional context" (p. 1). For example, Perreault (2004) describes soft skills as a type of personal quality or characteristics that has the potential to distinguish individuals with otherwise similar skills and experience levels. Soft skills, often referred to as employability skills, are vitally important in the workplace and critical to students' long-term success (Foster, Wiczer, & Eberhardt, 2019). According to Heckman and Kautz, "soft skills predict success in life...produce that success, and programs that enhance soft skills have an important place in an effective portfolio" (2012, p. 451). As a matter of definitions, this chapter encourages an intentionally reflective and broader, more culturally nuanced understanding of soft skills, as Hora, Benbow, and Smolarek (2018) suggest. Reflective of a broad interpretation, soft skills include the wide range of interpersonal and intrapersonal knowledge, ethical knowledge and decision-making skills, time management skills, organizational skills, oral and written communication, among many other attributes (Haddad & Marx, 2018). The Project, too, adopts a broad and culturally nuanced understanding of soft and transferable skills, both for definitional purposes as well as with respect to the ways such skills can be equitably incorporated into each component of a scaffolded, course-long project designed with all of the aforementioned goals in mind.

While James and James (2004) earlier described soft skills as an emerging trend that can describe a set of abilities or specific talents that can be applied successfully in the workplace, the long-term importance of, and demand durability for, soft skills have since been firmly established both as a practical and scholarly matter. For example, "[i]n repeated surveys—including one in 2016 by the Society for Human Resource Management—employers value these qualities as much, or more, than academic skills" (Foster at al., 2019, p. 54). Further, Foster et al. (2019) note that the demand and "clamor for soft skills in the workplace is only expected to increase, driven by such forces as automation and team-based decision-making" (p. 55).

Similarly, Pierce (2019) writes that employer demand for soft skills, including problem solving, critical thinking, and communication, "have grown in importance as rapid advancements in technology have transformed" business operations (p. 20). According to a National Association of Colleges and Employers survey, for example, "problem solving and the ability to work well in a team are the attributes that employers most desire among new hires. ... Yet, these are often the skills that employers struggle the most to fill" (p. 20). Similarly, as Fioravanti et al. (2020) write

[i]n today's rapidly changing global economy, organizations are fraught with an increasingly complex, and volatile, unpredictable, chaotic, and ambiguous (VUCA) business environment [2]. In this sense, the importance of soft skills has been expounded repeatedly as a crucial factor to thrive in the workplace, as opposed to mere knowledge of content, since it is important to be able to adapt to new situations. p. 1.

Despite their importance, soft skills are often lacking in new graduates' portfolios of finely developed and nurtured skills (Cook, 2015). Research suggests that persistent gaps remain a troubling trend and challenge (Foster, Wiczer, & Eberhardt, 2019; Stewart, Marciniec, Lawrence, & Joyner-McGraw, 2020).

More recently, the disproportionate impact of COVID-19 and associated lay-offs on underserved communities and minority populations has only compounded these challenges. For example, Guth (2020) writes,

[i]n San Diego, young people have been profoundly tested by pandemic-fueled equity issues, notes San Diego City College (SDCC) President Ricky Shabazz. California hotel, restaurant and tourism workers—mostly younger and more ethnically diverse than the general labor force—have faced the brunt of recent layoffs, he says. p. 10.

Oral and written communication and presentation skills are a critical component of workplace success (Rios et al., 2020; Sethi, 2016). Literature consistently emphasizes the importance of strong communication skills on success in business, legal, and other careers (Camacho, 2015; Clark & DeSanctis, 2013; Hampton, 2019; Vekaric & Jelic, 2013). However, despite the widely recognized and acknowledged importance of communication, written, and presentation skills, students often struggle in this area. Nolop (2013) describes a lack of strong writing skills as one of the most significant gaps in terms of workplace readiness. Leef (2015) also writes of persistent and widespread awareness regarding challenges on the part of educational systems and programs to successfully ensure students acquire strong and transferable written communication skills. Relatedly, Sethi (2016) discusses challenges students face in connection with soft skills and oral presentations.

Research has also found that concentrated writing instruction and associated writing skills on the part of students are often lacking in academic programs. According to Duchardt et al. (2016), for example, writing is under-emphasized in schools and across university syllabi despite the reality that students struggle with written communication across all educational levels, including higher education. Duchardt et al. (2016), for example, found that 60% of submitted writing samples failed to demonstrate complete sentence mastery with a majority of submitted samples failing to demonstrate mastery of complicated sentences as well as associated punctuation.

Not only have studies identified a concerning written communication skills deficit, research has also found a concerning lack of student awareness of the importance of strong communication skills. For example, Usoff and Feldmann (1998) surveyed 270 accounting students to assess their perceptions of the importance of nontechnical skills and found that students failed to fully appreciate the importance and relevance of communication skills on their long-term success (Camacho, 2015). In a 2013 survey, faculty ranked critical thinking, reading comprehension, and effective written communication as the three most critical skills (Jance & Morgan, 2013). However, this same survey found significant disparity between the perceived importance of these skills on the part of both faculty and students (Jance & Morgan, 2013).

Research has recommended that instructors design assignments in order to increase student awareness of the relative importance of communication as well as non-technical skills in accounting and related business fields (Anderson, 2013; Usoff & Feldmann, 1998). As data suggests, however, doing so is often challenging, especially in online environments. The Project is one example of how to actively encourage reflections in this area and, in part, address this challenge.

BACKGROUND LITERATURE

This section provides an overview of the theory and relevant literature that informed the development of the Project.

Student Self-Efficacy

Bandura (n.d.) wrote that "[a]mong the mechanisms of human agency, none is more central or pervasive than people's beliefs in their efficacy to influence events that affect their lives" (para. 1). Lent and Hacket (1987) describe self-efficacy expectations as "beliefs about one's own ability to perform a given behavior successfully" (p. 348). Student self-efficacy focuses on an individual's beliefs regarding the likelihood of being able to perform a task or learn material and, importantly, accepting related responsibility (Bandura, 1977). Self-efficacy is closed linked to intrinsic motivation and influences a wide range and variety of functions including cognitive, motivational, affective, emotional, and decisional functions (Bandura, 1994). Amabile and Kramer (2011) write on small wins over time as one way to enhance a growth mindset and related cognitive functions. Motivational functions relate closely to one's perception of obstacles, while emotional functions impact issues of emotional intelligence versus vulnerability. In connection with decision making, those with high levels of self-efficacy believe they build their environments (Bandura, n.d.).

Bandura describes self-efficacy as a belief in one's ability to influence events that affect one's life. "Self-efficacy has also been significantly implicated in career indecision (Lent & Hackett, 1987), indicating a need to develop self-efficacy through student experience. Lent and Hackett (1987) concluded acquisition of career skills could lead to greater self-efficacy, gained through enactive attainment (performance accomplishments). Acquisition of such performance accomplishments could occur through the Project.

According to Bandura (1977) self-efficacy can be strengthened in four ways, including mastery experience, vicarious experiences, verbal persuasion, and states of physiology. Mastery experiences include the influence of past experiences with both success and failure. Having successes through dedicated effort can positively impact self-efficacy (Bandura, 1977). Small wins are important in this context. That is, each time an individual achieves or reaches a goal a feeling of mastery and an associated positive impact on self- efficacy occurs. Vicarious experiences (observing others similar to us to succeed), verbal persuasion (support systems, positive cheer leaders, and recognition and praise from a teacher); as well as states of psysiology (good feelings that emerge when things are going well) all contribute to higher states of self-efficacy. Relatedly, Lent and Hackett (1987) note that greater efficacy attainment can be supported through, in part, performance accomplishments.

As "[g]reater perception of soft skill attainment, therefore, may lead to greater self-efficacy", it is important to provide such opportunities for students (Haddad and Marx, 2018, p. 162). As described in a later section of this chapters, possibilities might include experiences such as those created by and developed through the

Teach Me a Tech Tool Project. The Project was designed with the goal of, in part, supporting both the development of soft skills as well as the perception of soft skill attainment. In particular, student self-efficacy and associated strategies to both nurture and sustain student self-efficacy were a critical component of the project's design and development, as well as the course more generally. The chapter includes broadly applicable suggestions for bolstering student self-efficacy in connection with all elements of the Project and its associated leaning goals.

Feminist Digital Pedagogy

The Project was also grounded in principles of feminist digital pedagogy. Golden (2018) describes a feminist digital pedagogy as one that "engages goals, topics, and projects that demonstrate equality – fairly addressing students and texts, including formerly overlooked voices – using digital tools" (p. 42). Leckenby and Hesse-Biber (2007) write of feminist researchers as "an integral force" (p. 251) with powerful implications that include and even extend beyond concerns of sexism, oppression, patriarchal structures, and associated subjugation such as those described by hooks (2015). Characteristics of projects grounded in feminist digital pedagogy include having students see a project through from "beginning to end" (Golden, 2018, p. 42). Additionally, Pabon (2018) writes on the importance of ensuring students "engage the world outside of their world" and of encouraging "creativity in the process of knowledge production, comprehension, and analysis" (para. 3).

Bond (2019) writes that "[t]o encourages effective and engaging online environments, we must develop more purposeful pedagogies and practices—those that prioritize empowerment as an essential element of successful online teaching and learning" (para. 10). Further, Bond (2019) explains that "[m]uch of my strategy for increasing empowerment rests on shaking up the traditional submission standard, as well as building classroom spaces where students can be creators of curriculum and content" (para. 9). The breadth and potential power of feminist theory and feminist digital pedagogy, in particular, are not unlike that associated with reflexivity in similarly broad aspects of one's work and practice. Reinharz (2011) writes of reflexivity as both a theory and a process, where one's work incorporates intentional and conscious efforts to reflect on, consider, and account for the broad impact of one's thinking, actions, and perceptions on others.

The Project's design, described in detail in the following section, sought to address and incorporate the forgoing principles. In particular, feminist digital pedagogy was intentionally relied upon in connection with the development and delivery of the Project so as to help all individuals "find [their] voice" and "believe that [their] voice matters, even in this world where there are so many voices demanding to be heard" (Gay, 2014, p. x). hooks (1989) explain that

Feminist education — the feminist classroom — is and should be a place where there is a sense of struggle, where there is visible acknowledgment of the union of theory and practice, where we work together as teachers and students to overcome the estrangement and alienation that have become so much the norm in the contemporary university. p. 51

Feminist digital pedagogy (embracing feminism as a verb as Pabón-Colón (n.d.), Kreitler (2014) and others suggest) offers powerful opportunities to both acknowledge and actively support the union of theory and practice with the goal of positive change. Just as Pabón-Colón (n.d.) argues for the importance of understanding and appreciating "feminism as a verb, as an action" (Zipp, 2018, para. 3), the Project was designed intentionally to encourage active reflection and authentic audiences with the goal of supporting transferable skills.

In a manner that, like "feminist pedagogy is a pedagogy that is at-once reflective and realistic in its relationship to empowerment", the Project was designed with express acknowledgment and recognition of the fact that "[a]ttending to the naturalistic conditions and multiple layers of classroom life demands a subjective, holistic, and flexible approach" (Klehr, 2012, p. 123) and reflective of tenets "'core' to the feminist learning experience: breakdown of hierarchy, participatory learning, and social construction of knowledge" (Milanés & Denoyelles, 2014, para. 8). In particular, feminist digital pedagogy both supports educators' work "to develop transformative tenets for social justice and self-advocacy (Turpin, 2016), and productively integrate an intentional and empowering element into digitized learning encounters (Blackburn, 2012)" (Bond, 2019, para. 2). Core to the Project's learning experience and to the feminist learning experience were a "breakdown of hierarchy, participatory learning, and social construction of knowledge." (Milanés & Denoyelles, 2014, para. 1).

While scholars offer a wide range of suggestions for embracing a feminist digital pedagogy in course instruction, discussions, and assignments, the Project offers one possible example of the potential for feminist digital pedagogy to support the recognition and development of transferable skills for students. Moreover, the authentic nature of the work associated with the Project can empower "students, teaching them to intervene in the creation of meaning and distribution of power" (Golden, 2018, p. 43) and demonstrates how feminist digital pedagogy can have a public function and support work toward (p. 42). The Project was designed to "productively integrate an intentional and empowering element into digitized learning encounters (Blackburn, 2012)" (Bond, 2019, para. 2). Relatedly, the Project was also designed to help explore "how we can use digital tools to change the subject of what we teach and how we do so" in equitable ways and including in online spaces (Golden, 2018, p. 42).

Just as "[f]eminists are made, not born", so are, I believe, are students with strong soft skills researchers (hooks, 2015, p. 7) and feminist digital pedagogies. Leckenby and Hesse-Biber, along with research on feminist digital pedagogies in practice, in its many forms, offer guidance for the further growth and development of both.

PROJECT DESIGN AND FOCUS

Although written communication skills are desired by employers and widely recognized as critical to workplace success, students commonly underestimate the essential role of these skills on their careers (Anderson, 2013; Sarpparaje, 2016). Both raising student awareness and properly incentivizing students to seek improvements and transfer of such skills in equitable and inclusive ways are important components of long-term achievement in this context. This chapter describes a Project designed to support awareness, transfer, and empowerment in online learning contexts. The Project, drawing upon principles of feminist digital pedagogy and theory on self-efficacy, was designed to provide equitable, inclusive, and authentic opportunities (those that replicate use in the "real world" outside of the formal classroom) for students to both strengthen a wide variety of soft skills and deepen their appreciation of the importance of these skills in the workplace (Castillo Losado et al., 2016).

The Challenge

College classrooms have both an obligation and an opportunity to equitably support all students in the development of these skills as well as associated awareness and self-efficacy with respect to their importance and their achievement. Pierce (2019) writes on how employers are looking to community colleges for help teaching soft skills to students. According to Pierce, "[a]s these skills continue to grow in importance, employers are looking to community colleges for help in teaching and assessing them" (p. 21). Relatedly, Stewart et. al write that "[w]hile higher education doesn't disagree, it has done little to change its curriculum" (p. 78). However, tremendous opportunities remain, and all college classrooms have an opportunity to play a critically important role in this context.

Sample Responses

Explored solutions include internships and similar experiential learning opportunities (Khakurel & Porras, 2020). Stewart et al. (2020) offer a thinkubator approach while educational escape rooms have also been a topic of study (Morrell, Eukel, & Santurri, 2020). In a 2020 study, baccalaureate nursing students who had recently participated in a cardiovascular-themed educational escape room were purposefully recruited escape room (Morrell et al., 2020). However, these solutions are all supplemental in nature and occur outside of regular classroom instruction. While these are excellent strategies, many argue they are insufficient (Tomkins and Ulus, 2016) in course instruction, support, and awareness generation are also important and necessary opportunities.

Universities also often offer additional student support (typically through tutoring services, writing center coaching and/or library services) (Al Murshidi & Al Abd, 2014; Thonus, 2002). Services such as writing center coaching and interventions are valuable, but often are used in a reactive, rather than proactive manner. Students also often express dissatisfaction as well as limited awareness regarding the effective use of writing center interventions and feedback (Al Murshidi & Al Abd, 2014; Denny et al., 2018). Similarly, writing center tutors often lack avenues to track student improvement and implementation of shared strategies (Severino & Prim, 2016) and practice exercises and associated support resources are typically discipline-neutral (Hutchison, 2018).

In-course writing support has shown promise in a variety of settings (Hampton, 2019). Valuable opportunities to embed writing instruction in course experiences and simultaneously raise student awareness of the academic as well as professional relevance and impact of strong written communication skills remain. Additional solutions include course-long projects such as those encouraged by feminist digital pedagogues and where the development, awareness, and growth of soft-skills is embedded directly into the student course experience.

The remainder of this chapter details a project designed to do so in a community college classroom. Throughout, emphasized soft skills are aligned with those skills highlighted as most critical on the part of employers.

THE PROJECT

In a synchronous, online legal technology course, a course long project was designed and introduced to students with an express goal of raising awareness of the importance of soft skills and their associated transfer. This section provides an overview of the project components as well as resources to help others interested in adopting a similar type of project in other course contexts. This section also shares reflections and best practices, as well as pitfalls, for readers interested in incorporating a similar project into their own courses. Associated strategies for nurturing and supporting student self-efficacy, conception of self, and confidence in equitable and inclusive ways are shared throughout, as well.

Course and Project Overview

The course itself is a highly technical course. The course overview describes the course as "An introduction to the use of computers and legal specialty software programs in the contemporary law office and other legal environments. The course will examine applications involving office management, document management, electronic discovery and trial presentation. The course will also address legal ethical considerations in the use of computer technology". However, despite the course's emphasis on technical skills, valuable opportunities to raise awareness and teach and strengthen soft skills also exist.

The Project was designed to provide authentic opportunities (those that replicate use in the "real world" outside of the formal classroom) for students to both strengthen a variety of soft skills, including communication, creativity, problem solving, and flexibility, support the transfer of such skills, and deepen their appreciation of the importance of these skills in the workplace (Castillo Losado et al, 2016). Beyond the substantive goals directly aligned with course learning outcomes, related goals included (i) raising awareness of the importance of soft skills, (ii) developing those skills; and (iii) supporting the transfer of such skills going forward.

All Project components are scaffolded, and instruction is presented in a step-by-step fashion (Felsenburg & Graham, 2012). Lehman and Conceicao (2014) note that course design techniques that incorporate "chunking" (i.e., dividing course content into pieces called "chunks" and arranging these chunks into modules with a similar structure) tend to promote student motivation and simultaneously reduce cognitive overload. For example, students must first be taught that effective legal written communication depends more on the process of sound legal analysis than the adoption of any one specific form or style (Felsenburg & Graham, 2012). Other strategies to reduce cognitive load include maximizing signal to noise ratios, promoting generative strategies, providing scaffolding, creating opportunities for collaborative learning, and providing cognitive aids (Malamed, 2017).

Instructional Design Considerations

Clear and supportive instructional materials are provided in small units, requiring active interactions and engagement through class discussions (Gantt, 2007). Students who expect to receive information delivered by experts in the field are less likely to succeed than students who take an active and reflective role in their own learning (Felsenburg & Graham, 2012). Instruction also encourages active reflection and a meta-cognitive approach to learning (Gantt, 2007). Students also need to be taught (and reassured) that pre-writing both matters and requires a significant investment of time (Felsenburg & Graham, 2012).

Modeling is another important component of Project instruction. Studies have demonstrated the benefits of a see-do-teach methodology (Felsenburg & Graham, 2012; Coughlin, McElroy, & Patrick, 2009). For example, instruction should include in-depth use of examples (i.e., "see one"), drafting exercises (i.e., "do one"), and guided sessions to reinforce student learning (i.e., "teach one") (Coughlin et al., 2009). Studies have also found that video content can be an effective tool to improve student learning (Hegeman, 2015). Instructional content should be interactive, visual, and relevant. Modeling, visual video tutorials, and student generated video instruction are effective methods to engage learners in active learning and peer teaching (Dwyer, 2010). Weekly instruction adopted all of the aforementioned strategies, including examples of presentations and instruction on related legal technologies. A student toolkit for online presentations was developed and shared with students, as well.

Project Components

The Project includes several scaffolded components. This section provides an overview of each component as well as how each component supports awareness and development of associated soft skills.

Tool Selection. Early in the course, students are introduced to the Project and actively encouraged to think of legal technologies in the broadest sense. The class begins with a survey and exercises (both individual and collaborative) designed to identify and make visible, to both instructor and student, what students know about the course concepts (in this case, all related to legal technologies). Class discussions emphasize the broad nature of the legal technology field, as well as the breadth of tools and applications. The project has several components, with the first deliverable being the selection of a tool. Each student is asked to identify and describe a specific legal technology tool that they would like to research, experiment with, and then share (in a teaching presentation) with the class.

For many students, the selection of a tool of focus proved challenging. Students consistently emphasized the challenges that accompanied choice and multiple options. Class discussions were used to highlight strategies for tool selection. Lessons on pain points, simulated work challenges and scenarios, and exercises that encouraged critical thinking regarding use cases and expanded views of both existing tools as well as what was possible in terms of training on such tools supported students in the selection process. In addition to live, whole class discussions, individual meetings with students also helped narrow focus and explore options in collaborative ways. Collaborative testing of a sample collection of illustrative tools in addition to ongoing discussions regarding problem solving in simulated contexts also served to support student development of research, critical thinking, tool analysis, and tool selection skills. Class instruction relied upon constructionist principles and strategies that sought to support student use of reviewed legal technologies as an expressive medium to study other topics" and solve targeted and related problems, and "not just a skill to be learned for the sake of learning it. When submitting their selected tool, students were also asked to clarify their tool of choice, articulate their reasoning and interest in the tool in one to three sentences, and also identify the aligned course learning outcomes.

Presentation Component: In-Class Presentation and Presentation Selection Dates. A Google Document was used for students to self-select presentation dates. Supporting guidance was shared in connection with presentation content and technical requirements such as length and preferred manners of presentation. Students were required to properly manage their time so as to pace their research and their presentation development.

In general, the Presentation component asked students to teach one new legal technology to our class. Questions were encouraged. Shared guidelines suggested 10-12 minutes of presentation time, with clarification that more time was permitted, and 3-5 minutes of Question & Answer Period. In terms of presentation style, students were encouraged to be creative. Provided examples included sharing a PPT/Google Slides with voice-over, an original podcast or video, a traditional presentation, a game, or other creative examples. Students were encouraged to apply reflection and questioning strategies when considering how to design and develop their presentation. Suggested questions included: What type of teaching strategies do you most enjoy? How might you present your content in a creative, impactful way? Students were also encouraged to share resources and use visuals to engage with their audience.

For content, all suggestions were guides rather than requirements. Suggested content included: an overview of the selected tool, its purpose and use cases, how to use the tool, strengths and weaknesses, and applications in legal environments. Students were also encouraged to address history, trends, current applications and use in practice, ethical considerations, and competitors (both strengths and weaknesses).

Supporting documents encouraged students to reflect on the importance of presentation skills, communication skills, extended technological proficiencies, flexibility, and problem solving, among other skills, both in connection with the project presentation as well as more generally in the workplace. Attention to associated soft skills was woven throughout all elements of the project and supporting documentation.

The live presentations were valuable learning opportunities in ways that extended far beyond the knowledge associated with the newly introduced tools themselves. Presenting students developed their written and oral communication skills. Viewing students strengthened their listening and questioning skills. Critical thinking and problem solving were ongoing. Flexibility and adaptability were, as well. Students consistently indicated that watching their peers present was enormously helpful in a variety of ways including impact on efficacy, confidence, and modeling. Collaboration skills were also used extensively. Peers consistently helped each other troubleshoot technical challenges with the presentation software, video streaming, and sound, for example.

Presentation Confirmation. After their live presentation session, each student submitted a presentation confirmation via the course's learning management system. This was due within three days of their in-class presentation. In this confirmation, students were asked to submit a brief (three-four sentences is fine) reflection on the presentation experience; identify one-two things they felt went especially well during your presentation; and identify one to two things they might change if presenting again.

Peer Feedback. At the end of each live presentation, students welcomed questions and led a question-and-answer period. The instructor also supported the question-and-answer dialog. At the end of the presentation period, students uploaded their presentation resources (slides and supporting documents) to an online classroom forum.

The peer feedback experience contributed to a wide range of soft skill development including written communication (in online forums), oral communication (in live sessions), and critical thinking.

Final Submission. Students would use peer feedback from both the teaching session and the follow-up peer forum to revise, improve, and finalize their presentation for submission via the course's learning management system.

Project Reflection. The final element of the project was a reflection journal. In three to four paragraphs, students were asked to reflect on the project as a whole and consider: why/how they selected their teaching modality; why/how they selected their specific topic.

Publication Opportunities. In the final week of the course, students were invited to submit their presentations for publication on a standalone website. This provided both an authentic audience for students, an opportunity to see a project through from beginning to end, and authorship credit for the related publication of their work.

Assessment

All Project components were aligned with both course and program outcomes. Rubrics were developed for each Project component and shared with students. At the conclusion of the Project, students submitted reflections on their experience throughout the Project. Sample feedback comments are included on The Feedback Bank (https://www.thefeedbackbank.com/) under Digital Presentations.

Soft Skills

Soft skills development and awareness were incorporated throughout all aspects of the project. The following chart, modeled after a U.S. Department of Labor chart, highlights examples of how and where illustrative soft skills are nurtured and emphasized throughout the project.

Table 1. Key soft skills for workplace success: Characteristics

Soft Skill	Topic	Presentation Sign Up	Class Presentation	Post-Presentation Discussion	Peer Feedback	Presentation Reflection	Final Presentation Submission	Project
Written Communication	X				X	X	X	X
Verbal Communication			X	X				
Creativity	X		X				X	
Time Management	X	X	X	X	X	X	X	X
Problem Solving	X		X	X	X	X	X	
Comfort with Ambiguity	X		X	X	X			X
Confidence	X	X	X	X	X	X	X	X
Ethics	X	X	X	X	X	X	X	X
Collaboration			X	X	X			

LESSONS LEARNED

This section explores lessons learned as a result of the Project delivery and experience.

Student Reflections

Student reflections were reviewed, and codes were created to represent key concepts and thoughts expressed therein. High frequency codes were counted and documented. A thematic approach identified emerging and generated themes. Using coding tactics described in Merriam and Tisdell (2016) and Crabtree and Miller (1999), as well as tenets of phenomenology, an iterative process of codebook development was used to develop codes and categories for further analysis. Miles et al. (2013) explains that codes in qualitative research provides ways to provide meaning to individual pieces of data. After coding and analyzing the data, four major themes emerged. Each theme represents student reflections on the Project and the associated development and awareness of transferable soft skills. Notably, each theme is aligned with research and data on what employers are seeking in potential employees.

The following themes were identified in the shared reflections.

Greater Self-Confidence and Awareness in Navigating the Legal Field

Students consistently expressed improved confidence associated with a wide range of skills critical for navigation and success in the workplace. Student comments expressed greater confidence with research and technology (for example *"coming into this class, I was intimidated because I am not very computer savvy. I thought it would be difficult for me, but now my I have much more clarity than I had before. I learned a lot about some technology that I was not familiar with"* and *"I am more confident now because I am gaining a better understanding of how to utilize technology especially during these times. Technology use is the new norm so I am grateful to have some education in this field"* as well as greater awareness of the breath of the field (for example, *"going into this course I had very little idea of how utterly vast the selection of legal technology is. I also did not know how fascinating some of it was"* and *"I learned how quickly technology is changing the legal field. There are always new legal technologies available for us to consume, so it is important to always stay up to date. I didn't know, when I began this class, realize the legal aspects of many of the technologies I use daily".*

Students expressed associated improved confidence sorting throughout large quantities of information, processing information and more confidence in self, as well. For example, comments noted "*The field is more vast than I ever knew, with a lot of competing software available. I feel a lot more empowered entering the job knowing what is out there*" and

In order to stay abreast of trends in the legal tech field one step we can take is following blogs and websites that report news on it. For example, one can sign up for a newsletter that reports on legal tech in order to stay up to date. Another step one can take is research social media. Social media is a big platform and more people than ever use social media to market products or review them, someone could look up what's going on in the legal tech world on social media. One final step somebody could make is to just keep up with people in the legal tech field. Word of mouth has always been a useful way of sharing knowledge, and a paralegal could learn more about what's going on in the tech world by keeping up with a legal tech professional.

Relatedly, students also expressed increased confidence as future professionals in the field more broadly. For example, *"I would hate to imagine working in the legal world without using the Tech we've talked about and it's created more curiosity to learn more and more about the tech involved in the legal world".*

Increased Tolerance of Ambiguity

Student comments also suggested the Project experience contributed to increased tolerance of ambiguity, another skill importance to long term success in the workplace (Fioravanti et. al., 2020). VUCA is a term used to describe the emerging and future workplace, one that is volatile, uncertain, complex, and ambiguous (Fioravanti et. al., 2020). Increased tolerance for ambiguity and potential to thrive in a VUCA world was exhibited through problem solving, trouble shooting, and online presentations, among other experiences. Comments suggested an overall awareness of the presence of ambiguity in the workplace, as well as increased associated tolerance for such ambiguity as well as an associated broader understanding of its importance. Relatedly, students expressed deeper appreciation for collaboration (peer review, presentation to peers) and project success.

Commitment to Ongoing Learning / Self-Teaching

Feedback also suggested greater appreciation for self-initiated inquiry and enhanced self-awareness regarding the importance on self-initiated and sustained learning, with comments such as "*I will continue to follow current legal news topics and I will also make sure to keep in touch with my local paralegal chapter regarding possible trainings and conferences*". Additionally, student comments demonstrated increased confidence in connection with ability for ongoing learning.

Greater Awareness of Non-Technical Skills

Comments also suggested greater awareness of important non-technical skills such as oral communication, collaboration, time management, time management, and peer feedback. For example, a student noted the value of collaboration and collaborative learning by noting, *"After researching my own project, and especially seeing presentations of classmates, I have added much greater knowledge of the legal technology landscape"*. Students also expressed a deeper appreciation for the role legal technology can play in connection with time and project management, with comments such as *"I never would've realized or appreciated that had I not researched it for this assignment. So, the assignment created awareness of this for me."*

Student reflections consistently emphasized deeper appreciation for communication strategies as well as the associated value of collaboration, respectful dialogue, and constructively shared feedback. For example, students noted that *"I felt as though peer feedback makes a difference in how you feel about your performance"* and lessons learned in terms of how to "*control the narrative of in class presentation. The class was welcoming and respectful and I would do it again if I could."*

Positive reflections focused on the process of both receiving and providing feedback. For example, "*providing the feedback was helpful because I reviewed others' assignments before submitting my own. To that end, I was able to see how and what others were presenting on*" as well as an appreciation for collaboration and intentional encouragement of constructive feedback. For example, "*I also recognize that the feedback I gave did not contain much constructive criticism either; it is difficult and it can be uncomfortable to give criticism when you do not know the person well and you do not know how they will take it*" and I now plan to share work with notice that I am "*welcome to constructive criticism when [I] post [a] presentation on the discussion*".

CONCLUSION

Analysis of shared reflections suggests that a scaffolded, course long teaching and presentation project in a technical course can equitably and inclusively support digital literacy and student awareness of the importance of soft skills in both coursework and the workplace. Analysis also suggests that the individual project components as well as the sustained, course long nature of the Project contribute to ongoing skill development and associated transfer from academic to employment environments in this context.

REFERENCES

Al Murshidi, G., & Al Abd, K. (2014). UAE university students' awareness of using the writing center. *Higher Education Studies*, 4(3), 58–63. 10.5539/hes.v4n3p58

Anderson, M. O. (2013). Building accounting students' communication skills. *Management Accounting Quarterly*, 14(4), 32–43.

Bandura, A. (1977). Self-efficacy: Toward a unifying theory of behavioral change. *Psychological Review*, 84(2), 191–215. 10.1037/0033-295X.84.2.191847061

Bandura, A. (1994). Self-efficacy. In Ramachaudran, V. S. (Ed.), *Encyclopedia of human behavior* (Vol. 4, pp. 71–81). Academic Press.

Bandura, A. (n.d.). Self-efficacy. Professor Albert Andura. http://professoralbertbandura.com/albert-bandura-self-efficacy.html

Camacho, L. (2015). The communication skills accounting firms desire in new hires. *Journal of Business & Finance Librarianship*, 20(4), 318–329. 10.1080/08963568.2015.1072895

Castillo Losada, C. A., Insuasty, E. A., & Jaime Osorio, M. F. (2017). The impact of authentic materials and tasks on students' communicative competence at a Colombian language school. *PROFILE Issues in Teachers'. Professional Development (Philadelphia, Pa.)*, 19(1), 89–104. 10.15446/profile.v19n1.56763

Clark, J., & DeSanctis, C. (2013). Toward a unified grading vocabulary: Using rubrics in legal writing courses. *Journal of Legal Education*, 63(1), 3–35.

Cook, M. (2015, February 9). NWA job market calling for soft skills: today's students lacking in qualities sought by employers. *Arkansas Business, 32*(6).

Coughlin, C. N., McElroy, L. T., & Patrick, S. C. (2009). See one, do one, teach one: Dissecting the use of medical education's signature pedagogy in the law school curriculum. *Georgia State University Law Review*, 26(2), 361–416.

Denny, H., Nordlof, J., & Salem, L. (2018). "Tell me exactly what it was that I was doing that was so bad": Understanding the needs and expectations of working-class students in writing centers. *Writing Center Journal*, 37(1), 67–98. https://www.jstor.org/stable/26537363. 10.7771/2832-9414.1866

Duchardt, B., Furr, P., & Horton, S. G. (2016). A comparison of a progression of writing competencies in online undergraduate and graduate courses: Results and implications. *College Student Journal*, 50(4), 467–476.

Dwyer, F. (2010). Edgar Dale's cone of experience: A quasi-experimental analysis. *International Journal of Instructional Media*, 37(4), 431–437.

Felsenburg, M. E., & Graham, L. P. (2012). A better beginning: Why and how to help novice legal writers build a solid foundation by shifting their focus from product to process. *Regent University Law Review*, 24(1), 83–107.

Fioravanti, M. L., Sena, B., & Francine Barbosa, E. (2020). Assessing the Development of Soft Skills for Project Management using PBL: A Case Study. *2020 IEEE Frontiers in Education Conference (FIE), Frontiers in Education Conference (FIE)*. IEEE.

Foster, S. K., Wiczer, E., & Eberhardt, N. B. (2019). What's so hard about soft skills? *ASHA Leader*, 24(12), 52–60. 10.1044/leader.FTR2.24122019.52

Gantt, L. I. (2007). Deconstructing thinking like a lawyer: Analyzing the cognitive components of the analytical mind. 29. *Campbell Law Review*, (3), 413.

Golden, A. (2018). Feminist Digital Pedagogy. *Virginia Woolf Miscellany*, 93, 42–43.

Guth, D. J. (2020). BRIDGING THE WORKFORCE EQUITY GAP: Two-year colleges face challenges in drawing underserved students into job training programs. *Community College Journal*, 91(3), 10–15.

Haddad, B., & Marx, A. A. (2018). Student Perceptions of Soft Skills & Career Decision Self-Efficacy through Participation in SAE. *Journal of Agricultural Education*, 59(4), 159–176. 10.5032/jae.2018.04159

Hampton, M. D. (2019). A 5-Year Evaluation of Faculty Use of Practical Within-Course Writing Development Strategies in a DNP Program. *Nurse Educator*, 44(4), 197–201. 10.1097/NNE.0000000000000058930138150

Heckman, J., & Kautz, T. (2012). Hard evidence on soft skills. *Labour Economics*, 19(4), 451–464. 10.1016/j.labeco.2012.05.01423559694

Hegeman, J. S. (2015). Using instructor-generated video lectures in online mathematics courses improves student learning. *Online Learning : the Official Journal of the Online Learning Consortium*, 19(3), 70–87. 10.24059/olj.v19i3.669

hooks, b. (1989). *Talking Back: Thinking Feminist, Thinking Black*. Cambridge, Mass.: South End Press.

hooks, b. (2015). *Feminism is for everybody: Passionate politics*. New York, NY: Routledge.

Hora, M. T., Benbow, R. J., & Smolarek, B. B. (2018). Re-thinking Soft Skills and Student Employability: A New Paradigm for Undergraduate Education. *Change*, 50(6), 30–37. 10.1080/00091383.2018.1540819

Hutchison, A. (2018). Writing Support for the Online Technical Writing Service Course: A Feasibility Study. *2018 IEEE International Professional Communication Conference (ProComm), Professional Communication Conference (ProComm), 2018 IEEE International, PROCOMM*, (pp. 18–24). IEEE. 10.1109/ProComm.2018.00011

James, R. F., & James, M. L. (2004). Teaching Career and Technical Skills in "Mini" in Business World. *Business Education Forum*, 59(2), 39–41.

Jance, M., & Morgan, A. (2013). Critical learning skills for business students. *American Journal of Business Education*, 6(1), 25–32. 10.19030/ajbe.v6i1.7480

Khakurel, J., & Porras, J. (2020). The Effect of Real-World Capstone Project in an Acquisition of Soft Skills among Software Engineering Students. *2020 IEEE 32nd Conference on Software Engineering Education and Training (CSEE&T), Software Engineering Education and Training (CSEE&T)*. IEEE. https://doi-org.ezproxy.snhu.edu/10.1109/CSEET49119.2020.9206201

Leckenby, D., & Hesse-Biber, S. N. (2007). Feminist approaches to mixed-methods research. In Hesse-Biber, S. N., & Leavy, P. L. (Eds.), *Feminist research practice: A primer*. SAGE. 10.4135/9781412984270.n9

Leef, G. (2015). *Why colleges churn out poor writers and poor thinkers*. James G Martin. https://www.jamesgmartin.center/2015/08/why-colleges-churn-out-poor-writers-and-poor-thinkers/

Lehman, R. M., & Conceicao, S. C. O. (2014). *Motivating and retaining online students: Research-based strategies that work* (1st ed.). Jossey-Bass.

Lent, R., & Hackett, G. (1987). *Career self-efficacy: Empirical status and future directions*. Research Gate. https://www.researchgate.net/publication/223678204_Career_self-efficacy_Empirical_status_and_future_directions

Majid, S., & Eapen, C. M., Ei Mon Aung, & Oo, K. T. (2019). The Importance of Soft Skills for Employability and Career Development: Students and Employers' Perspectives. *The IUP Journal of Soft Skills*, 13(4), 7–39.

Malamed, C. (2017). *Six strategies you may not be using to reduce cognitive load*. The Learning Coach. https://theelearningcoach.com/learning/reduce-cognitive-load/

Miles, M., Huberman, M., & Saldana, J. (2013). *Qualitative data analysis: A methods sourcebook*. Sage Publications.

Morrell, B. L. M., Eukel, H. N., & Santurri, L. E. (2020). Soft skills and implications for future professional practice: Qualitative findings of a nursing education escape room. *Nurse Education Today*, 93, 93. 10.1016/j.nedt.2020.10446232791421

Nolop, B. (2013). *Our college graduates can't write.* WSJ. http://blogs.wsj.com/experts/2013/10/09/our-college-graduates-cant-write/

Pabón-Colón, J. (2018). https://jessicapabon.com/2018/08/21/why-i-use-digital-pedagogies-a-not-quite-manifesto-on-teaching-in-the-age-of-digital-feminist-movement/

Pabón-Colón, J. (n.d.). *Feminism is a verb.* JessicaPaBon. https://jessicapabon.com/

Perreault, H. (2004). Business Educators Can Take a Leadership Role in Character Education. *Business Education Forum*, 59(1), 23–25.

Pierce, D. (2019). What Employers Want: Employers are Looking to Community Colleges for Help in Teaching Soft Skills. *Community College Journal*, 89(3), 20–25.

Plant, K., Barac, K., & Sarens, G. (2019). Preparing work-ready graduates – skills development lessons learnt from internal audit practice. *Journal of Accounting Education*, 48, 33–47. https://doi-org.ezproxy.snhu.edu/10.1016/j.jaccedu.2019.06.001. 10.1016/j.jaccedu.2019.06.001

Reinharz, S. (2011). *Observing the observer: Understanding ourselves in field research.* Oxford University Press.

Rios, J. A., Ling, G., Pugh, R., Becker, D., & Bacall, A. (2020). Identifying Critical 21st-Century Skills for Workplace Success: A Content Analysis of Job Advertisements. *Educational Researcher*, 49(2), 80–89. 10.3102/0013189X19890600

Sarpparaje, M. (2016). Importance of enhancing communication skills among young graduates and how to make them career-ready & life-ready? *Language in India*, 16(4), 93.

Sethi, R. (2016). Importance of Soft Skills for Professional Students. *International Journal of Recent Research Aspects*, 113–115.

Severino, C., & Prim, S. N. (2016). Second language writing development and the role of tutors: A case study of an online writing center "Frequent Flyer.". *Writing Center Journal*, 35(3), 143. 10.7771/2832-9414.1844

Stewart, C., Marciniec, S., Lawrence, D., & Joyner-McGraw, L. (2020). Thinkubator Approach to Solving the Soft Skills Gap. *American Journal of Management*, 20(2), 78–89.

Thonus, T. (2002). *Tutor and student assessments of academic writing tutorials: What is "success"?* Science Direct. https://www.sciencedirect.com/science/article/pii/S1075293503000023

Tomkins, L., & Ulus, E. (2016). 'Oh, was that "experiential learning"?!' Spaces, synergies and surprises with Kolb's learning cycle. *Management Learning*, 47(2), 158–178. 10.1177/1350507615587451

Vekaric, G., & Jelic, G. (2013). Raising students' awareness of the importance of English language writing skills. *Activities in Physical Education & Sport*, 3(1), 29–31.

Zipp, M. (2018). *Feminism, Graffiti, Gender Fluidity: An Interview With Jessica Pabón-Colón, author of Graffiti Grrlz*. Got a Girl Crush. http://www.gotagirlcrush.com/archive/2018/5/20/feminism-graffiti-gender-fluidity-an-interview-with-jessica-pabn-coln-author-of-graffiti-grrlz

Chapter 15
The Internet Problem:
Pedagogical Solutions to the Information Problem

Julie Christina Tatlock
Mount Mary University, USA

ABSTRACT

This chapter explores the modern digital issues facing higher education including digital literacy and generative artificial intelligence. It argues that new technologies should not be avoided but incorporated into teaching and learning and institutions of higher education. It considers the role formative assessment can play in making digital skills integrated into curriculum. The chapter ends with a series of sample assignments demonstrating formative assessment and specifically formative assessment vis a vis the digital world.

DATA, INFORMATION, AND KNOWLEDGE

The ways in which our learning experience intersects with data/information has changed. So much is now available so fast. And, now we have generative artificial intelligence at our fingertips. While technological changes happen quickly, it is important to remember that we have been here before. As worries about artificial intelligence make their way through the halls of higher education, I am reminded of a time before Google, when the internet was also new and would irrevocably change our institutions. It did. And we adapted the way we teach and learn. The ways in which our learning experience intersects with data/information has changed

DOI: 10.4018/979-8-3693-2591-9.ch015

and will continue to be impacted by burgeoning technologies. Good teaching and learning have always had an answer: formative assessment.

Data is more prevalent in our everyday lives than ever before. It comes at us at unheard of speeds and from multiple sources, some reliable, some not. When we use data and put it into context, that data becomes information. The new question is, how does that information become knowledge, incorporated into a students' understanding of the world and usable in everyday situations? This manipulating of data into knowledge is the key in higher education. This is what we need to teach students. Digital natives, as they are called, are not as savvy as they are given credit for. The average student may be able to navigate social media sites with speed, but are they as capable of discerning what they are seeing and categorizing it appropriately as valid or not? Students have trouble finding reliable sources of information online. Those skills don't develop on their own. Like anything else they need to be taught and assessed. Students also to come with a variety of digital skills. Technology rarely spreads equally and we know that underprivileged students have less access to less technology than those from richer socio-economic backgrounds. The same will likely be true of generative artificial intelligence. Its use will not spread equally throughout the world.

In their study of scholarly work on digital literacy, Denhua Peng and Zhonggen Yu, authors of "A Literature Review of Digital Literacy over two Decades," found that the ability of students to successfully navigate online information depended on several factors including the social class their parents. Noting that all students don't come to college with the same set of digital comfort or skills, they suggest that a student's prior experience has a great deal to do with how successfully they will navigate digital space in higher education. Those with better backgrounds and models in this area are far more prepared to engage with the digital world in effective ways as part of a learning process. Given that "students' digital literacy positively affected their engagement, "having a strong sense of digital literacy is integral to creating a successful learning environment." (Peng, 2022). Students who are more confident in their digital skills also engage more effectively in classroom assignments. They can exercise more agency in digital spaces. Given the importance of digital skills, they must be worked in to our learning objectives so that all students have a solid base from which to work. Miah Doughtery and Laura Hanson, argue in "Teaching Digital Literacy is a 21st Century Imperative," that "inherent to being able to actively learn via technology is the ability to tap into the plethora of sources of information on the internet, allowing students a sense of agency in the selection of materials they use" (Doughtery, 2022). Students are more likely to have agency if they have had good experiences already, and if we want students to reach the point where they can take date and turn it into their own knowledge, agency is key to success.

Digital Literacy

The skill set we are defining is one of digital literacy and it is a skill that all our graduates will need to function effectively in the world. They will need to engage in the digital space on a regular basis. It is no longer possible to escape the online world completely, so pervasive has it become in our lives. Nieves, Gutierrez-Angel argues in "Digital Literacy in the University Setting" that "digital learning is understood as the set of technical-procedural, cognitive, and socio-emotional skills necessary to live, learn, and work in a digital society" (Nieves, 2022). We should be teaching students not only to use the internet for a specific discipline, but also how to approach the digital world and integrate into their lives effectively and in an emotionally mature way. Luci Pangrezio and Julian Sefton-Green argue in "Digital Citizenship and Digital Literacy: What's the Difference, that literacy is to "describe the individual's capacity to understand information and the social norms and conventions that surround it, as well as to demonstrate this knowledge through comprehension or writing (Pangrazio, 2021). In other words, students must be able to take in information and assess its position vis a vis other information and then to actually use that information, demonstrating understanding. They go on to say that "as the digital spaces, texts, and tools are continually changing and becoming more complex, so too is what it takes to be considered, 'literate' (Pangrazio, 2021). It is also true that what is involved in digital literacy will very likely continue to change as new technology develops. Students must then have the agility and adaptable to process in new ways.

The ability to critically assess information is even more important as the creation of knowledge has become democratized. Anyone can now create content. Martha Burke and Cristobel Cabo argue, in "Redefining Knowledge in the Digital Age, that "this phenomenon . . . has not only diversified the mechanism of knowledge production but has also disrupted what was traditionally understood as valid knowledge" (Burke, 2018). The concept of validity cannot be overstated. Exactly who can be an "authority" on a given subject is no longer as restricted as before. We have, to a large degree, democratized knowledge. The problem is that those who can make better decisions about data and information, those will strong digital literacy, will more successfully navigate the world. It is true that students can google anything and find an "answer." Perhaps this should change the way we teach in terms of spreading information. Do students need as much memorization work as in previous generations? Likely not. Do they need far more instruction in critically assessing information? Definitely so.

So important are digital skills, according to Romina Bandura and Elena Mendez in, "The Digital Literacy Imperative," that "digital literacy has become indispensable for every global citizen, whether to communicate, find employment, receive comprehensive education or socialize." They go on to say that "acquiring the right set of digital skills is not only important for learning and workforce readiness: digital skills are also vital to fostering more open, inclusive, and secure societies" (Bandura 2022).

The Role of Generative AI

We must now also consider the role of generative AI in our classrooms. Ai is the next frontier and advances will come quickly in the technology. AI can be used to source data/information and even write essays. The former is a legitimate use, much like doing a google search, the second is more problematic, raising questions about cheating and ethics. Charles Hodges and Ceren Oak, in "Integrating Generative AI Inter Higher Education," that "AI is not a device that can be banned, it is not a source that students can be instructed not to use, and its use cannot be discovered with crude plagiarism detection tools." They go on to say that "ignoring generative AI or banning its use on the academic side of higher education seems naïve and possible misguided." (Hodges, 2022). AI is here to stay, and students are going to use it. Coming to terms with that and finding ways to integrate AI into our classrooms will be the challenge going forward. Tom Farrelly and Nick Baker say it well in "Generative Artificial Intelligence: Implications and Considerations for Higher Education:

The truth (if indeed that is an appropriate term) is that the lines between artificial and reality are becoming increasingly blurred as we as individuals and as a collective may well need to adopt a new pragmatic approach to how we live, work, teach and study that recognizes the very real likelihood that GAI will become as ubiquitous as the internet itself I our everyday lives (Farrely, 2023).

Not only with AI continue to make advancements but using it effectively will become a necessary skill and a part of the new digital literacy. As always, machines are as good as the people using them. AI generates recommendations based on prompt input. You must ask it questions. Creating these prompts/questions is not straightforward and the response will only be as good as the crafting of the question. For example, if you asked generative AI to write a brief comparison of Athens and Spart in the Ancient World, it might not even pick up on the fact that the Helots, Spartan slaves, were important to why those distinctions occurred. Put another way, it will include only what it is prompted to include, leaving out potentially crucial information. Prompts must be very specific. They must also be written from multiple perspectives to avoid bias. In fact, according to Katia Ciampa, author of "ChatGPT in

Education," there is concern "about the potential of AI systems to reinforce existing inequalities and biases, particularly for marginalized students" (Ciampa, 2023).

Anthony He and Claire Thouary argue in "How AI Is Reshaping Higher Education," that student will need to "learn to establish context, define the task, and specify the desired outcome" (He, 2023). To this end students will continue to need to have a broad intellectual framework for information integration and strong critical thinking skills. What they may not needs is as much memorization. And Katia Ciampa argues that "we must ensure that our adolescent and adult learners learn how to use these technologies effectively, critically examining the information they encounter and develop the essential skill of actual thinking, particularly in the context of AI" (Campia, 2023). As always it is our job to know what students will need to succeed when they leave our institutions and provide a relevant education.

The Way Forward: Formative Assessment

To me, the biggest change in higher education in the last 15 years has been that students no longer just trust that those making the choices know what is best for them. The questioning of traditional authorities can be seen throughout our culture at this moment, and I am not sure they are entirely wrong to be skeptical. We do, after all want them to think critically. What it means is that we need to be far more explicit about why we are making the teaching choices we do in our classrooms. We need explain what we were teaching and why it is important and why how we are teaching it is effective. That may rub some academics the wrong way as we are experts in our field. But there is a richness that can develop in the classroom when everyone is on the same page and clarity of purpose can engage a student's agency in the classroom experience. Lucian Voinea argues in "Formative Assessment as Assessment for Learning Development," that "formative assessment is a continuous process, which is a constant companion of the instruction process and which has as the main aim the development of learning by orienting it and guiding it and by making it visible, explicit." Through a constant dialogue with our students, we are better able to gauge their understand and react appropriately. This dialogue also increases a student's agency.

Kim Schildkamp, Fabienne van der Kleij, Maaike Heitink, William Kippers, and Bernard Veldkamp, argue in "Formative Assessment: A Systematic Review of Critical Teacher Prerequisites for Classroom Practice that "It also requires a fundamental shift in the power relationship between teachers and students, in which teachers and students become jointly responsible for the quality of teaching and learning in the classroom" (Schildkamp, et al., 2023). This is one of the most important arguments that can be made for the use of more formative assessment as it involves highlighting the teaching moments in a class. Really engaging in assessment can bring forward the why of how we are teaching—to fill the gap between where a students' knowledge is and where it needs to be.

Traditional assessment is largely summative. But summative assessment can only go so far to gauge what students have truly learned. Learning is a process not necessarily just an outcome. Gavin Brown, in "The Past, Present and Future of Educational Assessment: A Transdisciplinary Perspective," contends that the "challenge for assessment lies in the conundrum that the material that is easy to test and score tends to be the material that is the least demanding or valuable in any domain" (Brown, 2023). In the digital age, this might be the information that students can easily find online. It is far harder and more complex to assess the processes by which students are learning and contextualizing the material. In "Formative vs. Summative Assessment," Ismail Seyed, D. R. Rahul, Idndrajit Petra and Ehsan Rezvani suggest that "Summative assessment is generally applied to give learners a numerical score with limited feedback. therefore, summative assessment is commonly used to measure learning and is rarely used for learning" (Seyed, 2022). Summative assessment also finds itself criticized for reflecting the bias of the elite classes. Standardized tests are often in a language that is not the student's primary language. The knowledge choices are based on the cultural assumptions of the dominant group. Creating more choice and variety of assignments and, thereby, assessments, can produce more equality in the assessment process.

Formative assessment answers many of these issues. Formative assessment differs from summative assessment in that it looks at several stages of a student's learning process and judges how well students are making progress. But that is not all. Its power lies in the ability of teachers to alter course when necessary to tailor learning to classroom needs. This might be as simple as reviewing a particularly difficult task or content item, or perhaps reteaching an entire lesson. It assumes that before new content is introduced, covered content has been mastered. "Formative assessment refers to frequent, interactive assessment of students' development and understanding to recognize their needs and adjust teaching appropriately." (Seyed, 2022) And, though there are several kinds of formative assessment, Kim Schildkamp argues that the "core unifying characteristic is the focus on gathering evidence about student learning and using this evidence to guide student learning" (Schildkamp, 2020).

There are many ways of achieving formative assessment in the classroom. They vary from very simple and quick assessments to semester-long projects. The goal would be to have both going on over the course of a semester depending on the learning outcomes you are trying to achieve. Below are a series of sample assignments for formative assessment.

Sample Formative Assessments

Quick Pole Assignment

This kind of assignment very quickly assess a classroom's comprehension. If there is traditional lecture or discussion, this can be a great way to gauge overall success. In this quick pole, you ask them to rate their understanding when they come into class and then at the end of the classroom lecture, discussion, or activity. If the score is low, you might want to consider a second activity to solidify the content before moving on.

On a scale of 1-10 how well did you understand the material before class? _________

On a scale of 1-10 how well did you understand the material after class? _________

Note-Taking Assignment

I find that if you do not assess a thing that thing might as well not exist. In most classes students put effort into what is graded. If you want students to take notes on the reading, for example, do a simple assessment of their notes. Note-taking is a great formative assessment, because you can easily see how much they are gleaning. Are they picking out the right information? Are they making associations with other content in the class? Are they integrating the information and making it relevant to their own lives?

Assignment: Take notes on Chapter Four. The notes can be in any format but be sure to cover the entire reading. You will be assessed on your ability to pull out the most important information and on your depth of coverage.

Journaling

In some classes, having students keep a reflective journal can be an effective formative assessment.

Typical Journal Assignment: As you reflect on today's material, think of a time in your life when what you learned might have impacted the situation. How would this knowledge have changed your participation in that event?

Self-Reflection and Assessment

Having students sit back and think about their own participation in the learning process is effective. It helps them see that they are agents in their own learning. Asking them how they are feeling about class and assignments also shows that you are truly interested in what is happening with them on an individual level. These reflections are really effective about a quarter of the way through a class, perhaps after the first big test.

Self-Reflective Assignment:

1. How do feel class is going overall? What assignments/content is going well for you? Which assignments/content are you struggling with?
2. Are your scores consistent with the work you are putting into learning the material?
3. What could you improve on to better your progress in class?
4. What can I, the instructor, do to help you improve your understanding?

Peer Feedback

Making time for peer reviews is also a great formative assessment tool. It is not as high stakes as the teacher's grading review and can show students where they can improve vis a vis someone in the same position.

Peer Review Assignment: In class today, you will pair off and each read each other's essay and offer critique. You must have three positive critiques and three constructive criticisms. By the end of class, each student will have two key revisions to their essay to work on over the next few days.

Progressive/Creative Assignment

This type of assignment is used all the time. It can be as simple as separating out the parts of the paper to be turned in over the course of a semester. For example, first a student turns in a bibliograph, then an outline, then a thesis, and finally a rough draft. You might also consider an iterative assignment with a creative bent. If the student repeats a similar assignment with slightly different parameters, you can judge their progress over the course of the term. You can start with a lower point value and move to a high one for the last iteration so that progress is rewarded in the grading scheme. You can also work with them in your feedback to address individual assessment needs.

Progressive/Creative Assignment (Used in a British Empire Class)

For your discussions throughout the semester, you will be creating a character. We will be traversing different centuries, so your character should be someone who can exist in any time. For example, you may choose a wealthy man, a poor woman, or someone from within the Empire-an American Colonist, a slave or free black from West Africa, and Indian Raja. You should feel free to run your choice by me if you are uncertain. This character will be with you for the semester, so try to choose a type of person that you are interested in learning more about. For example, you may be an indentured servant in America, then a servant on an English country estate, and finally, a servant in London in the modern era.

For the initial post, you will be introducing yourself in character by writing a letter of introduction. In it, you should include a description of who you are. Though you are a fictitious character, your ideas should be rooted in the time period, and you will have to do some research. You might comment on what kind of clothes you have, what instruments you might use, how you interact in society. You should also include in your introduction a description of your background, something about your family, or lack of family, personality traits, ambitions, and how your character feels about the current events as you have learned in the weekly course material.

You may use online sources and print sources for your weekly character research but do try to find **good** online sources. Stay away from Wikipedia and try museum sites, sites hosted by universities or professors, or government sites. You should provide a list of your resources in MLA format at the end of every post. Each post should address the material you read and watched that week.

Assessments for Digital Literacy

Digital Literacy Check

It is important to assess students' digital literacy, particularly in an online class, but also in any class where students will be using online tools, information, or media. I find this tool to be effective:

Critical Analysis of Digital Source Material
Your Name: ______________________________
Source Title: ______________________________
Source Author: ______________________________
Source Description:
Quotes/Information (at least 3):

AI Verification

AI generated content needs to be verified for a student to use it as a source. Having student's take this extra step encourages the proper use of AI and highlights the fact that generative AI is not infallible, nor is it the end of research.

If you used AI to collect data, you must verify each piece of information with other sources. Please list the content and how you verified it.

Content Piece:

AI System:
AI Prompt:

Verification Piece

Author:
Website:

Online Discussion with Digital Literacy Objective

The use of online discussions forums can be a great place to introduce digital literacy skills in research and writing. It is far more likely that students will do this kind of writing in their work lives and a rich series of discussion posts can replace a long research paper.

Choose any topic from this week's reading and develop further research. Your post should be analytical in style and should add substantially to the content of the research area.

Initial Post Requirements

1. Minimum of 500 words, maximum of 700 words.
2. Introduction with a thesis, a body, and a conclusion.
3. Times New Roman 12, double-spaced.
4. You must add **two additional online sources** to the topic discussion. These sources must be quality academic sources.

Table 1.

	Academic Source Rubric		
	Exceeds Expectation	**Meets Expectations**	**Does Not Meet Expectation**
	The web source is produced by an academic entity such as a research library, museum, or educational institution and the author of the content is readily available. The source has academic content that goes beyond mere description and surface analysis. The source either has a clearly stated bias or attempts to be neutral.	The Web source is clearly labeled, and you can tell which organization or author produced the content. The content is academic and goes beyond simple description. The source has a clearly stated bias or attempts to be neutral.	The web source is not clearly labeled, and you cannot tell who authored the material. The source is encyclopedic in nature or only has a simple description of the content. The source has hidden bias.

Response Post Requirements

1. Minimum of 250 words, maximum of 300 words.
2. You must substantially add to the other student's research by adding one quality academic source to the discussion (see above rubric).
3. Your post must in some way encourage further discussion.

Formative assessment can solve many of the issues we face in our classrooms, particularly in terms of raising the level of digital skills our students possess. The point is to not be afraid of technological change, but to find ways to integrate its use into the learning process. It will not replace traditional education; it will enhance it and allow us to continue to serve the needs of our students as they meet the world with confidence.

REFERENCES

Bandura, R., & Mendez Leal, E. L. (2022). *The Digital Literacy Imperative*. CSIS.

Burke, M. & Cobo, C. (2018). Redefining Knowledge in the Digital Age. *Journal of New Approaches in Educational Research, 7.*

Ciampa, K. (2023). ChatGPT in Education: Transforming Digital Literacy Practices. *Journal of Adult and Adolescent Literacy.*

Crompton, H. & Burke, D. (2023). Artificial Intelligence in Higher Education: The State of the Field. *Journal of Educational Technology in Higher Ed.*

Daughtery, M., & Hansen, L. B. (2022). *Teaching Digital Literacy is a 21st Century Imperative*. Transforming Education Through Technology.

Farrely, T., & Baker, N. (2023). Generative Artificial Intelligence: Implications and Considerations for Higher Education Practice. *Education Sciences*, 13(11), 1109. 10.3390/educsci13111109

Gutierrez-Angel, N. (2022). Digital Literacy in the University Setting: A Literature Review of Empirical Studies Between 2010 and 2021. *Front. Psychology.*

Pangrezio, Luci and Julian Sefton-Green. (2021). Citizenship and Digital Literacy: What's the Difference. *Journal of New Approaches in Educational Research, 1.*

Peng, D., & Yu, Z. (2022). A Literature Review of Digital Literacy over Two Decades. *Education Research International*, 2022, 1–8. 10.1155/2022/2533413

Schildkamp, K., van der Kleij, F. M., Heitink, M. C., Kippers, W. B., & Veldkamp, B. P. (2020). Formative Assessment: A Systematic Review of Teacher Prerequisites for Classroom Practice. *International Journal of Educational Research*, 103, 101602. 10.1016/j.ijer.2020.101602

Seyed, I. (2022). *Formative and Summative Assessment: Impacts on Academic Motivation, Attitudes Toward Learning, Test Anxiety, and Self Regulation Skills.* Sprinter Open.

Vonea, L. (2020). Formative Assessment as Assessment for Learning Development. *Jounral of Pedagogy.*

Compilation of References

Abu-Ghararah, A. H. (1998). *Teaching English as a foreign language: Procedures, techniques and activities*. Tawbah Library.

Adadi, A., & Berrada, M. (2018). Peeking inside the black-box: A survey on explainable artificial intelligence. *IEEE Access : Practical Innovations, Open Solutions*, 6(1), 52138–52160. 10.1109/ACCESS.2018.2870052

Aditya, B., & Permadi, A. (2020). Gender factor in designing features of a learning management system in higher education. *Proceedings of the International Conference on Online and Blended Learning 2019* (ICOBL 2019) IEEE. 10.2991/assehr.k.200521.006

Agung, A. S. N., Surtikanti, M. W., & Quinones, C. A. (2020). Students' perception of online learning during COVID-19 pandemic: A case study on the English students of STKIP Pamane Talino. *SOSHUM: Jurnal Sosial Dan Humaniora*, 10(2), 225–235. 10.31940/soshum.v10i2.1316

Ahmadi, D. M. R. (2018). The use of technology in English language learning: A literature review. *International journal of research in English education, 3*(2), 115-125.

Ahmad, K. S., Armarego, J., & Sudweeks, F. (2013). Literature review on the feasibility of mobile-assisted language learning (MALL) in developing vocabulary skills among non-English speaking migrant and refugee women. In *2013 International Conference on Research and Innovation in Information Systems (ICRIIS)* (pp. 336-341). IEEE. 10.1109/ICRIIS.2013.6716732

Ahmed, M., Siddique, M., & Tahira, Y. (2024). Impact of artificial intelligence-based writing assistant on the academic writing skills of University Faculty in Pakistan. *IJHS*, 4, 539–545.

Akgun, S., & Greenhow, C. (2022). Artificial intelligence in education: Addressing ethical challenges in K-12 settings. *AI and Ethics*, 2(3), 431–440. 10.1007/s43681-021-00096-734790956

Akorbi. (2024, July 11). *The Risk of Cultural Insensitivity in AI Translations*. Akorbi. https://akorbi.com/blog/the-risk-of-cultural-insensitivity-in-ai-translations/

Al Fadda, H. (2012). Difficulties in academic writing: From the perspective of King Saud university postgraduate students. *English Language Teaching*, 5(3), 123–130. 10.5539/elt.v5n3p123

Al Murshidi, G., & Al Abd, K. (2014). UAE university students' awareness of using the writing center. *Higher Education Studies*, 4(3), 58–63. 10.5539/hes.v4n3p58

Al Zumor, A. W. Q., Al Refaai, I. K., Eddin, E. A. B., & Al-Rahman, F. H. A. (2013). EFL students' perceptions of a blended learning environment: Advantages, limitations and suggestions for improvement. *English Language Teaching*, 6(10), 95–110. 10.5539/elt.v6n10p95

Alain, G., Coughlan, T., Adams, A., & Yanacopulos, H. (2018). *A Process for Co-Designing Educational Technology Systems for Refugee Children*. Science Open. .10.14236/ewic/HCI2018.162

Albu, D. (2019). *UNHCR Global trends report: forced displacement in 2018*. Drepturile Omului, 114. https://www.unhcr.org/statistics/unhcrstats/5d08d7ee7/unhcr-global-trends-2018.html

Alfadda, H. A., & Mahdi, H. S. (2021). Measuring students' use of zoom application in language course based on the technology acceptance model (TAM). *Journal of Psycholinguistic Research*, 50(4), 883–900. 10.1007/s10936-020-09752-133398606

Alkali, Y. E., & Amichai-Hamburger, Y. (2004). Experiments in digital literacy. *Cyberpsychology & Behavior*, 7(4), 421–429. 10.1089/cpb.2004.7.42115331029

Alshumaimeri, Y. A., & Alshememry, A. K. (2024). The extent of AI applications in EFL learning and teaching. *IEEE Transactions on Learning Technologies*, 17, 653–663. 10.1109/TLT.2023.3322128

Alvarez, J. (2007). *Du jeu vidéo au serious game: Approches culturelle, pragmatique et formelle*. [Thesis, Université de Toulouse].

Alzhanova, A., & Chaklikova, A. (2022). Multilingual education: Development of professional foreign language communicative competence of students in a digital environment. [IJWLTT]. *International Journal of Web-Based Learning and Teaching Technologies*, 17(1), 1–13. 10.4018/IJWLTT.294572

Aman, A., & Shiratuddin, N. (2020). Virtual reality and augmented reality create fair education opportunities for refugee children in camps. *IACSIT International Journal of Engineering and Technology*, 9(3), 665. 10.14419/ijet.v9i3.31003

Amoako, I. (2023). Global migration crisis: Challenges and opportunities for migrants and refugees. *Journal of the Neurological Sciences*, 455, 455. 10.1016/j.jns.2023.122664

Analytic Alpha. (n.d.). *Artificial Intelligence in Language, Culture & Literature Teaching*. Analytic Alpha. https://www.analyticalpha.nl/artificial-intelligence-in-language-culture-literature-teaching/

Ancheta-Arrabal, A., Pulido-Montes, C., & Carvajal-Mardones, V. (2021). Gender digital divide and education in Latin America: A literature review. *Education Sciences*, 11(12), 804. 10.3390/educsci11120804

Anderson, M. O. (2013). Building accounting students' communication skills. *Management Accounting Quarterly*, 14(4), 32–43.

Andujar, A., & Çakmak, F. (2023). Foreign language learning through instagram: A flipped learning approach. In I. *Management Association (Ed.), Research Anthology on Applying Social Networking Strategies to Classrooms and Libraries* (pp. 278-299). IGI Global.

Anthonysamy, L., Koo, A. C., & Hew, S. H. (2020). Self-regulated learning strategies in higher education: Fostering digital literacy for sustainable lifelong learning. *Education and Information Technologies*, 25(4), 2393–2414. 10.1007/s10639-020-10201-8

Arora, N. K., & Mishra, I. (2019). United Nations sustainable development goals 2030 and environmental sustainability: Race against time. *Environmental Sustainability*, 2(4), 339–342. 10.1007/s42398-019-00092-y

Arslantas, T. K. (2017). Foreign language education of visually impaired individuals: A review of pervasive studies. *Ihlara Journal of Educational Research, 2*(2), 95-104. http://ihead.aksaray.edu.tr/tr/download/article-file/396670

Atwood, M. (2004). *Strange Things. The Malevolent North in Canadian Literature*. Virago.

Aviram, A., & Eshet-Alkalai, Y. (2006). Towards a theory of digital literacy: Three scenarios for the next steps. *European Journal of Open, Distance and E-Learning, 9*(1).

Babcock, R. D., & Thonus, T. (2018). *Researching the Writing Center: Towards an Evidence-Based Practice* (Revised Edition). Peter Lang International Academic Publishers.

Backer, D. I., & Cairns, K. (2021). Social reproduction theory revisited. *British Journal of Sociology of Education*, 42(7), 1086–1104. 10.1080/01425692.2021.1953962

Bada, S. O., & Olusegun, S. (2015). Constructivism learning theory. *Journal of Research & Method in Education*, 5(6), 66–70.

Badawi, M. P. (2009). *Using language learning for enhancing EFL prospective teachers' pedagogical knowledge and performance*. Learning & Language - The Spirit of the Age, Ain Shams University Guest House, Cairo, Egypt.

Bai, H. (2009). Facilitating Students' Critical Thinking in Online Discussion: An Instructor's Experience. *Journal of Interactive Online Learning*, 8(2).

Bailey, D., Southam, A., & Costley, J. (2021). Digital storytelling with chatbots: Mapping L2 participation and perception patterns. *Interactive Technology and Smart Education*, 18(1), 85–103. 10.1108/ITSE-08-2020-0170

Bailin, A. (1988). Artificial intelligence and computer-assisted language instruction: A perspective. *CALICO Journal*, 5(3), 25–45. https://www.jstor.org/stable/24147434. 10.1558/cj.v5i3.25-45

Bali, M., Compton, M., Davis, M., Draper, M., Grove, M., Jones-Devitt, S., McArthur, J., Peddie, C., & Webb, M. (2024). *Navigating the complexities of the artificial intelligence era in higher education*. The Quality Assurance Agency for Higher Education.

Bandura, A. (n.d.). Self-efficacy. Professor Albert Andura. http://professoralbertbandura.com/albert-bandura-self-efficacy.html

Bandura, A. (1977). Self-efficacy: Toward a unifying theory of behavioral change. *Psychological Review*, 84(2), 191–215. 10.1037/0033-295X.84.2.191847061

Bandura, A. (1994). Self-efficacy. In Ramachaudran, V. S. (Ed.), *Encyclopedia of human behavior* (Vol. 4, pp. 71–81). Academic Press.

Bandura, R., & Mendez Leal, E. L. (2022). *The Digital Literacy Imperative*. CSIS.

Barkley, R. A. (1997). Behavioral inhibition, sustained attention, and executive functions: Constructing a unifying theory of ADHD. *Psychological Bulletin*, 121(1), 65–94. https://sciences.ucf.edu/psychology/childrenslearningclinic/wp-content/uploads/sites/24/2013/08/Barkley-1997-Psych-Bulletin.pdf. 10.1037/0033-2909.121.1.659000892

Barrantes, R. (2007). Analysis of ICT demand: What is digital poverty and how to measure it. *Digital poverty: Latin American and Caribbean perspectives*, 29-53.

Barrett, N., & Berger, E. (2021). Teachers' experiences and recommendations to support refugee students exposed to trauma. *Social Psychology of Education*, 24(5), 1259–1280. 10.1007/s11218-021-09657-4

Bartoli, T. (1970). Presencia hispánica en la costa noroeste de América (siglo XVIII). In Carlos H. Magis (Dir.), *Actas del Tercer Congreso Internacional de Hispanistas* (pp. 105-115). El Colegio de México.

Bath, D., & Bourke, J. (2010). *Getting started with blended learning*. Griffth University Press.

Bawden, D. (2008). Origins and concepts of digital literacy. *Digital literacies: Concepts, policies and practices, 30*(2008), 17-32.

Baysar, Z., Çavuşoğlu, İ. E., & Günaydın, E. (2023). Sürdürülebilir kalkınma amaçları ve göç. *Türkiye İnsan Hakları Ve Eşitlik Kurumu Akademik Dergisi*, 6(10), 43–84. 10.59162/tihek.1217860

Bedenlier, S., Bond, M., Buntins, K., Zawacki-Richter, O., & Kerres, M. (2020). Facilitating student engagement through educational technology in higher education: A systematic review in the field of arts and humanities. *Australasian Journal of Educational Technology*, 36(4), 126–150. 10.14742/ajet.5477

Belchior-Rocha, H., Casquilho-Martins, I., & Simões, E. (2022). Transversal competencies for employability: From higher education to the labour market. *Education Sciences*, 12(4), 255. 10.3390/educsci12040255

Bello, R., Brandau, F., & Horne, D. (2020). The enhancement of verbal immediacy in online university classes: A student-generated taxonomy. *International Journal of Communication*, 14, 17. 10.22237/ijoc.2020.14.17

Bellos, D. (2012). Is that a fish in your ear?: Translation and the meaning of everything. *Choice (Chicago, Ill.)*, 49(11), 49-6101. Advance online publication. 10.5860/CHOICE.49-6101

Bender, W. N. (2002). *Differentiating Instruction for Students with Learning Disabilities: best practices for general and special educators*. Corwin Press.

Bernacki, M. L., Greene, J. A., & Crompton, H. (2020). Mobile technology, learning, and achievement: Advances in understanding and measuring the role of mobile technology in education. *Contemporary Educational Psychology*, 60, 101827. 10.1016/j.cedpsych.2019.101827

Biasutti, M., Concina, E., & Frate, S. (2019). Working in the classroom with migrant and refugee students: The practices and needs of Italian primary and middle school teachers. *Pedagogy, Culture & Society*, 28(1), 113–129. 10.1080/14681366.2019.1611626

Biesta, G. J. J. (2013). Receiving the gift of teaching: From 'learning from' to 'being taught by'. *Studies in Philosophy and Education*, 32(5), 449–461. 10.1007/s11217-012-9312-9

Biletska, I. O., Paladieva, A. F., Avchinnikova, H. D., & Kazak, Y. Y. (2021). The use of modern technologies by foreign language teachers: Developing digital skills. *Linguistics and Culture Review*, 5(S2), 16–27. 10.21744/lingcure.v5nS2.1327

Black, L. T. (2004). *Russians in Alaska, 1732–1867*. University of Alaska Press.

Block, K., Cross, S., Riggs, E., & Gibbs, L. (2014). Supporting schools to create an inclusive environment for refugee students. *International Journal of Inclusive Education*, 18(12), 1337–1355. 10.1080/13603116.2014.899636

Boltenkova, J., Nevolina, A., Koksharov, V., Li, S., Rasskazova, T., Tkachuk, G., & Baliasov, A. (2020). Teaching EFL to blind and visually impaired students: An overview. *ICERI2020 Proceedings*, (pp. 5616-5623). IEEE. 10.21125/iceri.2020.1209

Booth, T., Ainscow, M., Black-Hawkins, K., Vaughan, M., & Shaw, L. (2000) *Index for Inclusion: Developing Learning and Participation in Schools*. Bristol: Centre for Studies on Inclusive Education Centre for Studies on Inclusive Education. https://www.csie.org.uk/inclusion/what.shtml

Borenstein, J., & Howard, A. (2021). Emerging challenges in AI and the need for AI ethics education. *AI and Ethics*, 1(1), 61–65. 10.1007/s43681-020-00002-738624388

Boring, A. (2017). Gender biases in student evaluations of teaching. *Journal of Public Economics*, 145(C), 27–41. 10.1016/j.jpubeco.2016.11.006

Borodkin, K., & Faust, M. (2014). Native language phonological skills in low proficiency second language learners. *Language Learning*, 64(1), 132–159. 10.1111/lang.12032

Bourdieu, P. (1986). The forms of capital. In Richardson, J. (Ed.), *Handbook of Theory and Research for the Sociology of Education* (pp. 241–258). Greenwood. https://www.marxists.org/reference/subject/philosophy/works/fr/bourdieu-forms capital.htm

Bourdieu, P., & Passeron, J.-C. (1977). *Reproduction in education, society, and culture*. Sage.

Bowles, S., & Gintis, H. (1976). *Schooling in capitalist America: Educational reform and the contradictions of economic life*. Basic Books.

Boyatzis, R. E. (1998). *Transforming qualitative information: Thematic analysis and code development*. Sage.

Boyd, P. W. (2008). Analyzing students' perceptions of their learning in online and hybrid first-year composition courses. *Computers and Composition*, 25(2), 224–243. 10.1016/j.compcom.2008.01.002

Bozkurt, A., & Sharma, R. C. (2020). Emergency remote teaching in a time of global crisis due to CoronaVirus pandemic. *Asian journal of distance education, 15*(1), i-vi.

Brayne, S. (2014). Surveillance and system avoidance: Criminal justice contact and institutional attachment. *American Sociological Review*, 79(3), 367–391. 10.1177/0003122414530398

Brinkmann, L., Baumann, F., Bonnefon, J. F., Derex, M., Müller, T. F., Nussberger, A. M., Czaplicka, A., Acerbi, A., Griffiths, T. L., Henrich, J., Leibo, J. Z., McElreath, R., Oudeyer, P.-Y., Stray, J., & Rahwan, I. (2023). Machine culture. *Nature Human Behaviour*, 7(11), 1855–1868. 10.1038/s41562-023-01742-237985914

Brookhart, S. M., & Durkin, D. T. (2003). Classroom assessment, student motivation, and achievement in high school social studies classes. *Applied Measurement in Education*, 16(1), 27–54. 10.1207/S15324818AME1601_2

Bruhn, J., López-Varela, A., & de Paiva Vieira, M. (Eds.). (2023). *The Palgrave Handbook of Intermediality*. Palgrave Macmillan. 10.1007/978-3-030-91263-5

Brunner, B. (2019). *Die Erfindung des Nordens. Kulturgeschichte einer Himmelsrichtung*. Verlag Galiani Berlin bei Kiepenheuer und Witsch.

Buchmüller, T., Lembcke, H., Ialuna, F., Busch, J., & Leyendecker, B. (2020). Mental Health Needs of Refugee Children in Specialized Early Education and Care Programs in Germany. *Journal of Immigrant and Minority Health*, 22(1), 22–33. 10.1007/s10903-019-00896-431089910

Bullen, M. (1998). Participation and critical thinking in online university distance education. *Journal of Distance Education*, 13, 1–32.

Burgstahler, S. (2013). Preface. In Burgstahler, S. (Ed.), *Universal design in higher education: Promising practices*. DO-IT, University of Washington. www.washington.edu/doit/preface-0

Burke, M. & Cobo, C. (2018). Redefining Knowledge in the Digital Age. *Journal of New Approaches in Educational Research, 7*.

Busch, J., Bihler, L. M., Lembcke, H., Buchmüller, T., Diers, K., & Leyendecker, B. (2018). Challenges and solutions perceived by educators in an early childcare program for refugee children. *Frontiers in Psychology*, 9, 378326. 10.3389/fpsyg.2018.0162130237777

Busch, J., Buchmüller, T., & Leyendecker, B. (2023). Implementation and quality of an early childhood education program for newly arrived refugee children in Germany: An observational study. *International Journal of Child Care and Education Policy*, 17(1), 3. 10.1186/s40723-023-00105-8

Busch, J., Cabrera, N., Ialuna, F., Buchmüller, T., & Leyendecker, B. (2022). Refugee Children's Early Development during Attendance of Specialized Preschool Programs and Transition into First Grade in Germany. *Early Education and Development*, 33(8), 1304–1325. 10.1080/10409289.2021.1970427

Busch, J., & Leyendecker, B. (2019). Socialization and Development of Refugee Children: Chances of Childcare. In Tulviste, T., Best, D., & Gibbons, J. (Eds.), *Children's Social Worlds in Cultural Context*. Springer. 10.1007/978-3-030-27033-9_14

Byram, M., & Golubeva, I. (2020). Conceptualising intercultural (communicative) competence and intercultural citizenship. In *The Routledge handbook of language and intercultural communication* (pp. 70–85). Routledge. 10.4324/9781003036210-6

Caeners, T. (2015). Memory and Memory Work. In Julian Wolfreys (Ed.), *Introducing Criticism in the 21st Century* (pp. 282-307). Edinburgh University Press.

Cai, L. J. (2017). Students' perceptions of academic writing: A needs analysis of EAP in China. *Asian-focused ELT research and practice: Voices from the far edge*, 127-151.

Camacho, L. (2015). The communication skills accounting firms desire in new hires. *Journal of Business & Finance Librarianship*, 20(4), 318–329. 10.1080/08963568.2015.1072895

Carillo-García, M. E., & Martínez-Ezquerro, A. (2018). Neurodidáctica de la lengua y la literatura. *Revista Iberoamericana de Educación*, 78(1), 149–164. 10.35362/rie7813243

Carlsen, L., & Bruggemann, R. (2022). The 17 United Nations' sustainable development goals: A status by 2020. *International Journal of Sustainable Development and World Ecology*, 29(3), 219–229. 10.1080/13504509.2021.1948456

Carpenter, J. (2024). The social accomplishment of the right to an education: Interviews with people who are blind in Japan. In Burke, A., Young, D., & Cook, M. (Eds.), *Barrier-free Instruction in Japan: Recommendations for Teachers at All Levels of Schooling* (pp. 164–179). Candlin & Mynard. 10.47908/30/8

Castaño-Muñoz, J., Colucci, E., & Smidt, H. (2018). Free digital learning for inclusion of migrants and refugees in Europe: A qualitative analysis of three types of learning purposes. *International Review of Research in Open and Distance Learning*, 19(2). 10.19173/irrodl.v19i2.3382

Castilho, S., Doherty, S., Gaspari, F., & Moorkens, J. (2018). Approaches to human and machine translation quality assessment. *Translation quality assessment: From principles to practice*, 9-38.

Castillo Losada, C. A., Insuasty, E. A., & Jaime Osorio, M. F. (2017). The impact of authentic materials and tasks on students' communicative competence at a Colombian language school. *PROFILE Issues in Teachers'. Professional Development (Philadelphia, Pa.)*, 19(1), 89–104. 10.15446/profile.v19n1.56763

Castle, A. (2006). Assessment of the critical thinking skills of student radiographers. *Radiography*, 12(2), 88–95. 10.1016/j.radi.2005.03.004

Cataleta, M. S. (2021). Artificial intelligence vs human intelligence. *Artificial intelligence vs human intelligence*, 107-116. NIH.

Cerna, L. (2019). *Refugee education: Integration models and practices in OECD countries*. OECD Education (Working Papers, 203), OECD Publishing.

Chambers, D. (2020). Assistive technology supporting inclusive education: Existing and emerging trends. In Chambers, D. (Ed.), *Assistive Technology to Support Inclusive Education* (pp. 1–16). Emerald. 10.1108/S1479-363620200000014001

Chan, C. K. Y., & Hu, W. (2023). Students' voices on generative AI: Perceptions, benefits, and challenges in higher education. *International Journal of Educational Technology in Higher Education*, 20(1), 43. 10.1186/s41239-023-00411-8

Chance, P. (1986). *Thinking in the Classroom: A Survey of Programs*. Teachers College Press.

Chang, M. M. (2005). Applying self-regulated learning strategies in a web-based instruction - An investigation of motivation perception. *Computer Assisted Language Learning*, 18(3), 217–230. 10.1080/09588220500178939

Chetty, K., Qigui, L., Gcora, N., Josie, J., Wenwei, L., & Fang, C. (2018). Bridging the digital divide: Measuring digital literacy. *Economics*, 12(1), 20180023. 10.5018/economics-ejournal.ja.2018-23

Chik, A. (2015). Recreational language learning and digital practices: Positioning and repositioning. In *Discourse and Digital Practices* (pp. 112–129). Routledge. 10.4324/9781315726465-8

Chine, D. R., Brentley, C., Thomas-Browne, C., Richey, J. E., Gul, A., Carvalho, P. F., Branstetter, L., & Koedinger, K. R. (2022). Educational Equity Through Combined Human-AI Personalization: A Propensity Matching Evaluation. In Rodrigo, M. M., Matsuda, N., Cristea, A. I., & Dimitrova, V. (Eds.), *Artificial Intelligence in Education* (pp. 366–377). Springer International Publishing. 10.1007/978-3-031-11644-5_30

Ching, C. C., Basham, J. D., & Jang, E. (2005). The legacy of the digital divide: Gender, Socioeconomic status and early exposure as predictors of full-spectrum technology use among young adults. *Urban Education*, 40(4), 394–411. 10.1177/0042085905276389

Chiu, T. K. F. (2023). The impact of Generative AI (GenAI) on practices, policies and research direction in education: A case of ChatGPT and Midjourney. *Interactive Learning Environments*, 1–17. 10.1080/10494820.2023.2253861

Cho, K., Van Merriënboer, B., Gulcehre, C., Bahdanau, D., Bougares, F., Schwenk, H., & Bengio, Y. (2014). *Learning phrase representations using RNN encoder-decoder for statistical machine translation.* arXiv preprint arXiv:1406.1078. 10.3115/v1/D14-1179

Choshanov, M. A. (2013). E-didactics: New view on education theory in digital technology era. Educational technologies and society. *Journal of Educational Technology & Society*, 16(3), 684–696.

Christison, M. A., & Krahnke, K. J. (1986). Student perceptions of academic language study. *TESOL Quarterly*, 20(1), 61–81. 10.2307/3586389

Chung, E. S., & Ahn, S. (2021). The effect of using machine translation on linguistic features in L2 writing across proficiency levels and text genres. *Computer Assisted Language Learning*, 35(9), 2239–2264. 10.1080/09588221.2020.1871029

Ciampa, K. (2023). ChatGPT in Education: Transforming Digital Literacy Practices. *Journal of Adult and Adolescent Literacy.*

Clark, C., & Gorski, P. (2002). Multicultural education and the digital divide: Focus on Socioeconomic class background. *Multicultural Perspectives*, 4(3), 25–36. 10.1207/S15327892MCP0403_6

Clarke, S., & Whittlestone, J. (2022). A survey of the potential long-term impacts of AI. *2022 AAAI/ACM Conference on AI, Ethics and Society*, (pp. 192-202). ACM. 10.1145/3514094.3534131

Clark, J., & DeSanctis, C. (2013). Toward a unified grading vocabulary: Using rubrics in legal writing courses. *Journal of Legal Education*, 63(1), 3–35.

Clark, R. C., & Mayer, R. E. (2016). *E-learning and the science of instruction: Proven guidelines for consumers and designers of multimedia learning*. John Wiley & Sons. 10.1002/9781119239086

Cleave, J. (2020). *Hats off to adaptive learning: Tailoring corporate training for each learner*. SweetRush.

Clegg, S. (2001). Theorising the Machine: Gender, education and computing. *Gender and Education*, 13(3), 307–324. 10.1080/09540250120063580

Clifford, J., Merschel, L., & Munné, J. (2013). Surveying the Landscape: What is the Role of Machine Translation in Language Learning? *@tic. revista d'innovació educativa*, (10), 108-121.

Cohen, I. (2011). Teacher-student interaction in classrooms of students with specific learning difficulties learning English as a foreign language. *Journal of Interactional Research in Communication Disorders*, 2(2), 271–292. 10.1558/jircd.v2i2.271

Colas, C., Karch, T., Moulin-Frier, C., & Oudeyer, P. Y. (2022). Language and culture internalization for human-like autotelic AI. *Nature Machine Intelligence*, 4(12), 1068–1076. 10.1038/s42256-022-00591-4

Collins, J. (2009). Social reproduction in classrooms and schools. *Annual Review of Anthropology*, 38(1), 33–48. 10.1146/annurev.anthro.37.081407.085242

Commission Européenne. (2007). *Compétences clés pour l'éducation et la formation au long de la vie. Un cadre de référence européen*. Office des Publications Officielles des Communautés Européennes.

Committee on the Rights of Persons with Disabilities. (2016). *General comment no. 4*. OHCHR. https://www.ohchr.org/en/hrbodies/crpd/pages/gc.aspx

Cook, M. (2015, February 9). NWA job market calling for soft skills: today's students lacking in qualities sought by employers. *Arkansas Business, 32*(6).

Cornell University Center for Teaching Excellence. (n.d.). *Inclusive Teaching Strategies*. Cornell University. https://www.cte.cornell.edu/teaching-ideas/building-inclusive-classrooms/inclusive-teaching-strategies.html

Correia, A. P. (2020). Healing the digital divide during the COVID-19 pandemic. *Quarterly Review of Distance Education*, 21(1).

Costa Lopes, A. M., Oliveira, A., Amante, F., Oliveira, I., Abrantes, J., Jesus Pato, M. L., Amaral, O., Relvas, S., Fidalgo, S., & Delplancq, V. (2018). Foreign languages and employability: A complex relationship: Case study in the region of Viseu (Portugal). *Proceedings of EDULEARN18.* IEEE. 10.21125/edulearn.2018.0246

Costa Lopes, A. M., Costa, C. A., Coutinho, E., Oliveira, I., Pereira, J., Gillain, R., Amante, S., Fidalgo, S., Relvas, S., & Delplancq, V. (2023). Looking into foreign languages and multimodal creativity as a tool for pedagogical innovation in higher education: The JASM Project – Open window onto the world. In Carrillo, M. E., & Garcés-Manzanera, A. (Eds.), *New approaches to the investigation of language teaching and literature* (pp. 141–153). IGI Publishing. 10.4018/978-1-6684-6020-7.ch008

Cotton, D., Falvey, D., & Kent, S. (2014). *Language Leader Intermediate*. Pearson Education.

Coughlin, C. N., McElroy, L. T., & Patrick, S. C. (2009). See one, do one, teach one: Dissecting the use of medical education's signature pedagogy in the law school curriculum. *Georgia State University Law Review*, 26(2), 361–416.

Council of Europe. (2020). *Common European Framework of Reference for Languages: Learning, teaching, assessment.* Council of Europe Publishing, Strasbourg. www.coe.int/lang-cefr

Cowling, M. A., Crawford, J., Vallis, C., Middleton, R., & Sim, K. N. (2022). The EdTech difference: Digitalisation, digital pedagogy, and technology-enhanced learning. *Journal of University Teaching & Learning Practice*, 19(2), 1–13. 10.53761/1.19.2.1

Crespi, J. (1774). *Diario que yo Fray Juan Crespi, Misionero del Apostólico Colegio de Propaganda Fide de Sn. Fernando de México, formo del viaje de la Fragata de Su magestad nombrada Santiago, alias la Nueva Galicia, mandada por su Capitán y Alférez de Fragata D. Juan Pérez... (Misión de San Carlos de Monterrey 5 octubre).* Archivo General de Indias (ref. AGI: Estado 43, n.º 10).

Creswell, J. W., & Creswell, J. D. (2018). *Research design: qualitative, quantitative, and mixed methods approaches* (5th ed.). SAGE Publications, Inc.

Criollo-C, S., Guerrero-Arias, A., Jaramillo-Alcázar, A., & Luján-Mora, S. (2021). Mobile learning technologies for education: Benefits and pending issues. *Applied Sciences (Basel, Switzerland)*, 11(9), 4111. 10.3390/app11094111

Croizet, J. C., Goudeau, S., Marot, M., & Millet, M. (2017). How do educational contexts contribute to the social class achievement gap: Documenting symbolic violence from a social psychological point of view. *Current Opinion in Psychology*, 18, 105–110. 10.1016/j.copsyc.2017.08.02528865350

Crompton, H. & Burke, D. (2023). Artificial Intelligence in Higher Education: The State of the Field. *Journal of Educational Technology in Higher Ed.*

Crompton, H., & Burke, D. (2022). Artificial intelligence in K-12 education. *SN Social Sciences*, 2(7), 113. 10.1007/s43545-022-00425-5

Cruz-Jesus, F., Vicente, M. R., Bacao, F., & Oliveira, T. (2016). The education-related digital Divide: An analysis for the EU-28. *Computers in Human Behavior*, 56, 72–82. 10.1016/j.chb.2015.11.027

Csizér, K., & Kontra, E. H. (2020). Foreign language learning characteristics of deaf and severely hard-of-hearing students. *Modern Language Journal*, 104(1), 233–249. 10.1111/modl.12630

Cullen, R. (2001). Addressing the digital divide. *Online Information Review*, 25(5), 311–320. 10.1108/14684520110410517

Cummins, J. (2000). *Language, power, and pedagogy: Bilingual children in the crossfire*. Multilingual Matters. 10.21832/9781853596773

Curtis, S., Gesler, W., Smith, G., & Washburn, S. (2000). Approaches to sampling and case selection in qualitative research: Examples in the geography of health. *Social Science & Medicine*, 50(7-8), 1001–1014. 10.1016/S0277-9536(99)00350-010714922

da Conceição, L. C. (2022). *As principais competências para um contexto profissional de alto desempenho – "Future of Work"*. [Dissertação de Mestrado, Instituto Universitário de Lisboa]. Repositório Iscte. http://hdl.handle.net/10071/26691

Darabi, A., Arrastia, M. C., Nelson, D. W., Cornille, T., & Liang, X. (2011). Cognitive presence in asynchronous online learning: A comparison of four discussion strategies. *Journal of Computer Assisted Learning*, 27(3), 216–227. 10.1111/j.1365-2729.2010.00392.x

Darling-Hammond, L. (2015). *Equity and Excellence in Education: The Role of High-Quality Instructional Materials*. Stanford Center for Opportunity Policy in Education.

Das, A. (2020). Neural Machine Translation (NMT): Inherent Inadequacy, Misrepresentation, and Cultural Bias. *International Journal of Translation*, 32(1-2).

Dasgupta, S., Lall, S., & Wheeler, D. (2005). Policy reform, economic growth and the digital divide. *Oxford Development Studies*, 33(2), 229–243. 10.1080/13600810500137889

Dash, N. (2006). *Inclusive Education for Children with Special Needs*. Atlantic Publishers and Distributors.

Dastjerdi, H. V. (2011). An investigation into the impact of traditional vs. blended teaching on EFL learners' vocabulary acquisition: M-learning in focus. *International Journal of Humanities and Social Science*, 1(15), 202–207.

Daugherty, M., & Funke, B. L. (1998). University faculty and student perceptions of Web-based instruction. *Journal of Distance Education*, 13(1).

Daughtery, M., & Hansen, L. B. (2022). *Teaching Digital Literacy is a 21st Century Imperative*. Transforming Education Through Technology.

Davies, J. A., Davies, L. J., Conlon, B., Emerson, J., Hainsworth, H., & McDonough, H. G. (2020). Responding to COVID-19 in EAP contexts: A comparison of courses at four Sino-foreign universities. *International Journal of TESOL Studies*, 2(2), 32–51.

Davies, S., & Aurini, J. (2010). *The Professionalization of Teaching in the Post-Secondary Sector*. Springer Science & Business Media.

Davis, F. D. (1985). *A technology acceptance model for empirically testing new end-user information systems: Theory and results* [Doctoral dissertation, Massachusetts Institute of Technology].

Davis, F. D. (1989). Perceived usefulness, perceived ease of use, and user acceptance of information technology. *Management Information Systems Quarterly*, 13(3), 319–340. 10.2307/249008

Davis, F. D. (1993). User acceptance of information technology: System characteristics, user perceptions and behavioral impacts. *International Journal of Man-Machine Studies*, 38(3), 475–487. 10.1006/imms.1993.1022

de Cervantes, M. (2004). *Los trabajos de Persiles y Sigismunda*. Cátedra.

de Mendoza, T. Luis (Ed.). (1866). *Colección de documentos inéditos, relativos al descubrimiento, conquista, y organización de las antiguas posesiones españolas en América y Oceanía, sacados de los Archivos del Reino, y muy especialmente del de Indias*. Imprenta de Frías y compañía.

de Montalvo, R. Garci (2003). *Sergas de Esplandián*. Castalia.

Dede, C. (2010). Comparing frameworks for 21st century skills. *21st century skills: Rethinking how students learn, 20*, 51-76.

Deleuze, G., & Guattari, F. (2007). *Mil planaltos: capitalismo e esquizofrenia 2*. Assírio & Alvim.

Delplancq, V., Costa Lopes, A. M., Pereira, J., & Fidalgo, S. (2023). Active foreign language learning practices in higher education: The perspectives of actors. In Carmo, M. (Ed.), *Education Applications & Developments VIII* (pp. 208–217). In Science Press.

Demaine, J. (2003). Social reproduction and education policy. *International Studies in Sociology of Education*, 13(2), 125–140. 10.1080/09620210300200107

Deng, X., & Yu, Z. (2022). A systematic review of machine-translation-assisted language learning for sustainable education. *Sustainability (Basel)*, 14(13), 7598. 10.3390/su14137598

Denny, H., Nordlof, J., & Salem, L. (2018). "Tell me exactly what it was that I was doing that was so bad": Understanding the needs and expectations of working-class students in writing centers. *Writing Center Journal*, 37(1), 67–98. https://www.jstor.org/stable/26537363. 10.7771/2832-9414.1866

Department for Education and Skills. (2004) *Removing Barriers to Achievement: The Governments Strategy for SEN* London: Department for Education and Skills Publications Department for Education and Skills [DfES].

Derry, S. J., Hmelo-Silver, C. E., Nagarajan, A., Chernobilsky, E., & Beitzel, B. D. (2006). Cognitive transfer revisited: Can we exploit new media to solve old problems on a large scale? *Journal of Educational Computing Research*, 35(2), 145–162. 10.2190/0576-R724-T149-5432

Desai, , S. (2013). Integrated systems oriented student-centric learning environment: A framework for curriculum development. *Campus-Wide Information Systems*, 31(1), 24–45. 10.1108/CWIS-01-2013-0002

Dillenbourg, P. (1999). What do you mean by "collaborative learning"? In Dillenbourg, P. (Ed.), *Collaborative Learning: Cognitive and Computational Approaches* (pp. 1–19). Elsevier.

DiMaggio, P. (1982). Cultural capital and school success: The impact of status culture participation on the grades of U.S. high school students. *American Sociological Review*, 47(2), 189–201. 10.2307/2094962

DiMaggio, P., Hargittai, E., Celeste, C., & Shafer, S. (2004). Digital Inequality: From Unequal Access to Differentiated Use. In Neckerman, K. (Ed.), *Social Inequality* (pp. 355–400). Russell Sage Foundation.

Divekar, R., Drozdal, J., Chabot, S., Zhou, Y., Su, H., Chen, Y., Zhu, H., Hendler, J., & Braasch, J. (2022). Foreign language acquisition via artificial intelligence and extended reality: Design and evaluation. *Computer Assisted Language Learning*, 35(9), 2332–2360. 10.1080/09588221.2021.1879162

Domagała-Zyśk, E. (2019). Vocabulary teaching strategies in English as a foreign language classes for Deaf and Hard-of-Hearing students. In Domagała-Zyśk, E., & Kontra, E. H. (Eds.), *English as a foreign language for Deaf and Hard-of-Hearing persons: Challenges and strategies* (pp. 135–150). Cambridge Scholars Publishing.

Dörnyei, Z. (2007). *Research methods in applied linguistics.*

Dresher, B. E., & Hornstein, N. (1976). On some supposed contributions of artificial intelligence to the scientific study of language. *Cognition*, 4(4), 321–398. 10.1016/0010-0277(76)90015-9

Drigas, A. S., & Ioannidou, R. E. (2012). Artificial intelligence in special education: A decade review. *International Journal of Engineering Education*, 28(6), 1366–1372.

Drolia, M., Papadakis, S., Sifaki, E., & Kalogiannakis, M. (2022). Mobile learning applications for refugees: A systematic literature review. *Education Sciences*, 12(2), 96. 10.3390/educsci12020096

Ducar, C., & Schocket, D. H. (2018). Machine translation and the L2 classroom: PedagogicalSolutions for making peace with Google Translate. *Foreign Language Annals*, 51(4), 779–795. 10.1111/flan.12366

Duchardt, B., Furr, P., & Horton, S. G. (2016). A comparison of a progression of writing competencies in online undergraduate and graduate courses: Results and implications. *College Student Journal*, 50(4), 467–476.

Dumaresq, C. C., & Tommasini, J. J. (2014) 'Inclusive Practices.' Retrieved 8th December 2016 from http://www.charterarts.org/wp-content/uploads/2014/09/Inclusive-Practices.pdf

Duong, T. M., & Tran, T. Q. (2023). Facebook-based language learning: Vietnamese university EFL students' attitudes and practices. In Bui, H. P., & Kumar, R. K. (Eds.), *Multidisciplinary applications of computer-mediated communication*. IGI Global. 10.4018/978-1-6684-7034-3.ch007

Duong, T. M., Tran, T. Q., & Nguyen, T. T. P. (2021). Non-English majored students' use of English vocabulary learning strategies with technology-enhanced language learning tools. [AJUE]. *Asian Journal of University Education*, 17(4), 455–463. 10.24191/ajue.v17i4.16252

Dwyer, F. (2010). Edgar Dale's cone of experience: A quasi-experimental analysis. *International Journal of Instructional Media*, 37(4), 431–437.

Ebadi, S., & Ghuchi, K. D. (2018). Investigating the effects of blended learning approach on vocabulary enhancement from EFL learners' perspectives. *Journal on English Language Teaching*, 8(2), 57–68. 10.26634/jelt.8.2.13981

Eco, U. (1979). *Lector in fabula. La cooperazione interpretativa nei testi narrativi*. Bompiani.

Eco, U. (2006). *La memoria vegetale e altri scritti di bibliofilia*. Rovello.

Emmerich, M., & Hormel, U. (2021). Unequal inclusion: The production of social differences in education systems. *Social Inclusion (Lisboa)*, 9(3), 432–442. 10.17645/si.v9i3.4322

English, J. A. (2016). *A digital literacy initiative in honors: Perceptions of students and instructors about its impact on learning and pedagogy*.

Ennis, R. H. (1962). A concept of critical thinking. *Harvard Educational Review*.

Erdemir, E. (2022). Summer Preschools for Syrian Refugee and Host Community Children in Turkey: A Model of Contextually Sensitive Early Intervention. *Early Education and Development*, 33(5), 912–938. 10.1080/10409289.2021.1961426

Ergün, S., & Ulukuş, G. (2022). Göç ve mülteci olgusu: Kavramsal çerçeve. *International Journal of Disciplines in Economics & Administrative Sciences Studies*, 6(24), 1063–1074.

Ertmer, P. A., Ottenbreit-Leftwich, A. T., Sadik, O., Sendurur, E., & Sendurur, P. (2012). Teacher beliefs and technology integration practices: A critical relationship. *Computers & Education*, 59(2), 423–435. 10.1016/j.compedu.2012.02.001

Ertmer, P., & Ottenbreit-Leftwich, A. (2010). Teacher Technology Change. *Journal of Research on Technology in Education*, 42(3), 255–284. 10.1080/15391523.2010.10782551

Eshet, Y. (2004). Digital literacy: A conceptual framework for survival skills in the digital era. *Journal of Educational Multimedia and Hypermedia*, 13(1), 93–106.

Euronews. (2020). *"Dünyada en fazla mülteciye ev sahipliği yapan ülke Türkiye, ilk 10'da Avrupa'dan sadece Almanya var".* Euronews. https://tr.euronews.com/2020/02/28/dunyada-en-fazla-multeciye-ev-sahipligi-yapan-ulke-turkiye-ilk-10-da-avrupa-sadece-almanya

European Agency for Development in Special Needs Education. (2010) *Teacher Education for Inclusion: International Literature Review*. Odense, Denmark: European Agency for Development in Special Needs Education.

European Commission, Directorate-General for Education, Youth, Sport and Culture. (2019). *Key competences for lifelong learning*. Publications Office.

European Labour Authority. (2023). *Unlock the power of a multilingual workforce*. ELA. https://eures.europa.eu/unlock-power-multilingual-workforce-2023-06-30_en

Evans, N., Broido, E. M., Brown, K. R., & Wilke, A. K. (2017). *Disability in higher education: A social justice approach*. Jossey-Bass.

Evans, S., & Morrison, B. (2011). The student experience of English-medium higher education in Hong Kong. *Language and Education*, 25(2), 147–162. 10.1080/09500782.2011.553287

Farrely, T., & Baker, N. (2023). Generative Artificial Intelligence: Implications and Considerations for Higher Education Practice. *Education Sciences*, 13(11), 1109. 10.3390/educsci13111109

Favilla, A. (2007). Novas tecnologias, velhas ideias: Notas para uma genealogia da arte computacional. Revista Nada. *Instituto Português do Livro e das Bibliotecas*, 9(2), 31–43.

Fedynich, L., Bradley, K. S., & Bradley, J. (2015). Graduate Students' Perceptions of Online Learning. *Research in Higher Education*, 27.

Fellmeth, G., Rose-Clarke, K., Zhao, C., Busert, L. K., Zheng, Y., Massazza, A., Sonmez, H., Eder, B., Blewitt, A., Lertgrai, W., Orcutt, M., Ricci, K., Mohamed-Ahmed, O., Burns, R., Knipe, D., Hargreaves, S., Hesketh, T., Opondo, C., & Devakumar, D. (2018). Health impacts of parental migration on left-behind children and adolescents: A systematic review and meta-analysis. *Lancet*, 392(10164), 2567–2582. 10.1016/S0140-6736(18)32558-330528471

Felsenburg, M. E., & Graham, L. P. (2012). A better beginning: Why and how to help novice legal writers build a solid foundation by shifting their focus from product to process. *Regent University Law Review*, 24(1), 83–107.

Fenner, A. B., & Newby, D. (2000). *Approaches to materials design in European textbooks: Implementing principles of authenticity, learner autonomy, cultural awareness*. Council of Europe Publishing.

Fernández-Batanero, J. M., Montenegro-Rueda, M., Fernández-Cerero, J., & Garcia-Martinez, I. (2022). Assistive technology for the inclusion of students with disabilities: A systematic review. *Educational Technology Research and Development*, 70(5), 1911–1930. 10.1007/s11423-022-10127-7

Fioravanti, M. L., Sena, B., & Francine Barbosa, E. (2020). Assessing the Development of Soft Skills for Project Management using PBL: A Case Study. *2020 IEEE Frontiers in Education Conference (FIE), Frontiers in Education Conference (FIE)*. IEEE.

Fitria, T. N. (2021). A review of machine translation tools: The translation's ability. *Language Circle: Journal of Language and Literature*, 16(1), 162–176. 10.15294/lc.v16i1.30961

Fitria, T. N. (2021). The use technology based on artificial intelligence in English teaching and learning. *ELT Echo*, 6(2), 213–223. 10.24235/eltecho.v6i2.9299

Flecha, R. (2011). The dialogic sociology of education. *International Studies in Sociology of Education*, 21(1), 7–20. 10.1080/09620214.2011.543849

Fortune, M. F., Spielman, M., & Pangelinan, D. T. (2011). Students' perceptions of online or face-to-face learning and social media in hospitality, recreation and tourism. *Journal of Online Learning and Teaching*, 7(1).

Foster, S. K., Wiczer, E., & Eberhardt, N. B. (2019). What's so hard about soft skills? *ASHA Leader*, 24(12), 52–60. 10.1044/leader.FTR2.24122019.52

Foucault, M. (1977). *Discipline and punish: The birth of the prison*. Pantheon Books.

Fránquiz, M. E., & Ortiz, A. A. (2017). Co-editors introduction: Who are the transfronterizos and what can we learn from them? *Bilingual Research Journal*, 40(2), 111–115. 10.1080/15235882.2017.1329378

Gall, M. D., Gall, J. P., & Borg, W. R. (2007). *Educational research: An introduction*. Allyn-Bacon.

Galvin, S., & Greenhow, C. (2020). Writing on social media: A review of research in the high school classroom. *TechTrends*, 64(1), 57–69. 10.1007/s11528-019-00428-9

Gantt, L. I. (2007). Deconstructing thinking like a lawyer: Analyzing the cognitive components of the analytical mind. 29. *Campbell Law Review*, (3), 413.

Gao, Y., & Bartlett, B. (2014). Opportunities and challenges for negotiating appropriate EAP practices in China. In *English for academic purposes (EAP) in Asia* (pp. 13-31). Brill Sense. 10.1007/978-94-6209-752-0_2

Garrison, D. R., & Vaughan, N. D. (2007). *Blended learning in higher education: Framework, principles and guidelines*. John Wiley and Sons. 10.1002/9781118269558

Gay, G. (2000). *Culturally responsive teaching: Theory, research, and practice*. Teachers College Press.

Gee, J. P. (2010). A situated-sociocultural approach to literacy and technology. *The new literacies: Multiple perspectives on research and practice, 165*, 193.

Gee, J. P. (2023). Discourse and 'the New Literacy Studies. In *The Routledge Handbook of Discourse analysis* (pp. 469–480). Routledge. 10.4324/9781003035244-39

Gefen, D., Karahanna, E., & Straub, D. (2003). Inexperience and experience with online stores: The importance of TAM and Trust. *IEEE Transactions on Engineering Management*, 50(3), 307–321. 10.1109/TEM.2003.817277

Gilliom, J., & Monahan, T. (2013). *SuperVision: An introduction to the surveillance society*. University of Chicago Press.

Glesne, C. (2015). *Nitel araştırmaya giriş* (A. Ersoy & P. Yalçınoğlu, Çev. Ed.). Ankara: Anı Yayıncılık.

Golden, A. (2018). Feminist Digital Pedagogy. *Virginia Woolf Miscellany*, 93, 42–43.

Goldstein, I., & Papert, S. (1977). Artificial intelligence, language, and the study of knowledge. *Cognitive Science*, 1(1), 84–123.

Golonka, E. M., Bowles, A. R., Frank, V. M., Richardson, D. L., & Freynik, S. (2014). Technologies for foreign language learning: A review of technology types and their effectiveness. *Computer Assisted Language Learning*, 27(1), 70–105. 10.1080/09588221.2012.700315

Gorski, P. (2005). Education equity and the digital divide. *AACE Journal*, 13(1), 3–45.

Government of Vietnam. (2021). *National Education Development Strategy 2021-2030*. Government of Vietnam. https://shorturl.at/g3sO5

Grace, S., & Gravestock, P. (2009). *Inclusion and Diversity: Meeting the Needs of All Students*. Routledge.

Graham, C. (2006). Blended learning systems. Definitions, current trends and future directions. In Bonk, C., & Graham, C. (Eds.), *The handbook of blended learning: Global perspectives, local designs*. John Wiley and Sons.

Graham, L. J. (2020). Inclusive education in the 21st century. In Graham, L. J. (Ed.), *Inclusive education for the 21st century: Theory, policy and practice* (pp. 3–26). Routledge. 10.4324/9781003116073-2

Grasmane, D., & Grasmane, S. (2011). Foreign language skills for employability in the EU labour market. *European Journal of Higher Education*, 1(2-3), 192–201. 10.1080/21568235.2011.629487

Gray, J. A., & DiLoreto, M. (2016). The effects of student engagement, student satisfaction, and perceived learning in online learning environments. *The International Journal of Educational Leadership Preparation*, 11(1), n1.

Grego, R., & Thompson, N. (1996). Repositioning remediation: Renegotiating composition's work in the academy. *College Composition and Communication*, 47(1), 62–84.

Grunhut, J., Marques, O., & Wyatt, A. T. M. (2022). Needs, challenges, and applications of artificial intelligence in medical education curriculum. *JMIR Medical Education*, 8(2), 35587. 10.2196/3558735671077

Grynyuk, S. (2016). Foreign language teaching for specific purposes: Basic aspects. *ScienceRise.*, 3/5(20), 18–23. 10.15587/2313-8416.2016.64803

Güçer, M., Karaca, S., & Dinçer, O. B. (2013). *Sınırlar arasında yaşam savaşı Suriyeli mülteciler alan çalışması.* International Strategic Research Organization (USAK). https://ecec-care.org/fileadmin/careproject/Publications/reports/new_version_CARE_WP4_D4_1_Review_on_the_effects_of_ECEC.pdf https://www.un.org/development/desa/dspd/wp-content/uploads/sites/22/2020/02/World-Social-Report-2020-Chapter-5.pdf

Guerra, J. C. (2004). *Putting literacy in its place: Nomadic consciousness and the practice of transcultural repositioning*. University of Washington.

Guilherme, A. (2019). AI and education: The importance of teacher and student relations. *AI & Society*, 34(1), 47–54. 10.1007/s00146-017-0693-8

Gupta, M., & Katarya, R. (2020). Social media based surveillance systems for healthcare using machine learning: A systematic review. *Journal of Ambient Intelligence and Humanized Computing*, 11(10), 4053–4069. 10.1007/s12652-020-01881-z32622833

Gustavsson, M., & Eriksson, A. F. (2010). Gendered learning environments in managerial work. *Studies in the Education of Adults*, 42(2), 141–158. http://urn.kb.se/resolve?urn=urn:nbn:se:liu:diva-64270. 10.1080/02660830.2010.11661594

Guth, D. J. (2020). BRIDGING THE WORKFORCE EQUITY GAP: Two-year colleges face challenges in drawing underserved students into job training programs. *Community College Journal*, 91(3), 10–15.

Gutierrez-Angel, N. (2022). Digital Literacy in the University Setting: A Literature Review of Empirical Studies Between 2010 and 2021. *Front. Psychology*.

Haddad, B., & Marx, A. A. (2018). Student Perceptions of Soft Skills & Career Decision Self-Efficacy through Participation in SAE. *Journal of Agricultural Education*, 59(4), 159–176. 10.5032/jae.2018.04159

Hajhashemi, K., Caltabiano, N., & Anderson, N. (2016). Integrating digital technologies in the classroom: Lecturers' views on the flipped classroom approach. *Australian and International Journal of Rural Education*, 26(3), 18–29. 10.47381/aijre.v26i3.74

Hampton, M. D. (2019). A 5-Year Evaluation of Faculty Use of Practical Within-Course Writing Development Strategies in a DNP Program. *Nurse Educator*, 44(4), 197–201. 10.1097/NNE.0000000000000058930138150

Hancı-Azizoglu, E. B. (2021). Emotional Intelligence and Empathic Linguistic Power in Times of Crisis. In *Rhetoric and Sociolinguistics in Times of Global Crisis* (pp. 100–115). IGI Global. 10.4018/978-1-7998-6732-6.ch006

Hargittai, E. (2005). Survey measures of web-oriented digital literacy. *Social Science Computer Review*, 23(3), 371–379. 10.1177/0894439305275911

Harker, M., & Koutsantoni, D. (2005). Can it be as effective? Distance versus blended learning in a web-based EAP programme. *ReCALL*, 17(2), 197–216. 10.1017/S095834400500042X

Harrington, S., Day, M., Rickly, R., & Bowen, B. (2000). *The online writing classroom*. Hampton Press.

Harris, J., Mishra, P., & Koehler, M. (2009). Teachers' technological pedagogical content knowledge and learning activity types: Curriculum-based technology integration reframed. *Journal of Research on Technology in Education*, 41(4), 393–416. 10.1080/15391523.2009.10782536

Hartley, J., McWilliam, K., Burgess, J., & Banks, J. (2008). The uses of multimedia: Three digital literacy case studies. *Media International Australia, Incorporating Culture & Policy*, 128(1), 59–72. 10.1177/1329878X0812800108

Hawthorne, N. (1987 [2013]). *Nathaniel Hawthorne's Tales*. W. W. Norton & Company.

Heckman, J., & Kautz, T. (2012). Hard evidence on soft skills. *Labour Economics*, 19(4), 451–464. 10.1016/j.labeco.2012.05.01423559694

Heffernan, N. (2005). Watching movie trailers in the ESL Class. *The Internet TESL Journal, 9*(3). https://bit.ly/3UW0sB5

Hegeman, J. S. (2015). Using instructor-generated video lectures in online mathematics courses improves student learning. *Online Learning : the Official Journal of the Online Learning Consortium*, 19(3), 70–87. 10.24059/olj.v19i3.669

Hernandez, J. (2021). Teachers' Perceptions of Integrating Digital Technology Tools [Doctoral dissertation, Concordia University Chicago].

Hernández, P., & José, H. (1774). *Continuación del diario que formó el Alferez graduado de Fragata Dn. Juan Perez, Primer Piloto del Departamento de Sn. Blas, con la titulada Santiago, alias la Nueva Galicia de su mando, que comprehende su salida de Monterrey á explorar la Costa Septentrional, y su regreso á este propio Puerto en 26 de Agosto de este año de 1774*. Archivo General de Indias (ref. AGI: Estado 38A, n.º 3).

Hertzberg, L. (1990). Artificial intelligence and the empiricist picture of thought. *Artifical Intelligence, Culture and Language: On Education and Work*, 9-12.

Hilgers, M., & Mangez, E. (Eds.). (2015). *Bourdieu's theory of social fields: Concepts and applications*. Routledge.

Hinkel, E. (2003). *Teaching academic ESL writing: Practical techniques in vocabulary and grammar*. Routledge. 10.4324/9781410609427

Hockly, N., & Dudeney, G. (2018). Current and future digital trends in ELT. *RELC Journal*, 49(2), 164–178. 10.1177/0033688218777318

Hodges, C. B., Moore, S., Lockee, B. B., Trust, T., & Bond, M. A. (2020). *The difference between emergency remote teaching and online learning*.

Hofstede, G. (1986). Cultural differences in teaching and learning. *International Journal of Intercultural Relations*, 10(3), 301–320. 10.1016/0147-1767(86)90015-5

Hoi, V. N. (2020). Understanding higher education learners' acceptance and use of mobile devices for language learning: A rasch-based path modeling approach. *Computers & Education*, 146, 146. 10.1016/j.compedu.2019.103761

Holmes, W., Anastopoulou, S., Schaumburg, H., & Mavrikis, M. (2018). *Technology-enhanced personalised learning: Untangling the evidence*.

Holmes, W., & Tuomi, I. (2022). State of the art and practice in AI in education. *European Journal of Education*, 57(4), 542–570. 10.1111/ejed.12533

Hong, H., & Cai, Q. (2023). Evidence-Based Educational Practices for Working With Refugee Children. *Journal of Research in Childhood Education*, 37(3), 405–422. 10.1080/02568543.2023.2211127

hooks, b. (1989). *Talking Back: Thinking Feminist, Thinking Black*. Cambridge, Mass.: South End Press.

hooks, b. (2015). *Feminism is for everybody: Passionate politics*. New York, NY: Routledge.

Hope, A. (2018). Creep: The growing surveillance of students' online activities. *Education and Society (Melbourne)*, 36(1), 55–72. 10.7459/es/36.1.05

Hora, M. T., Benbow, R. J., & Smolarek, B. B. (2018). Re-thinking Soft Skills and Student Employability: A New Paradigm for Undergraduate Education. *Change*, 50(6), 30–37. 10.1080/00091383.2018.1540819

House, J. (2001). Translation quality assessment: Linguistic description versus social evaluation. *Meta*, 46(2), 243–257. 10.7202/003141ar

Hrastinski, S., Olofsson, A. D., Arkenback, C., Ekström, S., Ericsson, E., Fransson, G., Jaldemark, J., Ryberg, T., Öberg, L. M., Fuentes, A., Gustafsson, U., Humble, N., Mozelius, P., Sundgren, M., & Utterberg, M. (2019). Critical imaginaries and reflections on artificial intelligence and robots in postdigital K-12 education. *Postdigital Science and Education*, 1(2), 427–445. 10.1007/s42438-019-00046-x

Hsu, T. C., Chang, C., & Jen, T. H. (2023). Artificial Intelligence image recognition using self-regulation learning strategies: Effects on vocabulary acquisition, learning anxiety, and learning behaviours of English language learners. *Interactive Learning Environments*, 1–19. 10.1080/10494820.2023.2165508

Hu, G., & Lei, J. (2014). English-medium instruction in Chinese higher education: A case study. *Higher Education*, 67(5), 551–567. 10.1007/s10734-013-9661-5

Hurley, J. J., Medici, A., Stewart, E., & Cohen, Z. (2011). Supporting Preschoolers and Their Families who are Recently Resettled Refugees. *Multicultural Perspectives*, 13(3), 160–166. 10.1080/15210960.2011.594400

Hutchins, W. J. (2023). Machine translation: History of research and applications. In *Routledge encyclopedia of translation technology* (pp. 128–144). Routledge. 10.4324/9781003168348-7

Hutchison, A. (2018). Writing Support for the Online Technical Writing Service Course: A Feasibility Study. *2018 IEEE International Professional Communication Conference (ProComm), Professional Communication Conference (ProComm), 2018 IEEE International, PROCOMM*, (pp. 18–24). IEEE. 10.1109/ProComm.2018.00011

Hwang, G. J., Sung, H. Y., Hung, C. M., Huang, I., & Tsai, C. C. (2012). Development of a personalized educational computer game based on students' learning styles. *Educational Technology Research and Development*, 60(4), 623–638. 10.1007/s11423-012-9241-x

Hwang, G. J., & Tu, Y. F. (2021). Roles and research trends of artificial intelligence in mathematics education: A bibliometric mapping analysis and systematic review. *Mathematics*, 9(6), 584. 10.3390/math9060584

Hwang, G. J., Xie, H., Wah, B., & Gasevic, D. (2020). Vision, challenges, roles and research issues of artificial intelligence in education. *Computers and Education: Artificial Intelligence*, 1(13), 1–5. 10.1016/j.caeai.2020.100001

Hyland, K. (2004). Genre and Second Language Writing. Diane Belcher and Jun Liu Series (Eds.), *Michigan Series on Teaching Multilingual Writers*. The University of Michigan Press. 10.3998/mpub.23927

Hyland, K. (2006). *English for academic purposes: An advanced resource book*. Routledge. 10.4324/9780203006603

Hysaj, A., Elkhouly, A., Qureshi, A. W., & Abdulaziz, N. A. (2019). Study of the impact of tutor's support and undergraduate student's academic satisfaction. *Am. J. Hum. Soc. Sci. Res*, 3(12), 70–77.

Iakimova, G., Koval-Saifi, N., Wittmann, M., & Guardiola, E. (2022). A game to promote literacy and psychosocial well-being among syrian refugee children. 10.31219/osf.io/7u946

Iivari, N., Sharma, S., & Ventä-Olkkonen, L. (2020). Digital transformation of everyday life–How COVID-19 pandemic transformed the basic education of the young generation and why information management research should care? *International Journal of Information Management*, 55, 102183. 10.1016/j.ijinfomgt.2020.10218332836640

Jaldemark, J. (2008). Participation and genres of communication in online settings of higher education. *Education and Information Technologies*, 13(2), 129–146. 10.1007/s10639-008-9057-9

James, R. F., & James, M. L. (2004). Teaching Career and Technical Skills in "Mini" in Business World. *Business Education Forum*, 59(2), 39–41.

Jance, M., & Morgan, A. (2013). Critical learning skills for business students. *American Journal of Business Education*, 6(1), 25–32. 10.19030/ajbe.v6i1.7480

Jarvis, H. (2001). Internet usage of English for academic purposes courses. *ReCALL*, 13(2), 206–212. 10.1017/S0958344001000623a

Jayakody, A., Lokuliyana, S., Sampath, A. A. T., Silva, G. T. S., Rajanthika, S. A. L., & Seneviratne, H. M. T. B. (2016). Mobile application for vision impaired people to facilitate to learn the English language. *International Journal of Computer Applications*, 138(12), 12–17. https://www.ijcaonline.org/research/volume138/number12/jayakody-2016-ijca-909025.pdf. 10.5120/ijca2016909025

Jenkins, R. (1992). *Pierre Bourdieu*. Routledge. 10.4324/9780203317471

Johns, M. A. (1997). *Text, Role and Context: Developing Academic Literacies*. Cambridge University Press. 10.1017/CBO9781139524650

Jones, R. H., Chik, A., & Hafner, C. A. (2015). *Discourse and digital practices: Doing discourse analysis in the digital age* (p. 262). Taylor & Francis.

Jones, R. H. (2016). Digital literacies. In *Handbook of research in second language teaching and learning* (pp. 286–298). Routledge. 10.4324/9781315716893-21

Joseph, N., Kar, A. K., & Ilavarasan, P. V. (2017, October). A model for prioritization and prediction of impact of digital literacy training Programmes and validation. In *Conference on e-Business, e-Services and e-Society* (pp. 227-238). Cham: Springer International Publishing. 10.1007/978-3-319-68557-1_21

Junaidi, J. (2020). Artificial intelligence in EFL context: Rising students' speaking performance with Lyra virtual assistance. *International Journal of Advanced Science and Technology Rehabilitation*, 29(5), 6735–6741.

Jungwirth, H. (1991). Interaction and gender — Findings of a microethnographical approach to classroom discourse. *Educational Studies in Mathematics*, 22(3), 263–284. 10.1007/BF00368341

Kamran, T. (2007). Islam, Urdu and Hindu as the Other: Instruments of Cultural Homogeneity in Pakistan. In Chandra, P., & Mahajan, S. (Eds.), *Composite Culture in a Multicultural Society* (pp. 93–122). Dorling Kindersley.

Kan, A. (2009). *Statistical procedures on measurement results. In the H. Atilgan. Assessment and evaluation in education*. Ani Publications.

Kaplan, I., Stolk, Y., Valibhoy, M., Tucker, A., & Baker, J. (2016). Cognitive assessment of refugee children: Effects of trauma and new language acquisition. *Transcultural Psychiatry*, 53(1), 81–109. 10.1177/136346151561293326563891

Kapur, R. (2018). *Significance of digital technology*. Research Gate.

Karataş, F., Abedi, F. Y., Ozek Gunyel, F., Karadeniz, D., & Kuzgun, Y. (2024). Incorporating AI in foreign language education: An investigation into ChatGPT's effect on foreign language learners. *Education and Information Technologies*, 1–24. 10.1007/s10639-024-12574-6

Kardeş, S., & Akman, B. (2018). Suriyeli Mültecilerin Eğitimine Yönelik Öğretmen Görüşleri. *Ilkogretim Online, 17*(3).

Karpava, S. (Ed.). (2022). *Handbook of research on multilingual and multicultural perspectives on higher education and implications for teaching*. IGI Global. 10.4018/978-1-7998-8888-8

Karsenti, T. (2019). Artificial intelligence in education: The urgent need to prepare teachers for tomorrow's schools. *Formation et Profession*, 27(1), 105–111. 10.18162/fp.2019.a166

Karsenti, T., Kozarenko, O. M., & Skakunova, V. A. (2020). Digital technologies in teaching and learning foreign languages: Pedagogical strategies and teachers' professional competence. *Education and Self Development*, 15(3), 76–88. 10.26907/esd15.3.07

Kasperski, R., Blau, I., & Ben-Yehudah, G. (2022). Teaching digital literacy: Are teachers' perspectives consistent with actual pedagogy? *Technology, Pedagogy and Education*, 31(5), 615–635. 10.1080/1475939X.2022.2091015

Kazim, R. (2017). *The issue of multi-linguality and challenges faced by working class students studying in an English medium school in Hyderabad*. Research Gate.

Kendrick, M., Early, M., Michalovich, A., & Mangat, M. (2022). Digital storytelling with youth from refugee backgrounds: Possibilities for language and digital literacy learning. *TESOL Quarterly*, 56(3), 961–984. 10.1002/tesq.3146

Kessler, M. (2022). *Multimodality.* ELT Journal. 10.1093/elt/ccac028

Khakurel, J., & Porras, J. (2020). The Effect of Real-World Capstone Project in an Acquisition of Soft Skills among Software Engineering Students. *2020 IEEE 32nd Conference on Software Engineering Education and Training (CSEE&T), Software Engineering Education and Training (CSEE&T)*. IEEE. https://doi-org.ezproxy.snhu.edu/10.1109/CSEET49119.2020.9206201

Khan, G. Z., & Mahmood, A. (2022). The role of assistive technology in the English language learning experience of blind and visually impaired students in Pakistan: A qualitative study. *Journal of Social Sciences Review*, 2(4), 313–321. 10.54183/jssr.v2i4.106

Khasawneh, M. A. S. (2021). Problems teaching English to deaf students. *Indonesian Journal of Creative Counseling*, 1(1), 32–42. 10.47679/ijcc.v1i2.107

Khodabandeh, F., & Mombini, A. (2024). Exploring the effect of augmented reality technology on high school students' vocabulary learning, personality traits, and self-efficacy in flipped and blended classes. *Education and Information Technologies*, 1–24. 10.1007/s10639-024-12486-5

Khodadady, E., & Gholamian, M. (2014). Motivations underlying blind students' English language learning: A theoretical and factorial analysis. *International Journal of Applied Psychology*, 4(5), 169–180. 10.5923/j.ijap.20140405.01

Kids Together. (2010) *Benefits of Inclusive Education*. Kids Together. http://www.kidstogether.org/inclusion/benefitsofinclusion.htm

Kim, H. S., & Kim, H. (2017). A study of Korean English teachers' future readiness for the fourth industrial revolution. *Multimedia-Assisted Language Learning*, 20(3), 179–205.

Kim, N. Y., Cha, Y., & Kim, H. S. (2019). Future English learning: Chatbots and artificial intelligence. *Multimedia-Assisted Language Learning*, 22(3), 32–53.

Koehn, P. (2020). *Neural machine translation*. Cambridge University Press. 10.1017/9781108608480

Kohnke, L., & Jarvis, A. (2021). Coping with English for academic purposes provision during COVID-19. *Sustainability (Basel)*, 13(15), 8642. 10.3390/su13158642

Kormos, J. (2017a). *The second language learning processes of students with specific learning difficulties*. Routledge.

Kormos, J. (2017b). The effects of specific learning difficulties on processes of multilingual language development. *Annual Review of Applied Linguistics*, 37, 30–44. 10.1017/S026719051700006X

Kormos, J., & Smith, A. M. (2024). *Teaching languages to students with specific learning differences* (2nd ed.). Multilingual Matters. 10.21832/9781800418622

Korteling, J. H., van de Boer-Visschedijk, G. C., Blankendaal, R. A., Boonekamp, R. C., & Eikelboom, A. R. (2021). Human-versus artificial intelligence. *Frontiers in Artificial Intelligence*, 4, 622364. 10.3389/frai.2021.62236433981990

Krakouer, J., Mitchell, P., Trevitt, J., Kochanoff, A., & Children, S. (2017). *Early years transitions : Supporting children and families at risk of experiencing vulnerability : Rapid literature review.* State of Victoria: Department of Education and Training. http://research.acer.edu.au/cgi/viewcontent.cgi?article=1015&context=early_childhood_misc

Kress, G. (2003). *Literacy in the New Media Age*. Routledge.

Kress, G., & van Leeuwen, T. (2001). *Multimodal Discourse*. Routledge.

Krumsvik, R. J. (2008). Situated learning and teachers' digital competence. *Education and Information Technologies, 13*(4), 279-290. 10.1007/s10639-008-9069-5

Krutka, D., Manca, S., Galvin, S., Greenhow, C., Koehler, M., & Askari, E. (2019). Teaching «against» social media: Confronting problems of profit in the curriculum. *Teachers College Record*, 121(14), 1–19. 10.1177/016146811912101410

Kühl, N., Goutier, M., Baier, L., Wolff, C., & Martin, D. (2022). Human vs. supervised machine learning: Who learns patterns faster? *Cognitive Systems Research*, 76, 78–92. 10.1016/j.cogsys.2022.09.002

Kuhn, D. (1991). *The skills of argument*. Cambridge University Press. 10.1017/CBO9780511571350

Kuiken, F., & Vedder, I. (2021). The interplay between academic writing abilities of Dutch undergraduate students, a remedial writing programme, and academic achievement. *International Journal of Bilingual Education and Bilingualism*, 24(10), 1474–1485. 10.1080/13670050.2020.1726280

Kumar, A. H. S. (2023). Analysis of ChatGPT tool to assess the potential of its utility for academic writing in biomedical domain. *BEMS Reports*, 9(1), 24–30. 10.5530/bems.9.1.5

Lahcen, A. A. (2023). *The Impact of Machine Translation on Cultural Transfer in Literary Texts*. Research Gate. https://www.researchgate.net/publication/374910874_The_Impact_of_Machine_Translation_on_Cultural_Transfer_in_Literary_Texts/citation/download

Láinez, M. (2009). *Banderas lejanas. La exploración, conquista y defensa por España del territorio de los actuales Estados Unidos*. Crónicas de la Historia.

Land, S. (2004). *Effective Teaching Practices for Students in Inclusive Classrooms*. WM. https://education.wm.edu/centers/ttac/resources/articles/inclusion/effectiveteach/

Lane-Mercier, G. (2014). Global and Local Languages. *A Companion to Translation Studies*, 217-229. Wiley.

Lankshear, C., & Knobel, M. (2014). Englishes and digital literacy practices. In *The Routledge Companion to English Studies* (pp. 451–463). Routledge.

Lantolf, J. P., & Thorne, S. L. (2006). *Sociocultural Theory and the Genesis of Second Language Development*. Oxford University Press.

Laslett, B., & Brenner, J. (1989). Gender and social reproduction: Historical perspectives. *Annual Review of Sociology*, 15(1), 381–404. https://www.jstor.org/stable/2083231. 10.1146/annurev.so.15.080189.00212112316382

Laura-De La Cruz, K., Noa-Copaja, S., Turpo-Gebera, O., Montesinos-Valencia, C., Bazán-Velasquez, S., & Pérez-Postigo, G. (2023). Use of gamification in English learning in higher education: A systematic review. *Journal of Technology and Science Education*, 13(2), 480–497. 10.3926/jotse.1740

Laura, R. S., & Chapman, A. (2009). The technologisation of education: Philosophical reflections on being too plugged in. *International Journal of Children's Spirituality*, 14(3), 289–298. 10.1080/13644360903086554

Laurel, B. (2013). *Computers as theatre*. Addison-Wesley.

Lawrence, G., Haque, E., King, J., & Rajabi, S. (2014). Exploring the feasibility of e-learning in Ontario ESL programs. *Contact (Thousand Oaks, Ventura County, Calif.)*.

Lea, M., & Street, B. (1998). Student writing in higher education: An academic literacies approach. *Studies in Higher Education*, 23(2), 157–172. 10.1080/03075079812331380364

Leckenby, D., & Hesse-Biber, S. N. (2007). Feminist approaches to mixed-methods research. In Hesse-Biber, S. N., & Leavy, P. L. (Eds.), *Feminist research practice: A primer*. SAGE. 10.4135/9781412984270.n9

LeCun, Y., Bengio, Y., & Hinton, G. (2015). *Deep learning. nature, 521*(7553), 436-444.

Leef, G. (2015). *Why colleges churn out poor writers and poor thinkers*. James G Martin. https://www.jamesgmartin.center/2015/08/why-colleges-churn-out-poor-writers-and-poor-thinkers/

Lee, S. M. (2020). The impact of using machine translation on EFL students' writing. *Computer Assisted Language Learning*, 33(3), 157–175. 10.1080/09588221.2018.1553186

Lehman, R. M., & Conceicao, S. C. O. (2014). *Motivating and retaining online students: Research-based strategies that work* (1st ed.). Jossey-Bass.

Leibrandt, I. M. (2019). Postmodern Literacy. Multimodal, Hypertextual, Intertextual Reading. In Romero, E. D., Bobkina, J., & Stefanova, S. (Eds.), *Teaching Literature and Language Through Multimodal Texts* (pp. 258–276). IGI Global. 10.4018/978-1-5225-5796-8.ch014

Lent, R., & Hackett, G. (1987). *Career self-efficacy: Empirical status and future directions*. Research Gate. https://www.researchgate.net/publication/223678204_Career_self-efficacy_Empirical_status_and_future_directions

Lentz, B. K., Dreshler, D. D., & Kissam, B. R. (2004) *Teaching Content to All: evidence-based inclusive practices in middle and secondary schools*. Boston, MA: Pearson Education Merriam-Webster Dictionary. https://www.merriam-webster.com/dictionary/disadvantaged

Lerga, R., Candrlic, S., & Jakupovic, A. (2021). A review of assistive technology for students with dyslexia. *Proceedings of the 13th Conference on Computer Supported Education,* (pp. 64-72). ACM. 10.5220/0010434500640072

Leung, L. (2010). Telecommunications across borders: Refugees' technology use during displacement. *Telecommunications Journal of Australia*, 60(4), 58.1–58.13. 10.2104/tja10058

Lewis, K., & Thacker, S. (2016). ICT and the Education of Refugees: A Stocktaking of Innovative Approaches in the MENA Region. World Bank. 10.1596/26522

Lillis, T., & Turner, J. (2001). Student writing in higher education: Contemporary confusion, traditional concerns. *Teaching in Higher Education*, 6(1), 57–68. 10.1080/13562510020029608

Lim, K., Nam, Y.-O., Eom, S., Jang, Y., Kim, D., & Kim, M. (2020). Structural gender differences in LMS use patterns among college students. *Sustainability (Basel)*, 12(11), 4465. 10.3390/su12114465

Lindström, N. B., Hashemi, S. S., Bartram, L., & Bradley, L. (2017). Mobile resources for integration: how availability meets the needs of newly arrived Arabic-speaking migrants in Sweden. *CALL in a climate of change: adapting to turbulent global conditions–short papers from EUROCALL*, 40-45.

Liu, J., & Sadler, R. W. (2003). The effect and affect of peer review in electronic versus traditional modes on L2 writing. *Journal of English for Academic Purposes*, 2(3), 193–227. 10.1016/S1475-1585(03)00025-0

Liu, Z. J., Tretyakova, N., Fedorov, V., & Kharakhordina, M. (2020). Digital literacy and digital didactics as the basis for new learning models development. [iJET]. *International Journal of Emerging Technologies in Learning*, 15(14), 4–18. 10.3991/ijet.v15i14.14669

Łoboda, K., & Mastela, O. (2023). Machine translation and culture-bound texts in translator education: A pilot study. *The Interpreter and Translator Trainer*, 17(3), 503–525. 10.1080/1750399X.2023.2238328

Longoria, A.-I., Inés, B.-B., Rogelio, R.-M., Soledad, M., & Molina, A. (2022). Systematic Mapping of Digital Gap and Gender, Age, Ethnicity, or Disability. *Sustainability (Basel)*, 14(3), 1–20. 10.3390/su14031297

Lonn, M. R., & Dantzler, J. Z. (2017). A Practical Approach to Counseling Refugees: Applying Maslow's Hierarchy of Needs. *Journal of Counselor Practice*, 8(2).

Loo, D. B. (2020). Integrating critical thinking in online language tasks: Considerations for an academic writing class. *International Journal of TESOL Studies*, 2(2), 52–61.

Lopes, D. M. (2010). *A Philosophy of Computer Art*. Routledge.

Lotherington, H., & Jenson, J. (2011). Teaching multimodal and digital literacy in L2 settings: New literacies, new basics, new pedagogies. *Annual Review of Applied Linguistics*, 31, 226–246. 10.1017/S0267190511000110

Lyon, D. (2022). Surveillance. *Internet Policy Review*, 11(4). Advance online publication. 10.14763/2022.4.1673

Lythreatis, S., Singh, S. K., & El-Kassar, A. N. (2022). The digital divide: A review and future research agenda. *Technological Forecasting and Social Change*, 175, 121359. 10.1016/j.techfore.2021.121359

Mackey, A., & Gass, M. S. (2005). *Second language research: Methodology and design*. Lawrence Erlbaum Associates.

Magis, C. H. (Dir.). (1970). *Actas del Tercer Congreso Internacional de Hispanistas*. El Colegio de México.

Ma, J. K. H. (2021). The digital divide at school and at home: A comparison between schools by socioeconomic level across 47 countries. *International Journal of Comparative Sociology*, 62(2), 115–140. 10.1177/00207152211023540

Majid, S., & Eapen, C. M., Ei Mon Aung, & Oo, K. T. (2019). The Importance of Soft Skills for Employability and Career Development: Students and Employers' Perspectives. *The IUP Journal of Soft Skills*, 13(4), 7–39.

Malamed, C. (2017). *Six strategies you may not be using to reduce cognitive load.* The Learning Coach. https://theelearningcoach.com/learning/reduce-cognitive-load/

Manovich, L. (2001). *The Language of New Media.* MIT Press.

Manyika, J., Chui, M., Miremadi, M., Bughin, J., George, K., Willmott, P., & Dewhurst, M. (2017). *A future that works: Automation, employment, and productivity.* McKinsey Global Institute.

Marcus, M., Santorini, B., & Marcinkiewicz, M. A. (1993). Building a large annotated corpus of English: The Penn Treebank. *Computational Linguistics*, 19(2), 313–330.

Margaryan, A., Littlejohn, A., & Vojt, G. (2011). Are digital natives a myth or reality? University students' use of digital technologies. *Computers & Education*, 56(2), 429–440. 10.1016/j.compedu.2010.09.004

Marín, V. I., & Castaneda, L. (2023). Developing digital literacy for teaching and learning. In *Handbook of open, distance and digital education* (pp. 1089–1108). Springer Nature Singapore. 10.1007/978-981-19-2080-6_64

Mariscal, J., Mayne, G., Aneja, U., & Sorgner, A. (2019). Bridging the Gender Digital Gap. *Economics*, 13(1), 2–12. 10.5018/economics-ejournal.ja.2019-9

Martin, A. (2008). Digital literacy and the "digital society". *Digital literacies: Concepts, policies and practices, 30*(2008), 151-176.

Martin, A., & Grudziecki, J. (2006). DigEuLit: Concepts and tools for digital literacy development. *Innovation in teaching and learning in information and computer sciences, 5*(4), 249 -267.

Martin, A., & Grudziecki, J. (2006). DigEuLit: Concepts and tools for digital literacy development. *Innovation in teaching and learning in information and computer sciences, 5*(4), 249-267.

Martin, J. R., & Rose, D. (2007). *Genre Relations.* Equinox.

Marzuki, W., Widiati, U., Rusdin, D., Darwin, , & Indrawati, I. (2023). The impact of AI writing tools on the content and organization of students' writing: EFL teachers' perspective. *Cogent Education*, 10(2), 1–17. 10.1080/2331186X.2023.2236469

Massey, G. & Ehrensberger-Dow, M. (2017). Learning machines and teaching humans. International Conference: Points of View in Translation and Interpreting, Kraków, Poland. https://digitalcollection.zhaw.ch/handle/11475/3278

Maton, K. I. (2008). Empowering community settings: Agents of individual development, community betterment, and positive social change. *American Journal of Community Psychology*, 41(1-2), 4–21. 10.1007/s10464-007-9148-618175215

Maura, J. (2022). Gestación del mito de las "Siete Ciudades" en Naufragios de Alvar Núñez Cabeza de Vaca. *Lemir*, (26), 405-420.

Maura, J. F. (2016). Sobre el origen hispánico del nombre "Canadá.". *Lemir*, (20), 17–52.

Maura, J. F. (2021). *Españoles y portugueses en Canadá en tiempos de Cristóbal Colón*. Universitat de València.

McCarthy, J. (2007). From here to human-level AI. *Artificial Intelligence*, 171(18), 1174–1182. 10.1016/j.artint.2007.10.009

McDowell, J. (1998). *José Narváez: The Forgotten Explorer*. The Arthur H. Clark Company.

Mendoza-Fierro, L. E. (2020). *The Digital Literacy Practices of Transfronterizx ESOL College Students: Los De ESOL* [Doctoral dissertation, The University of Texas at El Paso].

Merriam, S. B. (2013). *Nitel araştırma desen ve uygulama için bir rehber (S. Turan, Çev.)*. Nobel Akademik Yayıncılık.

Messmer, R., & Schmitz, S. (2004). Gender demands on e-learning. *WIT Transactions on Information and Communication Technologies*, 31. Advance online publication. 10.2495/CI040261

Meyer, A., Rose, D. H., & Gordon, D. (2014). *Universal design for learning: Theory and Practice*. CAST Professional Publishing.

Meyerhoff, M. (2011). *Introducing Sociolinguistics*. Taylor & Francis.

Meyer, K. A. (2003). Face-to-face versus threaded discussions: The role of time and higher-order thinking. *Journal of Asynchronous Learning Networks*, 7(3), 55–65.

Michinov, N., Brunot, S., Le Bohec, O., Juhel, J., & Delaval, M. (2011). Procrastination, participation, and performance in online learning environments. *Computers & Education*, 56(1), 243–252. 10.1016/j.compedu.2010.07.025

Miles, M., Huberman, M., & Saldana, J. (2013). *Qualitative data analysis: A methods sourcebook*. Sage Publications.

Milton, M., & Vozzo, L. (2013). Digital literacy and digital pedagogies for teaching literacy: Pre- service teachers' experience on teaching rounds. *The Journal of Literacy and Technology*, 14(1), 72–97.

Mirete, A. B., Maquilón, J. J., Mirete, L., & Rodríguez, R. A. (2020). Digital competence and university teachers' conceptions about teaching. A structural causal model. *Sustainability (Basel)*, 12(12), 4842. 10.3390/su12124842

Mohammed Nuri, H. S., Azeez, N., & Mustafa, A. (2023). The effectiveness of blended learning in improving the vocabulary range of postgraduate students. *Journal of Garmian University*, 10(2), 1015–1022. 10.24271/garmian.2023.10281

Moinolnolki, N., & Han, M. (2017). No Child Left Behind: What About Refugees? *Childhood Education*, 93(1), 1, 3–9. 10.1080/00094056.2017.1275231

Monahan, T. (2011). Surveillance as cultural practice. *The Sociological Quarterly*, 52(4), 495–508. 10.1111/j.1533-8525.2011.01216.x22175064

Montgomery, M. A., Jackson, C. T., & Kelvin, E. A. (2014). Premigration harm and depression: Findings from the New Immigrant Survey, 2003. *Journal of Immigrant and Minority Health*, 16(5), 773–780. 10.1007/s10903-013-9810-z23504372

Monty, R. W. (2015). Everyday borders of transnational students: Composing place and space with mobile technology, social media, and multimodality. *Computers and Composition*, 38, 126–139. 10.1016/j.compcom.2015.09.013

Moreno, D. (2019). *Teaching Literature and Language Through Multimodal Texts*. IGI Global.

Morrell, B. L. M., Eukel, H. N., & Santurri, L. E. (2020). Soft skills and implications for future professional practice: Qualitative findings of a nursing education escape room. *Nurse Education Today*, 93, 93. 10.1016/j.nedt.2020.10446232791421

Mossberger, K., Tolbert, C. J., & Hamilton, A. (2012). Broadband adoptionl measuring digital citizenship: Mobile access and broadband. *International Journal of Communication*, 6, 37.

Mpofu, J., & Chimhenga, S. (2013). Challenges faced by Hearing Impaired pupils in learning: A case study of King George VI Memorial School. *IOSR Journal of Research & Method in Education*, 2(1), 69–74. 10.9790/7388-0216974

Munro, K. (2019). Social reproduction theory, social reproduction, and household production. *Science and Society*, 83(4), 451–468. 10.1521/siso.2019.83.4.451

Murphy, J., & Dodd, B. (2010). A diagnostic challenge: Language difficulties and hearing impairment in a secondary-school student from a non-English-speaking background. *Child Language Teaching and Therapy*, 26(3), 207–220. 10.1177/0265659009349977

Murray, J. S. (2019). War and conflict: Addressing the psychosocial needs of child refugees. *Journal of Early Childhood Teacher Education*, 40(1), 3–18. 10.1080/10901027.2019.1569184

Nagata, N. (1996). Computer vs. workbook instruction in second language acquisition. *CALICO Journal*, 14(1), 53–75. 10.1558/cj.v14i1.53-75

Nanjundaswamy, C., Baskaran, S., & Leela, M. H. (2021). Digital pedagogy for sustainable learning. *Shanlax International Journal of Education*, 9(3), 179–185. 10.34293/education.v9i3.3881

Nash, R. (1999). Bourdieu, "Habitus", and educational research: Is it all worth the candle? *British Journal of Sociology of Education*, 20(2), 175–187. 10.1080/01425699995399

National Health Service. (2012). *What is Equality and Diversity?* NHS. http://www.faculty.londondeanery.ac.uk/e-learning/diversity-equal-opportunities-and-human-rights/what-is-equality-and-diversity

Nawaz, A., & Kundi, G. M. (2010). Digital literacy: An analysis of the contemporary paradigms. *Journal of Science and Technology Education Research*, 1(2), 19–29.

Nazzal, K. H., Forghany, M., Charis Geevarughese, M., Mahmoodi, V., & Wong, J. (2014). An innovative community-oriented approach to prevention and early intervention with refugees in the United States. *Psychological Services*, 11(4), 477–485. 10.1037/a003796425384000

Negroponte, N. (1996). *Ser Digital*. Editorial Caminho.

Nesi, H., & Gardner, S. (2012). *Genres across the disciplines: Student writing in higher education*. Cambridge University Press. 10.1017/9781009030199

Nguyen, H. T. T., Sivapalan, S., Hiep, P. H., Van Anh, P. T., & Lan, N. T. M. (2021). Teaching English as a second language in Vietnam: Transitioning from the traditional learning approach to the blended learning approach. In *SHS Web of Conferences* (*Vol. 124*, p. 01003). EDP Sciences.

Nguyen, P. V., Naleppa, M., & Lopez, Y. (2021). Cultural competence and cultural humility: A complete practice. *Journal of Ethnic & Cultural Diversity in Social Work*, 30(3), 273–281. 10.1080/15313204.2020.1753617

Nida, E. A. (1993). *Language, Culture and Translating*. Shanghai Foreign Language Education Press.

Niño, A. (2009). Machine translation in Foreign Language Learning: Language Learners' and tutors' perceptions of its advantages and disadvantages. *ReCALL*, 21(2), 241–258. 10.1017/S0958344009000172

Nolop, B. (2013). *Our college graduates can't write*. WSJ. http://blogs.wsj.com/experts/2013/10/09/our-college-graduates-cant-write/

North, B., & Piccardo, E. (2016). *Developing illustrative descriptors of aspects of mediation for the CEFR*. Education Policy Division, Council of Europe.

Not, L. (2013). *Las pedagogías del conocimiento[The pedagogies of knowledge]*. (Sergio, R. M. B., Trans.). Fondo de Cultura Económica de México.

O'Connor, F. (1971). *The Complete Stories*. Farrar, Straus and Giroux.

OECD. (2021). *21st-century readers: Developing literacy skills in a digital world*. OECD. https://www.oecd.org/publications/21st-century-readers-a83d84cb-en.htm

Oktradiksa, A., Bhakti, C. P., Kurniawan, S. J., Rahman, F. A., & Ani, . (2021). Utilization artificial intelligence to improve creativity skills in society 5.0. *Journal of Physics: Conference Series*, 1760(1), 012032. 10.1088/1742-6596/1760/1/012032

Ono, Y., & Ishihara, M. (2012). Integrating mobile-based individual activities into the Japanese EFL classroom. *International Journal of Mobile Learning and Organisation*, 6(2), 116. 10.1504/IJMLO.2012.047597

Organisation for Economic Co-operation and Development (OECD). (2015). *Students, Computers and Learning: Making the Connection*. OECD Publishing.

Ovcharuk, O., Ivaniuk, I., Soroko, N., Gritsenchuk, O., & Kravchyna, O. (2020). The use of digital learning tools in the teachers' professional activities to ensure sustainable development and democratization of education in European countries. *E3S Web of Conferences, 166*(10019).

Pabón-Colón, J. (n.d.). *Feminism is a verb*. JessicaPaBon. https://jessicapabon.com/

Pabón-Colón, J. (2018). https://jessicapabon.com/2018/08/21/why-i-use-digital-pedagogies-a-not-quite-manifesto-on-teaching-in-the-age-of-digital-feminist-movement/

Pally, M. (1997). Critical thinking in ESL: An argument for sustained content. *Journal of Second Language Writing*, 6(3), 293–311. 10.1016/S1060-3743(97)90016-3

Palou, F. (1774). *Relación de la expedición de la fragata la "Nueva Galicia" en el año 1774 al descubrimiento de la costa del norte, cuyo capitán era el primer piloto D. Juan Pérez... Copia de lo particular que vio la expedicion de mar en las costas del Norte, sacado del Diario original, que se formo abordo de la Fragata por los P.P. Fr. Juan Crespi, y Fr. Tomas de la Peña, que iban en la dicha expedición.* Museo Naval de Madrid (ref. M. N. Ms. 335, doc. 40, f. 99-105).

Palou, F. (1787). *Relación histórica de la vida y apostólicas tareas del Venerable Padre Fray Junípero Serra, y de las misiones que fundó en California septentrional, y nuevos establecimientos de Monterrey.* Imprenta de Don Felipe Zúniga.

Pangrezio, Luci and Julian Sefton-Green. (2021). Citizenship and Digital Literacy: What's the Difference. *Journal of New Approaches in Educational Research, 1.*

Paniagua, A., & Istance, D. (2018). *Teachers as designers of learning environments. The importance of innovative pedagogies. Educational Research and Innovation.* OECD Publishing.

Papendieck, A. (2018). Technology for equity and social justice in education: A critical issue overview. *Texas Education Review (Austin, Tex.).*

Papert, S. (1972). Teaching Children to be Mathematicians Versus Teaching About Mathematics. *International Journal of Mathematical Education in Science and Technology*, 31(3), 249–262. 10.1080/0020739700030306

Park, J. H., & Shin, N. M. (2017). Students' perceptions of artificial intelligence technology and artificial intelligence teachers. *The Journal of Korean Teacher Education*, 34(2), 169–192.

Patton, M. Q. (2014). Nitel mülakat yapma. (M. Çakır & S. İrez, Çev.). M. Bütün & S. B. Demir (Çev. Ed.). *Nitel araştırma ve değerlendirme yöntemleri içinde* (s. 339-422). Ankara: Pegem Akademi.

Pearce, A. (2020). The Digital Gap Still Exists, Generationally, Rurally, and Academically. In *ICETC '20: Proceedings of the 12th International Conference on Education Technology and Computers* (pp. 215-222). Association for Computing Machinery. 10.1145/3436756.3437048

Pecora, V. P. (2002). The Culture of surveillance. *Qualitative Sociology*, 25(3), 345–358. 10.1023/A:1016081929646

Peña-López, I. (2010). From laptops to competences: Bridging the digital divide in education. *Rev. U. Soc. Conocimiento*, 7, 21.

Peng, D., & Yu, Z. (2022). A Literature Review of Digital Literacy over Two Decades. *Education Research International*, 2022, 1–8. 10.1155/2022/2533413

Peres, R., Schreier, M., Schweidel, D., & Sorescu, A. (2023). On ChatGPT and beyond: How generative artificial intelligence may affect research, teaching, and practice. *International Journal of Research in Marketing*, 40(2), 269–275. 10.1016/j.ijresmar.2023.03.001

Perreault, H. (2004). Business Educators Can Take a Leadership Role in Character Education. *Business Education Forum*, 59(1), 23–25.

Pethick, D. (1976). *First Approaches to the Northwest Coast*. J.J. Douglas.

Pham, T. T. H. (2019). Applying blended learning method in teaching English at the University of Da Nang, Vietnam. *Educational Review*, 1, 1–5. 10.26855/er.2019.01.002

Phuong, H. Y., Huynh, M. H., & Huynh, C. M. H. (2019). Students' perceptions of a blended learning environment for English training at a university in Vietnam. *Can Tho University Journal of Science*, 11(3), 57–64. 10.22144/ctu.jen.2019.039

Pierce, D. (2019). What Employers Want: Employers are Looking to Community Colleges for Help in Teaching Soft Skills. *Community College Journal*, 89(3), 20–25.

Pinkwart, N. (2016). Another 25 years of AIED? Challenges and opportunities for intelligent educational technologies of the future. *International Journal of Artificial Intelligence in Education*, 26(2), 771–783. 10.1007/s40593-016-0099-7

Plant, K., Barac, K., & Sarens, G. (2019). Preparing work-ready graduates – skills development lessons learnt from internal audit practice. *Journal of Accounting Education*, 48, 33–47. https://doi-org.ezproxy.snhu.edu/10.1016/j.jaccedu.2019.06.001. 10.1016/j.jaccedu.2019.06.001

Pokrivcakova, S. (2019). Preparing teachers for the application of AI-powered technologies in foreign language education. *Journal of Language and Cultural Education*, 7(3), 135–153. 10.2478/jolace-2019-0025

Polybius, . (2010). *The Histories*. Oxford University Press.

Polyportis, A. (2024). A longitudinal study on artificial intelligence adoption: Understanding the drivers of ChatGPT usage behavior change in higher education. *Frontiers in Artificial Intelligence*, 6, 1–10. 10.3389/frai.2023.132439838249792

Pordata, Base de Dados Portugal Contemporâneo. (n.d.). *Fundação Francisco Manuel dos Santos*. Pordata. https://www.pordata.pt/db/municipios/ambiente+de+consulta/tabela/5839568

Portes, A. (1998). Social capital: Its origins and applications in modern sociology. *Annual Review of Sociology*, 24(1), 1–24. 10.1146/annurev.soc.24.1.1

Putri, R. S., Purwanto, A., Pramono, R., Asbari, M., Wijayanti, L. M., & Hyun, C. C. (2020). Impact of the COVID-19 pandemic on online home learning: An explorative study of primary schools in Indonesia. *International Journal of Advanced Science and Technology*, 29(5), 4809–4818.

Qashou, A. (2021). Influencing factors in M-learning adoption in higher education. *Education and Information Technologies*, 26(2), 1755–1785. 10.1007/s10639-020-10323-z

Qiao, H., & Zhao, A. (2023). Artificial intelligence-based language learning: Illuminating the impact on speaking skills and self-regulation in Chinese EFL context. *Frontiers in Psychology*, 14, 1255594. 10.3389/fpsyg.2023.125559438022973

Qinda, S. (2018). The Effects of blended learning on EFL students' usage of grammar in context. *The Eurasia Proceedings of Educational & Social Sciences (EPESS), 10*(2587 – 1753), 11-22.

Qobilovna, A. M. (2023). Communicative competence as a factor of teacher's professional competency. *American Journal of Social Sciences and Humanity Research*, 3(09), 32–44.

Rafalow, M. H. (2020). *Digital divisions: How schools create inequality in the tech era*. University of Chicago Press. 10.7208/chicago/9780226726724.001.0001

Rafalow, M. H., & Puckett, C. (2022). Sorting machines: Digital technology and categorical inequality in education. *Educational Researcher*, 51(4), 274–278. 10.3102/0013189X211070812

Rafner, J., Dellermann, D., Hjorth, A., Verasztó, D., Kampf, C., Mackay, W., & Sherson, J. (2021). Deskilling, upskilling, and reskilling: A case for hybrid intelligence. *Morals & Machines*, 1(2), 24–39. 10.5771/2747-5174-2021-2-24

Rapley, T. J. (2001). The art(fulness) of open-ended interviewing: Some considerations on analysing interviews. *Qualitative Research*, 1(3), 303–323. 10.1177/146879410100100303

Reay, D. (2004). It's all becoming a habitus: Beyond the habitual use of habitus in educational research. *British Journal of Sociology of Education*, 25(4), 431–444. 10.1080/0142569042000236934

Regan, P. M., & Jesse, J. (2019). Ethical challenges of edtech, big data and personalized learning: Twenty-first century student sorting and tracking. *Ethics and Information Technology*, 21(3), 167–179. 10.1007/s10676-018-9492-2

Reinharz, S. (2011). *Observing the observer: Understanding ourselves in field research.* Oxford University Press.

Remond, E., Massou, L., & Bonfils, P. E. H. (2021). Enseignement supérieur et numérique. Mondialisation, mobilités. In *Colloque international Pédagogie et numérique: l'enseignement supérieur au défi de la mondialisation?* Presses universitaires de Nancy-Éditions universitaires de Lorraine.

Rensburg, H., & Son, J. (2010). Improving English Language and Computer Literacy Skills in an Adult Refugee Program. *International Journal of Pedagogies and Learning*, 6(1), 69–81. 10.5172/ijpl.6.1.69

Rice, M., & Cun, A. (2023). Leveraging digital literacies to support refugee youth and families' success in online learning: A theoretical perspective using a socio-ecological approach. *Online Learning : the Official Journal of the Online Learning Consortium*, 27(3). 10.24059/olj.v27i3.3628

Richardson, J. C., & Ice, P. (2010). Investigating students' level of critical thinking across instructional strategies in online discussions. *The Internet and Higher Education*, 13(1-2), 52–59. 10.1016/j.iheduc.2009.10.009

Ridgeway, C. L. (2001). Gender, status, and leadership. *Journal of Social issues, 57*(4), 637-655. https://psycnet.apa.org/doi/10.1111/0022-4537.00233

Riordan, D. P. (2022). *Emergency Remote Instruction During the COVID-19 Pandemic: An Analysis of Access and Learning Outcomes* [Doctoral dissertation, University of Houston].

Rios, J. A., Ling, G., Pugh, R., Becker, D., & Bacall, A. (2020). Identifying Critical 21st-Century Skills for Workplace Success: A Content Analysis of Job Advertisements. *Educational Researcher*, 49(2), 80–89. 10.3102/0013189X19890600

Rodríguez-Sala, M. L. (Ed.). (2006). *De San Blas hasta la Alta California. Los viajes y diarios de Juan Joseph Pérez Hernández*. Universidad Nacional Autónoma de México.

Rogers, A. (2006). Lifelong learning and the absence of gender. *International Journal of Educational Development*, 26(2), 189–208. 10.1016/j.ijedudev.2005.07.025

Rose, D. H., & Meyer, A. (2002). *Teaching Every Student in the Digital Age: Universal Design for Learning*. Association for Supervision and Curriculum Development.

Roshanaei, M., Olivares, H., & Lopez, R. R. (2023). Harnessing AI to Foster Equity in Education: Opportunities, Challenges, and Emerging Strategies. *Journal of Intelligent Learning Systems and Applications*, 15(4), 123–143. 10.4236/jilsa.2023.154009

Roxas, K., & Fruja, R. (2019). *Teacher Education and Refugee Students*. Oxford Research Encyclopedia of Education., 10.1093/acrefore/9780190264093.013.285

Rubtsova, A., Almazova, N., Bylieva, D., & Krylova, E. (2019). Constructive model of multilingual education management in higher school. *IOP Conference Series. Materials Science and Engineering*, 940(1), 012132. 10.1088/1757-899X/940/1/012132

Rusmiyanto, R., Huriati, N., Fitriani, N., Tyas, N., Rofi'i, A., & Sari, M. (2023). The role of artificial intelligence (AI) in developing English language learner's communication skills. *Journal of Education*, 6(1), 750–757. 10.31004/joe.v6i1.2990

Ryberg, T., & Georgsen, M. (2010). Enabling Digital Literacy. *Nordic Journal of Digital Literacy*, 5(2), 88–100. 10.18261/ISSN1891-943X-2010-02-02

Sage, R. (2007). *Inclusion in Schools: Making a Difference*. Network Continuum Education.

Sala, A., Punie, Y., & Garkov, V. (2020). *LifeComp: The European framework for personal, social and learning to learn key competence. EUR 30246 EN*. Publications Office of the European Union.

Salajan, F. D., Schönwetter, D. J., & Cleghorn, B. M. (2010). Student and faculty inter-generational digital divide: Fact or fiction? *Computers & Education*, 55(3), 1393–1403. 10.1016/j.compedu.2010.06.017

Samania, S. (2011). Family process and content model: A contextual model for family studies. *Procedia: Social and Behavioral Sciences*, 30, 2285–2292. 10.1016/j.sbspro.2011.10.446

Sanchez-Prieto, J., Trujillo-Torres, J. M., Gómez-García, M., & Gómez-García, G. (2020). The Generational Digital Gap within Dual Vocational Education and Training Teachers. *European Journal of Educational Research*, 9(4), 1557–1567. 10.12973/eu-jer.9.4.1557

SánchezR, ,. (2021). Lorenzo Ferrer Maldonado: El almeriense que descubrió el Estrecho de Bering. *REAL.Revista de Estudios Almerienses*, (1), 6–52.

Sarpparaje, M. (2016). Importance of enhancing communication skills among young graduates and how to make them career-ready & life-ready? *Language in India*, 16(4), 93.

Saswandi, T., & Ningsih, P. E. A. (2023). The effect of using blended learning strategy toward the students' vocabulary mastery at tenth grade of SMKN 2 *Sungai Penuh.Jurnal Ilmiah Wahana Pendidikan*, 9(2), 633–643.

Sawant, S. (2021). Online collaborative learning tools and types: Their key role in managing classrooms without walls. In *Human-computer interaction and technology integration in modern society* (pp. 12–41). IGI Global. 10.4018/978-1-7998-5849-2.ch002

Schildkamp, K., van der Kleij, F. M., Heitink, M. C., Kippers, W. B., & Veldkamp, B. P. (2020). Formative Assessment: A Systematic Review of Teacher Prerequisites for Classroom Practice. *International Journal of Educational Research*, 103, 101602. 10.1016/j.ijer.2020.101602

Schmidt, T., & Strasser, T. (2022). Artificial intelligence in foreign language learning and teaching: A CALL for intelligent practice. *Anglistik*, 33(1), 165–184. 10.33675/ANGL/2022/1/14

Schumm, W. R., Webb, F. J., Turek, D. E., Jones, K. D., & Ballard, G. E. (2006). A comparison of methods for teaching critical thinking skills for US Army officers. *American Journal of Distance Education*, 20(1), 39–50. 10.1207/s15389286ajde2001_4

Schwab, K., & Zahidi, S. (2020). *The future of jobs report 2020*. World Economic Forum.

Selwyn, N. (2010). Looking beyond learning: Notes towards the critical study of educational technology. *Journal of Computer Assisted Learning*, 26(1), 65–73. 10.1111/j.1365-2729.2009.00338.x

Selwyn, N. (2011). *Education and technology: Key issues and debates*. Continuum International Publishing Group.

Selwyn, N. (2016). *Is technology good for education?* Wiley.

Senowarsito, S., & Ardini, S. N. (2023). The use of artificial intelligence to promote autonomous pronunciation learning: Segmental and suprasegmental features perspective. *IJELTAL*, 8(2), 133–147. 10.21093/ijeltal.v8i2.1452

Séror, J. (2012). Show me! Enhanced feedback through screencasting technology. *TESL Canada Journal*, •••, 104–104.

Sethi, R. (2016). Importance of Soft Skills for Professional Students. *International Journal of Recent Research Aspects*, 113–115.

Severiens, S., & Ten Dam, G. (1998). Gender and learning: Comparing two theories. *Higher Education*, 35(3), 329–350. Advance online publication. 10.1023/A:1003033003124

Severino, C., & Prim, S. N. (2016). Second language writing development and the role of tutors: A case study of an online writing center "Frequent Flyer.". *Writing Center Journal*, 35(3), 143. 10.7771/2832-9414.1844

Seyed, I. (2022). *Formative and Summative Assessment: Impacts on Academic Motivation, Attitudes Toward Learning, Test Anxiety, and Self Regulation Skills*. Sprinter Open.

Sharma, P. (2010). Blended Learning. *ELT Journal*, 64(4), 456–458. 10.1093/elt/ccq043

Sharpe, R., & Benfield, G. (2005). The student experience of e-learning in higher education. *Brookes eJournal of Learning and Teaching, 1*(3), 1-9.

Shebansky, W. J. (2018). Blended learning adoption in an ESL context: Obstacles and guidelines. *TESL Canada Journal*, 35(1), 52–77. 10.18806/tesl.v35i1.1284

Shekhar, A., & Marsden, N. (2018). Cognitive walkthrough of a learning management system with gendered personas. *Proceedings of the 4th Conference on Gender & IT*. ACM. 10.1145/3196839.3196869

Shi, G., Ke, S., & Banozic, A. (2022). The role of assistive technology in advancing sustainable development goals. *Frontiers in Political Science*, 4, 859272. 10.3389/fpos.2022.859272

Sindoni, M. G., Adami, E., Karatza, S., Moschini, I., & Petroni, S. (2022). Theory and practice of the common framework of reference for intercultural digital literacies. In Sindoni, M. G., & Moschini, I. (Eds.), *Multimodal literacies across digital learning contexts* (pp. 166–184). Routledge. 10.4324/9781003134244-13

Singh, S. (2010). Digital divide in India: Measurement, determinants and policy for addressing the challenges in bridging the digital divide. [IJIDE]. *International Journal of Innovation in the Digital Economy*, 1(2), 1–24. 10.4018/jide.2010040101

Sinnayah, P., Rathner, J. A., Loton, D., Klein, R., & Hartley, P. (2019). A combination of active learning strategies improves student academic outcomes in first-year paramedic bioscience. *Advances in Physiology Education*, 43(2), 233–240. 10.1152/advan.00199.201831088160

Sirin, S. R., & Rogers-Sirin, L. (2015). *The Educational and Mental Health Needs of Syrian Refugee Children.* Research Gate. https://www.researchgate.net/profile/Selcuk_Sirin/publication/287998909_The_Educational_and_Mental_Health_Needs_of_Syrian_Refugee_Children/links/567ccd6c08ae19758384e4bf.pdf

Siu, S. C. (2023). Revolutionizing translation with AI: Unravelling neural machine translation and generative pre-trained large language models. *SSRN* 4499768. 10.2139/ssrn.4499768

Slavkov, N. (2015). Sociocultural Theory, the L2 Writing Process, and Google Drive: Strange Bedfellows? *TESL Canada Journal*, 32(2), 80–94. 10.18806/tesl.v32i2.1209

Smith, A. M. (2018). *Inclusive practices.* Oxford University Press.

Snyder, L. G., & Snyder, M. J. (2008). Teaching critical thinking and problem solving skills. *The Journal of Research in Business Education*, 50(2), 90.

Soomro, K. A., Kale, U., Curtis, R., Akcaoglu, M., & Bernstein, M. (2020). Digital divide among higher education faculty. *International Journal of Educational Technology in Higher Education*, 17(1), 1–16. 10.1186/s41239-020-00191-5

Sparks, J. R., Song, Y., Brantley, W., & Liu, O. L. (2014). *Assessing written communication in higher education: Review and recommendations for next-generation assessment* (ETS Research Report No. RR-14-37). Princeton: Educational Testing Service. 10.1002/ets2.12035

Sparks, R. L., Ganschow, L., Kenneweg, S., & Miller, K. (1991). Use of an orton-gillingham approach to teach a foreign language to dyslexic/learning-disabled students: Explicit teaching of phonology in a second language. *Annals of Dyslexia*, 41(1), 96–118. https://link.springer.com/article/10.1007/BF02648080. 10.1007/BF0264808024233759

Srimongkontip, S., & Wiriyakarun, P. (2014). Measuring vocabulary size and vocabulary depth of secondary education students in a Thai-English bilingual school. *Art journal Abulratchathani University, 10*(2), 181-209.

Stacey, E. (2002, January). Learning links online: Establishing constructivist and collaborative learning environments. In *Proceedings of the International Education & Technology Conference: Untangling the web-establishing learning links* (pp. 1-6). ASET.

Stanton-Salazar, R. D., & Dornbusch, S. M. (1995). Social capital and the reproduction of inequality: Information networks among Mexican-origin high school students. *Sociology of Education*, 68(2), 116–135. 10.2307/2112778

Stapleton, P. (2003). Assessing the quality and bias of web-based sources: Implications for academic writing. *Journal of English for Academic Purposes*, 2(3), 229–245. 10.1016/S1475-1585(03)00026-2

Starr-Glass, D. (2014). Internalizing cross-cultural sensitivity: Reflective journals of migrant students. *Journal of International Education in Business.*

Steding, S. (2009). Machine translation in the German classroom: Detection, reaction, prevention. *Die Unterrichtspraxis/Teaching German, 42*(2), 178–189. 10.1111/j.1756-1221.2009.00052.x

Steedman, C. (1998). The Place of Memory: In an Archive. *History of the Human Sciences*, 11(4), 65–83. 10.1177/095269519801100405

Stevens, K. E., Siraj, I., & Kong, K. (2023). A critical review of the research evidence on early childhood education and care in refugee contexts in low- and middle-income countries. *International Journal of Child Care and Education Policy*, 17(1), 7. 10.1186/s40723-023-00109-4

Stewart, C., Marciniec, S., Lawrence, D., & Joyner-McGraw, L. (2020). Thinkubator Approach to Solving the Soft Skills Gap. *American Journal of Management*, 20(2), 78–89.

Stolk, Y., Kaplan, I., & Szwarc, J. (2023). Majority language acquisition by children of refugee background: A review. *International Journal of Inclusive Education*, 1–24. 10.1080/13603116.2023.2210593

Stone, P., Brooks, R., Brynjolfsson, E., Calo, R., Etzioni, O., Hager, G., Hirschberg, J., Kalyanakrishnan, S., Kamar, E., Kraus, S., Leyton-Brown, K., Parkes, D., Press, W., Saxenian, A., Shah, J., Tambe, M., & Teller, A. (2022). *Artificial intelligence and life in 2030: The one hundred year study on artificial intelligence*. Standford University.

Sujarwo, S., Sukmawati, S., Akhiruddin, A., Ridwan, R., & Siradjuddin, S. S. S. (2020). An analysis of university students' perspective on online learning in the midst of covid-19 pandemic. *Jurnal Pendidikan Dan Pengajaran*, 53(2), 125–137. 10.23887/jpp.v53i2.24964

Sumakul, D. T. Y. G., Hamied, F. A., & Sukyadi, D. (2022). Artificial Intelligence in EFL classrooms: Friend or foe? *LEARN Journal*, 15(1), 232–256.

Sun, H. (2011). On Cultural Differences and Translation Methods. *Journal of Language Teaching & Research*, 2(1), 160–163. 10.4304/jltr.2.1.160-163

Suraci, C., Pizzi, S., Montori, F., Di Felice, M., & Araniti, G. (2022). 6G to take the digital divide by storm: Key technologies and trends to bridge the gap. *Future Internet*, 14(6), 189. 10.3390/fi14060189

Swales, J. (1990) Genre Analysis: English in academic and research settings. (Cambridge Applied Linguistics) Cambridge: Cambridge University Press.

Swan, K. (2003). Learning effectiveness online: What the research tells us. *Elements of quality online education, practice and direction, 4*(1), 13-47.

Swisher, M. V. (1989). The language-learning situation of deaf students. *TESOL Quarterly*, 23(2), 239–257. 10.2307/3587335

Szente, J., Hoot, J., & Taylor, D. (2006). Responding to the Special Needs of Refugee Children: Practical Ideas for Teachers. *Early Childhood Education Journal*, 34(1), 15–20. 10.1007/s10643-006-0082-2

Taftaf, R., & Williams, C. (2020). Supporting Refugee Distance Education: A Review of the Literature. *American Journal of Distance Education*, 34(1), 18–5. 10.1080/08923647.2020.1691411

Tahir, A., & Tahir, A. (2023). AI-driven advancements in ESL learner autonomy: Investigating student attitudes towards virtual assistant usability. *Linguistic Forum -. Journal of Linguistics*, 5(2), 50–56. 10.53057/linfo/2023.5.2.8

Tang, K. Y., Chang, C. Y., & Hwang, G. J. (2023). Trends in artificial intelligence-supported e-learning: A systematic review and co-citation network analysis (1998–2019). *Interactive Learning Environments*, 31(4), 2134–2152. 10.1080/10494820.2021.1875001

Taylor, S. (1982). Schooling and social reproduction. *Australian Journal of Education*, 26(2), 144–154. 10.1177/000494418202600204

Thonus, T. (2002). *Tutor and student assessments of academic writing tutorials: What is "success"?* Science Direct. https://www.sciencedirect.com/science/article/pii/S1075293503000023

Tight, M. (2023). Employability: A core role of higher education? *Research in Post-Compulsory Education*, 28(4), 551–571. 10.1080/13596748.2023.2253649

Toktarova, V. I., & Semenova, D. A. (2020, November). Digital pedagogy: Analysis, requirements and experience of implementation. *Journal of Physics: Conference Series*, 1691(1), 012112. 10.1088/1742-6596/1691/1/012112

Tomkins, L., & Ulus, E. (2016). 'Oh, was that "experiential learning"?!' Spaces, synergies and surprises with Kolb's learning cycle. *Management Learning*, 47(2), 158–178. 10.1177/1350507615587451

Tomlinson, C. (2009). Differentiating instruction as a response to academically diverse student populations. *On excellence in teaching,* 247-268.

Tovell, F. M. (2008). *At the Far Reaches of Empire: The Life of Juan Francisco De La Bodega Y Quadra*. University of British Columbia Press. 10.59962/9780774855952

Tran, N. K. N. (2016). The adoption of blended e-learning technology in Vietnam using a revision of the Technology Acceptance Model. *Journal of Information Technology Education*, 15, 253–282. 10.28945/3522

Tran, T. Q., Duong, T. M., & Nguyen, D. T. H. (2023). The use of Edtech Apps in English language learning: EFL learners' perspectives. *Theory and Practice in Language Studies*, 13(5), 1115–1123. 10.17507/tpls.1305.04

Tran, T. Q., & Nguyen, V. L. T. (2023). Insights into Vietnamese bilingual students' Quizlet-based English vocabulary learning. *Journal of Language Teaching and Research*, 14(3), 682–688. 10.17507/jltr.1403.15

Trejo Guzmán, N. P., Mora Vázquez, A., & Andrade Rubio, K. L. (2023). Navigating the transition from the American into the Mexican educational system: Transnational students' experiences. *Bilingual Research Journal*, 46(1-2), 142–157. 10.1080/15235882.2023.2225455

Trigueros, Gómez, María, Isabel, & de Aldecoa, Yáñez, Cristina. (2022). La brecha digital en el contexto educativo: Formación y aprendizaje de la ciudadanía digital. *REALIA.Research in Education and Learning Innovation Archives*, (30), 39–45.

Trussler, S., & Robinson, D. (2015) *Inclusive Practice in the Primary School: A Guide for Teachers*. London: Sage Publications Ltd.

Tsai, S. C. (2019). Using google translate in EFL drafts: A preliminary investigation. *Computer Assisted Language Learning*, 32(5–6), 510–526. 10.1080/09588221.2018.1527361

Tsai, Y. R. (2015). Applying the Technology Acceptance Model (TAM) to explore the effects of a Course Management System (CMS)-Assisted EFL writing instruction. *CALICO Journal*, 32(1), 153–171. 10.1558/calico.v32i1.25961

Tunç, A. (2015). Mülteci davranışı ve toplumsal etkileri: Türkiye'deki Suriyelilere ilişkin bir değerlendirme. *Tesam akademi dergisi, 2*(2), 29-63.

Türkiye Cumhuriyeti İçişleri Bakanlığı Göç İdaresi Başkanlığı. (2024) https://www.goc.gov.tr/gecici-koruma5638

Tursunovich, R. I. (2022). Linguistic and cultural aspects of literary translation and translation skills. *British Journal of Global Ecology and Sustainable Development*, 10, 168–173.

Tyack, D. B., & Cuban, L. (1997). *Tinkering toward utopia: A century of public school reform*. Harvard University Press. 10.4159/9780674044524

UNESCO. (2021). *Understanding the impact of COVID-19 on the education of persons with disabilities: Challenges and opportunities of distance education*. UNESCO. https://iite.unesco.org/publications/the-impact-of-covid-19-on-the-education-of-persons-with-disabilities/

UNESCO. (2022). *Leveraging innovative technology in literacy and education programmes for refugees, migrants and internally displaced persons*. UNESCO. https://eric.ed.gov/?id=ED627597 Erişim 23.03

UNESCO. (2023). *2023 global education monitoring report*. UNESCO. https://gem-report-2023.unesco.org/

UNESCO. (2024). *Digital literacy*. UNESCO. https://uis.unesco.org/en/glossary-term/digital-literacy

UNICEF. (2018). *Türkiye'de çocukların eğitim yoluyla korunması*. UNICEF. https://www.unicef.org/turkiye/hikayeler/t%C3%BCrkiyede-%C3%A7ocuklar%C4%B1n-e%C4%9Fitim-yoluyla-korunmas%C4%B1

UNICEF. (2022). *The use of assistive technology in education: A guide for teachers and schools*. UNICEF. https://www.unicef.org/eca/media/30671/file/Teacher's%20guide%20for%20building%20capacity%20for%20assistive%20technology.pdf

United Nations. (2024). *Goal 4: Quality education*. UN. https://unric.org/en/sdg-4/

United Nations. (n.d.). *Convention on the rights of persons with disabilities and optional protocol*. https://www.un.org/disabilities/documents/convention/convoptprot-e.pdf

Urlaub, P., & Dessein, E. (2022). Machine Translation and foreign language education. *Frontiers in Artificial Intelligence*, 5, 936111. 10.3389/frai.2022.93611135937139

Vairaperumal, V. (2023, December 15). *AI in Education: Reimagining the Role of Teachers*. Integra. https://bit.ly/4byG3Ze

van de Werfhorst, H. G., & Hofstede, S. (2007). Cultural capital or relative risk aversion? Two mechanisms for educational inequality compared. *The British Journal of Sociology*, 58(3), 391–415. 10.1111/j.1468-4446.2007.00157.x17727500

van Laar, E., van Deursen, A. J. A. M., van Dijk, J. A. G. M., & de Haan, J. (2020). Determinants of 21st-century skills and 21st-century digital skills for workers: A systematic literature review. *SAGE Open*, 10(1), 1–14. 10.1177/2158244019900176

Vasbieva, D. G., Klimova, I. I., Agibalova, E. L., Karzhanova, N. V., & Bírová, J. (2016). Enhancement of students' vocabulary learning through a blended learning approach. *International Electronic Journal of Mathematics Education*, 11(5), 1195–1203.

Vekaric, G., & Jelic, G. (2013). Raising students' awareness of the importance of English language writing skills. *Activities in Physical Education & Sport*, 3(1), 29–31.

Venkatesh, V., & Davis, F. D. (1996). A model of the antecedents of perceived ease of use: Development and test. *Decision Sciences*, 27(3), 451–481. 10.1111/j.1540-5915.1996.tb01822.x

Verdú, E., Regueras, L. M., Gal, E., de Castro, J. P., Verdú, M. J., & Kohen-Vacs, D. (2017). Integration of an intelligent tutoring system in a course of computer network design. *Educational Technology Research and Development*, 65(3), 653–677. 10.1007/s11423-016-9503-0

Vermeulen, M. (2018). *Une approche meta-design des learning games pour développer leur usage* [PhD final thesis]. Université de la Sorbonne.

Volkom, M. V., Stapley, J. C., & Amaturo, V. (2014). Revisiting the digital divide: Generational differences in technology use in everyday life. *North American Journal of Psychology*, 16(3).

Vonea, L. (2020). Formative Assessment as Assessment for Learning Development. *Jounral of Pedagogy*.

Votruba-Drzal, E., Coley, R. L., Collins, M., & Miller, P. (2015). Center-based preschool and school readiness skills of children from immigrant families. *Early Education and Development*, 26(4), 549–573. 10.1080/10409289.2015.1000220

Wadmany, R., & Kliachko, S. (2014). The Significance of Digital Pedagogy: Teachers' Perceptions and the Factors Influencing Their Abilities as Digital Pedagogues. *Journal of Educational Technology*, 11(3), 22–33.

Waller, M., & Waller, P. (2020). *Why predictive algorithms are so risky for public sector bodies*. Social Science Research Network. 10.2139/ssrn.3716166

Walsh, M. (2010). Multimodal literacy: What does it mean for classroom practice? *Australian Journal of Language and Literacy*, 33(3), 211–239. 10.1007/BF03651836

Walter, Y. (2024). Embracing the future of artificial intelligence in the classroom: The relevance of AI literacy, prompt engineering, and critical thinking in modern education. *International Journal of Educational Technology in Higher Education*, 21(1), 15. 10.1186/s41239-024-00448-3

Walther-Thomas, C., Korinek, L., McLoughlin, V. L., & Williams, B. (2000). *Collaboration for Inclusive Education: Developing Successful Programs*. Allyn & Bacon.

Wang, H. Y., Sigerson, L., & Cheng, C. (2019). Digital nativity and information technology addiction: Age cohort versus individual difference approaches. *Computers in Human Behavior*, 90, 1–9. 10.1016/j.chb.2018.08.031

Warnock, S. (2009). *Teaching writing online: How and why*. National Council of Teachers of English.

Warschauer, M. (2004). *Technology and Social Inclusion: Rethinking the Digital Divide*. MIT Press.

Warschauer, M., Knobel, M., & Stone, L. (2004). Technology and equity in schooling: Deconstructing the digital divide. *Educational Policy*, 18(4), 562–588. 10.1177/0895904804266469

Warschauer, M., & Matuchniak, T. (2010). New technology and digital worlds: Analyzing evidence of equity in access, use, and outcomes. *Review of Research in Education*, 34(1), 179–225. 10.3102/0091732X09349791

Watson, J. (2008). *Blended learning: The convergence of Online and face to face education*. North American Council for Online Learning. https://files.eric.ed.gov/fulltext/ED509636.pdf

Wayman, J. C., Midgley, S., & Stringfield, S. (2007). *Technology Applications in Education: A Learning View*. Lawrence Erlbaum Associates.

Weiss, H. (2021) “Social reproduction”. In Stein, F. (Ed) *The Open Encyclopedia of Anthropology* Facsimile of the first edition in *The Cambridge Encyclopedia of Anthropology*. Cambridge. 10.29164/21socialrepro

Wells, G. (2000). Dialogic inquiry in education. *Vygotskian perspectives on literacy research*, 51-85.

Wells, N. (2022). Translation as Culture in the Age of the Machine. *Wasafiri*, 37(3), 77–80. 10.1080/02690055.2022.2067244

Wesołowska, A., & Jedynak, M. (2014). FL vocabulary learning strategies used by blind, partially blind and normally sighted learners of English. In Paradowski, M. (Ed.), *Teaching Languages off the Beaten Track* (pp. 306–328). Peter Lang.

Widhiarso, W. (2016). Comparing the performance of synonym and antonym tests in measuring verbal abilities. *TPM. Testing, Psychometrics, Methodology in Applied Psychology*, 23(3).

Wildhagen, T. (2010). Capitalizing on culture: How cultural capital shapes educational experiences and outcomes. *Sociology Compass*, 4(7), 519–531. 10.1111/j.1751-9020.2010.00296.x

Wilson, J., Ahrendt, C., Fudge, E. A., Raiche, A., Beard, G., & MacArthur, C. (2021). Elementary teachers' perceptions of automated feedback and automated scoring: Transforming the teaching and learning of writing using automated writing evaluation. *Computers & Education*, 168, 104208. 10.1016/j.compedu.2021.104208

Wolfreys, J. (Ed.). (2002). *Introducing Criticism in the 21st Century*. Edinburgh University Press.

Woodrich, M. P., & Fan, Y. (2017). Google Docs as a tool for collaborative writing in the middle school classroom. *Journal of Information Technology Education*, 16, 391–410. 10.28945/3870

Woolcock, M. (1998). Social capital and economic development: Toward a theoretical synthesis and policy framework. *Theory and Society*, 27(2), 151–208. 10.1023/A:1006884930135

World Health Organization. (2024). *Assistive technology*. WHO. https://www.who.int/europe/health-topics/assistive-technology#tab=tab_1

Wright, K. B. (2005). Researching Internet-based populations: Advantages and disadvantages of online survey research, online questionnaire authoring software packages, and web survey services. *Journal of Computer-Mediated Communication*, 10(3), JCMC1034. 10.1111/j.1083-6101.2005.tb00259.x

Wu, K. (2022). An exploration of the educational experiences of refugee children. *International Journal of Education and Humanities*, 5(2), 304–307. 10.54097/ijeh.v5i2.2194

Wu, T. J., Wang, L. Y., Gao, J. Y., & Wei, A. P. (2020). Social support and well-being of chinese special education teachers-An emotional labor perspective. *International Journal of Environmental Research and Public Health*, 17(18), 6884. 10.3390/ijerph1718688432967136

Xiu, P., & Xeauyin, L. (2018). Human translation vs machine translation: The practitioner phenomenology. *Linguistics and Culture Review*, 2(1), 13–23.

Xu, J. (2021). Chinese university students' L2 writing feedback orientation and self-regulated learning writing strategies in online teaching during COVID-19. *The Asia-Pacific Education Researcher*, 30(6), 563–574. 10.1007/s40299-021-00586-6

Yao, B., Jiang, M., Yang, D., & Hu, J. (2023). *Empowering LLM-based machine translation with cultural awareness.* arXiv preprint arXiv:2305.14328.

Young, D. (2024). Awareness of inclusive education policy among postsecondary English language teachers in Japan. In Peking University-Waseda University Joint Research Initiative (Eds.), *Renewing Governance Mechanism in Asia-Pacific* (pp. 338-355). Waseda University Press.

Young, D., & Burke, A. (2024). Conceptualizing inclusive practices for English language teachers. In Burke, A., Young, D., & Cook, M. L. (Eds.), *Barrier-free Instruction in Japan: Recommendations for Teachers at all Levels of Schooling* (pp. 86–104). Candlin & Mynard. 10.47908/30/3

You, X. (2004). New directions in EFL writing: A report from China. *Journal of Second Language Writing*, 13(4), 253–256. 10.1016/j.jslw.2004.09.002

Yu, J., Xu, G., & Bai, F. (2011). Exploring the problems and countermeasures of Chinese students' English academic writing. [ ]. *Teaching Research*, 6, 41–44.

Yung, K. W. H., & Fong, N. (2019). Learning EAP at university: Perceptions of high-achieving first-year ESL undergraduates. *ELT Journal*, 73(3), 306–315. 10.1093/elt/ccz019

Yurdakul, A., & Tok, T. N. (2018). Öğretmen Gözüyle Göçmen/Mülteci Öğrenci. *Adnan Menderes Üniversitesi Eğitim Fakültesi Eğitim Bilimleri Dergisi*, 9(2), 46–58.

Zebroski, J. T. (1986). The uses of theory: A Vygostkyan approach to composition. *Writing Instructor*, 5, 57–67.

Zhang, R., & Zou, D. (2020). Types, purposes, and effectiveness of state-of-the-art technologies for second and foreign language learning. *Computer Assisted Language Learning*, 35(4), 696–742. 10.1080/09588221.2020.1744666

Zhang, W., & Luo, L. (2004). Some thoughts on the development and current situation of college English teaching in China. *Foreign Language World*, 3, 2–7.

Zhang, W., & Zhu, C. (2018). Comparing learning outcomes of blended learning and traditional face-to-face learning of university students in ESL courses. *International Journal on E-Learning*, 17(2), 251–273. https://www.learntechlib.org/primary/p/171512/

Zhao, Y., & Frank, K. A. (2003). Factors affecting technology uses in schools: An ecological perspective. *American Educational Research Journal*, 40(4), 807–840. 10.3102/00028312040004807

Zipp, M. (2018). *Feminism, Graffiti, Gender Fluidity: An Interview With Jessica Pabón-Colón, author of Graffiti Grrlz*. Got a Girl Crush. http://www.gotagirlcrush.com/archive/2018/5/20/feminism-graffiti-gender-fluidity-an-interview-with-jessica-pabn-coln-author-of-graffiti-grrlz

Zúñiga, V., & Hamann, E. T. (2009). Sojourners in Mexico with US school experience: A new taxonomy for transnational students. *Comparative Education Review*, 53(3), 329–353. 10.1086/599356

About the Contributors

Katelyn Prager is an Assistant Professor in the Department of English and Communication Studies at the Fashion Institute of Technology (SUNY) based in New York, New York. She received her PhD in Composition and Rhetoric from the University of Rhode Island. Her research explores issues of digital pedagogy, equitable teaching practices, and the impact of generative AI in the classroom. This research is informed by her experience teaching a variety of digital writing and rhetoric courses. There, she focuses on topics related to digital literacy, participatory culture, and digital activism.

Nurhayat Bilge is an Assistant Professor at SUNY - Fashion Institute of Technology based in New York City, New York.

***

Berra Nur Acay is currently working as a research assistant at Cappadocia University in the Department of English Translation and Interpreting, and she graduated from Hacettepe University, which is the top tier university in the field of languages and linguistics in Turkiye. Her fields of interest are Artificial Intelligence, Applied Linguistics, Language Education, and Adapting AI into innovative language teaching practices.

Feyza Aydin Bölükbaş completed her undergraduate education at Gazi University Faculty of Education, Preschool Education Programme in 2015. In 2018, she completed her master's degree at Gazi University Institute of Educational Sciences, Department of Preschool Education. In 2018, she started her doctorate education in Gazi University Institute of Educational Sciences, Preschool Education programme and completed it in 2023. She has been working on mathematics education and science education in preschool children and taking part in projects related to technology integration in education. She is currently working as a research assistant at Aksaray University.

Emine Bozkurt Polat graduated from Necmettin Erbakan University, Department of Preschool Education in 2012 and was appointed as a research assistant at Kahramanmaraş Sütçü İmam University in the same year. After completing his master's degree in Necmettin Erbakan University Preschool Education Department in 2016, he was appointed as a research assistant to Gazi University Preschool Education Department in the same year and started his doctorate education. She worked as the education coordinator at Gazi Practice Kindergarten for 1 year in the 2018-2019 academic year. The author is still working as a research assistant at Gazi University. As an academician, he has publications on technology, augmented reality, robotic coding values education in preschool children. She worked on robotic coding in her doctoral thesis.

José Manuel Correoso-Rodenas holds a PhD in English (Universidad de Castilla-La Mancha, Spain) and he is currently an Assistant Professor of English at the Universidad Complutense de Madrid (Spain). His areas of interest and research are mainly Gothic Literature and Native American Studies, in which he has presented several papers at national and international conferences. Among his recent publications, some of the most outstanding examples are: Edición y estudio de La fe del Cristiano y La religion pura (1699), de Cotton Mather (Editorial Sindéresis) and "'The very land of romance': Original Compositions on Spain and the Spanish in The Southern Literary Messenger (1834-1864)" (EJAS. European Journal of American Studies). He has also edited the volume Teaching Language and Literature On and Off-Canon (IGI Global). He is currently the Academic Secretary of the scholarly journal Amaltea. Revista de Mitocrítica.

Steven D'Agustino holds a doctorate from Fordham University's Graduate School of Education and is the Director of Online Learning for the Office of the Provost where his responsibilities include supporting the development of distance learning programs across Fordham University. He has published research in the area of instructional enhancement through the integration of technology and has been awarded a number of grants while at Fordham, the largest of which was a 2.5 million dollar grant to provide access to technology through online learning. Dr. D'Agustino is the editor of two books: Adaptation, Resistance and Access to Instructional Technologies and Immersive Environments, Augmented Realities, and Virtual Worlds: Assessing Future Trends in Education published in 2010 and 2012, respectively. His most recent publications, both in 2013, include "Toward a course conversion model for distance learning: a review of best practices" in Frontiers of Distance Learning in Business Education and "Providing innovative opportunities and options through online credit recovery and afterschool programs" in Expanding Minds and Opportunities.

Véronique Delplancq is full professor at the Department of Language Sciences at the Higher School of Education of the Polytechnic Institute of Viseu. She holds a PhD in Psycho-pedagogy (phonetics) from Mons University in Belgium (BE) and in Romanesque Linguistics (accreditation granted by the University of Lisbon). Professor Véronique Delplancq carries out professional and research activities at national and international levels in the areas of spoken communication, teaching and learning of FL in higher education and inter / multi culturality.

Kübra Engin graduated from Hacettepe University, Department of Preschool Education, at the undergraduate level in 2014. She completed her master's degree in the Department of Preschool Education at Gazi University between 2016-2019. She has been working as a research assistant in the field of Preschool Education at Gazi University since 2017 and has been continuing his doctoral studies in the same department since 2019. Family education, social and emotional development, emotional intelligence and self-compassion are among his academic interests. The author has taken part in various projects on technology integration (digital stories, augmented reality applications and coding) and has carried out studies on this subject.

Susana Fidalgo is a full professor in the Language Sciences Department at the School of Education of the Polytechnic Institute of Viseu. She holds a PhD in Didactics from the University of Aveiro. Her intervention and research areas are the teaching of English as a foreign language, extensive reading and the acquisition of a foreign language and early foreign language teaching.

Romain Gillain is an Associate Professor at the School of Education and Social Sciences of the Polytechnic Institute of Leiria. He holds a PhD in Spanish Philology from Oviedo University. His intervention and research areas include lexicography, sport terminology, Franco-Belgian comics and the teaching of Spanish and French as foreign languages.

Eda Başak Hancı-Azizoglu gained her Ph.D. in English Language from Indiana University of Pennsylvania with a double major in Rhetoric and Applied Linguistics/ TESOL. She is an expert on global perspectives on language and literacy policies and English language learning and writing programs. She has given master's level courses to certified American school teachers to provide them leadership and skills on language teaching methods for their multicultural students. She is currently working as an associate professor in the English Language Teaching Department at Mediterranean University, Türkiye. Her research interests are artificial linguistic intelligence, linguistic analysis, the poetic and creative function of English as an additional language.

Ana Lopes is a full professor at the Department of Language Sciences at the Higher School of Education of the Polytechnic Institute of Viseu, Portugal. She holds a PhD in American Studies - American History, Culture and Literature. In addition to the research Professor Ana Maria Costa Lopes has been carrying out in the context of American culture and literature, mainly with regard to the work of the novelist Sinclair Lewis, she has recently been doing research in the field of Portuguese literature, specifically with regard to the function of space as a structuring category of the narrative.

Nguyen Phuong Thao is a full-time lecturer and a coordinator of student support activities at Language Institute – Van Lang University. She graduated in English Linguistics and Literature from the University of Social Sciences and Humanities – Ho Chi Minh City. Currently, she is teaching General Academic English courses and organizing support activities for students in English language learning methods. As a student support coordinator, she is responsible for designing extra courses and hosting workshops to enhance students' learning skills and motivation in learning English. Her research interests focus on education leadership and professional development.

José Pereira is an associate professor at the Department of Communication and Art at the Higher School of Education of the Polytechnic Institute of Viseu, Portugal. He holds a PhD in Fine Arts (Multimedia Art expertise), by the Fine Arts College of Lisbon University. Professor José Pereira carries out professional / research / artistic activity in the areas of Fine Arts (with particular emphasis on the fields of Photography, Digital Art and New Media Art), Art Theory and Art Essay.

Julie Tatlock is an Associate Professor of History at Mount Mary University in Milwaukee, WI. Her most recent publications include Restructuring Core Curricula (IGI Global, 2024) and World Civilizations (Rice University/OpenStax, 2023). Her interests are primarily in finding new and creative ways to engage students in good online and writing as well as creating unique online education spaces. Research areas in addition to pedagogy are World History, British History and Gender History.

Thao Quoc Tran is currently working at HUTECH University, Vietnam. He has been teaching English for 20 years, and he is experienced in teaching English to both local and international students. His research areas are discourse analysis, English language skills, teacher professional development, and instructional design models.

Ilkay Ulutaş received an undergraduate degree in the Child Development and Education Teaching program at Gazi University. She completed her master's degree in child development at Ankara University and her PhD in Child Development and Education at Gazi University. In 2009, she conducted a postdoctoral study on emotional intelligence at the University College London Department of Psychology within the scope of the TUBITAK Scientist Support Department International Postdoctoral Research Scholarship Program. Her studies focus on the emotional intelligence in preschool children, Montessori education, mathematics education in early childhood education, arts in early childhood education, early childhood quality, and technology in early childhood education. She has also recently carried out projects on digital mathematics stories in early childhood education, augmented reality applications in early childhood mathematics education, and cultural heritage and technology (coding, digital storytelling) in early childhood education. She currently works as a professor at the Early Childhood Education Department at Gazi University. She received her PhD in early childhood education at Gazi University in 2005. She did post-doctoral studies at the Trait Emotional Intelligence laboratory of K. V. Petrides in 2009 at University College London. Her research interest focuses mainly on emotional intelligence in early childhood. She also has studies on early childhood quality, visual arts education in early childhood, mathematics education in early childhood, and Montessori education. She teaches undergraduate and graduate courses as a professor at the Department of Early Childhood Education at Gazi University. She also participates in international conferences and carries out various national projects.

Chenghao Wang is a PhD student in the department of Applied Linguistics, Xi'an Jiaotong-Liverpool University, Suzhou, China. His research interests include Computer-Assisted Language Learning (CALL), AI-assisted language learning and teaching, EAP and WTC.

Luyue Wang holds a Masters degree in TESOL from Xi'an Jiaotong-Liverpool University. Currently, she works as an English teacher at the NO.1 Middle School of Suzhou New District. Her research interests lie in the fields of Computer-Assisted Language Learning, Artificial Intelligence,and English language teaching.

Bin Zou received his PhD degree in TESOL and Computer Technology from the University of Bristol, UK. He is a Senior Associate Professor and PhD supervisor at the Department of Applied Linguistics, Xi'an Jiaotong-Liverpool University. His research interests include Computer-Assisted Language Learning (CALL), AI, EAP and ELT. He is the Founding Editor and Co-Editor-in-Chief of two international journals: the International Journal of Computer-Assisted Language Learning and Teaching and the International Journal of EAP: Research and Practice.

Index

E

F

G

H

I

L

T

V

www.ingramcontent.com/pod-product-compliance
Lightning Source LLC
LaVergne TN
LVHW080609300926
849162LV00005B/1094
9798369325919